Cocoa and Objective-C: Up and Running

Cocoa and Objective-C: Up and Running

Scott Stevenson

O'REILLY®

Beijing · Cambridge · Farnham · Köln · Sebastopol · Taipei · Tokyo

Cocoa and Objective-C: Up and Running
by Scott Stevenson

Published by O'Reilly Media, Inc., 1005 Gravenstein Highway North, Sebastopol, CA 95472.

O'Reilly books may be purchased for educational, business, or sales promotional use. Online editions are also available for most titles (*http://my.safaribooksonline.com*). For more information, contact our corporate/institutional sales department: (800) 998-9938 or *corporate@oreilly.com*.

Editor: Brian Jepson
Production Editor: Adam Zaremba
Copyeditor: Nancy Kotary
Proofreader: Sada Preisch

Indexer: Ellen Troutman Zaig
Cover Designer: Karen Montgomery
Interior Designer: David Futato
Illustrator: Robert Romano

Printing History:

April 2010:	First Edition.

 This book uses RepKover™, a durable and flexible lay-flat binding.

ISBN: 978-0-596-80479-4

[M]

1271195397

Table of Contents

Preface

I'm not sure if this is the first book you've picked up to learn Cocoa, but I think it's the one that will get you started writing apps. I started teaching Cocoa and Objective-C in 2004, and I have worked with a lot of people who wanted to learn how to write software so that they could get their ideas onto the screen. But there's a problem.

There are two kinds of people who want to learn programming. Those in the first group are wired for the algorithmic mindset; they're interested in data and the inner workings of things for their own sake. When they see a dog catch a Frisbee, they think of the calculations the dog does to catch it. Programming is a natural extension of this mindset. My guess is around five percent of the population is actually built this way.

The second (much larger) group has ideas for software that they desperately want to make real. They're often graphic or interaction designers. You probably have ideas about a fantastic Mac, iPhone, or iPad app that you want to create, but you don't have a million dollars to hire an engineering staff. It's very likely that you even like programming and data in addition to several other interests, but you don't see everything in terms of algorithms.

The problem is that most technical books are written by and for people in the first group. That means most of the material is being created for those who need the least help. As a result, a lot of books on programming go unread. In fact, there's this unspoken honor given to anyone who actually finishes reading one: "Wow, he must be really motivated."

My problem with this is that there are a lot of people with great ideas in the second group. Many of my favorite Mac and iPhone apps today come from developers without a formal computer science background, most likely because they bring different experiences into the mix. I want to encourage more of this. Fortunately, the good folks at O'Reilly agree with me.

So here's the deal. I wanted to write this book because I want to help you learn how to write Mac, iPhone, and iPad apps. I want you to read it so that I get to use whatever software you end up creating.

This book is made to be accessible to new programmers, but it's not watered down. You're learning to use the same things the professionals use. My job is to make sure that each page says something useful. For each paragraph, I've asked myself, "Does this help you write your app?" Anything that didn't meet that standard got cut. But I haven't sold you short; if there's something you need to know to be a good Mac programmer, I've at least told you about it. However, I haven't spent time on minutiae that don't matter for Cocoa.

The content of this book is based on Cocoa tutorials I wrote between 2003 and 2009. Many of these were published at my personal site, Theocacao (*http://theocacao.com*), and some of the longer ones were published at Cocoa Dev Central (*http://cocoadevcentral.com*), a site I didn't originally create but have run since 2004. I've refined the tutorials based on a one-on-one mentoring program that I ran over the same period of time. You get the benefit of all those efforts in a single condensed book.

Your job is to go write world-class Mac, iPhone, and iPad apps, and to tell everyone else how great Cocoa is. Let's get started.

Who This Book Is For

This book is for people who want to learn to make great Cocoa apps. I don't assume that you already know how to program, or anything about Objective-C or C. You do need to own an Intel-based Mac running Mac OS X 10.6 Snow Leopard, and you must know how to install software, launch apps, edit and save files, and so on. Essentially, you have to know how to use a Mac.

If you know any computer languages at all (even HTML), things will make more sense from the start. If not, you'll still be able to make it through this book, but you may find some parts challenging. Even though Cocoa makes many common tasks easy, your brain has to adjust to the basic concepts of programming.

To be clear, though, this book is not exclusively for novice programmers. Depending on your experience level, you can skip a few of the chapters that are designed for beginners and jump right to the parts that are relevant to your experience.

If you already know C but haven't done object-oriented programming, start with Chapter 1, which will walk you through creating a basic Cocoa application. Then move onto Chapter 4, which introduces object-oriented concepts.

If you know C and at least one object-oriented language (such as Java, Ruby, or C++), you can start with Chapter 1 for the basic orientation, and then jump ahead to Chapter 5, which introduces Objective-C.

How This Book Is Organized

The chapters in this book are organized as follows:

Chapter 1

To build Cocoa apps, you'll need to know your way around Xcode. Although we'll get into Xcode more deeply later, this chapter gives you a quick tour.

Chapter 2

Before you can start programming in Objective-C (the native programming language used with Cocoa), you'll need a background in programming as well as in the C language. This chapter gets you started with the basics of programming in C.

Chapter 3

A programming language spends all its time moving things around in memory. This chapter explains how C manages memory and also explains pointers, which let you work directly with memory locations. Although you won't need all the low-level memory manipulation that C is capable of, an understanding of it will help you better understand Objective-C.

Chapter 4

Here's where we take a detour from the C language and get into the object-oriented world. In this chapter, you'll learn about classes, inheritance, objects, and more.

Chapter 5

Now that you have a basic understanding of object-oriented concepts, it's time to move on to Objective-C. This chapter explains Objective-C's syntax for calling methods, defining classes, and creating objects.

Chapter 6

Before you can get into Cocoa, there are a few more things you need to learn about Objective-C. This chapter introduces some intermediate Objective-C concepts, including memory management, categories, selectors, and more.

Chapter 7

Although you can (and sometimes will) use standard C types in your Cocoa apps, Objective-C offers a rich set of classes for working with primitive values, such as integers, floating-point numbers, and strings. This chapter shows you how to use these value classes.

Chapter 8

Cocoa's AppKit user interface layer allows you to create applications with rich user interfaces. This chapter prepares you to work with the built-in controls and connect them with actions you define in your code.

Chapter 9

Model-View-Controller is the mindset that guides the way you'll put your Cocoa apps together. In this chapter, you'll learn how to write code that coordinates your data and user interfaces.

Chapter 10

Cocoa includes a rich set of classes for displaying graphics in your apps. In this chapter, you'll learn how to work with shapes, images, gradients, and more.

Chapter 11
> Now that you've read through the book, you're ready to write some apps. This short chapter gives you a few last pointers to help you on your way.

Conventions Used in This Book

The following typographical conventions are used in this book:

Italic
> Indicates new terms, URLs, email addresses, filenames, and file extensions.

`Constant width`
> Used for program listings, as well as within paragraphs to refer to program elements such as variable or function names, databases, data types, environment variables, statements, and keywords.

`Constant width bold`
> Shows commands or other text that should be typed literally by the user.

`Constant width italic`
> Shows text that should be replaced with user-supplied values or by values determined by context.

 This icon signifies a tip, suggestion, or general note.

 This icon indicates a warning or caution.

Using Code Examples

This book is here to help you get your job done. In general, you may use the code in this book in your programs and documentation. You do not need to contact us for permission unless you're reproducing a significant portion of the code. For example, writing a program that uses several chunks of code from this book does not require permission. Selling or distributing a CD-ROM of examples from O'Reilly books does require permission. Answering a question by citing this book and quoting example code does not require permission. Incorporating a significant amount of example code from this book into your product's documentation does require permission.

We appreciate, but do not require, attribution. An attribution usually includes the title, author, publisher, and ISBN. For example: "*Cocoa and Objective-C: Up and Running* by Scott Stevenson. Copyright 2010 Scott Stevenson, 978-0-596-80479-4."

If you feel your use of code examples falls outside fair use or the permission given above, feel free to contact us at *permissions@oreilly.com*.

Safari® Books Online

Safari Books Online is an on-demand digital library that lets you easily search over 7,500 technology and creative reference books and videos to find the answers you need quickly.

With a subscription, you can read any page and watch any video from our library online. Read books on your cell phone and mobile devices. Access new titles before they are available for print, and get exclusive access to manuscripts in development and post feedback for the authors. Copy and paste code samples, organize your favorites, download chapters, bookmark key sections, create notes, print out pages, and benefit from tons of other time-saving features.

O'Reilly Media has uploaded this book to the Safari Books Online service. To have full digital access to this book and others on similar topics from O'Reilly and other publishers, sign up for free at *http://my.safaribooksonline.com*.

How to Contact Us

Please address comments and questions concerning this book to the publisher:

O'Reilly Media, Inc.
1005 Gravenstein Highway North
Sebastopol, CA 95472
800-998-9938 (in the United States or Canada)
707-829-0515 (international or local)
707-829-0104 (fax)

We have a web page for this book, where we list errata, examples, and any additional information. You can access this page at:

http://www.oreilly.com/catalog/9780596804794/

A full site dedicated to the book is available from the author, and may include additional examples and announcements about Cocoa user groups and other information you may find useful as a developer. This book site is at:

http://cocoabook.com

To comment or ask technical questions about this book, send email to:

bookquestions@oreilly.com

You can email the author directly at:

cocoahelp@me.com

For more information about our books, conferences, Resource Centers, and the O'Reilly Network, see our website at:

http://www.oreilly.com

Acknowledgments

My education didn't follow the normal path. I taught myself how to program and learned how to run a business mostly by trial and error. In the end, I think this is the only option that would have worked for me, but it was possible only because of my extremely patient and understanding family: my mom, Peggy; my dad, Alan; and my sister, Jamie. You would not be reading this now if it was not for their support.

There are so many people that have helped me in my work life, but there are a few that have had a direct impact on this book.

Michael Lopp and Angela Muller were ongoing sources of encouragement and inspiration. This book first came into being over lunch when Michael mentioned something along the lines of "everyone wants an animal on the cover of their book," referring to the iconic O'Reilly covers. By incredible coincidence, Brian from O'Reilly emailed me about two weeks later. Had Michael not made that comment, this might not have happened.

I had world-class tech reviewers for this project: Joar Wingfors, Michael Jurewitz, Rob Rhyne, and Tim Triemstra. Joar, who I originally met through the tutorials I posted online, tirelessly reviewed an ever-changing book, provided a wealth of essential comments and suggestions, and even helped me fix some bugs in the code. He's one of the most talented engineers I know, and I am thrilled to have been able to get his help on this.

Though he wasn't involved in this project, I owe a lot to John Mora. He has an ability to look an impossibly large task in the face and just do it, despite the usual doubts about whether you know enough or have enough time. It is one of the most impressive traits I know of, and John has it in spades. Thankfully, I think some of that rubbed off on me over the 15 years I've known him.

Thanks to Kip Krueger for patiently helping me figure out the low-level details of memory and offering pointers when I was learning C. His mentoring is the reason I'm able to teach these topics to you now.

When I first started learning Cocoa, there were only two books out on the topic. I chose Aaron Hillegass's book *Cocoa Programming for Mac OS X* (Addison-Wesley). Not only was it the first Mac programming book I read, it was the first technical book I actually enjoyed. His book proved to me that you could write in a direct and personal style and still be taken seriously. Having spent time with him in person, I can also add that he's a great guy. There's no doubt that his influence is weaved into the tutorials I've written.

Brian Jepson is simply a superhero among editors. I'm not sure there's enough space to list all of the things he did to make sure this project was a success, but I certainly could not have done it without him. For any part of the book that you really like, there's a good chance he had a hand in it. Follow him on Twitter: *@bjepson*.

Finally, to the thousands of people who have emailed me over the years with questions or suggestions about tutorials, I owe a lot to you as well. You helped me refine everything that ended up in this book, and by extension, helped a new generation of Cocoa developers learn how to program.

This book is dedicated to Gina and Ilya, who both taught me that life's too short to not be spent with the people you want to be with.

Thank you.

CHAPTER 1

Setup and First Run

I know you want to start writing apps as soon as possible, but there are three things you need to know first:

I don't assume you already know how to program.
> You don't need to have existing experience with Objective-C, Cocoa, Xcode, or even C. If you have some familiarity with a computer language (even HTML), it will help you. You do need to be a reasonably proficient Mac user. If you show up with the desire to learn Mac programming, I'll walk you through what you need to know.

The chapters are modular.
> If you know C and object-oriented concepts, but not Objective-C specifically, you can skip to Chapter 5 after learning about Xcode in this chapter. If you've already dabbled in Mac or iPhone programming, and know your way around Objective-C and some basic Cocoa topics, you can probably jump to Chapter 7. Otherwise, start right here.

You need a Mac running Snow Leopard.
> All of the chapters assume that you're running Mac OS X 10.6 Snow Leopard, which runs only on Intel-based Macs.

All set? Good, let's get Xcode running.

Download and Install Xcode

You can either get Xcode from the Mac OS X install DVD or download it from the official Mac Dev Center website. The version on the website will always be the newest one, but the download may take several hours. If you want to get started right away, you can install from the DVD.

If you're running Snow Leopard and already have the iPhone SDK installed, you have everything you need to write Mac apps. You can skip ahead to "Your First Application" on page 4.

To download the newest version of Xcode, go to *http://developer.apple.com* and click on Mac Dev Center. The layout of the site changes regularly, but you should look for a link that says "Register" to create an account. There is a paid membership that offers access to prerelease software and training videos, but you can start with the free membership, which requires you only to fill out some basic contact information. After you've registered, return to *http://developer.apple.com* and log in. Once you're logged in, look for a link for downloading Xcode.

If you have a slow Internet connection and want to save yourself a few hours, put the Snow Leopard Install DVD in the drive and open the folder called *Optional Installs* as shown in Figure 1-1.

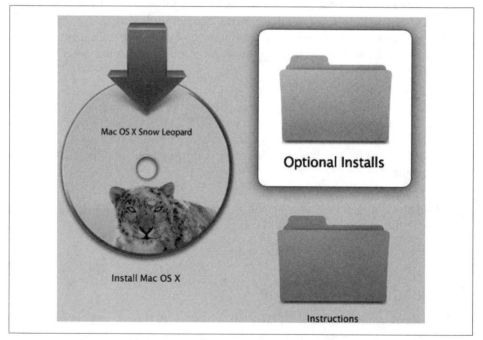

Figure 1-1. The Optional Installs folder on the Snow Leopard Install DVD

Inside the Optional Installs folder is a package called *Xcode.mpkg*. Double-click it to open the installer (see Figure 1-2).

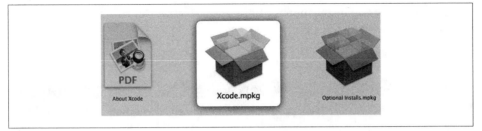

Figure 1-2. The Xcode.mpkg package inside the Optional Installs folder

 The version of Xcode on the DVD is usually older than what is available on the developer site, so you should upgrade Xcode as soon as you have the time to download it. The Xcode download at the Mac Dev Center will show you the version number that's available. When you run Xcode, the version number is displayed on the Welcome window below "Welcome to Xcode."

Once the installer is running, you can just accept all of the default options. You will likely need several gigabytes free for installation. Figure 1-3 shows the installer running.

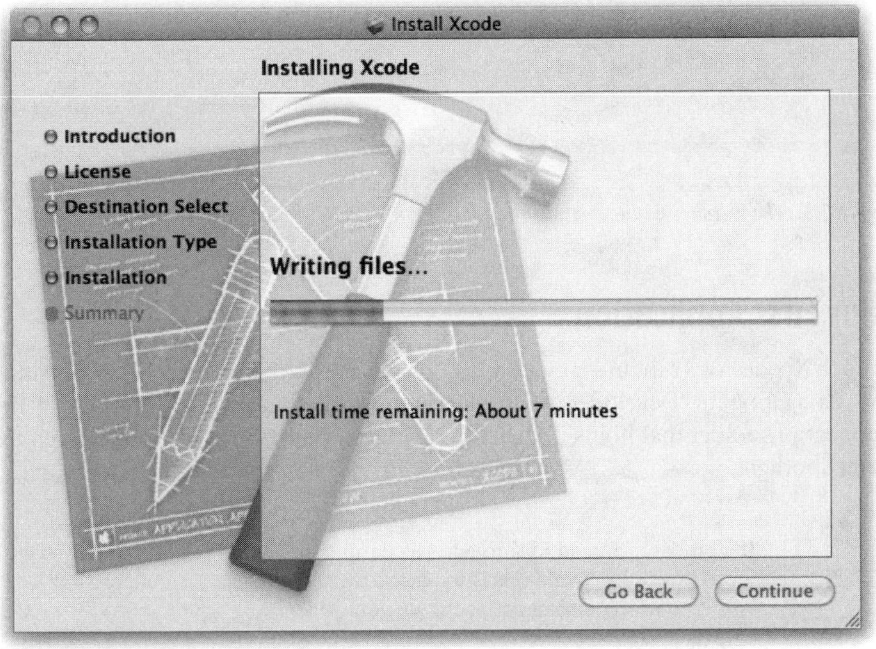

Figure 1-3. An Xcode install in progress

Once the window says installation is complete (see Figure 1-4), go ahead and close the window.

Figure 1-4. The installer window confirming that Xcode was installed

Your First Application

Launch Xcode. You can find it by clicking on your hard drive icon in the Finder sidebar and navigating to Developer → Applications. This is *separate* from the general Applications folder that holds things like Safari and iTunes. You can also search for it using Spotlight.

 It's probably a good idea to add Xcode to your Dock since it's a few levels down. In theory, this is for easy access, but it's also a good conversation starter if someone sees it on your Mac.

If Xcode asks you for any initial configuration preferences, simply accept the defaults. Each time Xcode runs you will see a Welcome window that looks something like Figure 1-5.

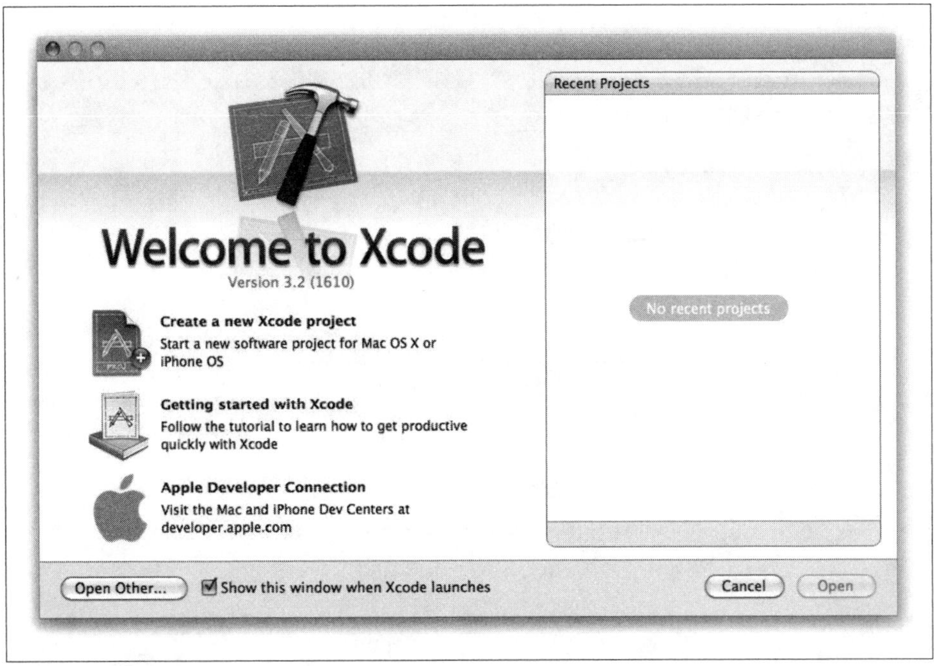

Figure 1-5. The Xcode Welcome window after the first launch

The left side of the window has a few items to help you get started, and the right side lists projects that you've used recently. The list will be empty the first time you run Xcode. Click on "Create a new Xcode project" to get started.

If you closed the Welcome window, you can start a new project by choosing File → New Project from the menu. You can open the Welcome window again by choosing Help → Welcome to Xcode.

In the New Project window, click on Application under the Mac OS X section and select the Cocoa Application icon as shown in Figure 1-6.

Click the Choose button, and you'll be asked to select a location for the project. Go to your home folder and create a folder called *CocoaBook* (you can do this within the Save dialog). Select the CocoaBook folder as the save location and enter "TextEditNano" as the project name (see Figure 1-7).

The layout of the New Project window has changed significantly in the 3.*x* releases of Xcode. If your window doesn't look similar to the screenshot in Figure 1-6, download a newer version of Xcode from *http://developer.apple.com*.

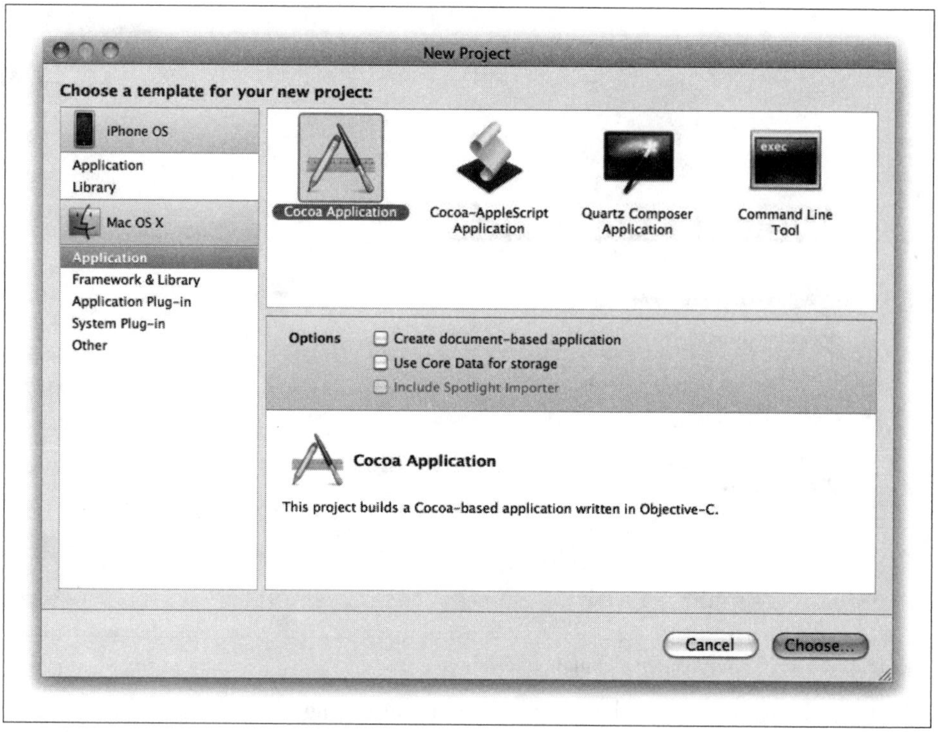

Figure 1-6. The New Project window in Xcode

After you click Save, you'll see the main Xcode window come up, which looks like Figure 1-8.

Go ahead and click the Build and Run icon in the toolbar to try the app out. You should see a blank window come up, as shown in Figure 1-9.

This obviously isn't a useful window, but if it shows up, you know Xcode is working and you're ready to start writing Mac apps. Close the application and return to the main Xcode window.

To close an app that's running inside of Xcode, you can either choose Quit from the application's menu, or just click the Tasks stop sign toolbar icon in Xcode, which is shown in Figure 1-10.

It's called Tasks because you may have several things going on in Xcode, and if you click and hold on this icon, you can select *which* task you want to stop.

> If your application crashes or stops responding, you won't be able to use Quit from the application menu. If that happens, just use the Tasks toolbar item. This is equivalent to a Force Quit, so the application won't have a chance to save any data or preferences before closing.

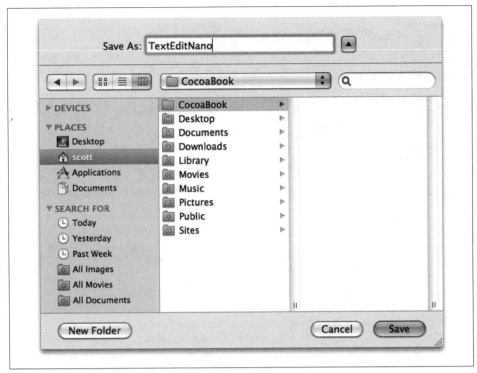

Figure 1-7. Create a CocoaBook folder for your projects, and name the project "TextEditNano"

Create the Interface

At the heart of every great Mac app is a great user interface. You might design the interface in an image editing program, on a napkin, or just in your head, but eventually you'll want to make it real. In Cocoa, there are two ways to create a user interface.

You can manually enter configuration details for controls in your application code (you'll learn more about writing code in the next chapter), or you can visually arrange controls in *Interface Builder*. In my experience, novice programmers usually jump at the chance to work visually, but experienced developers sometimes take a bit more convincing.

Some new programmers think that writing software the hard way makes you a better programmer, but expert Mac developers measure success by how quickly they can deliver great results. Interface Builder is *not* training wheels for Cocoa; it's a tool to reduce the amount of "busy work" you have to do when setting up your user interface (UI), which means you can work more quickly and avoid trivial errors. That leaves you free to focus on the *real* work.

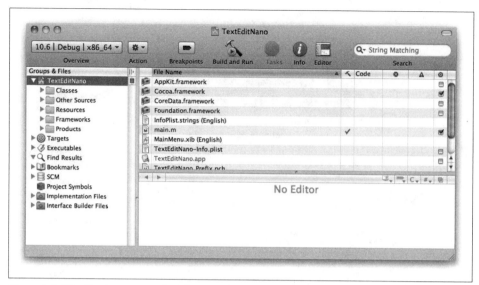

Figure 1-8. The Xcode main window showing the TextEditNano project

 Eliminating busy work is the most important idea in Cocoa. A programmer who doesn't need to waste time on tedious tasks is free to focus on creating features that make her app unique.

Xcode includes an Interface Builder document with each new project, but as you've seen from the blank window, there's not much to it. In the main Xcode window, click the disclosure triangle to the left of the blue TextEditNano project icon in the sidebar to display its contents. Now open the Resources group and double-click the *MainMenu.xib* file to open it in Interface Builder. You'll see a window that looks something like Figure 1-11.

Double-click the Window icon (circled) to open the main window for the TextEdit-Nano application. It should look exactly like the blank window you saw when you first ran the application. This window is your canvas. You can add any UI elements here that you want to use in your application.

Interface Builder works differently than some other visual development tools. It doesn't *generate* Objective-C code. Instead, it takes snapshots of the *state* of the objects. The configuration of all of the controls, including all of their positioning information, is saved in the *MainMenu.xib* file and loaded by Cocoa when your app is launched.

Figure 1-9. The blank window you see the first time you run TextEditNano

Figure 1-10. The Tasks button in the Xcode toolbar

The *.xib* file format is an XML version of the standard *.nib* format that was Interface Builder's native format in earlier versions of Mac OS X. The XML version is easier to use in version control systems, but when Xcode builds your app, it actually converts XIB files into NIB files. The original XIB file is preserved, though.

Open Interface Builder's Library window by choosing Tools → Library from the menu. The Library window contains ready-to-use UI elements that are built into Cocoa. You can also download third-party plug-ins or create your own. Type "text view" into the search field at the bottom of the window to bring up the Text View item, as shown in Figure 1-12.

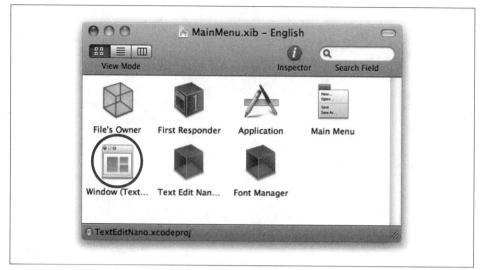

Figure 1-11. The MainMenu.xib file for TextEditNano

 If nothing shows up when you search for the text view, make sure that the Objects tab is selected at the top of the window, and the Library item is selected in the drop-down menu below it.

Drag the Text View item from the Library window into the application window. This might be obvious, but you need to drag it to your "prototype" application window that appeared when you double-clicked on Window in Interface Builder (Figure 1-13), not the real one from the running application (which you hopefully already closed).

Move the text view so that it's near the top-left edge of the window. Use the handles around the outside to resize it so it nearly fills the window, but leave a little bit of space at the bottom. The exact size isn't important—just do whatever you think looks right.

Select File → Simulate Interface from the menu, or press Command-R. This will display the window in Interface Builder's *simulator test mode*. The application isn't actually running, but you can see a preview of what it will look like and can even type in the text field. If you try to resize the window, though, you can see that the text view doesn't resize with it. Press Command-Q to close the simulator, and we'll fix this.

Set sizing properties

Select the text view by clicking on it in the prototype window, and choose Tools → Size Inspector from the menu, or press Command-3. The Inspector window's title is "Scroll View Size," but that's OK (you may have expected it to be named "Text View Size"). The scroll view is wrapped around the text view to provide scrolling support for long runs of text.

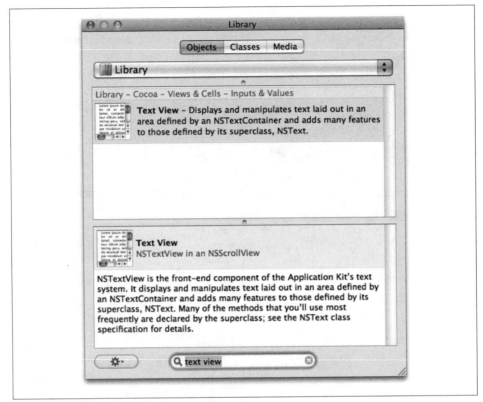

Figure 1-12. Search for "text view" in the Library window

The Autosizing section of the Inspector controls resizing. The outer anchors control which edges the view *moves* with, and the inner arrows control which edges the view *resizes* with. That may not make sense when you read it, but fortunately the Inspector window shows you a live preview as you make changes. You can turn each anchor on or off by clicking it. Click both sets of internal arrows so the view resizes with the window. It should look Figure 1-14 when you're done.

Run the test mode again by pressing Command-R. If you resize the window, the text view should now resize with it. Press Command-Q to close the simulator, then Command-S to save the *MainMenu.xib* file. Switch back to Xcode.

Run the Finished Application

Back in Xcode, click the Build and Run icon in the toolbar (or just press Command-R) to build the application and run it. This time when the window comes up, you should see the text view you added. Choose Format → Font → Show Fonts to choose a font, then type something in the text field (see Figure 1-15).

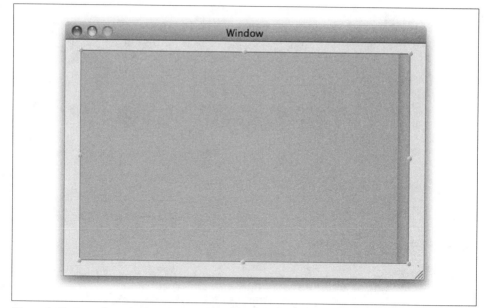

Figure 1-13. Drag the text view icon into the prototype window

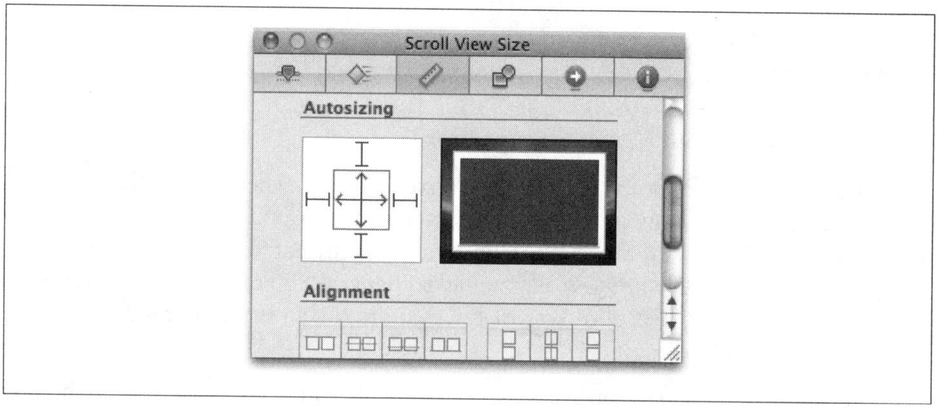

Figure 1-14. Click both sets of arrows to enable resizing

Even though you haven't written a single line of code yet, you already have a real Cocoa application. It can't save files, but it uses Cocoa's built-in text view so you can use fonts, colors (Shift-Command-C), international text, and spellchecking. It also supports drag-and-drop, text search (try Command-F), and many other features.

Figure 1-15. Cocoa has built-in support for advanced text effects

You can also create PDFs from the text and even print. Choose File → Print to bring up the standard print dialog, and click Preview to convert the text into a PDF as shown in Figure 1-16.

The document can use features like any other PDF, including text selection, searching, and annotation. Remember, this is *your application* that you just made from scratch.

Figure 1-16. Basic PDF generation and printing is built in

CHAPTER 2

Thinking in Code: Basic C

As a Cocoa programmer, your job is to get your ideas onto the screen. When you write an essay, you use sentences and paragraphs. Writing software works the same way, though you write *lines of code* instead. Each line performs a task, such as opening a file or displaying an image. When you put enough of these lines of code together, you eventually have an application.

You write these instructions using a programming language. Most Mac and iPhone apps are written in Objective-C, so that's what you'll use in this book. The process of converting your ideas into code is called, literally, *writing code*, and the result is *source code*. For example, to make your application play the alert sound, you write this line of code:

```
NSBeep();
```

There's one important detail, though. Objective-C is based on a simpler language, called C. In fact, Objective-C isn't just based on C; it's *all* of C plus some other stuff. Programmers like to say it's a *strict superset* of C.

So before you start writing Cocoa apps, it helps to learn some C. I'm not going to lead you into the outer limits of the language; you'll see just enough to get started. If you already know C, you can safely skim this chapter.

 If this seems confusing, just remember that Objective-C is the language that defines *how* you format your code—the grammar. Cocoa defines *what* you can make your code do—the overall vocabulary. You create a Cocoa app by writing code in the Objective-C language.

How Code Works

Mac OS X contains special folders for programmers called *frameworks*. A framework helps you do things like animate graphics, display web pages, and create PDFs. These aren't just for third-party developers; the built-in applications use them too. Applications can also include their own custom frameworks that aren't provided by Mac OS X.

You might be used to thinking of Cocoa as a single tool for building Mac apps. In reality, it's the foundation for many different frameworks—an entire ecosystem. In fact, there are more than 90 frameworks in Snow Leopard, and some of those contain *sub*frameworks.

Each one is designed to help you do something different. For example, the *Core Video* framework helps you write an application that can apply real-time special effects to video. A single Mac application may use *many* different frameworks, though almost all inherit basic infrastructure from Cocoa.

 The frameworks built into Mac OS X are in */System/Library/Frameworks* (Figure 2-1). Developers can also create their own frameworks and install them in */Library/Frameworks*. Feel free to look around in there, even if you don't know what the frameworks do yet.

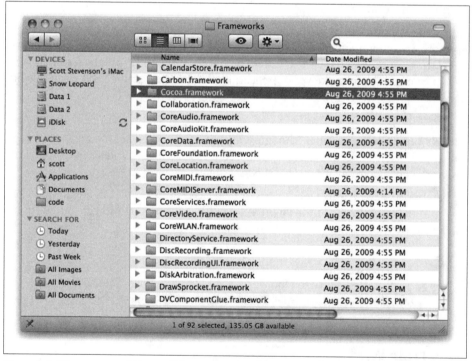

Figure 2-1. The contents of /System/Library/Frameworks on Snow Leopard

When you write a line of Objective-C code, you are usually asking a framework to do something for you. For example, these lines of code download an image from a website and save it as a TIFF file on my desktop:

```
id url   = [NSURL URLWithString:@"http://cocoabook.com/test.png"];
id image = [[NSImage alloc] initWithContentsOfURL:url];
id tiff  = [image TIFFRepresentation];

[tiff writeToFile:@"/Users/scott/test.tiff" atomically:YES];
```

If you've never written code before, this probably all looks pretty strange. It's a lot like when you see algebra or a foreign language for the first time. Even though it's new, there *is* a consistent structure that you can learn. Here's what Cocoa does for you when you write and run the example lines of code:

1. Finds the IP address for the host cocoabook.com
2. Establishes an HTTP connection to the server at that IP address
3. Creates an image to hold the data
4. Downloads the data, bit by bit, and places it in memory
5. Saves the image data to a TIFF image file on the local disk

Incredibly, you don't need to know the HTTP protocol, how to resolve IP addresses, or how to create a TCP connection. Frameworks are designed to abstract these kinds of details from you so that you can focus on what makes your app unique. As Cocoa and other frameworks are improved with each new version of Mac OS X and iPhone OS, your app will often pick up new features without any additional work.

So making Mac apps is really about writing code that uses frameworks. You type specific instructions into a file in Xcode, then click Build and Run to try them out. When you do this, Xcode *compiles* your code into an application, which can be double-clicked on a Mac, tapped on an iPhone's home screen, or even run from the command line in Mac OS X's Terminal application.

In a sense, the lines of code you write are the "raw materials" of your application. Xcode then acts as an assembly line, compiling your code into the final product. Compilation is a fairly complex process, but Xcode handles the basic cases with very little effort on your part.

How to Format Code

Xcode and Cocoa do a lot of work for you, but you have to do your part by writing accurate code. If we stay with the theme of you supplying raw materials and Xcode assembling them, you have to be sure the materials are "built to spec." In other words, you need to write code that Xcode can understand.

Appropriately, when Xcode processes your code it generates something called *assembly code*. This is harder for humans to read, but perfect for computers. You can see this by opening a source code file and choosing Build → Show Assembly from the menu.

Some programming languages have very complex formatting rules, but C and Objective-C are pretty simple. That doesn't mean they're always easy to use, just that they have fewer grammar rules than many other languages. We'll start with something basic. Let's say you have some driving instructions:

1. Enter I-280 South.

2. Exit at the De Anza ramp.

3. Make a U-turn at Mariani Avenue.

4. Turn right into Infinite Loop.

Anybody who knows English can read these steps, but I can't compile them. I'll convert them to code:

```
enterFreeway          ( "I-280 South" );
exitFreewayAtRamp     ( "De Anza" );
performUTurnAtStreet  ( "Mariani Ave" );
turnRightAtStreet     ( "1 Infinite Loop" );
```

This program won't actually run, because it assumes four hypothetical actions that aren't supported by any framework you're likely to find on a Mac or iPhone.

Written languages are flexible. Even if you misspell a word or structure a sentence strangely, the reader usually knows what you mean. For example, a person knows that "Mariani *Ave*" and "Mariani *Avenue*" are the same, but programming languages are usually more strict. When Xcode compiles your code, it can't make conceptual leaps about what your intentions are.

Word spacing is another key difference. In English, each word is separated by a space or hyphen, but many programming languages combine several words into one big noun or verb, such as `mailboxSearchField`. There's a consistent pattern to the code: an action, sometimes followed by additional details. Here's the first line of that code again:

```
enterFreeway ( "I-280 South" );
```

The line starts with `enterFreeway`, which is the name of an action. These actions are called *functions*. The second part of the line describes *which* freeway to enter: I-280 South. The technical term for this is an *argument* or *parameter*, but I think those are pretty awkward terms. You can just think of it as an *input value*.

Each instruction ends with a semicolon. In C, a semicolon is like a period at the end of a sentence. Just like sentences, a single instruction can span multiple lines, but almost all instructions end with a semicolon.

 The compiler converts source code into working programs. When you click Build in the toolbar, Xcode uses the compiler to do a lot of the low-level work. Besides abstracting a lot of these tedious details, Xcode also packages up the program as a proper Mac app.

If you write a line of Xcode that isn't correct, Xcode will display an error when you try to build. You won't be able to run your app until you fix the error. These kinds of mistakes are known as *build errors* (Figure 2-2).

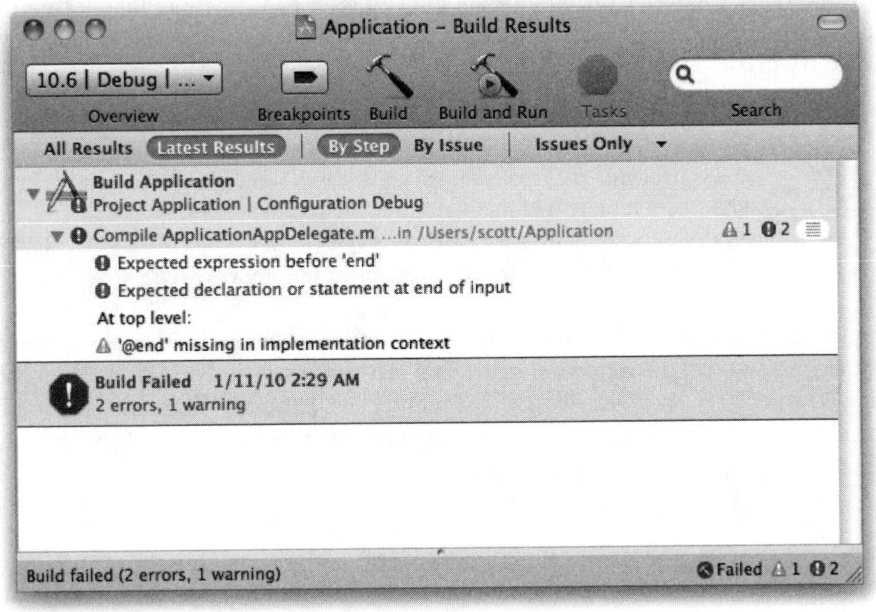

![Screenshot of the Xcode Application – Build Results window showing a build error. The toolbar shows Overview, Breakpoints, Build, Build and Run, Tasks, Search. Tabs show All Results, Latest Results, By Step, By Issue, Issues Only. The results show Build Application, Project Application | Configuration Debug, Compile ApplicationAppDelegate.m ...in /Users/scott/Application with errors: Expected expression before 'end', Expected declaration or statement at end of input, At top level: '@end' missing in implementation context. Build Failed 1/11/10 2:29 AM, 2 errors, 1 warning. Status bar: Build failed (2 errors, 1 warning).]

Figure 2-2. A build error in Xcode

Even the best programmers make mistakes like this every day, but many are easy to fix. You'll learn more about this as you use Xcode to build applications.

One thing that C *is* flexible about is how you use whitespace. All of the lines in the following example will produce exactly the same result:

```
enterFreeway            ( "I-280 South" );
enterFreeway (     "I-280 South"    );
enterFreeway("I-280 South");
```

Programmers use whitespace to make the intentions of their code more clear, though there are a lot of different opinions on what "clear code" is. You can usually use whatever style works best for you. Teams of programmers usually try to agree on a style that everyone in the group uses, though there is always room for flexibility in how you format your code.

Instead of listing every single C formatting rule here, I'm going to move on to more practical concepts and show you these rules by example. If you ever have trouble typing in a sample correctly, you can download a working version from the book's companion website (see the Preface for information on obtaining the sample code).

Variables

A *variable* is a container for a piece of data, such as a block of text, an image, or a web page. You give each variable a name so you can refer to it in code. Like formatting, there are different conventions for naming variables. When writing Mac software, you should try to use the same conventions that Cocoa itself uses.

 Cocoa is designed to make very large projects manageable, and encourages you to write code that's easy to understand. Some applications are made up of hundreds of thousands or millions of lines of code. Using consistent, clear naming conventions makes it easier for many programmers to collaborate on a project.

Giving names to things with varying definitions makes them easier to refer to: you see *a movie*, eat *a meal*, drive down *a street*. It's just easier to say "breakfast" than "that thing we did yesterday where we ate bacon and eggs." You can share information between different parts of an application using variable names instead of the data they contain. Let's start with a simple line of code:

```
emailMessageToFriend ( "Hi there!", "test@example.com" );
```

This seems reasonable. I call the function `emailMessageToFriend()`, with one input item for the message and another for the email address. But what if I want to send a different message, or send the message to a different person? I'd need to change the code, recompile it, and rerun it. Clearly, this won't work.

Variables make it possible to write one piece of code for many different situations by using a name as a *placeholder* for the real data. Here's what the previous line of code looks like if I use variables instead:

```
message = "Hi there";
address = "test@example.com";

emailMessageToFriend ( message, address );
```

I can use the variables `message` and `address` to refer to the email contents and recipient without having to know what they will be ahead of time. I can also make the code more useful by reusing the `message` variable as-is, but *changing* the `address` variable to send the same email to other people:

```
message = "Welcome to Cupertino!";
address = "gina@example.com";
emailMessageToFriend ( message, address );

address = "fred@example.com";
emailMessageToFriend ( message, address );

address = "sarah@example.com";
emailMessageToFriend ( message, address );
```

If I ever want to change the welcome message, I have to update it in only one place instead of three.

 In a real program, I would make a window that allows the user to select whom they want to send messages to, ideally using the Mac OS X Address Book database to choose from a list of existing contacts.

Types

In C, variables have a *type*, which describes what kind of data the variable contains. C has a handful of built-in types for common things like numbers and text, but you can also create your own.

There are two steps to using a variable in C: *declare* it, then *assign* a value to it. You can change the value of a variable as many times as you want, which is actually what the term "variable" means. Here's an example of declaring a variable and assigning it a value in one step:

```
int milesPerGallon = 35;
```

This code creates a new `int` variable with the name `milesPerGallon`, and assigns it an initial value of 35. On a Mac running Snow Leopard, this variable can store any whole integer up to 2,147,483,647.* *No, you don't need to memorize this.*

For floating-point numbers (numbers with decimal points), C has a *float* type. Here's an example:

```
float exchangeRate = 1.618;
```

The `milesPerGallon` and `exchangeRate` variables have different *types*, but they do the same thing: store a value. You can also declare a variable and assign it a value in separate steps:

---

* You can see the actual definition for the maximum value in */usr/include/i386/limits.h*. Just look for `INT_MAX`.

```
int milesPerGallon;
float exchangeRate;

milesPerGallon = 35;
exchangeRate = 1.618;
```

Here's an example of declaring a variable once, assigning it a value, then reassigning it a new value several times:

```
int milesPerGallon;

milesPerGallon = 35;
milesPerGallon = 27;
milesPerGallon = 81;

float exchangeRate;

exchangeRate = 1.120;
exchangeRate = 1.114;
exchangeRate = 1.618;
```

If you try to assign the wrong type of data to a variable, C will usually try to do some conversion, but you may lose information in the process. For example, if you try to assign the value 24.5 to milesPerGallon, it will be stored as 24 because int variables only store *whole* numbers. Some conversions are not possible, and Xcode will warn you about these when you compile your application (when Xcode wants to show you warnings or error messages, it calls your attention to them in the status bar at the bottom of the window).

Some successful conversions will give a different result than you expect. Most of the time, assigning an int value to a float variable does what you expect. However, if you divide one integer value by another integer value, you'll always get a integer result, *even if* you assign the result to a float:

```
int miles = 366;
int gallons = 8;
float milesPerGallon = miles / gallons;
```

The milesPerGallon variable will contain the value 45 instead of 45.75. You can use the *cast* operation (specify the name of the desired type in parentheses) to force a specific type conversion. This example converts both miles and gallons to float values before it performs the division:

```
float milesPerGallon = (float) miles / (float) gallons;
```

Technically, you don't need to cast both values, because the compiler is smart enough to treat both as float values if you cast at least one of them:

```
float milesPerGallon = (float) miles / gallons;
```

Table 2-1 contains a list of some of the most common "primitive" types used in C.

Table 2-1. Basic C data types

Type	Description	Examples
int	Integer numbers, including negatives	0, 78, −1400
unsigned int	Integer numbers (no negatives)	0, 46, 900
float	Floating-point decimal numbers, including negatives	0.0, 1.618, −1.4
char	Single text character or symbol	a, D, ?

In addition to the types listed in the table, there's also a type called `double`, which is a version of `float` that can hold larger decimal point numbers, and `long`, which is a larger version of `int`. Cocoa has special variable types that automatically adapt to different sizes as necessary, which you'll learn about in Chapter 7. I'll also show you how to make your *own* types in Chapter 3.

Constants

In computer programming, *constants* are variables that can't be modified once you've assigned a value to them. C has a keyword `const` that behaves like a constant most of the time. For example, the compiler won't let you change the value of an `int` that you've declared as `const`:

```
int currentSpeed = 55;
currentSpeed = 65;

const int maximumSpeed = 75;
maximumSpeed = 80;
```

If you try to compile this, you'll get the error: `assignment of read-only variable`. Changing `currentSpeed` is fine, but trying to change the constant `maximumSpeed` won't work. Constants are a way to prevent your code from accidentally changing important variables. Another way to define a constant in C and Objective-C is to use `#define`, which is a *preprocessor directive*. By convention, these are usually in all capital letters:

```
#define MAX_MPG 120
if (milesPerGallon > MAX_MPG) {
  errorMessage = "You appear to have a nuclear-powered car.";
}
```

The preprocessor is a tool that runs behind the scenes when you compile an application. It does a number of different things, such as handling `#include` statements, but also does a search and replace on placeholders you've specified with `#define`. So the `#define` directive doesn't create real variables; it just replaces one string of text with another before the compiler gets its hands on the code. Here's what the preceding example looks like by the time it's handed off to the compiler:

```
if (milesPerGallon > 120) {
  errorMessage = "You appear to have a nuclear-powered car.";
}
```

In general, #define is common in pure C programs, but it's not considered such great style in Cocoa apps. It's not outright wrong, just considered a bit clumsy or inelegant. My experience is that const is generally better for Objective-C, especially because Xcode can do a better job with helping you write code if you use real variables.

Enumerated Types

If you have a group of related values (such as days of the week), you can use C's enum keyword to create a group of constant values that you can use in your programs. These enumerations are integer types, and the values can be used wherever you would use an integer:

```
enum { monday, tuesday, wednesday, thursday,
       friday, saturday, sunday };

int day = saturday;
```

Typedefs

C lets you define your own types with the typedef statement. You can use this to create aliases to some of the basic types in C, which lets you write code that's somewhat self-documenting:

```
typedef int Distance;
Distance home_to_office = 30;
Distance office_to_cafe = 3;
```

What's more, you can combine typedef and enum to create your own type that can only be assigned one of the values listed in the enum. Doing so eliminates the need to define the day variable shown earlier as an int, and makes for a more self-documenting program:

```
typedef enum {
  monday, tuesday, wednesday, thursday,
  friday, saturday, sunday
} DayOfWeek;

DayOfWeek day = saturday;
```

Functions

The previous example programs were just flat lists of instructions. That's fine for very simple cases, but you need some sort of structure to manage all of the code in a real application. A *function* is a way to group multiple instructions together so they can be used with a single line of code.

When someone asks you what you did today, you might say something like "I went to the grocery." You probably don't say "I opened the door, walked outside, closed the door, locked it, walked to the car, opened the car door…" because that level of detail isn't relevant to the conversation. Once somebody understands what the phrase "I went to the grocery store" means, they know that it contains a sensible series of steps. Let's see how that might look as a list of steps first:

```
Buy Groceries

    Open front door
    Walk out front door
    Close front door
    Lock front door

    Walk to car
    Open car door
    Enter car
    Close car door
```

I know this seems like a ridiculous level of detail, but this is how a computer programmer thinks. In general, software cannot make conceptual leaps. You need to spell out *exactly* how the application should work. For example, if I wrote out the exact steps to display a PNG image on screen, they would probably look like this:

```
Display Image

    Save file path as a variable
    Make sure the path to the file is valid
    Make sure the file at the path is a PNG image

    Reserve memory for an image
    Read data from the file, one byte at a time
    When all data is read in, close the file

    Open a new window to display the image
    Draw the contents of the image into the window
```

The good news is that frameworks like Cocoa have already done a lot of the groundwork for you. Cocoa has defined what many of these "lists of tasks" are, and they're ready for you to use. That's what allows you to place an image in a window without knowing details like the refresh rate of the user's display.

Now let's go back and translate the "Buy Groceries" steps into something that looks more like C code. I'll create a function called buyGroceries() that itself calls a series of other functions:

```
void buyGroceries() {

    openFrontDoor();
    walkOutFrontDoor();
    closeFrontDoor();
    lockFrontDoor();

    walkToCar();
    openCarDoor();
    enterCar();
```

```
    closeCarDoor();
  }
```

There are a few things that may look new here, but you can probably still get the gist of what's going on. My `buyGroceries()` function is calling other functions like `openFrontDoor()` and `walkOutFrontDoor()`. This pattern of functions calling other functions is the essence of structured programming. Let's take a look at the first line again:

❶ void **❷** buyGroceries() **❸** {

There are three things to notice here:

❶ The word `void` is the *return type* for the function. The return type could also be `int`, `float`, `char`, or any other C type. The value a function returns is called a *result*. When a function doesn't return anything, the return type is `void`. Yes, it's a slightly strange convention, but this is just one of the delightful quirks of C.

❷ The function name is followed by a pair of parentheses: `buyGroceries()`.

❸ Programmers usually call the { symbol a "curly brace." All of the instructions in a function must be inside of a pair of curly braces. It's easy to forget to add a curly brace to the *end* of the function. So check this first if Xcode shows you an error when compiling your app.

Let's look at a few actual functions with return values:

```
int numberOfPeople () {
   return 3;
}


float dollarsAndCents () {
   return 10.33;
}
```

We're using all of the same conventions here as in the previous example. In fact, the only difference is now we're using the *return statement*, which sends a result back to the caller and ends the function.

 There's a subtle point here. The `return` statement returns a result to the caller, but it will also *immediately* end the function. If you have any code after the `return` statement, that code will not run.

When you call a function, you can capture the result in variable of the same type. Here are some examples:

```
int count;
count = numberOfPeople();

float totalCost;
totalCost = dollarsAndCents();
```

I declared `count` as an `int` because the `numberOfPeople()` function returns an `int`. You can also create functions that *input* values. In the following sample, I have a function that multiplies the input value by 10, and returns the result. In C, the asterisk character multiplies two numbers:

```
int timesTen (int input) {
   return input * 10;
}
```

Here's how I can call the function, providing input and capturing the output:

```
int outputValue = timesTen( 18 );
```

 When you're capturing the result of a function, give the variable a type that matches the return type of the function. So if the function returns an `int` value, declare the variable as an `int`, too.

You can also provide a variable as input:

```
int inputValue;
int outputValue;

inputValue  = 18;
outputValue = timesTen ( inputValue );
```

After this code runs, the variable `outputValue` will contain the value 180. This is a common pattern in programming: you provide input to a function; it does a calculation of some sort and returns a result that you store in a variable. You can also make functions that take multiple input values. You separate input values with commas:

```
int difference ( int input1, int input2 ) {
   return input1 - input2;
}
```

Here's how to use this function:

```
int originalCount = 100;
int itemsSold = 10;

// currentStock will contain the value 90
int currentStock = difference ( originalCount, itemsSold );
```

The example code has a line of descriptive text with two slashes at the beginning. This is called a *comment*:

```
// currentStock will contain the value 90
```

Software can get very complex, and comments help you explain to other people reading your code what various parts of the program do. It can also help *you* remember what the code does. Comments don't affect how the program runs at all, and you can generally write whatever you want. There are two styles: *single-line* and *multiple-line*:

```
// single-line comment
// another single-line comment

/* multiple-line comment
    same multiple-line comment continued */
```

Many Cocoa programmers seem to use the single-line style, because the slashes at the beginning of each line make it clear that the rest of the line is not actual code that's being used. Use whichever one you prefer.

Declaring Functions

Like variables, functions have to be declared before they can be used. A declaration is basically just the first line of the function. Here are some examples of declarations for functions we've already used:

```
int     numberOfPeople    ();
float   dollarsAndCents   ();
int     timesTen          ( int x );
int     difference        ( int input1, int input2 );
```

Remember that C is generally very flexible about how you use whitespace. I spaced the code here so that it lines up and is a bit easier to read, but the declarations would work exactly the same if written like this:

```
int numberOfPeople ();
float dollarsAndCents ();
int timesTen ( int x );
int difference ( int input1, int input2 );
```

You need to be sure that the input and output types in the function *declaration* match those in the function *implementation*; otherwise, Xcode will display errors. For example, this is incorrect, and will generate errors if you try to compile it:

```
// this is incorrect. the declaration says the return type is 'float'
// but the implementation says it is 'int'.

float numberOfPeople ();

int numberOfPeople () {
  return 3;
}
```

Example: FirstProgram

Now you're going to take everything we've learned about types, variables, and functions and put together a small sample program that displays values on the command line in the Terminal. For this example, I'm going to have you use Xcode for editing the files, but use the command line to actually compile the program. In addition to giving us a bit of insight about what Xcode is doing behind the scenes, it will also help us stay focused on the basics of C.

Go to your *CocoaBook* folder in the Finder. If you haven't created the *CocoaBook* folder in your home directory yet, do so now. Then, create a new subfolder inside *CocoaBook* called *ch02*. Now open Xcode and choose File → New File. In the template window, choose Mac OS X → C and C++ → C File, then click Next. See Figure 2-3.

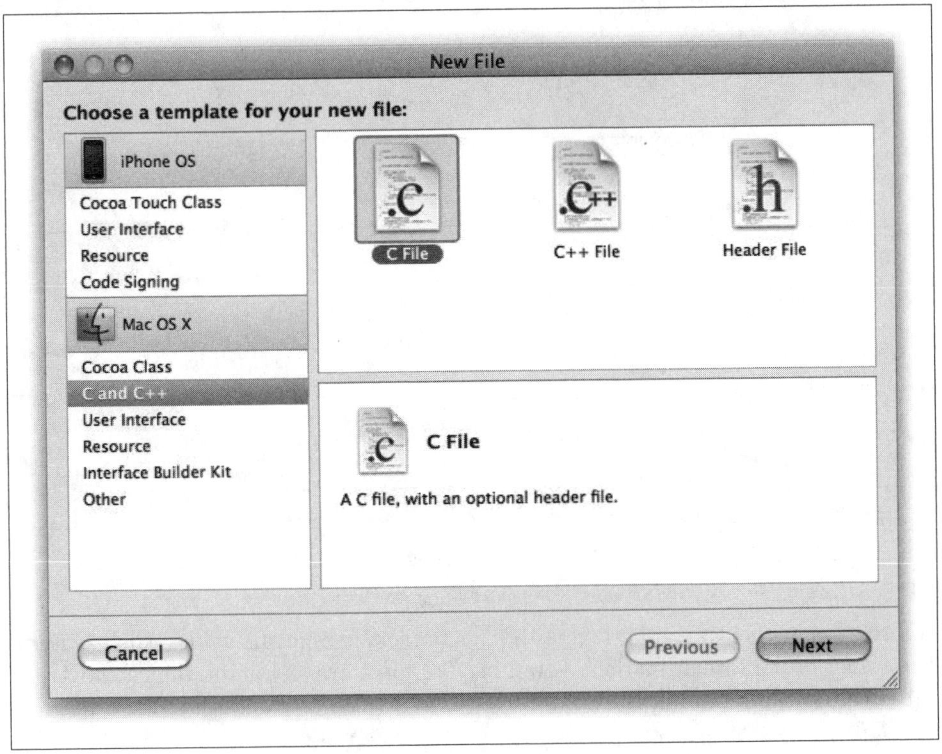

Figure 2-3. Create a new C file in Xcode

In the New File window, type *FirstProgram.c* into the File Name field, and *uncheck* the checkbox labeled "Also create FirstProgram.h."

Next, type *~/CocoaBook/ch02/* into the Location field. If you want to navigate to the path visually, click the Choose button and find the folder. Leave all other options in the window at their default settings and click Finish (Figure 2-4).

Displaying Values on the Command Line

To display values in the Terminal's command-line environment, we'll use a built-in C function called `printf()`. Programmers often say "print" to refer to displaying values on the command line. The "f" stands for "format." So `printf()` takes a *format string*, and "prints" the result.

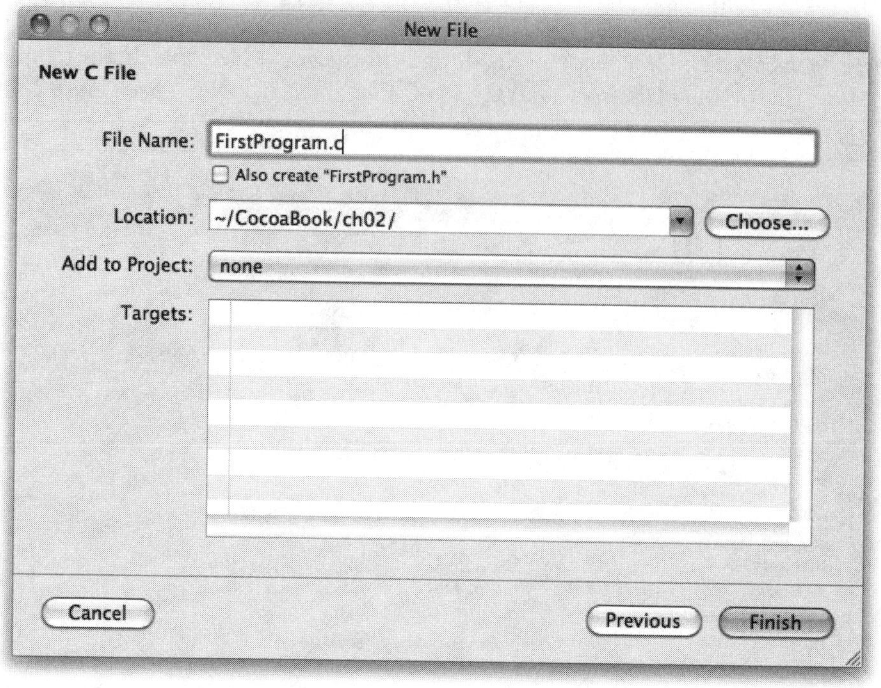

Figure 2-4. Name the file FirstProgram.c and save it in ~/CocoaBook/ch02/

A format string is just regular text with placeholders for specific values, such as numbers. Two of the format markers you'll use the most are %i for int values and %f for float values. Here's a simple example:

```
printf ( "The first value is: %i", 8+2 );
```

Here's the output:

```
The first value is: 10
```

Here's another example:

```
printf ( "The second value is: %f", 100.0 / 4.0 );
```

And the result:

```
The second value is: 25.000000
```

The printf() function is somewhat special, because it takes a *varying number of input values*. That is, for each marker, you need to supply one additional input value:

```
printf ( "First: %i Second: %i Third: %i\n", 10, 100, 1000 );
```

In this example, I provided the format string, plus three additional input values: 10, 100, and 1000. This may be the first time you've seen the \n *newline character*. Even though it takes two separate key presses on the keyboard, a newline is treated as one character by C. This kind of character is call an *escape sequence*. The backslash right before the n tells `printf()` not to treat it as a normal character, but to give it special status.

The newline character simply creates a new line in the output. Here's what multiple calls to `printf()` look like without it:

Code:

```
printf ( "First line" );
printf ( "Second line" );
printf ( "Third line" );
```

Result:

```
First lineSecond lineThird line
```

When I add the \n symbol back in, everything looks right:

Code:

```
printf ( "First line\n" );
printf ( "Second line\n" );
printf ( "Third line\n" );
```

Result:

```
First line
Second line
Third line
```

Now let's put all of this to use in a real program. Type the code from Example 2-1 into the *FirstProgram.c* file you just created in Xcode. I'll describe each part individually.

Example 2-1. FirstProgram.c

```
#include <stdio.h>

int sum ( int x, int y );

main () {
  int total = sum (2, 10);
  printf ( "Total: %i \n", total );
}

int sum ( int x, int y ) {
  return x + y;
}
```

The first line has something we haven't seen yet: the `#include` statement. This allows us to use code that's built into C, or code written by other programmers. The *stdio.h* file contains declarations for functions related to standard input and output. In this case, we need *stdio.h* to use the `printf()` function. Next is the declaration for the `sum()` function:

```
int sum ( int x, int y );
```

You've seen this before. This declares a function with two input values. Now let's look at something else that's new: the `main()` function:

```
main () {
  int total = sum (2, 10);
  printf ( "Total: %i \n", total );
}
```

The `main()` function is always the first thing that gets run in a C program. It's the starting point. *Inside* the function is the same stuff you've seen before. You declare the `total` variable and use it to capture the result of the `sum()` function. Then use `printf()` to display the result in the Terminal window. Finally, you have these lines of code:

```
int sum ( int x, int y ) {
  return x + y;
}
```

This is your implementation of the `sum()` function. You just take two input values, add them together, and return the result. Even though this function appears at the bottom of the file, you can still call it within `main()`. The declaration of the `sum()` function at the beginning of the file is what makes this possible. If you're used to other programming languages, declaring functions may seem like an odd requirement, but it is something that's necessary to write in C code.

Compile and Run the Example

To keep things simple, and learn about how things are working at a lower level, you're going to compile a few programs at the Unix command line. On Mac OS X, you can get to the command line using the Terminal application in Applications → Utilities. When you launch it, you'll see a prompt like the one in Figure 2-5.

If you don't know how to use the command line, don't worry—I'll tell you exactly what to type. If you haven't already done so, save the *FirstProgram.c* file. In Terminal, change to the folder where the file is by typing this command:

```
my-mac:~ scott$ cd ~/CocoaBook/ch02/
```

 Everything before the **$** is the *shell prompt* and will look slightly different on your computer. You should only type what's shown to the right of the shell prompt in listings you see in this book.

To compile the application, we're going to use a command-line program called *GCC* (*http://gcc.gnu.org*). The GCC compiler is a low-level program tool used by Xcode, although it's used by other programming environments as well. Type the following command into the Terminal:

```
my-mac:~ scott$ gcc FirstProgram.c -o FirstProgram
```

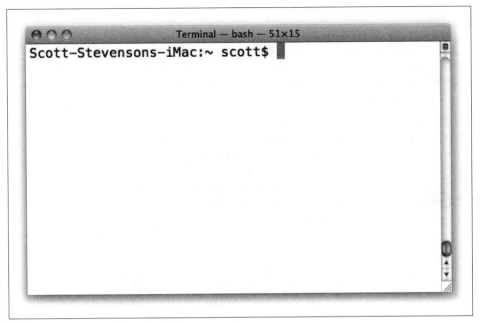

Figure 2-5. The command line in the Terminal application

To try it out, type the following:

```
my-mac:~ scott$ ./FirstProgram
```

 At the command line, Mac OS X searches for programs in a variety of locations on your computer, but not your current directory. Using *./* tells Mac OS X to run a program that's in your current directory.

You should see something on the screen like this:

```
Total: 12
```

You are now officially a programmer. A *new* programmer, but a programmer just the same. If you have any typos in your code, you might see some odd errors, such as these:

```
FirstProgram.c: In function 'main':
FirstProgram.c:8: error: expected ';' before '}' token
```

We'll look at how to fix these sort of errors soon enough, but for now, just go back and compare your code, one line at a time, to the code in the book. If you still can't get it to work, you can download a working version from the companion website mentioned in the Preface.

Scope

When speaking out loud, you sometime use *scope* to imply what you mean without explaining it in detail. For example, if I'm standing in a house, saying "the house" probably means the house I'm currently in. But if I'm standing on a street, "the house" could mean any house on that street.

In programming, scope is a general term for the *visibility* of different variables. A *global variable* is visible anywhere in the application. Any function anywhere in the program can use it. A *local variable* is visible only within a single function.

 Local variables will not usually keep their values after the function ends. That means that if you call a function multiple times, you should set the values each time. A variable may *happen* to have the same value, but the value could also be random data, which can cause incorrect results or cause the program to crash.

How do you know which is which? It all depends on where you declare the variable. If you declare a variable *outside* of any functions (typically near the top), it's global. If you declare it *inside* a function, it's local. Example 2-2 uses both.

Example 2-2. LocalGlobalVariable.c

```
#include <stdio.h>

int globalCount = 0;
void addToGlobal ();

main () {

  printf ( "global: %i \n", globalCount );
  addToGlobal();
  printf ( "global: %i \n", globalCount );
}

void addToGlobal () {

  int localCount = 100;
  globalCount = globalCount + localCount;
}
```

I declared the globalCount at the top of the file—not inside a function—so it has *global visibility*, which means all functions can see it. The localCount variable is declared inside addToGlobal() so it's visible only within that function—which is called *local visibility*. In fact, you can declare another local variable inside main() with the same name as a local variable in addToGlobal(). They have different scope, so there's no conflict:

```
main () {
  int localCount = 80;
}
```

```
void declareLocalVariable () {
  int localCount = 100;
}
```

Variables names don't have to be unique across the entire application. The names have to be unique only in their scope. So you can't have two *global* variables with the same name, and you can't have two local variables in the same function with the same name:

```
void declareTwoLocalVariables () {

    // This will cause an error. Two variables
    // can't have the same name in the same scope.
    int localCount = 100;
    int localCount = 80;
}
```

This also touches on another subtle point. You can't change the *kind* of data a variable holds after you've declared it. If you make it an `int`, you can't later declare it as a `float` somewhere else in the program.

Static Variables

If you want a local variable to keep its value even after the function ends, you can use the *static* keyword in front of it. You can specify an initial value for a static variable, but that value is only set the first time the function is called:

```
#include <stdio.h>

void myFunction () {

    static int numberOfCalls = 1;
    printf("This function has been called %i times\n", numberOfCalls);

    numberOfCalls = numberOfCalls + 1;
}

main () {

    myFunction();
    myFunction();
    myFunction();
}
```

Here's the result of this code:

```
This function has been called 1 times
This function has been called 2 times
This function has been called 3 times
```

If you use the `static` keyword with a *global variable*, it will only be visible *within the same file*. This is important for larger programs (especially Cocoa projects), those in which multiple files are combined into a single application. Marking global variables as `static` means they won't collide with global variables in other files.

Conditionals

One thing I haven't talked about yet is how you deal with special cases in your code. For example, what if you have an email application, and don't want to let the user send a message with an empty subject line? In English, a requirement might look something like this:

```
Only send the message if it has a subject
```

In C, you use an `if` statement to do this. An `if` statement is one type of *conditional*. For this example, I want to make sure that the subject line isn't empty. Here's how that looks in code:

```
if ( lengthOfSubjectLine > 0 ) {
  sendMessage();
}
```

The `if` statement starts with the keyword `if`, followed by parentheses, which contain a comparison test, a function, or a variable. Here are some more examples:

```
// is one less than two? YES.

if ( 1 < 2 ) {
  ...
}


// is three greater than four? NO.

if ( 3 > 4 ) {
  ...
}


// is firstNumber less than secondNumber? YES.

int firstNumber  = 18;
int secondNumber = 36;

if ( firstNumber < secondNumber ) {
  ...
}


// is firstNumber equal to secondNumber? YES.

firstNumber  = 12;
secondNumber = 12;

if ( firstNumber == secondNumber ) {
  ...
}
```

In this last example, I'm using the *equality operator*, which is simply a double equals sign. It tests whether the number on the left is equal to the number on the right:

```
if (1 == 2) // NO.
if (2 == 2) // YES.
```

This double equals sign thing looks a little weird, right? Why not just use the regular single equals sign? It turns out you already use that to *assign* a value, so if you tried to use it to test equality too, C wouldn't know what you were trying to do. You use == to specifically test for equality. Even experienced programmers occasionally use the single equals sign when they mean to use the equality operator, so be *extra* careful when writing if statements.

You may also want to *negate* a comparison:

```
if ( dayOfWeek != 5 ) {
   printf ( "Today is not Friday \n" );
}

if ( dayOfWeek == 5 ) {
   printf ( "Today is Friday \n" );
}
```

The *inequality operator* (!=) is just an exclamation mark paired with an equals sign. You use it when you want to check whether two things are *not equal* to each other.

There's one important thing to be aware of with the if statement, though. It looks like an if statement is looking for a "yes" or "no" answer, but what it's really checking for is whether the result is zero or *anything else*.

Read that again: an if statement doesn't check for "yes" or "no"; it checks for zero or *nonzero*. In programming, nonzero means "anything other than zero."

C *really* likes numbers. Everything boils down to a number at some level, so even true/false statements are ultimately a 1 (true) or 0 (false). As a result, this code is *technically* correct:

```
// 1 is the same as YES.

if ( 1 ) {
  ....
}

// even 95014 is treated as YES by C.

if ( 95014 ) {
  ....
}
```

Some programmers use this quirk to take shortcuts in code, but you should try to avoid it. Instead, use only comparisons that result in reasonable "yes" or "no" answers. You will make the world a better place if you do. I'm serious.

By the way, this little detail can really trip you up if you accidentally use the single equals sign instead of the equality operator:

```
int firstNumber  = 0;
int secondNumber = 1;

// I've _accidentally_ used the single equals sign, so I'm
// _assigning_ the value of 'secondNumber' to 'firstNumber'.
// This will always resolve to '1', which is the same as 'YES'.

if ( firstNumber = secondNumber ) {
  sendMessage();
}

// This is what the code should look like.

if ( firstNumber == secondNumber ) {
  sendMessage();
}
```

This may seem obscure, but it's an invaluable bit of knowledge if your app doesn't seem to be doing the right thing. These mistakes are hard to find because it's *technically* correct, so the compiler will allow it.

Sometimes you need to check for more than one thing. For that, you use the *logical "and" operator*, which is just two ampersands together: &&.

```
if ( dayOfWeek == 5 && dayOfMonth < 8 ) {
  printf ( "It's the first Friday of the month! \n" );
}
```

And if you want to check for one of two things to be true, you can use the *logical "or" operator*, which is two pipes together: ||.

```
if ( dayOfWeek == 6 || dayOfWeek == 7 ) {
  printf ( "It's the weekend!\n" );
}
```

You can, of course, make any combination of these operators, but there will be plenty of time to get into that later. For now, let's move on to the final part of the if statement: the *else clause*. You can think of "else" as "otherwise." So instead of just silently ignoring the message if the subject line is missing, we can use an else clause to do something as a fallback case:

```
if ( lengthOfSubjectLine > 0 ) {

  sendMessage();

} else {

  printf ("You forgot a subject line\n" );

}
```

An `else` clause doesn't have a set of parentheses, because there's nothing to evaluate. It just specifies what happens when the `if` statement ends up with a false. There's also a combination of the two, called the `else if` clause:

```
if ( dayOfWeek == 6  ||  dayOfWeek == 7 ) {

    printf ( "It's the weekend! \n" );

} else if ( dayOfWeek == 5 ) {

    printf ( "It's Friday \n" );

} else {

    printf ( "No weekend yet, but it's only a matter of time. \n" );

}
```

You can include any number of `else if` clauses, but the initial `if` must always come first. The final `else` isn't required, but if you have one, it must be at the end.

Example: ShoppingTrip

Developers need hardware to do their programming, so let's write a small C program to calculate the cost of hardware you'll need to make some great apps. This example will use all of the concepts from the chapter. This may seem like quite a bit of typing, but every time you type a line of code, you're burning it into your brain.

As before, go into Xcode and choose File → New File. In the template window, choose Mac OS X → C and C++ → C File, then click Next.

In the New File window, type *ShoppingTrip.c* into the File Name field. Uncheck the checkbox labeled "Also create ShoppingTrip.h."

Next, type ~/*CocoaBook/ch02/* into the Location field. Leave all other options in the window at their default settings and click Finish. Type the code from Example 2-3 into the *ShoppingTrip.c* file.

Example 2-3. ShoppingTrip.c

```
#include <stdio.h>

// global variables. these are visible from any function.

int    totalItems  = 0;
float  totalCost    = 0.0;
float  salesTax     = 0.0925;

// declare the functions we're going to use.
// we don't need to declare main() because it's built in.

void addToTotal (float cost, int quantity);
```

```
float costWithSalesTax ( float price );

// this is where the program starts when it runs.

main () {
  float budget = 10000.00;

  // make a new line.
  printf ("\n");

  // set the prices of each item.
  float laptopPrice    = 1799.00;
  float monitorPrice   = 499.80;
  float phonePrice     = 199.00;

  // for each line item, call the addToTotal() function,
  // specifying the item and quantity.

  addToTotal ( laptopPrice,  2 );
  addToTotal ( monitorPrice, 1 );
  addToTotal ( phonePrice,   4 );

  // display a line and then the final total.
  printf ("------------\n");
  printf ("TOTAL for %i items: $%5.2f\n\n", totalItems, totalCost);

  if ( totalCost < budget ) {
    printf ("You came in under budget!\n\n");

  } else {
    printf ("You're over budget. Time to talk to finance.\n\n");
  }
}

void addToTotal (float cost, int quantity) {

  printf ("Adding %i items of cost $%5.2f\n", quantity, cost );

  // find the cost for this item by multiple cost by quantity.
  // then get the real cost by applying sales tax.
  float calculatedCost = cost * quantity;
  float realCost = costWithSalesTax ( calculatedCost );

  // add this amount to the total, and increase the total number
  // of items purchased.

  totalCost  = totalCost + realCost;
  totalItems = totalItems + quantity;

  printf ("Subtotal for %i items: $%5.2f\n", totalItems, totalCost);
}

float costWithSalesTax ( float price ) {

  // remember, 'salesTax' is a global variable.
```

```
    float taxAmount = price * salesTax;
    float subtotal  = price + taxAmount;

    return subtotal;
}
```

Compile and Run

If you haven't already done so, save the file. Now launch Terminal and change to the folder where the file is:

```
my-mac:~ scott$ cd ~/CocoaBook/ch02/
```

Type the following command to compile the program:

```
my-mac:~ scott$ gcc ShoppingTrip.c -o ShoppingTrip
```

Now try it out:

```
my-mac:~ scott$ ./ShoppingTrip
```

You should see something like this on the screen:

```
Adding 2 items of cost $1799.00
Subtotal for 2 items: $3930.81
Adding 1 items of cost $499.80
Subtotal for 3 items: $4476.85
Adding 4 items of cost $199.00
Subtotal for 7 items: $5346.48
------------
TOTAL for 7 items: $5346.48

You came in under budget!
```

The only convention in this example that we haven't covered yet is the %5.2f in this line:

```
printf ("TOTAL for %i items: $%5.2f\n\n", totalItems, totalCost);
```

You already know that %f is a placeholder for a float variable, but the 5.2 is new. This just describes how many digits should appear on each side of the decimal point. Without this, we'd see strange dollars amounts on the screen:

```
$3930.814941
```

The 5.2 formats the amounts as we're used to seeing in currency: two digits after the decimal point. The 5 could be a larger number for bigger shopping trips, but you'd most likely keep two digits to the right of the decimal point for dollar amounts.

If there's anything else in this example that doesn't make sense, take a few minutes now to go back and review the earlier parts of the chapter, such as those covering variable scope and functions.

Wrap Up

Welcome back from your whirlwind tour of the basics of C programming. Keep in mind that the C language has been in use for decades, and there is a lot more to it than what we've covered here. The goal is to give you just the slices of C that are relevant for day-to-day work with Objective-C and Cocoa.

At this point, we're going to look at a few more advanced C topics, and then it's straight on to Objective-C and Cocoa.

CHAPTER 3

Memory and Pointers: Advanced C

You technically know enough C now to start writing Objective-C code, but I've seen a lot of brand-new Cocoa programmers quickly get in over their heads because they were missing key C concepts. So to help you avoid that phase, I'm introducing you to a few *hand-picked* advanced C techniques. Nothing is in this chapter by accident. If it's here, I'm confident you will need it.

This is *not* a complete course in C. These are just the parts that are likely to help you in day-to-day Cocoa programming. You're probably eager to jump right into Cocoa, so I've done everything I can to condense the fundamentals of C into two chapters instead of an entire book. If you're already an expert C programmer, though, you can safely move on to the next chapter.

Arrays

So far, you've only used variables that hold a single value, but real programs need to handle many values at the same time. For example, in a photo sharing application, each album has some number of photos, but you don't want to make a separate variable for each photo in each album.

To manage large groups of data in C, you use *arrays*. Unlike a normal variable, a single array can hold many values at the same time. You can create an array of just about anything: `int` values, `float` values, or any other C type. But the key is that an array isn't a series of multiple variables. It's a *single variable* that contains *multiple values*.

You can think of a normal variable as a four-door car—a single vehicle with one shared space for everyone inside. It has only one "compartment." If you want to carry more people or things, you need a whole separate car. If you want to store two values, you need two variables.

By contrast, an array is more like a train with many cars attached. An array is a single variable with many separate individual compartments, or *slots*. No matter how many cars you add to a train, the *whole thing* is still called a train. The same is true for an array; no matter how many values you add to it, it's still a single array (see Figure 3-1).[*]

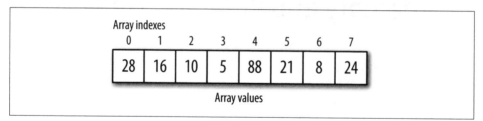

Figure 3-1. *An array stores multiple values in a single variable*

Some arrays hold only a few values, but you can create arrays that hold hundreds or thousands of values. In fact, on a modern Mac, an array could theoretically hold millions of values or more.

Arrays in C provide very few conveniences or safeguards, but the upside is that they're extremely fast. Cocoa has a smarter kind of array called an NSArray, but I want to teach you about the lower-level C version first, because it's a good way to learn about *memory management*. Let's start by declaring an array of float values:

```
float amounts[4];
```

This is an array called amounts, which can hold multiple float values. The 4 in the square brackets specifies that this array can hold up to four values. You can also *assign* values at the same time that you declare an array:

```
float amounts[4] = {10.45, 1.618, 81.81, 14.44};
```

If you declare an array and assign values to it at the same time, you can let C figure out the number of slots automatically (note the square brackets are empty):

```
float amounts[] = {10.45, 1.618, 81.81, 14.44};
```

You can assign and reassign new values to an array whenever you like, but when you're getting or setting a value in an array, you need to specify a slot, also called an *array index*. Just to be clear, *index* and *value* are separate things. A value is *at* an index in an array. In the following example, I'm setting a new value at each index, in order:

```
amounts[0] = 2.1;
amounts[1] = 3.4;
amounts[2] = 212.14;
amounts[3] = 556.21;
```

You don't have to set array values sequentially, though. You don't even have to set all of them at the same time:

[*] An especially geeky real-world example of an array is the Very Large Array (VLA) in New Mexico. The VLA is actually 27 *separate* radio antennas that act as a *single* massive dish. You can learn more about the VLA at *http://www.vla.nrao.edu*.

```
amounts[2] = 3.4;
amounts[1] = 212.14;
amounts[3] = 556.21;
amounts[0] = 2.1;

amounts[2] = 3.4;
amounts[1] = 212.14;
```

I use 0 in the brackets to get to the first slot in an array. You might expect that 1 would be first, but arrays start counting at zero. As a result, the last index is one less than what you'd expect. For example, if an array can hold four values, the first value is at index 0, and the last one is at index 3.

You can also copy a value from an array to use in another variable, like this:

```
float oneValue = amounts[3];
```

As with all variables in C, you can't *redeclare* an array once you've created it. In other words, if you declare an array with 100 values, you can't change it to 150 several lines later:

```
// set this array to hold 100 values.
float amounts[100];

// this will cause an error. you can't redeclare arrays.
float amounts[150];

// this array is implicitly declared to have four slots,
// because four values are supplied.
float timeSamples[] = { 40.1, 200.80, 1.45, 14.6 };

// this array was declared to have four values. you can't redeclare it.
float timeSamples[10];
```

Now that you can store values in an array, you need a way to read and write the values. You *could* write a separate line of code for each value when there are only four of them, but it's not practical for an array with thousands of values. This is where *loops* come in.

Loops

A loop runs the same lines of code a certain number of times. This can make it much easier to write code that uses arrays. For example, adding five numbers in an array looks like this:

```
int values[5] = {12,14,18,21,64};
int total = 0;

total = total + values[0];
total = total + values[1];
total = total + values[2];
total = total + values[3];
total = total + values[4];
```

```
printf ("Total is: %i \n", total);
```

With a loop, you can just do this instead:

```
int values[5] = {12,14,18,21,64};
int total = 0;

int i;
for ( i = 0; i < 5; i++ ) {

    total = total + values[i];
}

printf ("Total is: %i \n", total);
```

This may not seem like much less code with such a small array, but the important idea is that this loop will work just as well for a thousand values as it does for five. In fact, loops and arrays are frequently used together, because they complement each other so perfectly. An array *stores* a series of values, and a loop provides a way to *act on* each value. Here's a typical for loop:

```
int i;
for ( i = 0; i < 5; i++ ) {

    total = total + values[i];
}
```

First, I declare an int variable called i. Cocoa programmers usually choose more descriptive names for variables, but using i for a loop is so common that it's effectively exempt from the rule. You can think of i as standing for "iteration," but the name doesn't matter as much as what it *does*: keeps track of the current "lap" of a loop.

Picture an athlete running around a track during training. Each time she crosses the finish line, the coach advances his counter by 1 to keep track of how many laps she has completed. In C, the i variable is the C equivalent of that counter. It increases by 1 each time the loop runs.

Here's what the for statement itself looks like:

```
for ( i = 0; i < 5; i++ )
```

It *almost* looks like a function, but the items in the parentheses are a bit different. There are three sections in the for statement, with a semicolon (instead of a comma) between each section. The first section sets the counter to zero:

```
i = 0
```

The next part is the "test." It's evaluated before each lap to see whether the loop should continue:

```
i < 5
```

In this case, the `for` loop checks to see whether `i` is less than `5`. If it is, the code inside the loop runs for another lap. Otherwise, it ends and the next line of code *after* the loop runs.

Finally, this advances the `i` counter by 1:

```
i++
```

This is C shorthand for "add 1 to `i`," and you can use it outside of loops, too. This is the equivalent of the coach pressing the clicker as the runner passes. Then you get to the core of the loop:

```
total = total + values[i];
```

This line of code will run for every iteration of the loop. One item from the `values` array will be added to `total` each time through. Something's different here, though. Usually when you want to specify an index in an array, you put a number inside of the brackets, like this:

```
values[4];
```

But here, I'm using the variable `i` instead:

```
values[ i ];
```

The `i` counter starts at zero and increases by 1 each time until the loop is complete. So each time this line of code runs, `i` will be one number higher, and we'll automatically get the next value in the array:

```
total = total + values[i];
```

In fact, it's simpler to write it this way, which has the exact same effect:

```
total += values[i];
```

In the first trip through the loop, the `i` variable is equal to `0`, so this line adds the contents of `value[0]`. In the next trip, `i` will be set to `1`, so it adds the contents of `value[1]`. The `i` variable works as a stand-in for the index so you can read and write all of the values with very little code.

Text Strings

I very quickly introduced you to the `char` data type in the previous chapter. It holds a single character:

```
char firstLetter = 'a';
char lastLetter  = 'z';
```

You can also create *arrays* of `char` values:

```
char word[5];
word[0] = 'C';
word[1] = 'o';
word[2] = 'c';
word[3] = 'o';
```

```
    word[4] = 'a';

    char anotherWord[] = {'C','o','c','o','a'};
```

With one change, an array of char values becomes a *string*. A string is simply a collection of text. Strings are used everywhere in programming: for button labels, usernames, search terms, and so on. Anywhere text is used, a string is involved.

To make an array of char values a real string, you add a *null terminator* to the end. Like the newline character, a null terminator is an escape character with a backslash: \0. Without the backslash, this would be just a normal zero. *With* the slash, it becomes the "end cap" on a string:

```
    char fullString[] = {'C','o','c','o','a','\0'};
```

This is still an array of char values, but the null terminator on the end means that it's been promoted to a string. This syntax is fairly awkward. Fortunately, there's a simpler way to create strings:

```
    char fullString[] = "Cocoa";
```

Unlike single char values, a full string is wrapped in *double quotes*. When you use double quotes, C automatically adds the null terminator, but the terminator still needs an extra slot. So even though there are *five characters* in "Cocoa", the char array actually has *six slots* because there's an extra slot reserved for '\0' at the end to make it a string.

The printf() marker for strings is %s:

```
    char fullString[] = "Cocoa";
    printf ( "New word: %s \n", fullString );
```

The code will display this on the command line:

```
    New word: Cocoa
```

There's one very important detail here. You *can't* return these kinds of strings from a function the way you can return numbers. It may cause your application to crash or behave unpredictably. There *is* a way to create strings that stay around, though. You'll find out about that later in the chapter.

 Modern C programs need to handle *Unicode* when dealing with international text. Fortunately, Cocoa does most of the hard work for you. Because you're learning to write Cocoa apps specifically, you can assume that Unicode support is handled for you for the purposes of this book. In fact, the application you built in the first chapter used Unicode without you even knowing it.

Multidimensional Arrays

Many applications need to store "arrays of arrays." A spreadsheet has an array of rows, and each row has an array of column values. An array in which each slot contains a nested set of arrays is called a *multidimensional array*. A multidimensional array with two rows and three columns is declared like this:

```
int cells[2][3];
```

You can fill in a multidimensional array just like you would a normal array, except that you specify index numbers for *both* dimensions (see Figure 3-2):

```
// first row.
cells[0][0] = 12;   // first column.
cells[0][1] = 24;   // second column.
cells[0][2] = 36;   // third column.

// second row.
cells[1][0] = 48;   // first column.
cells[1][1] = 96;   // second column.
cells[1][2] = 112;  // third column.
```

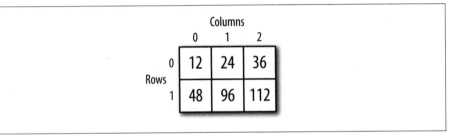

Figure 3-2. A multidimensional array as a grid

You can also *assign* values to a multidimensional array when you declare it:

```
int cells[2][3] = { {12,24,36}, {38,96,112} };
```

To assign values to this multidimensional array, you describe a *parent array* that contains two *child arrays*, each surrounded by a set of brackets. The child arrays are separated by commas.

Pointers

Pointers have a reputation for being difficult to learn, but the idea behind them is simple. A pointer works just a like a mirror: you point it at something, and it will simply reflect whatever value it's pointing at. If you change the value of the thing it refers to, the pointer will reflect that new value. It's a lot like a Mac file alias or a filesystem link in Unix. Here's a simple example of a pointer declaration:

```
int* numberPointer;
```

Most of the variables you've seen store simple values: integers, floating-point numbers, and characters. A pointer, though, stores a *memory address*. A memory address is a unique identifier, like a car license plate, phone number, or package tracking number. They *refer* to something else—a car, a phone, or a package.

Every piece of data in every application currently running on your Mac or iPhone has a memory address. Memory addresses are usually displayed as hexadecimal numbers, like 0x7fff5fbffa6c. In C, all hexadecimal numbers start with 0x.

 HTML and CSS use hexadecimal values for RGB colors. The value #ff0000 has the highest possible value (ff) for the red channel, and the lowest values for green and blue. Black is #000000 and white is #ffffff.

Even though they look strange, hexadecimal numbers are still just numbers with *16* values per digit instead of 10. You use letters to represent digits with values higher than 9:

```
Hexadecimal digits
 0 1 2 3 4 5 6 7 8 9 a b c d e f
```

Every variable you create receives a memory address when the program runs (the actual address is usually different for each run), such as 0x7fff5fbffa6c. A pointer stores a memory address so that it can refer back to the original data later. I know that may sound like a strange idea, because variables *already* refer to data. So is a pointer just a variable that points to another variable? Essentially, yes. But that's just one part of a bigger picture.

The Purpose of Pointers

When I was first learning about pointers, I understood how they worked but it wasn't clear to me why I was using them. So first I'm going to tell you *why* you need pointers, then I'll show you how to use them.

Remember that local variables are not guaranteed to keep their value each time a function runs, and that they're visible only inside their own function. But you still may want to share data between functions. You can use return, but that works only for a single value. You can also use global variables, but if all of your data has to live in global variables and you have thousands of different things to store, you soon have a mess.

What you need is a local variable with *shared storage* that other functions can get to on demand. You want to create the data once and just pass around the memory address (the unique ID). In terms of Cocoa, that's the most important purpose of a pointer—to share data in many different places in a program.

Using Pointers

Here's a simple example of creating and using a pointer variable. This example uses just local data, but it makes more sense if you start small:

```
int  number = 4;
int* numberPointer = &number;
```

```
printf ("number: %i \n", number);
printf ("numberPointer: %i \n\n", *numberPointer);

number = 16;
printf ("number: %i \n", number);
printf ("numberPointer: %i \n", *numberPointer);
```

This code displays the following output on the command line:

```
number: 4
numberPointer: 4

number: 16
numberPointer: 16
```

The numberPointer variable is pointing at the same data as the number variable, so they stay in sync. When the value of number changes to 16, numberPointer picks it up, too. To link a pointer to a variable, you put an ampersand in front of the target variable. When used like this, the ampersand is called the *address-of operator*:

```
numberPointer = &number;
```

The address-of operator returns the memory address for a variable. But there's something else that looks a bit strange at first. The asterisk is being used *both* in the declaration of numberPointer *and* when you display its value with printf():

```
int  number       = 4;
int* numberPointer = &number;
printf ("numberPointer: %i \n", *numberPointer);
```

In this context, the asterisk is called the *dereference operator*. Dereferencing means we're *resolving* the pointer to get the actual data that it's linked to. If you use printf() to display numberPointer without the dereference operator, you'll see something like this:

```
numberPointer: 1606417004
```

This is the *memory address* of the data (in this case, it's in 10-digit decimal format instead of hexadecimal). You dereference the pointer to get the actual data.

Let's be clear on one point: *this is all very confusing*. If pointers seem complex, it's not just you. The way they're expressed in C is not intuitive, because the asterisk is used for three *separate* purposes:

Declaring a pointer

When you declare a pointer variable, you put an asterisk after the type name and before the variable name:

```
int* numberPointer;
```

By the way, the whitespace between the type, the asterisk, and the variable name doesn't matter. You'll see int* numberPointer, int *numberPointer, and even int * numberPointer. They all work the same.

Dereferencing a pointer
You use an asterisk in front of a pointer variable to get the *data it refers to*. This is not a declaration, so there's no type name used:

```
printf ("numberPointer: %i \n", *numberPointer);
```

Standard multiplication
The asterisk is also used for general-purpose multiplication. This has nothing to do with pointer variables at all:

```
int hoursInWeek = 24 * 7;
```

So there are actually three *separate* ways the asterisk is used in C, and they each do something different. This is easily one of the most confusing parts of C, but fortunately, it's a temporary state of confusion. Once you get it, you *get it*. If it makes the learning process easier (and this is entirely up to you), every time you see a declaration like this:

```
int* number;
```

think this:

```
int POINTER number;
```

When you see this:

```
printf ("numberPointer: %i \n", *numberPointer);
```

think this instead:

```
printf ("numberPointer: %i \n", ACTUAL_VALUE(numberPointer) );
```

You should *never write code like this*, but if you temporarily do this mapping in your head, the concepts will quickly sink in.

Pointers and the const Keyword

When you use pointers with the `const` modifier, it behaves slightly differently from what you saw in "Constants" on page 23. Just as with the example shown there, you can't change the value through a pointer that's been declared `const`. This will generate a compile-time error:

```
int start_speed = 55;
int max_speed   = 75;

const int *mph = &start_speed;
*mph = max_speed;
```

But if you change *what the pointer points at*, you can effectively change its value without getting a compiler error:

```
int start_speed = 55;
int max_speed   = 75;

const int *mph = &start_speed;
mph = &max_speed;
```

Because pointers give you a level of indirection, there are two ways of changing the value they point to: modifying the value itself, or modifying what the pointer points to. With a const pointer, you can't change the value through the pointer, but you can always point it at something else.

Dynamic Memory

So far, you've used only *fixed-size* arrays. That's fine for simple examples, but we don't live in a fixed-size world. If you're writing a music player application, your code needs to be able to handle thousands of songs, but you can't possibly know the exact number ahead of time.

Dynamic memory enables you to work with large amounts of data and calculate the exact size as the program is running. Doing this with Cocoa and Objective-C is nearly transparent, but those conveniences will make more sense if you know how C manages memory at a lower level.

At the center of all of this is the malloc() function, which stands for "memory allocate." You use malloc() to request dynamic memory. Here's an example of requesting memory to store 10 int values:

```
int* numbers;
numbers = malloc ( sizeof(int) * 10 );
```

In C, you refer to memory blocks using memory addresses. I start by creating an int pointer variable called numbers, then use the malloc() function to request a block of memory that is the *size of* 10 int values. The sizeof() function determines how much memory a particular kind of value needs. I multiply that by the number of values I want to store, and pass the result to malloc() as a total number of *bytes*.

The malloc() function reserves a block of memory at least as big as the size I request, and returns the address of the new memory block. I then assign the address to the numbers pointer variable (remember that pointers store memory addresses). Because malloc() returns a memory address directly, I don't need to use the address-of operator (&).

In this case, the asterisk is being used for multiplication to figure out how big the memory block should be. The equation is:

```
sizeof ( data type ) * number of items
```

It's easy to get tripped up on this, though, because just one line earlier, I used the asterisk to *declare* a pointer variable. These are *separate* tasks that both use the asterisk character.

Now that I have a memory block and have assigned its address to the numbers pointer variable, I'm ready to use it. To do this, I take advantage of the fact that pointers are *movable*. The `numbers` variable initially points at the first "slice" of the memory block, and I can use the dereference operator to set a value at that first slice:

```
*numbers = 280;
```

Then I can *move* the pointer to the next slice, and set another value:

```
// move the pointer to the next 'slice' of the memory block.
numbers++;

// set the value at this slice.
*numbers = 230;
```

Just like I used `i++` to advance the counter in a loop, I can use `numbers++` to move the pointer to a new part of the memory block (see Figure 3-3).

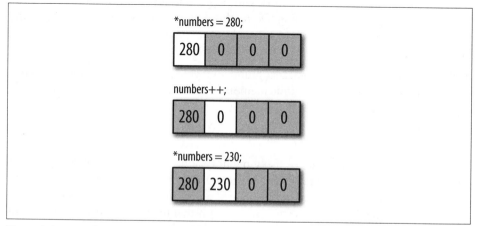

Figure 3-3. Move the pointer to the next slot by incrementing the variable

This dynamic memory block now works like an array: it's a single variable with multiple slots. You can also jump ahead to a specific value in the memory block. Here's how you can move straight to the fifth value (just like arrays, the first value is at zero):

```
numbers += 4;
```

Although you can store large amounts of data using `malloc()`, you need to `free()` the memory when you're done with it. If you don't, your application will start taking more and more memory, and will eventually cause the whole machine to run very slowly or the application will simply crash (or both). This is called a *memory leak*. To use `free()`, pass in a variable that points to the beginning of the memory block—that is, the *first* value:

```
free ( numbers );
```

This will work only if the `numbers` variable is currently pointing at the *beginning* of the memory block. Here's an example of code that *isn't* using `free()` correctly (if you want to try this example out, be sure to `#include <stdlib.h>` at the top):

```
// declare an int pointer and create a block of memory
// to hold 10 int values.

int* numbers;
numbers = malloc ( sizeof(int) * 10 );

// set the first value, move the pointer forward, and
// set the second value.

*numbers = 100;
numbers++;
*numbers = 200;

// this is incorrect. 'numbers' is currently pointing at the
// second value instead of the first value at the beginning
// of the memory block.

free ( numbers );
```

If you were to run the code as-is, you would probably see an error like this:

```
malloc: *** error for object 0x100100084: pointer being freed was not allocated
```

This error is saying "there's no memory block at this memory address that I can free." Or more specifically, no memory block *starts* at this memory address. In this case, I tried to free a memory block when the pointer's not at the beginning. One way to solve this is to create a *separate* variable that always points at the beginning. This example shows one correct approach:

```
int* numbers;
numbers = malloc ( sizeof(int) * 10 );

// create a _second_ variable to always point
// at the beginning of same memory block.
int* numbersStart;
numbersStart = numbers;

*numbers = 100;
numbers++;
*numbers = 200;

// use the 'numbersStart' variable to free the memory instead.
free ( numbersStart );
```

When you use pointers and dynamic memory, you're working at a very low level. It's easy to make mistakes. If you reserve a block of memory for 10 values, and then write 15 values, the results are unpredictable. You'll be using memory that you haven't set up for this purpose.

Your program may crash, or it may occasionally work fine purely by chance. But you should *never* write code that just happens to work some of the time. Fortunately, Cocoa and Objective-C provide much more supervision.

Strings and Dynamic Memory

Programmers often need to create *arrays of strings*. For example, if you are making an address book program, you will probably have an array of names. There's no way to know ahead of time how many names the user will want to store or how long each name will be, so you need to use dynamic memory.

To make strings of varying lengths, I'll use a new function called `asprintf()`. Roughly, the name stands for *"allocate dynamic memory for a string using* `printf` *conventions."* You can see why they shortened it.

Like `printf()`, the `asprintf()` function takes a format string, but instead of displaying the result, it creates a memory block large enough to hold all of the characters, plus a null terminator. When you're done, you just need to `free()` the string:

```
char* fullName;

asprintf ( &fullName, "Albert Einstein" );
printf   ( "%s \n", fullName );

free ( fullName );
```

There's one new convention here. I'm calling the function and providing the variable `fullName` as input, but putting the address-of operator in front of `fullName`. The `asprintf()` function works a bit differently than the other ones you've used. Instead of returning the new string directly, it *returns by indirection*. This means that a function effectively *reroutes* a pointer by changing the memory address it's pointing at.

In this case, `asprintf()` reroutes the `fullName` variable to point at the memory block that contains the new string.

 There's no one rule for which C functions return directly and which return by indirection. You often have to look it up in the documentation of the function you're using. You can find details on standard C functions by searching for them in the Xcode documentation window, which you can bring up via Help → Developer Documentation.

Because `asprintf()` accepts format strings the way `printf()` does, you can include other kinds of values in the final formatted string:

```
// declare an int and a float variable.
int   total = 81;
float ratio = 1.618;

// declare a string pointer and use asprintf() to
// format the string and reserve dynamic memory.
char* result;
asprintf ( &result, "total: %i, ratio: %f", total, ratio );

// display the 'result' string and free the memory.
```

```
printf ( "%s \n", result );
free ( result );
```

The result of this code is:

```
total: 81, ratio: 1.618000
```

You can use all of the same format markers with `asprintf()` that you can with `printf()`. You should usually avoid adding \n at the end of a format string when using `asprintf()`. It's better to add the newlines when you call `printf()`.

Returning Strings from Functions

Earlier in the chapter, I mentioned that you can't return standard strings from a function safely, because local strings can go away when the function ends:

```
// this won't work.
char[] myFunction () {

    char myString[5] = "Hello";
    return myString;
}
```

But I told you that there *is* a safe way to do it. This is it:

```
char* myFunction () {

    char* greeting;
    asprintf ( &greeting, "Hello" );
    return greeting;
}
```

Strings created with `asprintf()` *can* be returned, because the data is reserved by `malloc()` and won't go away until you call `free()` on it. When you return this kind of string, you're returning *a pointer to the memory that was allocated* for the string.

Expert C programmers will be quick to remind you that there are a lot of subtle details when returning strings from functions or simply dealing with strings in C in general. But the idea is that, *conceptually*, you understand that dynamically allocated memory will not go away until you free it. And that last point is important. Eventually, you must call `free()` on any string you create with `asprintf()`.

Again, I'm intentionally glossing over many of the low-level details here, because C-style strings aren't something you have to use frequently in Cocoa. I just want you to understand the basic concept, and you can always research it in more detail later if you like.

Arrays of Strings

Now that you've learned how to create arrays and strings from dynamic memory, let's combine the two. As you know, a string is basically just an array of char values. If you want an *array of strings*, you need a *multidimensional* array of char values:

```
char names[10][10];
```

This is like the spreadsheet example I talked about earlier in the chapter, where each item in a multidimensional array was a cell in a grid. Instead of an array of rows, though, I have an array of *names*, and instead of column values, each name string is an array of char values. But names can be any length, and you won't know ahead of time how many strings the user will want to store. This is how you create a variable-size array of strings:

```
int count = numberOfNames();
char* arrayOfStrings[ count ];
```

Again, remember that a string created from dynamic memory is a char* variable, so we're just creating an array of those. An "easy" dynamic array of char values isn't a good fit for a string, because a multidimensional array would force us to declare a size for all of the child arrays as well. This is a problem, because each name is a different length. You need the full flexibility of dynamic memory.

To try this out, we're going to allow the program to accept names that the user types on the command line. Our goal is to do be able to do something like this:

```
my-mac:~ scott$ ./names Peggy Alan Jamie
```

Fortunately, C gives us a way to get input from the command line. It provides it as input to the standard main() function that every C program uses. Here's how you can capture that input as variables:

```
#include <stdio.h>
main ( int inputCount, char* inputValues[] ) {

    // we don't want to count the program itself as a name,
    // so our nameCount will be the total inputCount, minus one.
    int nameCount = (inputCount - 1);

    // loop through and print out one string each time.
    int i;
    for ( i = 0; i < nameCount; i++ ) {

        // print each name. we use inputValues[i+1]
        // because the first string is the program name.
        printf ( "%s\n", inputValues[i+1] );
    }
}
```

The inputCount variable tells you *how many* items the user typed. For this program, each input item is a name for our address book. The inputValues variable is an array of strings that has the *actual names* that were typed in.

I used the variable names `inputCount` and `inputValues` here for clarity, but most C programs call them `argc` and `argv`, for argument count and argument values. I know, right? You can call them whatever you like.

You can use a loop to get the strings from the `inputValues` array using `inputCount` to determine how many times the loop should run. The only catch is that the program name *itself* is the first string (item 0) in the `inputValues` array. For example, if the program is called "names", the first string in `inputValues` will be "names". The code needs to skip the first item by adding 1 to `i` each time through the loop.

In the following example program, I'll reformat the input strings and add them to a new array.

Example: AddressBook

Open Xcode and choose File → New File. In the template window, choose Mac OS X → C and C++ → C File, then click Next (see Figure 3-4).

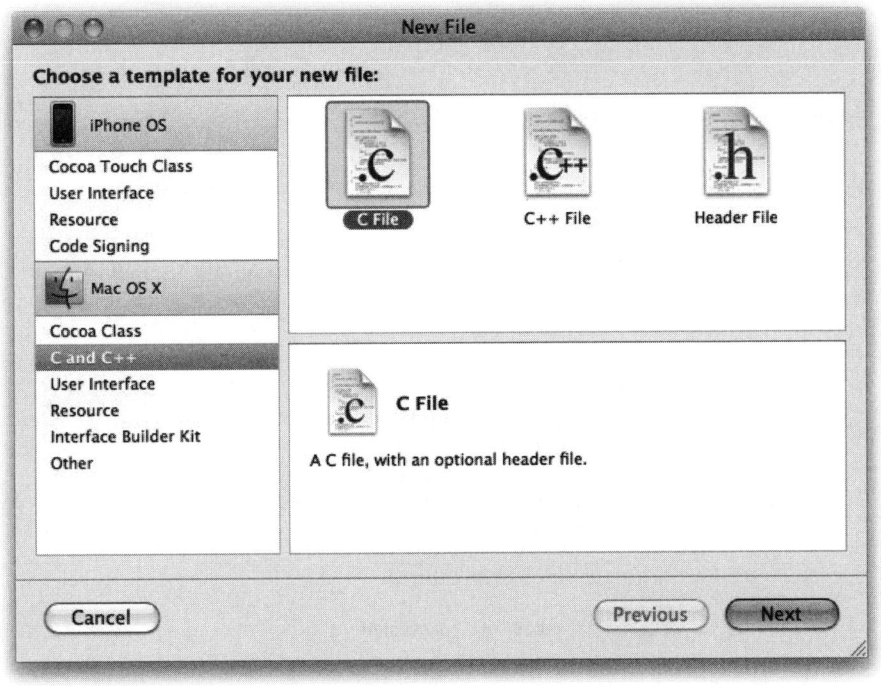

Figure 3-4. Create a new C file in Xcode

In the New File window, type *AddressBook.c* into the File Name field. *Uncheck* the checkbox labeled "Also create AddressBook.h" (see Figure 3-5).

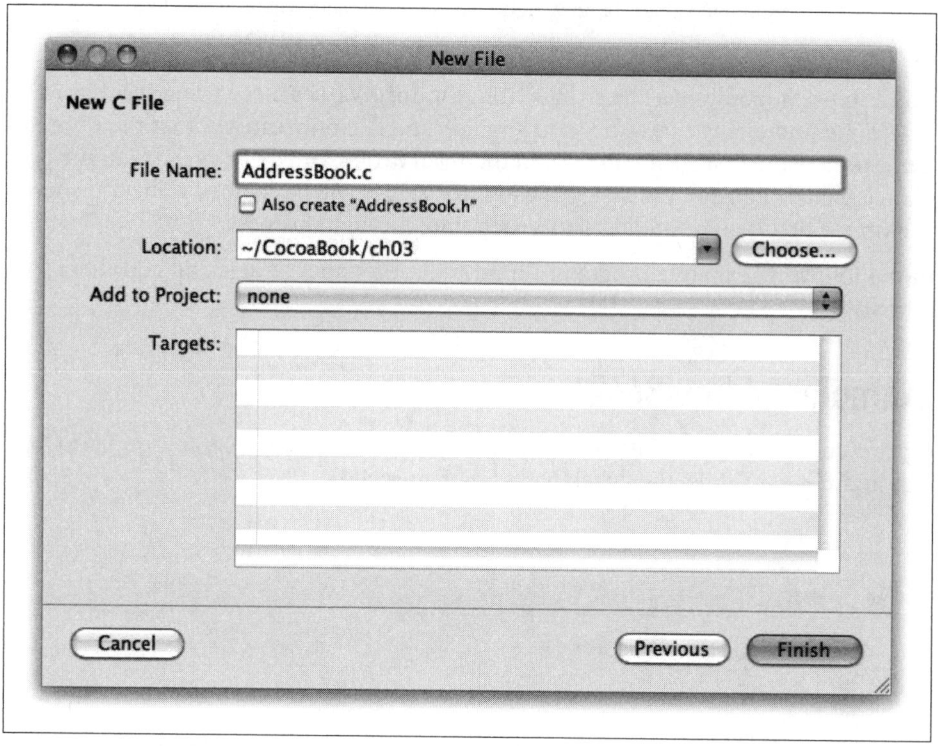

Figure 3-5. Name the file AddressBook.c and uncheck the option to add AddressBook.h

Next, type *~/CocoaBook/ch03/* into the Location field. Leave all other options in the window at their default settings and click Finish. Type the following into *AddressBook.c*:

```c
#include <stdio.h>

main ( int inputCount, char* inputValues[] ) {

  // we don't want to count the program itself as a name,
  // so our nameCount will be the total inputCount, minus one.
  int nameCount = (inputCount - 1);

  // tell the user how many names they entered.
  if ( nameCount > 0 ) {
    printf ( "You entered %i names \n", nameCount );

  } else {
    printf("You didn't enter any names.\n");

  }
```

```
// create an array that's large enough to hold the names.
char* formattedNames[ nameCount ];

int i;
for ( i = 0; i < nameCount; i++ ) {

  // create a new formatted name. we use inputValues[i+1]
  // for the slot because the first string is the program name.
  char* currentName = inputValues[i+1];
  asprintf ( &formattedNames[i], "Name %i: %s", i, currentName );
}

// display the final result.
for ( i = 0; i < nameCount; i++ ) {

  printf ( "%s \n", formattedNames[i] );
}

// free the memory for each string created by asprintf.
for ( i = 0; i < nameCount; i++ ) {

  free ( formattedNames[i] );
}
}
```

Compile and Run the AddressBook Example

If you haven't already done so, save the file. Now launch Terminal and change to the folder where the file is and compile the program:

```
my-mac:~ scott$ cd ~/CocoaBook/ch03/
my-mac:~ scott$ gcc AddressBook.c -o AddressBook
```

To try it out, type the following into the Terminal:

```
my-mac:~ scott$ ./AddressBook Alan Peggy Jamie
```

You should see something like this:

```
You entered 3 names
Name 0: Alan
Name 1: Peggy
Name 2: Jamie
```

This is the most complex part of the AddressBook program:

```
char* currentName = inputValues[i+1];
asprintf ( &formattedNames[i], "Name %i: %s", i, currentName );
```

These two lines grab a name from the inputValues array, reformat it, and add the reformatted string to the formattedNames array.

The first step of this is to capture one name in a temporary variable called currentName. It actually isn't strictly necessary to create a temporary holding variable, but it does make the code easier to understand.

Because the first string in `inputValues` is the name of the program itself, you always want to get the value at one index *higher* than the current value of i—effectively skipping the first value—so you use i+1 instead of just i.

The `asprintf()` function returns by indirection, so you provide a variable name with the address-of operator in front. But you don't want to change the *whole array* each time, so you specify an index number, too. You want to write a value to a different index for each iteration of the loop, so you use the i in place of a number in the brackets.

The format pattern is `Name: %i: %s`, which creates strings like `Name 1: Jamie`. You provide two variables to `asprintf()` to fill in the markers in the format string. The i variable contains the current iteration of the loop, and `currentName` contains one of the names typed in by the user.

The last step is to release the memory for the reformatted name strings. Although our new, easy-to-use dynamic arrays automatically clean up their memory, the strings created with `asprintf()` do not. You need to `free()` them manually.

 Memory management is hard. Even the best programmers regularly make mistakes when dealing with memory. Fortunately, it's much easier to manage memory in Cocoa and Objective-C than in plain C.

Structs

Arrays can hold a lot of data, but all of the values have to be the same *type*. Sometimes you want to store *different kinds* of values in the same variable. A *struct* is a structured group of values. Here's an example of a struct that stores details about a song:

```
typedef struct {
    char* title;
    int   lengthInSeconds;
    int   yearRecorded;
} Song;
```

At first glance, this looks like two int variables and a char* variable, but it's actually a new type of variable that contains *multiple values* of different types. The `typedef` statement names the struct. In this case, the name is Song.

Unlike in an array, each value in a struct has a name, also known as a *field name*. A field in a struct can be any type, even pointers or other nested structs. Just like functions, you need to declare structs before you can use them, so it's usually best to put them at the top of a file.

You can use structs nearly anywhere you'd use int, float, or char. A struct is basically a template that you can use to create as many *instances* as you want. Each Song instance has its own values for title, lengthInSeconds, and yearRecorded. You assign a value to field in a struct using the *dot syntax* convention:

```
Song song1;
song1.title            = "Hey Jude";
song1.lengthInSeconds  = 425;
song1.yearRecorded     = 1968;

Song song2;
song2.title            = "Let It Be";
song2.lengthInSeconds  = 243;
song2.yearRecorded     = 1970;
```

In this example, I created a Song instance called song1, and used the dot syntax to set values for its title, lengthInSeconds, and yearRecorded fields. I then created a second Song instance, called song2. When you change the values of one Song instance, the others are unaffected.

You can make functions that take structs as input, as well as functions that return them as output. For example, here's a function that takes length and year values and returns a new Song instance:

```
Song createSong ( int length, int year ) {

    Song mySong;
    mySong.lengthInSeconds = length;
    mySong.yearRecorded    = year;
    return mySong;
}
```

You can then use the function to make a new Song instance:

```
Song mySong = createSong ( 324, 2004 );
```

Here's a function that accepts a Song as input and displays it:

```
void displaySong (Song theSong) {

    printf ("The song is %i seconds long ", theSong.lengthInSeconds);
    printf ("and was recorded in %i. \n", theSong.yearRecorded);
}
```

I can then take the instance created with createSong(), and use it as input for displaySong():

```
Song mySong = createSong ( 324, 2004 );
displaySong ( mySong );
```

The program will then display this on the command line:

```
The song is 324 seconds long and was recorded in 2004.
```

To make this even simpler, I can change the createSong() function to directly call displaySong() each time it creates a new instance:

```
Song createSong ( int length, int year ) {

    Song newSong;
    newSong.lengthInSeconds = length;
    newSong.yearRecorded    = year;
```

```
    // display the new song that was created.
    displaySong ( newSong );
    return newSong;
}
```

Now you don't need to call displaySong() separately—it will happen automatically. Programmers call this sort of arrangement *encapsulation*. The goal of encapsulation is to write functions that are smart enough to manage the tedious bits transparently. In plain English, encapsulation means "handle the details for me."

For example, if you decided to add a creation date field to the Song struct, you would usually have to update all of the places in code a Song instance is created. Because we're using the createSong() function, though, you can make the change in one place and all the other parts of the program that use createSong() will get the benefits.

Encapsulation is one of the most important ideas in Cocoa, and is one of the reasons you can get fairly sophisticated applications up and running quickly.

Header Files

As you need to declare functions, structs, and globals before you can use them, it helps to have all of these things in one place. This is what *header files* do. Header files are very useful in large projects, because they help you understand what the code does without having to look through every single line—sort of a "table of contents" for one part of a program. They usually have a *.h* file extension.

Use Xcode to create a new file named *MathFunctions.c*. This time, though, leave the "Also create MathFunctions.h" checkbox *activated* so that Xcode creates the *MathFunctions.h* header file, too. We'll use this in an example program shortly. Save the files in *~/CocoaBook/ch03/*. If you need reminders about how to create files in Xcode, flip back a few pages to an example earlier in the chapter.

Type the following into *MathFunctions.h*:

```
int sum ( int values[], int count );
float average ( float values[], int count );
```

This header file contains the declarations for two functions we're going use in this program. When you create the file, you can either keep the comments Xcode automatically adds or remove them. They won't affect the way the program runs. Save the file and open *MathFunctions.c*.

 Xcode has a shortcut for switching back and forth between a pair of *.h* and *.c* files: Option-Command-↑.

Type the code from Example 3-1 into *MathFunctions.c* (note that the `#include` directive is already in the file).

Example 3-1. MathFunctions.c

```
int sum (int values[], int count) {

  int i;
  int total = 0;

  for ( i = 0; i < count; i++ ) {

    // add each value in the array to the total.
    total = total + values[i];
  }

  return total;
}

float average (float values[], int count ) {

  int i;
  float total = 0.0;

  for ( i = 0; i < count; i++ ) {

    // add each value in the array to the total.
    total = total + values[i];
  }

  // calculate the average.
  float average = (total / count);
  return average;
}
```

Both functions take an array of values and a count. The sum() function takes an array of int values, and the average() function takes an array of float values. Save the file when you're done, then use Xcode to create a new file called *HeaderFileTest.c* in the same folder. This is the *main program file*, so you don't need a matching header file. You can *deactivate* the checkbox that provides that option. Type the code from Example 3-2 into the file.

Example 3-2. HeaderFileTest.c

```
#include <stdio.h>
#include "MathFunctions.h"

main () {

  int wholeNumbers[5] = {2,3,5,7,9};
  int theSum = sum (wholeNumbers, 5);
  printf ("The sum is: %i ", theSum);

  float fractionalNumbers[3] = {16.9, 7.86, 3.4};
```

```
  float theAverage = average (fractionalNumbers, 3);
  printf ("and the average is: %f \n", theAverage);
}
```

After the standard *stdio.h*, I added an include statement for *MathFunctions.h*. This allows the program to call the sum() and average() functions. When you include a header file specific to a program, put the filename in double quotes. When it's a header file from a library—such as the *stdio.h* header from the C standard library itself—put the file name in angle brackets.

Compile and Run the HeaderFileTest Example

If you haven't already done so, save all of the source files you have open. Now launch Terminal and change to the folder where the file is:

    my-mac:~ scott$ cd ~/CocoaBook/ch03/

Type the following command into the Terminal to compile the program. Note that this time you're combining *multiple* C files into a single program:

    my-mac:~ scott$ gcc HeaderFileTest.c MathFunctions.c -o HeaderFileTest

To try it out, type the following on the command line:

    my-mac:~ scott$ ./HeaderFileTest

You should see something like this:

    The sum is: 26 and the average is: 9.386666

One thing you might notice here is that I didn't ask you to specify the *.h* header files as part of the gcc compile command. That's because the #include statement figures that stuff out for us. You just need to tell gcc about the *.c* files.

Create Files for the Song Struct

To work up to the final example in the chapter, you're going to create a pair of files that encapsulate everything involving the Song struct. They will contain the declaration of the struct itself, as well as functions for creating and displaying Song instances.

Use Xcode to create a new file called *Song.c* and the matching *Song.h* header file, and put both in *~/CocoaBook/ch03/*. Type the code from Example 3-3 into the *.h* file.

Example 3-3. Song.h

```
typedef struct {
  char* title;
  int lengthInSeconds;
  int yearRecorded;
} Song;
```

```
Song createSong ( char* title, int length, int year );
void displaySong ( Song theSong );
```

Now type the code from Example 3-4 into *Song.c* (the `#include` statement for *Song.h* will already be in the file).

Example 3-4. Song.c

```
#include <stdio.h>

Song createSong (char* title, int length, int year) {

  Song mySong;
  mySong.lengthInSeconds = length;
  mySong.yearRecorded    = year;
  mySong.title           = title;

  displaySong (mySong);
  return mySong;
}

void displaySong (Song theSong) {

  printf ("'%s' is %i seconds long ", theSong.title, theSong.lengthInSeconds);
  printf ("and was recorded in %i\n", theSong.yearRecorded);
}
```

Now let's create a simple program to test whether the `Song` files are set up correctly. Use Xcode to make a file called *SongTest.c* in *~/CocoaBook/ch03/*. This is the main program file, so you don't need a header file to go with it. Type the code from Example 3-5 into *SongTest.c*.

Example 3-5. SongTest.c

```
#include <stdio.h>
#include "Song.h"

main () {

  Song allSongs[3];

  allSongs[0] = createSong ( "Hey Jude", 210, 2004 );
  allSongs[1] = createSong ( "Jambi", 256, 1992 );
  allSongs[2] = createSong ( "Lightning Crashes", 223, 1997 );
}
```

Save all the files you have open, then type the following commands into the Terminal to compile the program. Remember that you're combining *multiple* C files into a single program:

```
my-mac:~ scott$ cd ~/CocoaBook/ch03/
my-mac:~ scott$ gcc SongTest.c Song.c -o SongTest
```

To try it out, type the following into the Terminal to run the program:

```
my-mac:~ scott$ ./SongTest
```

You should see something like this:

```
'Hey Jude' is 210 seconds long and was recorded in 2004
'Jambi' is 256 seconds long and was recorded in 1992
'Lightning Crashes' is 223 seconds long and was recorded in 1997
```

In some cases, you might see an error like this:

```
Song.h:15: error: conflicting types for 'Song'
Song.h:15: error: previous declaration of 'Song' was here
```

If you do see this, you might have duplicate #include statements. Check your code to make sure you're not including *Song.h* more than once.

Final Example

This example program uses the files you created earlier in the chapter, and covers nearly everything we've learned about C. If this example makes sense to you, you're ready to move on to object-oriented programming.

Nearly of the conventions used here were described earlier in the book. If anything is unclear, go back and review what you've already read. The one thing I haven't covered, though, is the rand() function. You use this function to generate random numbers.

However, convincing a computer to generate a *truly* random number is not trivial. You can get better random numbers from rand() if you "seed" it first by calling the sranddev() function. You need to seed it only once per run of the program, though.

You can also control the maximum value of the random number using the *modulus operator*, which, confusingly, is actually the percent symbol: %. The whole sequence looks like this:

```
// seed the random number generator.
sranddev();

// get a random number, with a maximum of 500.
int randomNumber = rand() % 500;
```

 The modulus operator returns the remainder of integer division (no decimal point), which also can limit the maximum value. For example, 499 divided by 500 is 0 with a remainder of 499. But 500 divided by 500 is 1, with a remainder of 0. So any positive number *modulo 500* is limited to the range 0 to 499. You can also use this to "wrap around" larger numbers: 1,499 modulo 500 is 499, and 1,501 modulo 500 is 1.

Use Xcode to create a new file called *FinalProgram.c*, and type the code from Example 3-6 into the file. I realize this is a fair amount of code, but actually typing code helps you learn programming much more quickly than just reading about it.

Example 3-6. FinalProgram.c

```c
#include <stdio.h>
#include <stdlib.h>
#include "MathFunctions.h"
#include "Song.h"

// global variables.
int  yearCount = 12;
int* allYears;

// utility functions.
void setupYears();
int randomSongYear();


main ( int inputCount, char* inputValues[] ) {

  // we don't want to count the program itself as a song name.
  int songCount = (inputCount - 1);

  // tell the user how many song names they entered.
  if ( songCount > 0 ) {
    printf ( "You entered %i song names \n", songCount );

  } else {
    printf ( "Didn't enter any song names. \n" );
    exit(1);
  }

  // fill in the global 'allYears' array.
  setupYears();

  // seed the random number generator,
  // and get a random number.
  sranddev();
  int randomNumber = rand() % 500;

  // create an "easy" dynamic array of all of the songs,
  // and a separate array of just the song lengths.
  Song allSongs[ songCount ];
  int songLengths[ songCount ];

  int i;
  for (i = 0; i < songCount; i++) {

    // choose a random length in seconds (up to 500)
    // and a random song year.
    int length = rand() % 500;
    int year = randomSongYear();

    // get the song name.
    char* songName = inputValues[i+1];

    // create the Song instance using all of the other values.
    allSongs[i] = createSong ( songName, length, year );
```

```
    // finally, copy the length to the 'songLengths' array.
    songLengths[i] = length;
  }

  // display the total length of all songs.
  int combinedLength  = sum (songLengths, songCount);
  printf ("The total length of all songs is %i seconds\n", combinedLength);

  // loop through the songs again and make an array of float values.
  float songLengthsAsFloats[ songCount ];

  for (i = 0; i < songCount; i++) {
    songLengthsAsFloats[i] = songLengths[i];
  }

  // calculate the average length.
  float averageLength = average (songLengthsAsFloats, songCount);
  printf ("The average length is: %.2f seconds\n", averageLength);

  // clean up the memory we malloc'd.
  free ( allYears );
}

void setupYears () {

  // reserve memory for all of the year values. we can't use
  // the "easy" dynamic array because 'years' is a global variable.
  allYears = malloc ( sizeof(int) * yearCount );

  // choose the starting year.
  int oneYear = 2000;

  // loop through and fill in each value.
  int i;
  for ( i = 0; i < yearCount; i++ ) {

    oneYear++;
    allYears[i] = oneYear;
  }
}

int randomSongYear () {

  // get a random value between 0 and (yearCount-1).
  int yearIndex = rand() % (yearCount-1);

  // now use the index to get a year out of the 'allYears' array.
  int year = allYears[ yearIndex ];

  return year;
}
```

Type the following commands into the Terminal to compile the program. Note that this time we're combining *multiple* C files into a single program:

```
my-mac:~ scott$ cd ~/CocoaBook/ch03/
my-mac:~ scott$ gcc FinalProgram.c MathFunctions.c Song.c -o FinalProgram
```

To try it out, type the following into the Terminal to run the program:

```
my-mac:~ scott$ ./FinalProgram "Hey Jude" "Jambi" "Lightning Crashes"
```

You should see something similar to the following, but remember that the song lengths and years are random, so yours will probably be different:

```
You entered 3 song names
'Hey Jude' is 409 seconds long and was recorded in 2001
'Jambi' is 445 seconds long and was recorded in 2009
'Lightning Crashes' is 213 seconds long and was recorded in 2001
The total length of all songs is 1067 seconds
The average length is: 355.67 seconds
```

Remember: if any of this code doesn't make sense, go back and review the earlier parts of the book to find something you may have skimmed over. If you can't get the code to compile, you can get a working version from the book's companion site (see the Preface for details).

CHAPTER 4

Thinking in Objects

A funny thing happened on the way to the future. Computers became much more powerful, and developers decided to take advantage of this potential by making software that did a lot more than just process one instruction at a time on the command line.

They built more sophisticated interfaces that could do a lot of things at once. This allowed software to tackle complex tasks like nonlinear video editing and 3D modeling. But creating programs with such sophisticated user interfaces required a lot of code.

Expert engineers love simplifying code. They're *obsessed* with it. Good programmers think of ways to write code more quickly, but great engineers think of ways to write less code to do the same job. There's a good reason for this. The less code you have, the easier it is to understand and improve.

The functions in earlier chapters do a calculation and return a result. You store the result in a variable, and then pass it into another function, like this:

```
#include <stdio.h>
#include "types.h"

main () {

    char* itemType     = "Document";
    int   itemCount    = countForItemType     ( itemType );
    int   itemTotal    = totalForCountOfType   ( itemCount, itemType );
    char* totalString  = formattedTotalForType ( itemTotal, itemType );

    printf ("The total for %s is %s", itemType, totalString);
    free   ( totalString );
}
```

C is a *procedural* language, which means that functions and the data are separate, and the code is fairly linear. You can also say that C is a *static language*. This means that all functions have to exist before you call them, and when you call a function, it *will* run. There's no reinterpretation as the program is running. Also, all variables have to be a specific type, which is called *static typing*.

The upside of this is that the code is predictable and you have complete control. The downside is that you have manage all of the details manually, which means you end up doing a lot of busywork. This is hard to picture when working with very small programs, but it's very clear when working with programs that are made up of hundreds of thousands or millions of lines of code.

 I think of this as a CEO of a 2,000-person company answering support calls. He may be good at it, but it's probably better for everyone if he runs the company instead. You are the CEO of your application. If you spend time on low-level details, you may never be able to take on the bigger tasks. Instead, you delegate the lower-level details to Cocoa.

So engineers started trying to think up better ways to program, and two ideas that took hold are *object-oriented programming* and *dynamic languages*. Standard C had the seeds of object-oriented concepts with structs. Each struct definition is a template for a certain kind of thing, like a movie or a document. You create a variable of that struct type, and you have another *instance* of the struct with its own set of values. From that single struct, you can store data for any number of different movies.

By convention, developers started writing functions that used structs instead of individual `char` and `int` variables. You did this with the `createSong()` and `displaySong()` functions in the previous chapter. Objective-C took this convention and formalized it.

Objective-C also added dynamic features, which means that not everything in your code has to be defined when you compile. You can declare "typeless" variables and can use classes and methods that don't exist yet. This allows the design of the application to be more flexible, making it much easier to implement things like plug-in support. A lot of the thinking behind Cocoa is based on the dynamic features of Objective-C.

Structs and Classes

Because you already know how C works from the earlier chapters, the easiest way to introduce object-oriented concepts is to compare them to structs and functions.

I'm not going into detail about the Objective-C language in this chapter. I'm just using it as a way to show you object-oriented concepts. This means you will see parts that don't make sense yet, such as the @ symbol and square brackets. I'll cover these and the rest of the language in detail in the following chapters. For now, just focus on the concepts.

The *Song.h* file from Chapter 3 looks like this:

```
typedef struct {
  char* title;
  int   lengthInSeconds;
  int   yearRecorded;
} Song;
```

```
Song createSong ( char* title, int length, int year );
void displaySong ( Song theSong );
```

In Objective-C, the equivalent *Song.h* file looks like this:

```
@interface Song : NSObject ❶

  @property char* title; ❷
  @property int   lengthInSeconds;
  @property int   yearRecorded;

+ (Song *) song; ❸
- (void) display;

@end
```

This is called a *class*, and you may notice that it looks a lot like a struct. This class *interface* is the part of the class that goes in the header file. It's a lot like declaring structs and functions in a header file. The class implementation goes in a separate file.

❶ This line declares the class name and defines which class it inherits from (see "Inheritance" on page 78).

❷ *Instance variables* or *properties* are very similar to fields in a struct. I'll describe properties in more detail in the following chapters; for now, just know that the intent of struct fields and class properties is the same: to store a unique set of values for each instance.

❸ *Methods* are similar to functions, though methods are not freestanding. Each method belongs to a class. That means that two classes can have `display` methods that do completely separate things. Methods have direct access to the class's properties, so you don't need to pass any of those values in when calling a method.

I used a `char*` C string in this example because you're already familiar with it, but you won't see this in the source code for most Cocoa applications. You *can* use C strings in Objective-C, but Cocoa has its own type for strings, which I'll describe in the following chapters. Other than this one detail, though, this is very much like a class you'd find in any Cocoa application.

Each instance of a class is called an *object*. Even though you have only one Song class (the blueprint), you can have many Song *objects*. Here's how you make a Song struct in C code, compared to making a Song *object* in Objective-C code:

```
// creating a Song struct in C.
Song mySong;
mySong.title           = "Hey Jude";
mySong.lengthInSeconds = 425;
mySong.yearRecorded    = 1968;
displaySong ( mySong );

// creating a Song object in Objective-C.
Song* mySong           = [Song song];
```

```
mySong.title          = "Hey Jude";
mySong.lengthInSeconds = 425;
mySong.yearRecorded   = 1968;
[mySong display];
```

 The rules about including Objective-C class headers are the same as
including C headers with struct definitions. If you refer to a class literally
in code, you have to include its header file. If you don't include the file,
you will see a build error.

The Song object variable is a pointer. All object variables in Objective-C are pointers
because they're always stored in dynamic memory—just as if you had allocated them
with the malloc() function. In fact, deep down in Objective-C, that's exactly what's
happening.

Designing Classes

At first, classes look like a way to group functions and variables together. That's *technically* true, but not really the main point. The idea is that if you want to describe
something like a photo, it's easier to create a Photo class with all of the methods and
properties related to that concept rather than a series of structs and functions that
simulate a photo class.

When I first create a class, I don't think about which methods (functions) it will have.
Instead, I focus on the kind of data it needs to store. So if I'm designing a Game class, I
know it will need at least two player names, two scores, and a game duration. So I just
start with that:

```
@interface Game : NSObject

    @property char* playerOne;
    @property char* playerTwo;
    @property int   playerOneScore;
    @property int   playerTwoScore;
    @property int   durationInSeconds;

@end
```

A class isn't just a big box to put a bunch of things in. Novice programmers may be
tempted to do something like this, because it seems convenient to put everything in
one class:

```
@interface Game : NSObject

    @property char* playerOne;
    @property char* playerTwo;
    @property int   playerOneScore;
    @property int   playerTwoScore;
    @property int   durationInSeconds;
```

```
// these are not part of a 'Game' so they're not appropriate for this class.
@property char*   computerName;
@property int     cpuCount;
@property char*   userName;
@property char*   userPassword;
```

    @end

The problem with this is that the computer name, CPU count, user name, and user password have nothing to do with the Game class. Even if you use them in the same *application*, they don't belong in the same *class*. Instead, create a separate class for each distinct kind of data:

```
@interface Game : NSObject

    @property char* playerOne;
    @property char* playerTwo;
    @property int   playerOneScore;
    @property int   playerTwoScore;
    @property int   durationInSeconds;

@end

@interface Computer : NSObject

    @property char*   name;
    @property int     cpuCount;

@end

@interface User : NSObject

    @property char*   name;
    @property char*   password;

@end
```

If each kind of data is separate from the others, the overall design of your application is much more flexible. You can change how the Computer class works without affecting the Game class or the User class. This is very important when creating Mac and iPhone apps.

Accessors

In the previous chapter, I described how encapsulation is a way to separate the *what* from the *how*. In one example, I showed you how adding a `printf()` call *inside* the `createSong()` function allowed you to automatically display the Song instance when it's created.

Accessors are "gatekeepers" for properties. If you use accessors, the details of *how* the data is stored is separate from *what* the data is. For example, here is a pair of accessor methods for a `title` property of the `Photo` class:

```
- setTitle: newTitle {
    title = newTitle;
}

- title {
    return title;
}
```

The `setTitle:` accessor method takes an input value and assigns it to the instance variable (the actual variable that stores the property data). This is called a *setter* accessor method. The `title` method is the *getter* accessor method, and it simply returns the instance variable's value.

 In other object-oriented languages, it's more common to have a `getValue` method and a `setValue` method, but Objective-C methods rarely have `get` as a prefix. It's used only when returning a value through indirection.

Now imagine after you wrote this code, you decided to store all your data in a database. Instead of going and changing every part of the program that sets or gets a photo's title, you can just change the accessors in one place:

```
- setTitle: newTitle {
    saveTitleValueToDatabase(newTitle);
}

- title {
    return titleValueFromDatabase();
}
```

Software changes a *lot*. One of the best things you can do as a programmer is make it easy to change the code. Even though you start out with an idea of how your program will work, you will probably change your mind later. It's often hard to "see" the whole thing in your head before you start (though you'll get better at this).

Good code is written with a pencil: *easily changed*. Bad code is written in ink: *difficult to change*. If you need to change good code, you can just erase a few things and continue on. If you need to change bad code, you're often better off just throwing it out and starting with a blank slate.

Inheritance

One of the key concepts in object-oriented programming is *inheritance*, which allows you to pull in properties and methods from a "parent" class, also known as a *superclass*. For example, if you have both a Song class and a Movie class in your application, it might make sense to create a Media superclass that both Song and Movie inherit from, because they're both logically an extension of a more generic "media" type. They can then share instance variables and methods:

```
@interface Media : NSObject

    @property int     duration;
    @property char*   format;

    - (void) play;
    - (void) pause;
    - (void) rewind;

@end
```

All of these things make sense for both Song and Movie objects, but each class can also add its own functionality. For example, Movie might add properties like aspectRatio and framesPerSecond, as well as a method called enableSubtitles. The new class, including inherited methods, would look like this:

```
@interface Movie : Media

    @property float aspectRatio;
    @property int   framesPerSecond;

    - (void) enableSubtitles;

    // inherited from Media.

    @property int    duration;
    @property char* format;

    - (void) play;
    - (void) pause;
    - (void) rewind;

@end
```

 You usually don't redeclare methods or properties that you inherit from a superclass. I added the declarations here for clarity.

In this example, Movie is a *subclass* of Media. Another class could be a subclass of Movie, bringing in everything from *both* the Movie class and the Media class. The whole tree is called a *class hierarchy*. Most frameworks have a "root" object that all other classes inherit from. Cocoa actually has two root classes: NSObject and NSProxy, but almost all of your classes will inherit from NSObject.

Some object-oriented languages have *multiple inheritance*, which allows you to inherit from more than one class. Not everyone agrees on whether this a good or bad thing, though, and the creators of Objective-C decided not to include it in the language.

In addition to *adding* methods, subclasses can also *override* methods from a superclass. It's common to override methods when you want to customize existing behavior. For example, if you want to use a standard Mac OS X button in your application, but would like to change the clicking behavior, you could create a subclass of `NSButton` and override the methods related to clicking.

You don't use superclasses just to share code, though. A subclass should only inherit from a class that it's a logical extension of. For example, you shouldn't create a subclass of `Media` called `Camera`, because a camera is not a kind of media. Instead, you could make a generic `Device` class, and create subclasses for `Camera`, `Phone`, and so on.

Composition

Classes can have properties that refer to instances of other classes. This is called *composition*, because you're combining different kinds of objects together to accomplish a task:

```
@interface User : NSObject

  @property char*  name;
  @property char*  password;

@end

@interface Game : NSObject

  @property User* playerOne;
  @property User* playerTwo;
  @property int   playerOneScore;
  @property int   playerTwoScore;
  @property int   durationInSeconds;

@end
```

When you want to use methods and properties from another class, but it logically doesn't make sense to inherit from that class (a camera isn't a kind of media), you can create a property for the other kind of object instead:

```
@interface Device : NSObject

  @property char* name;
  @property int   minFocalDistance;

@end
```

```
@interface Media : NSObject

    @property int      duration;
    @property char*    format;
    @property Device*  recordingDevice;

@end
```

This way, a Media object can *use* a Device object, but it doesn't have to *be* a Device object, which makes much more sense. Cocoa encourages you to use composition much more frequently than subclassing, because subclassing can add complexity, which means it's harder to create great software.

Object Lifetime

The last building block concept is *object lifetimes*. Just like in C, you need to clean up the memory of objects when you're no longer using them. The actual process of reserving and freeing memory in Objective-C is easier than in C, but the trade-off is that there are usually more cleanup tasks.

In Objective-C and most other object-oriented languages, a class almost always has an *initialization method*. If you don't add one to your class, you typically inherit it from the root object. You create an initialization method when you want to set up default values for things. For example, you might want to set the initial title value for a Photo object to "Untitled Photo" so it's not just blank:

```
- init {
  title = "Untitled Photo";
}
```

The counterpart to the initialization method is a "cleanup" method, which you create if you want to clean up memory for any data you have, or maybe display a message in the console that the object is shutting down:

```
- dealloc {
  printf ("Deallocating Photo\n");
}
```

There are some more advanced techniques in Cocoa that we will use the cleanup methods for, but you need to learn about Objective-C before we can go into that in detail.

Built-in Classes

Most of Cocoa is available to you as *classes*. Cocoa has hundreds of different classes that do things like display web pages, record video, create PDFs, and search for files on the user's computer. The process of becoming a better Cocoa programmer is really about learning how these classes work. There are *some* C functions and structs, too, but Cocoa is designed as an object-oriented framework.

For example, I can make a window object using the `NSWindow` class (I'll tell you more about windows in Chapter 8). In three lines of code, I can create a window object, set its size and position, and display it on the screen:

```
id myWindow = [[NSWindow alloc] init];
[myWindow setFrame:NSMakeRect(100, 100, 400, 300) display:YES];
[myWindow orderFront:nil];
```

I can also set properties on the window, like the title:

```
myWindow.title = @"An Empty Space";
```

Once I've done that, I can see the window on the screen (Figure 4-1).

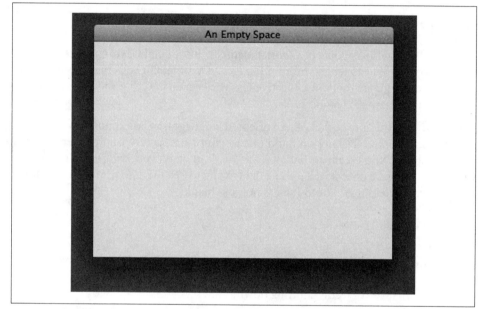

Figure 4-1. A window object displayed on the screen

A lot of the code you write in Objective-C is very similar to this. You create an object, set some properties on it, and then the user can start interacting with the object on screen. I'll introduce you to many different Cocoa classes as you continue through the book.

CHAPTER 5

Basic Objective-C

When I was first learning Cocoa, some very smart people told me that Objective-C is *C with objects*. I hear that now and it sounds like describing the desert as "a place with a lot of sand." It's technically a true statement, but it doesn't really tell you much about the language.

Writing a Cocoa app is nothing like writing software with standard C libraries. The C foundation is just a vehicle, not the basis for how you design your application. In my experience, there are three standout features of Objective-C:

Compiled speed, dynamic features
> Objective-C has the compiled speed of C with many of the features of a dynamic scripting language. You can use static typing for variables if you want, but the types are not strictly enforced. You can also load classes and methods as the application is running, or generate them on the fly.

Compatibility with C and C++
> You can freely use C types and libraries within Objective-C classes, as well as integrate with existing C++ code. In fact, some frameworks in Mac OS X are written in C.

Cocoa integration
> Cocoa is designed for Objective-C, and Objective-C is evolving around Cocoa. You have other options for languages, but in my opinion, the two are much more powerful together than they are apart.

The first two points are interesting, but the most important feature of Objective-C is its tight integration with Cocoa. The majority of Mac and iPhone apps are written in Objective-C, including Xcode itself. Cocoa apps *can* be written with languages like Ruby and Python—and some developers do just that and create great software—but Objective-C is the native tongue of Cocoa.

Even if you later decide to write Mac applications in another language, you should still learn Objective-C first. It will help you understand how Cocoa works, and you can transfer what you learn to iPhone development. It's also important because most of the existing sample and open source code for Cocoa is written in Objective-C.

 Objective-C is open source. If you're an experienced C programmer and want to see how everything works, go to *http://opensource.apple.com/ source/objc4/*.

One thing you should know before we start is that, *at first*, the language syntax will look really weird. But trust me, this is a temporary state of confusion that almost everyone gets over in just a few days.

When I was getting ready to write the book, I did a quick survey online of about 120 developers, asking what their biggest initial stumbling block was for learning Cocoa.[*] The most common response, by a wide margin, was that Objective-C "seemed strange at first."

However, *none* of the developers said they still feel that way now. So the confusion you might feel at first is totally normal. A tiny percentage of your time goes into learning the language. Most of the effort goes into finding out which of the hundreds of classes in Cocoa are the right match for a task, and how to use the class once you find it.

NSString Basics

Most of the examples in this chapter use `NSString` objects to store text. I only use it in a very basic way in this chapter, but I'll explain the class in more detail in Chapter 7. `NSString` objects are so common in Cocoa than they have a special syntax. Here's an example:

```
// a famous quote by Alan Kay.
NSString* quote = @"The best way to predict the future is to invent it.";
```

The `@"string"` shortcut creates an `NSString` object that you can either pass directly into a method or assign to a variable. You'll see more examples in the following chapters, but this is enough to get started.

Using Methods

If you're familiar with a language like C, C++, Java, or PHP, you're probably used to seeing methods or functions called like this:

```
displayNames();
displayNamesWithPrefix( prefix );
addressBook.displayNames();
addressBook.displayNamesWithPrefix( prefix );
```

---

[*] "What Do People Find Challenging About Cocoa?" (*http://theocacao.com/document.page/605*).

This is how you call methods in Objective-C:

```
[addressBook displayNames];
[addressBook displayNamesWithPrefix: prefix];
```

Many experienced programmers get tripped up on the method syntax during the first day or so, then realize it's not actually that different. The syntax is:

```
[object method];
[object methodWithInput: inputValue];
```

Objective-C is a dynamic language, so *technically* you're not calling a method directly when you use this syntax; you're actually *sending a message*. Calling a method is basically issuing an *order*, whereas sending a message is more like making a *request*.

When you send a message to an object, the object may call a method with the same name, it may call another method instead, or it may even redirect the entire request to another object. There's a lot of flexibility in Objective-C for interpreting messages.

 Sending a message usually calls the method with the same name, so many programmers use the terms "message" and "method" interchangeably. Dynamic messaging enables some great features in Cocoa, but it's not something you have to really think about on a minute-to-minute basis.

Methods can, of course, also return values:

```
names = [addressBook names];
names = [addressBook namesWithPrefix:prefix];
```

In addition to calling methods on objects, you can call methods on *classes*, too, which is how you create objects. In the following example, I use the `string` method on the `NSString` class, which returns a new `NSString` object:

```
id myString = [NSString string];
```

The `id` type declares that the `myString` variable can refer to *any kind of object*, so the actual class of the object isn't known ahead of time. In this example, it's clear that the object will be an `NSString`, so I'll add the type:

```
NSString* myString = [NSString string];
```

This is now an `NSString` variable, so Xcode will warn me if I try to send a message to an object that `NSString` doesn't support. But it's just a warning, not an error. Because Objective-C is a dynamic language, methods can be added to classes as the program is running, so new methods may show up later.

You might have also noticed that there's an asterisk to the right of the object type. All Objective-C object variables are pointer types. The `id` type is predefined as a pointer, so there's no need to add the asterisk to it.

In Chapter 3, I said that Cocoa makes it easier to use dynamic memory. When you create an `NSString` object with the string method, Cocoa allocates a memory block for the object and returns the address. That's why all object variables are pointers.

Nested Method Calls

In many languages, nested method or function calls look like this:

```
stringWithFormat ( format() );
```

The result of `format()` is passed as input to `stringWithFormat()`. In Objective-C, nested messages look like this:

```
[NSString stringWithFormat:[prefs format]];
```

You should avoid nesting more than two methods calls, because it's usually very hard to read.

Multi-Input Methods

Some methods take multiple input values. In Objective-C, a method name can be split up into several segments. The declaration for a multi-input method looks like this:

```
-(BOOL)writeToFile:(NSString *)path atomically:(BOOL)useAuxiliaryFile;
```

Here's how you call the method:

```
BOOL result = [myData writeToFile:filePath atomically:NO];
```

These are not just named values. The method itself is actually called `-writeTo File:atomically:`, and Xcode will warn you if you misspell any part of it.

Accessors

All instance variables are *protected* in Objective-C by default, so you should always use accessors to get and set values. You should even use them when getting and setting values *within* the object itself. This is partially just because it's better encapsulation, but the other reason is that Cocoa offers some more advanced "generic programming" features that depend on using accessors properly. Here's an example of using accessors for the `caption` instance variable:

```
[photo setCaption:@"Day at the Beach"];
currentCaption = [photo caption];
```

Calling [photo caption] does not read the instance variable directly. It actually calls the *method* named `caption`. In most cases, you don't add the "get" prefix to accessors in Objective-C. It's important that you use standard naming conventions for accessors, because it enables Cocoa to automate a lot of work for you.

The "get" prefix is used on some methods that return values by indirection, such as -[NSArray getObjects:range:], which writes directly to a memory address that you provide.

Dot Syntax

The dot syntax for accessors is part of Objective-C 2.0, which was introduced in Mac OS X 10.5 Leopard and the first version of the iPhone SDK. This syntax is optional, and produces the same end result as the traditional style:

```
photo.caption = @"Day at the Beach";
output = photo.caption;
```

When you use the dot syntax, you don't add the "set" prefix to the property name. Many Cocoa programmers have an opinion on which accessor style is better, but there is no performance difference at all. It just comes down to what you find more readable. Personally, I like using the dot syntax, because it reduces the amount of special characters needed to make nested calls. For example, both of these do the same thing:

```
[[[properties regions] us] setTitle: @"United States"];
```

```
properties.regions.us.title = @"United States";
```

This is just my opinion, though. You can use either style, but choose only one for each project to keep the code consistent. Most importantly, the dot syntax should only be used for setters and getters, *not* for general-purpose methods. Xcode may let you get away with it, but it's exceptionally bad style:

```
// INCORRECT: do not use dot syntax for general methods.
addressBook.rebuildIndex;

// CORRECT: dot syntax should be used for getters and setters only.
// use the brackets for all other methods.
allNames = addressBook.names;
addressBook.names = allNames;

[addressBook rebuildIndex];
```

In other words, you should use dot syntax only when assigning or retrieving a value. As an advanced technique, it's acceptable to mix and match the two styles. Both of these are correct:

```
names = [[[system storage] addressBook] namesWithPrefix:prefix];
names = [system.storage.addressBook namesWithPrefix:prefix];
```

Again, this is an advanced technique and you are never *required* to use it. I'm just mentioning it here so you know it's an option.

Creating Objects

There are two main ways to create an object. The first is the one you saw before:

```
NSString* myString = [NSString string];
```

This is the more convenient automatic style. In this case, you are creating an *autoreleased* object, which means that its memory will be freed automatically. In many cases, though, you need to create an object using the manual style:

```
NSString* myString = [[NSString alloc] init];
```

This is a nested method call. The first is a call to `alloc`, which reserves memory for the object. It's a class method, so it's called on the `NSString` class itself. The second piece is a call to `init` on the new object. The `init` method for a class usually does basic setup, such as setting default values for instance variables. In some cases, you may use a different version of `init` that takes input:

```
NSNumber* value = [[NSNumber alloc] initWithFloat:1.0];
```

Virtually all classes support the manual `alloc` style, but not all provide the autoreleased style. The documentation and header file for each class tells you specifically whether it supports both, but I'll teach you about the most common cases. If a class supports both styles, there are trade-offs for each:

Autoreleased style: +string

>   Requires fewer lines of code, and reduces the possibility that you'll forget to release the memory for an object later. This convenience comes at a small performance cost. The difference is usually minuscule, but you *can* run into significant slowdowns when dealing with thousands of objects or more. See the following section for more details on freeing memory.

Manual style: +alloc

>   Is slightly faster on a per-object basis than the autoreleased style. More importantly, some classes offer certain initialization options only in the manual style, in the form of `[[MyClass alloc] initWithFirstName:name]`, but this varies by class. I tend to use this style more often to get whatever performance benefits I can.

Basic Memory Management

If you're writing an application for Mac OS X, you have the option to enable *garbage collection*, which means that you generally don't have to think about memory management until you get to more complex cases. However, that's not always an option. For example, the iPhone SDK does not support garbage collection, or you may find yourself maintaining an application written by someone who didn't use garbage collection.

The rest of the examples in this book do not use garbage collection. My reason for this is that you will probably work with a lot of code that uses conventional memory management. It's much easier to learn the conventional system from the start than to try to insert it into your understanding after using garbage collection.

The conventional, non-garbage-collected memory management system is called *reference counting*. It's similar to using `malloc()` and `free()`, but Objective-C has a slightly different challenge than standard C. In an object-oriented framework, many parts of the application share the same data, so it's challenging for you (as the programmer) to know when an object is no longer being used and can safely be freed.

In the reference counting system, each part of the application keeps track of only its *own* references for an object rather than the total in use throughout the entire application. The Objective-C runtime takes responsibility for freeing the memory when *all* of the references are released. This means you can focus on very isolated cases without being overwhelmed by all of the places the object is possibly being used (see Figure 5-1).

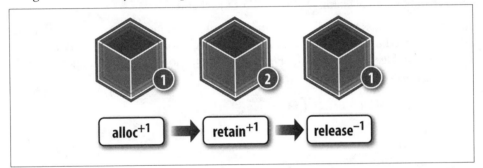

Figure 5-1. The +alloc method creates an object with a retain count of 1; the +retain method increases the retain count by 1 (a total of 2), and the -release method reduces it back to 1

It sounds very complicated, but the mechanics are extremely simple. If you create an object using the manual `alloc` style, you need to *release* the object later. Here are two examples:

```
NSString* string1 = [NSString string];      // automatic.

    // (code that uses string1 runs here.)

NSString* string2 = [[NSString alloc] init]; // manual.

    // (code that uses string2 runs here.)

[string2 release];
```

You might be tempted to manually release an autoreleased object just to be sure that it's been cleaned up, but doing that will cause a crash. There's more to learn about memory management, but let's first take a look at a few more key concepts.

Using Autorelease Directly

I'll walk you through memory management in more detail in the next chapter, but there's one thing that's useful to mention here. If you create an object using the manual +alloc style, you can directly call -autorelease on it. As a result, these two lines of code are essentially equivalent:

```
NSString* string1 = [NSString string];
NSString* string2 = [[[NSString alloc] init] autorelease];
```

This doesn't save you much typing and is harder to read, but it *is* important to use this technique in certain cases. There's a class method in the example at the end of the chapter that creates a new object and returns it as autoreleased.

Declaring a Class

I'm going to show you some examples of how to create basic classes, but at this point you can just follow along and take in the examples. You don't need to actually create the files until the final example at the end of the chapter.

An Objective-C class is usually made up of two files. The instance variables and methods are declared in the *ClassName.h* file, and the method implementations are in the *ClassName.m* file. Here's what the *Photo.h* header file looks like for the Photo class:

```
#import <Cocoa/Cocoa.h> ❶

@interface Photo : NSObject { ❷

    id caption; ❸
    id photographer;
}
@end ❹
```

❶ Most Objective-C classes import *Cocoa.h* at the top. Unlike #include in C, the #import statement prevents a file from being included multiple times.

❷ The @interface statement declares the actual class name, Photo. To the right of that is a colon and the superclass name, NSObject.

❸ Inside the curly brackets are two instance variables: caption and photographer. Both are generic id object types, but instance variables are usually declared to be specific types like Cocoa's NSString class, or C types like int and float.

❹ Finally, the @end statement ends the class declaration.

Some new programmers mistakenly swap the class name with the filename. For example, they might try to declare a class called *Photo.h* instead of Photo. Remember *.h* and *.m* are for *filenames* only, not class names.

Add Methods

Now that I have some instance variables, I'll add accessors to retrieve the values:

```
#import <Cocoa/Cocoa.h>

@interface Photo : NSObject {
  id caption;
  id photographer;
}

- caption;
- photographer;

@end
```

Remember, you don't add the "get" prefix to Objective-C methods except in certain specific cases. A *plus symbol* before a method name means it's a *class method*. A *minus symbol* before a method name means it's an *instance method*:

```
+ classMethod;
- instanceMethod;
```

You call class methods on the class itself, such as `+[NSString string]`. Many of these methods exist only to create instances of the class as objects. Instance methods are used on objects that are instances of a class, such as `-[object release]`.

When declaring a method, ask yourself this: *does the method apply to only one instance or all instances of the class?* If it applies to *all instances*, it's usually better as a *class method*. Otherwise, it should be an instance method. Most methods you create in Objective-C will probably be instance methods.

Objective-C assumes that all input and output values are `id` objects, so you're not strictly required to provide types. The previous example is technically correct, but it's unusual. I'll add specific types for the instance variables and their accessors:

```
#import <Cocoa/Cocoa.h>

@interface Photo : NSObject {
  NSString* caption;
  NSString* photographer;
}

- (NSString*) caption;
- (NSString*) photographer;

@end
```

Now I'll add setters:

```
#import <Cocoa/Cocoa.h>

@interface Photo : NSObject {
  NSString* caption;
  NSString* photographer;
```

```
}
- (NSString*) caption;
- (NSString*) photographer;

- (void) setCaption: (NSString*)input;
- (void) setPhotographer: (NSString*)input;

@end
```

Setters don't return a value, so I just set the return type to **void**. If you're thinking that a lot of this code is redundant, you're right. There are simpler ways to declare accessors that you'll learn about in the next chapter, but it's easier to learn the basics first.

Implementing a Class

Now that the class name, instance variables, and methods are declared in *Photo.h*, I can add the method implementation in *Photo.m*:

```
#import "Photo.h" ❶

@implementation Photo ❷

- (NSString*) caption { ❸
    return caption;
}

- (NSString*) photographer {
    return photographer;
}

@end ❹
```

❶ A class implementation starts by importing the header file, which in this case is *Photo.h*.

❷ Next is the `@implementation` statement and the class name, `Photo`.

❸ After that are any number of method implementations; in this case, these are `-caption` and `-photographer`.

❹ The `@end` statement at the very bottom ends the class implementation.

 It's easy to type `@interface` when you mean to use `@implementation`, so be careful. Xcode usually fills this part in for you, but if you type it in wrong by hand, you'll see all sort of cryptic errors. Remember this: *.h* has the `@interface` and *.m* has the `@implementation`.

The getters themselves are very simple—they just return the instance variable. I'm going to move on to the setters, which I need to spend a bit more time explaining:

```
- (void) setCaption: (NSString*)input {
```

```
    [caption autorelease];
    [input retain];
    caption = input;
}

- (void) setPhotographer: (NSString*)input {

    [photographer autorelease];
    [input retain];
    photographer = input;
}
```

A setter's job is to swap the old value with the new value. Objective-C objects are different than an `int` or `float`, though. When you an assign an object to a variable, it doesn't get the *value* (such as the number 12 or the string "Cupertino"); it gets a *reference* to the object.

It's as if somebody writes down her phone number on a piece of paper and hands it to you. You don't get the phone, you get a *reference* to it so that you can call it later.

In technical terms, an object variable is actually a *pointer* that refers to the memory block where the object is. You can then "dial up" that memory block to get the object, though Objective-C does that part for you behind the scenes.

So instead of assigning *values*, a setter for an object variable actually assigns *references*. It's like scribbling out the phone number on the paper and writing a new one. For example, this is the code inside the setter for the **caption** instance variable:

```
    [caption autorelease];
    [input retain];
    caption = input;
```

I no longer need the old **NSString** object that **caption** refers to, so I call **autorelease** on it. I then call **retain** on the **input** object because I'm going to assign it to the instance variable and need it to stay around.

Finally, I set the **caption** instance variable to be equal to **input**. Because these are both objects, the **caption** now *refers* to the same object that **input** does. I can simplify this, though:

```
    [caption autorelease];
    caption = [input retain];
```

Because the **retain** method returns a reference to the object, I **retain** the new object and *assign* it to the **caption** instance variable in one step.

This is very common in Cocoa programs. It may seem confusing, but it will make more sense as you see examples in context. Don't feel obligated to figure it all out now. You can always come back to this section later to review.

I use the -autorelease method here instead of -release for several different reasons (most of which are too involved to explain at this point), but the most important is that caption and input might be the *same object*. If that was true, and you were to -release the caption object, it could immediately be freed and the next line of code would crash the application. Using -autorelease guarantees that the object will stay around at least until the setter is done running.

init

Classes usually have an init method to set initial values for its instance variables or do other setup tasks.

```
- (id) init {

    if ( self = [super init] ) { ❶

        [self setCaption:@"Default Caption"]; ❷
        [self setPhotographer:@"Default Photographer"];
    }

    return self; ❸
}
```

❶ Inside the if statement, there's a single equals sign that assigns the result of [super init] to self. The self variable refers to the object that the current method belongs to. Usually a *single* equals sign inside an if statement is a typo, but this one is actually intentional.

I combine the assignment and the test to make sure the assignment worked. You use the **super** variable to call the superclass's version of a method. You should always call [super init] in your own init method so the superclass can do some basic configuration for you. If [super init] fails for some reason, it will return nil, which is equal to zero. That would prevent the code inside the brackets from running.

Although it looks like an advanced trick, this is the *standard* way to write an init method. I'd usually try to steer you away from combining two actions into one because it can be confusing, but this one is so common that it's more confusing to do something else.

You usually shouldn't try to make up your own Objective-C conventions unless you're sure they're substantially better than the ones in use. The thing that makes large Cocoa projects (meaning hundreds of thousands of lines of code or more) manageable is that most Objective-C code looks the same, so you don't have to constantly switch between different styles.

❷ Instance variables are set to nil automatically, so inside the brackets, I set better default values for caption and photographer. Some Cocoa programmers set the instance variables directly inside of -init, but I think using the setters is cleaner and generally more predictable.

❸ The last part of this method is the statement return self. Any init method you create has to return self at the end. Your implementation calls the superclass version of init and captures the result, so you need to actually return the new object to whoever requested it.

Of course, you can get into a logical paradox as to how the method runs at all if self is defined inside of it, but explaining the nature of self is outside of the scope of this book.

 Objective-C's nil keyword is similar to NULL in other languages like C and Java. The difference is that it's perfectly safe to call methods on nil. If any method that returns an object is called on nil, you will receive a nil back. Methods that return primitive values like int or float will return 0 or 0.0. This is slightly more complex for methods that return structs, but this book does not cover that part of Objective-C. To keep things simple, avoid calling methods that return structs on objects that might be nil.

dealloc

The dealloc method is called on an object when it is being removed from memory. You should add this method to your classes and clear references to all of your instance variables that are objects:

```
- (void) dealloc {

    [caption release];
    [photographer release];

    [super dealloc];
}
```

The goal of Objective-C memory management is to balance every alloc or retain with either a release or autorelease. We don't need to use autorelease here, and the standard release is a bit faster. After you release the instance variables, call [super dealloc] so the Objective-C runtime can actually free the memory. This should always be the last line of your dealloc method. Another way to do this is to simply set the instance variables to nil:

```
- (void) dealloc {

    [self setCaption:nil];
    [self setPhotographer:nil];

    [super dealloc];
}
```

I think this is slightly safer, because any code that happens to try to access the instance variable will get a `nil` instead of random memory. The setter will `release` the old value, call `retain` on `nil` (which does nothing), and then continue on.

Some Cocoa programmers feel that it's better to call `-release` on instance variables here because the object might be in a different state inside `-dealloc` than it normally is. As far as I know, `-release` is the most common style. In reality, either will probably work fine.

 The `dealloc` method is not called on objects if garbage collection is enabled. Instead, you can implement the `finalize` method. You usually don't need to clean up Objective-C objects in `finalize`, but you might need to do other housekeeping tasks.

Example: PhotoInfo

Launch Xcode and click "Create a new Xcode project," or choose File → New Project from the menu. In the New Project window, click Application under the Mac OS X section and select the Cocoa Application icon, as shown in Figure 5-2.

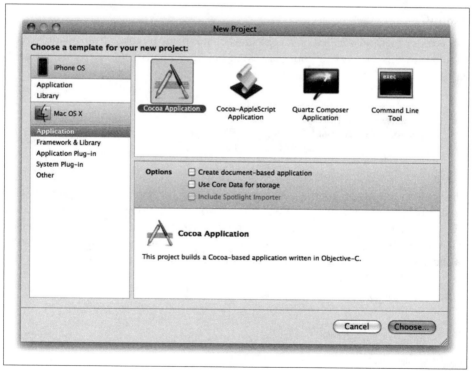

Figure 5-2. The New Project window in Xcode

Click the Choose button, and you'll be asked to select a location for the project. Go to the *CocoaBook* folder you created at the beginning of the book, and create a new subfolder called *ch05*. Select the *CocoaBook/ch05/* folder as the save location and enter "PhotoInfo" as the project name. Click Save.

At this point, you can press Command-R to quickly build and run the application to make sure that everything works. You should just see a blank window. Quit the test application, or click the Tasks stop button in the Xcode toolbar.

This example uses the `NSLog()` function, which works just like `printf()` with the exception that you can provide a `%@` marker for any object. This will cause `NSLog()` to call the `-description` method on the object you pass in for that marker and display the return value in the console.

Create a new Objective-C class file by choosing File → New File from the menu. In the New File window (Figure 5-3), select Cocoa Class under the Mac OS X section, then select the "Objective-C class" icon and click Next.

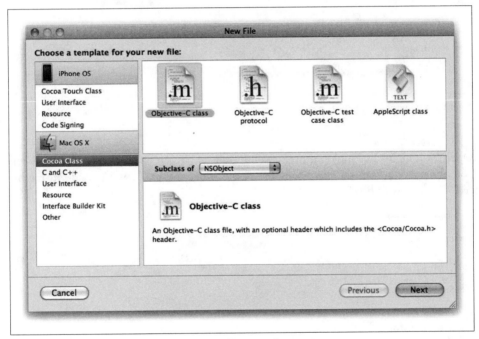

Figure 5-3. Creating a new Objective-C class file in Xcode

Name the file *Photo.m*, and you can accept all of the default options, as shown in Figure 5-4. Click Finish.

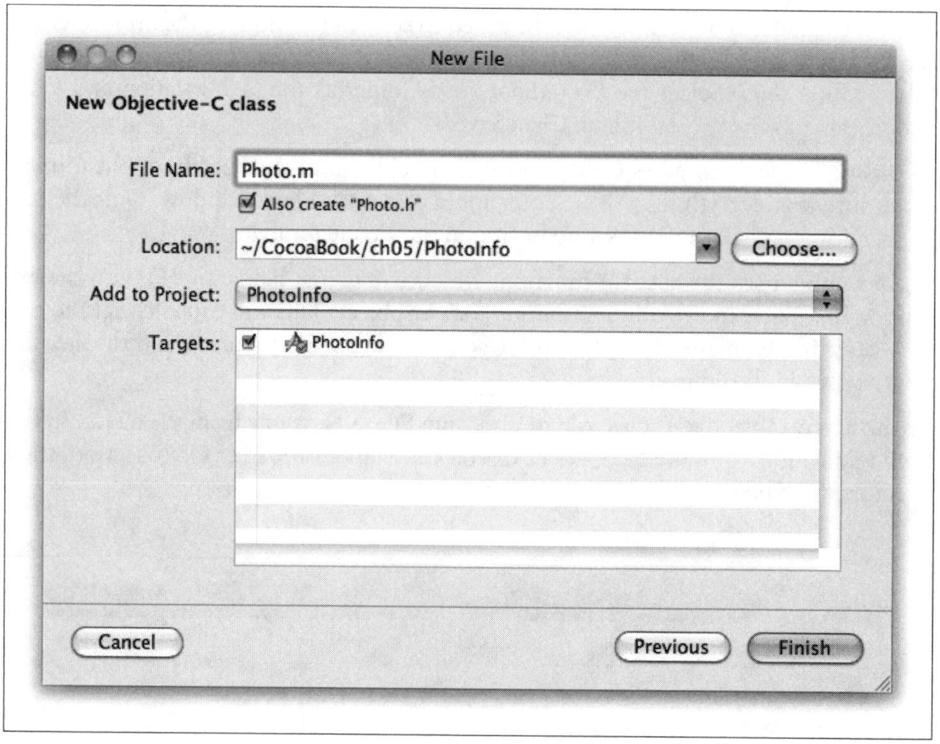

Figure 5-4. Name the file Photo.m and accept all of the default options

Open *Photo.h* by clicking on it in the Xcode sidebar. If you had a group selected when you chose New File, the class files may be in that group. Type the code in Example 5-1 into *Photo.h*.

Example 5-1. Photo.h

```
#import <Cocoa/Cocoa.h>

@interface Photo : NSObject {
  NSString* caption;
  NSString* photographer;
}

+ (Photo*) photo;

- (NSString*) caption;
- (NSString*) photographer;

- (void) setCaption: (NSString*)input;
- (void) setPhotographer: (NSString*)input;

@end
```

Now click *Photo.m* in the Xcode sidebar to start editing it, and type the code from Example 5-2 into the file.

Example 5-2. Photo.m

```
#import "Photo.h"

@implementation Photo

- (id) init {

    if ( self = [super init] ) {

        [self setCaption:@"Default Caption"];
        [self setPhotographer:@"Default Photographer"];
    }

    return self;
}

+ (Photo*) photo {

    Photo* newPhoto = [[Photo alloc] init];
    return [newPhoto autorelease];
}

- (NSString*) caption {
  return caption;
}

- (NSString*) photographer {
  return photographer;
}

- (void) setCaption: (NSString*)input {

  [caption autorelease];
  caption = [input retain];
}

- (void) setPhotographer: (NSString*)input {

  [photographer autorelease];
  photographer = [input retain];
}

- (void) dealloc {

    [self setCaption:nil];
    [self setPhotographer:nil];

    [super dealloc];
}

@end
```

You're almost done. Next, in the Classes group in the Xcode sidebar, open the *PhotoInfoAppDelegate.m* file. This class is automatically generated by Xcode when you create the project, and acts as a sort of "control center" of the application. The one built-in method is -applicationDidFinishLaunching:, which is the first thing that is called when the application is actually running and ready to do things. Type the Example 5-3 version of -applicationDidFinishLaunching: into *PhotoInfoAppDelegate.m*, completely replacing the existing version of -applicationDidFinishLaunching: but leaving the rest of the file untouched.

Example 5-3. PhotoInfoAppDelegate.m

```
- (void)applicationDidFinishLaunching:(NSNotification *)aNotification {

    Photo* photo1 = [[Photo alloc] init];

    NSLog( @"photo1 caption: %@", photo1.caption );
    NSLog( @"photo1 photographer: %@", photo1.photographer );

    photo1.caption      = @"Overlooking the Golden Gate Bridge";
    photo1.photographer = @"(Your name here)";

    NSLog( @"photo1 caption: %@", photo1.caption );
    NSLog( @"photo1 photographer: %@", photo1.photographer );

    [photo1 release];


    Photo* photo2  = [Photo photo];

    NSLog( @"photo2 caption: %@", photo2.caption );
    NSLog( @"photo2 photographer: %@", photo2.photographer );

    photo2.caption      = @"Moffett Field";
    photo2.photographer = @"(Your name here)";

    NSLog( @"photo2 caption: %@", photo2.caption );
    NSLog( @"photo2 photographer: %@", photo2.photographer );
}
```

 You will see a few things in the file that you don't recognize yet, such as the @synthesize statement. I'll cover that in the next chapter.

Finally, add the #import statement for the Photo class header at the top of *PhotoInfoAppDelegate.m*, as shown in Example 5-4.

Example 5-4. Top of PhotoInfoAppDelegate.m

```
#import "PhotoInfoAppDelegate.h"
#import "Photo.h"

@implementation PhotoInfoAppDelegate
```

Now save any files that you've edited and run the project by pressing Command-R. If you see any errors, double-check that you typed in the code exactly as shown previously. When you run the application, the main window will still be blank, but you can see the output from NSLog() in the console by going back to Xcode and pressing Command-Shift-R:

```
photo1 caption: Default Caption
photo1 photographer: Default Photographer
photo1 caption: Overlooking the Golden Gate Bridge
photo1 photographer: (Your name here)
photo2 caption: Default Caption
photo2 photographer: Default Photographer
photo2 caption: Moffett Field
photo2 photographer: (Your name here)
```

Not all of the code snippets in this book are set up as full examples, but if you'd like to try them out as you go, you can paste them into the -application DidFinishLaunching: method here and rerun. This won't work with every single code snippet in the book because some depend on other pieces of code (in which case you would see a build error), but it *should* work in the vast majority of cases.

CHAPTER 6

More Objective-C

Now that all of the basic building blocks are in place, I can show you some of the more technical details of how Objective-C works. I'm going to fine-tune your code, talk more about reference counting, and then look at some unique features.

Most of the sections in this chapter describe techniques that you will use on a regular basis. A few of the topics are more advanced and you may not use them often, but if you need them, you *really* need them. All of them help you understand how Cocoa works.

More on Memory Management

In Chapter 5, I walked you through Objective-C's traditional memory management system, called *reference counting*. Each object has a *retain count*, which is ostensibly the number of other things that are currently using it. The good news is that you don't need to constantly check the retain count. You need to keep track of only your *own* references; Cocoa will do the rest.

 You can call the retainCount method on any object, but don't read too much into what it returns. It may not always reflect the *exact* number of retains and releases you have issued. Cocoa intervenes in certain cases.

The retain count starts at 1 when you create an object with alloc. It goes up and down as you call retain, release, and autorelease. When the retain count reaches 0, the Objective-C runtime will call dealloc on the object so that it can be removed from memory (see Figure 6-1).

The point of all this is that you're trying to *balance* all of your memory management calls. So for every alloc or retain, you must issue exactly one call to either release or autorelease.

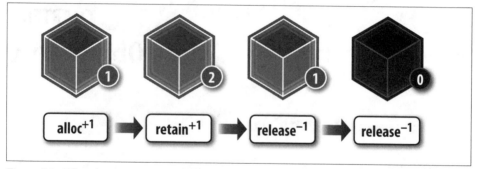

Figure 6-1. When the retain count reaches 0, the dealloc method is called and the object is removed from memory

That's the most common explanation of Cocoa memory management, and I didn't want to leave out such a crucial bit of lore. That said, I think it's easier to explain this in terms of what you need to do instead of how it works internally.

In plain terms, there are usually* only two reasons that you would create an object in a Cocoa application:

- To keep it as an instance variable (long term)
- To use it temporarily inside a method (short term)

In most cases, the setter method for an instance variable should just `autorelease` the old object and `retain` the new one. You then just make sure to `release` it in `dealloc`, as well:

```
- (void) setTotalAmount: (NSNumber*)input {

    [totalAmount autorelease];
    totalAmount = [input retain];
}

- (void) dealloc {

    [totalAmount release];
    [super dealloc];
}
```

That just leaves the case of a "short-term" object that you need only temporarily. For this scenario, there's only one rule: if you create an object with `alloc` or `copy`, then you need to call `release` or `autorelease` on it by the end of the method. If you create an object *any other way, do nothing*:

```
NSNumber* value1 = [[NSNumber alloc] initWithFloat:8.75];
NSNumber* value2 = [NSNumber numberWithFloat:14.78];
```

---

* The word "usually" is important here. There *are* cases where things are a bit more complex, but these basic rules work the vast majority of the time, and the others are fairly easy to pick up as you encounter them.

```
// only release value1, not value2.
[value1 release];
```

Here's a combination case: start with a "short-term" object and set it as a "long-term" instance variable:

```
// create a number and set it as the 'total' instance variable.
NSNumber* value1 = [[NSNumber alloc] initWithFloat:8.75];
[self setTotal:value1];

// create another number and set it as the new 'total'.
NSNumber* value2 = [NSNumber numberWithFloat:14.78];
[self setTotal:value2];

// only release the object created with 'alloc'.
[value1 release];
```

Notice how the rules for managing the "short-term" references are exactly the same, regardless of whether you end up setting them as instance variables. If you removed the lines that contain setTotal, the code would still be correct.

The setters are self-contained, so you don't need to think about how they are managing memory internally. If you understand this, you understand 90 percent of everything you need to know about Objective-C memory management.

The Life of an Instance Variable

To help put all of these concepts together, here's a brief walkthrough of all of the stages of an instance variable. For the discussion, I'll call this instance variable title, and it will be an NSString.

1. Because it's an instance variable, title starts out as nil.
2. The setter for title is called inside the parent object's -init method. The setter autoreleases the existing object (nil, which does nothing), and retains the new NSString object: @"Cupertino".
3. At some point while the program is running, the user types a new value into a text field, which triggers the setter to be called again with a new NSString object: @"Sunnyvale". The old value is autoreleased, and the new object is retained. The old object may get deallocated at this point, but you don't have to think about that; you've released *your reference* to it.
4. Finally, when -dealloc is called on the parent object, it calls the setter for title one last time using a input value of nil. The setter autoreleases the old value, and retains the input value (nil, which does nothing). The -dealloc method could also just call -release on title directly, which usually has the same effect.

Copying Objects

Many classes support copying with the -copy method, which creates a new instance of an object with most the same data as the original. I say "most" because certain values should not be copied, such as a unique identifier. You manage the memory of a copy just as if you had created a new object with +alloc:

```
NSString* originalString = [[NSString alloc] init];
NSString* copyOfString   = [originalString copy];

[originalString release];
[copyOfString release];
```

Classes you create will usually not support copying until you implement the -copyWithZone: method. Here's a simple implementation for the Photo class from the previous chapter.

```
- (id) copyWithZone:(NSZone *)zone {

    Photo* newPhoto         = [[Photo allocWithZone:zone] init];
    newPhoto.caption        = self.caption;
    newPhoto.photographer   = self.photographer;
    return newPhoto;
}
```

You can now make copies of Photo objects:

```
Photo* photo1        = [Photo photo];
photo1.caption       = @"Golden Gate Park";
photo1.photographer = @"(Your name here)";

NSLog( @"photo1 caption: %@", photo1.caption );
NSLog( @"photo1 photographer: %@", photo1.photographer );

Photo* photo2 = [photo1 copy];
NSLog( @"photo2 caption: %@", photo2.caption );
NSLog( @"photo2 photographer: %@", photo2.photographer );
[photo2 release];
```

Here's the result in the console:

```
photo1 caption: Golden Gate Park
photo1 photographer: (Your name here)
photo2 caption: Golden Gate Park
photo2 photographer: (Your name here)
```

The NSZone class represents a "memory zone." The idea is to keep related objects close together in memory to improve performance when system resources are constrained. You'll rarely see this class used outside of the -copyWithZone: method.

Class Name Prefixes

Objective-C does not implement namespaces, which means that all class names and global variables are in the same global pool. This means that if you are creating a class with a very general name, such as `Image`, you want to add a custom prefix to avoid colliding with classes built into Cocoa, as well as other third-party frameworks you may decide to use. If you collide with a built-in class name when compiling, you will see a build error in Xcode (Figure 6-2).

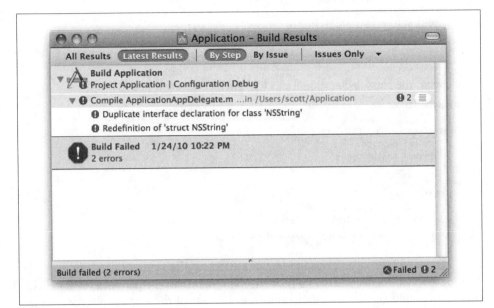

Figure 6-2. A build error in Xcode describing a duplicate class name

To avoid this, prefix your class names with something specific to you or your application. For example, if my application is called "Photo Stacks," I could prefix all of the classes in the project with `PS`. So the `Image` class would instead be called `PSImage`. If wanted to reuse this class in several chapters of this book, I could also use the prefix `CB` for Cocoa Book. The exact prefix doesn't matter, as long as it's unique. It's better to do this from the beginning rather than going back and renaming your classes later.

Properties

When I added the accessor methods for `caption` and `photographer` in the previous chapter, you might have noticed that the same code was repeated in the accessor methods for each class. *Properties* are a feature of Objective-C that, among other things, allow you to automatically create accessors in your implementation (*.m* file). Here's the original class declaration (*Photo.h*):

```
#import <Cocoa/Cocoa.h>

@interface Photo : NSObject {
  NSString* caption;
  NSString* photographer;
}

+ (Photo*) photo;

- (NSString*) caption;
- (NSString*) photographer;

- (void) setCaption: (NSString*)input;
- (void) setPhotographer: (NSString*)input;

@end
```

Here's what the class declaration looks like once I convert it to use properties:

```
#import <Cocoa/Cocoa.h>

@interface Photo : NSObject {
  NSString* caption;
  NSString* photographer;
}

+ (Photo*) photo;

@property (retain) NSString* caption;
@property (retain) NSString* photographer;

@end
```

The @property directive declares a property. The retain in the parentheses states that the setter should retain the input value, and the rest of the line simply specifies the type and the name of the property. Properties are not methods—they're a way to declare data that the object stores. But you can use them to generate accessors in the implementation file.

 If you are creating software exclusively for 64-bit Macs (see "64-Bit Objective-C" on page 111), you can use @property declarations to automatically generate instance variables as well, eliminating the last bits of redundant code. For compatibility reasons, this is not available for 32-bit applications.

Here's the implementation of the class (*Photo.m*):

```
#import "Photo.h"

@implementation Photo

  @synthesize caption;
  @synthesize photographer;
```

```
- (id) init {

  if ( self = [super init] ) {

      [self setCaption:@"Default Caption"];
      [self setPhotographer:@"Default Photographer"];
  }

  return self;
}

+ (Photo*) photo {

    Photo* newPhoto = [[Photo alloc] init];
    return [newPhoto autorelease];
}

- (void) dealloc {

    [caption release];
    [photographer release];
    [super dealloc];
}

@end
```

The @synthesize directive automatically generates the setters and getters, so all you have to implement in this case is the dealloc method. What's particularly nice is that the system will generate only accessors that you don't create yourself. So if you use @synthesize and then add your own custom getter, the compiler will generate only the setter.

Property Options

The property declarations give you a few options for controlling how the accessors are generated. The simplest version of a property looks like this:

```
@property id name;
```

The most complex version looks like this:

```
@property (
    retain,  ❶
    getter=firstName, setter=setFirstName, ❷
    nonatomic, ❸
    readwrite ❹
) NSString* name; ❺
```

❶ This describes the memory management that will be used by the setter. The options are retain, copy, and assign. For most object properties, use retain or assign, which work just like the methods by the same names. The assign keyword does no memory management at all. It just sets the property to the given value. Use this for nonobject values like float, int, and BOOL.

If you don't specify which memory management option you want, the property will default to assign. This is usually not what you want unless you're using garbage collection, so look here first if your application is crashing. Also, if you implement a custom setter, you should respect the keyword used here. So if you use copy, make sure your custom setter uses -copy and not -retain.

❷ This allows you to specify the getter and setter names that will be generated. One of the most common uses for this is to wrap a BOOL property like enabled in a getter called isEnabled, which is better Objective-C style.

❸ By default, all properties are *atomic*, meaning that access to that property is thread-safe. It's effectively the same as putting a lock around instance variable access in the getter and setter. The official documentation points out that this doesn't mean the entire *class* is thread-safe, though. In a conventional, non-garbage-collected environment, there is a performance cost to make this work. If you're *not* using threads, you can specify nonatomic for better performance. If you're using garbage collection, there's no overhead for using atomic properties. Thread safety is an advanced topic that is not covered in this book.

❹ By default, properties are readwrite, which means that other classes can freely get and set the value. Some properties are just designed to provide information, such as an application version number. If you don't want any outside classes to set the property value, you can specify readonly.

❺ This is the property type and name.

In most cases, the defaults work fine. For properties that represent object values, though, you almost always want to at least specify retain or copy.

Options for accessor implementations

You have two main options for properties on the implementation side. By default, the @synthesize directive looks for an instance variable with the same name as the property. For example:

```
@interface Photo : NSObject {
    NSString* name;
    NSString* storedName;
}
@property (retain) NSString* name;
@end

@implementation Photo
@synthesize name;
@end
```

If I want the accessors for the name property to use the storedNamed instance variable instead, I can specify it manually:

```
@implementation Photo
@synthesize name=storedName;
@end
```

In some advanced cases, you may know that accessors for a property will be generated while the program is running, but you still want to use the property in code. To compile that code without errors or warnings, you can use @dynamic instead of the @synthesize directive:

```
@implementation Photo
@dynamic name;
@end
```

This effectively disables all compiler-generated warnings about accessors for this property. They will not be generated for you, and you don't have to implement them yourself either. However, if the method is *not* generated as the program is running, an error will be raised, which will probably prevent the program from running correctly.

64-Bit Objective-C

Most of the Macs sold since 2006 are 64-bit capable. Starting with Snow Leopard, most of the built-in Mac OS X applications run in 64-bit mode (the fact that the kernel itself will start up in 32-bit mode on many Macs does not affect this; it's the CPU architecture that matters). That opens up a lot of possibilities for processing power in general, but it has special meaning for Cocoa programmers. The 64-bit version of Objective-C revamps the low-level bits of the runtime to improve speed and overall flexibility. A few highlights:

Synthesized instance variables

You can use properties to generate both accessor methods *and* the instance variable itself. Here's the 64-bit version of the *Photo.h* file:

```
#import <Cocoa/Cocoa.h>

@interface Photo : NSObject
@property (retain) NSString* caption;
@property (retain) NSString* photographer;
@end
```

Yes, feel free to offer this feature a round of applause. Keep in mind that you can still declare the instance variables manually if you want—you just don't have to.

Faster method lookup

The revamped runtime allows a set number of commonly used methods to be stored in an extra-fast cache. For the most part, this is automatic, so all you know is that your code runs faster.

Unified geometry variable types

There are two sets of geometry types on the Mac: those defined by Cocoa, and those defined by a framework called CoreGraphics (which is used by the iPhone

SDK as well). In a 32-bit app, you need to convert between these types manually. In 64-bit, you can use them interchangeably.

Other than these additional features, writing 64-bit Cocoa apps is basically the same as writing 32-bit apps. By design, Cocoa and Objective-C abstract you from most of the lower-level details. There are some differences with C primitive types, though. You can find out about Cocoa's solution to this in Chapter 7.

 The Snow Leopard kernel (the very core of the system) starts up in 32-bit mode by default on some machines for compatibility reasons, but this doesn't directly affect you as a Cocoa developer. The only requirement for running 64-bit Cocoa apps is that the Mac itself must be 64-bit capable.

Enabling 64-Bit

Xcode creates hybrid 32-bit/64-bit projects by default on modern hardware. To check which architecture a project is currently using, highlight the Project icon in the sidebar of the main Xcode project window, and choose File → Get Info (or Command-I) to open the Inspector. Click on the Build tab to see the project's build settings, as shown in Figure 6-3.

▼ Architectures	
Additional SDKs	
Architectures	Standard (32/64-bit Universal)
Base SDK	Mac OS X 10.6
Build Active Architecture Only	☑
Valid Architectures	i386 ppc ppc64 ppc7400 ppc970 x86_64

Figure 6-3. The Architectures option in Project Inspector's Build tab; the Base SDK is set to Mac OS X 10.6, but this works for 10.5, too

This project is set up for "32/64-bit Universal," which means that Xcode will create a single application that runs on Intel or PowerPC-based Macs, including 32-bit and 64-bit versions.[†]

This hybrid setting is basically a compromise, though. Your software will run on most Macs, and you will get a speed boost on newer machines, but you won't be able to use 64-bit specific features in your project. This means you won't get synthesized instance variables or unified Cocoa/CoreGraphics types. To do that, you need to change this field to *64-bit Intel*.

---

† The term "universal" means that the app will run on both Intel and PowerPC chips. It's not directly related to 32-bit versus 64-bit.

Once you've done that, the compiled software will *run only* on Macs introduced since 2006. Some early models of MacBook Pro, for example, will not be able to run the software. You can always go back and change this setting later, but you might have to make some changes to your code to restore 32-bit compatibility.

 There's a subtle point here. Even if the Architectures field includes both 32-bit and 64-bit, the Build Active Architecture Only checkbox will override that and compile for your machine architecture only. This checkbox is on by default in the Debug configuration, but off in Release.

You can leave this checkbox on during development to shorten compile times, but switch back to the Release target occasionally to make sure that everything builds correctly. See "Preparing for Release" on page 303 for details on how to do this.

Should I Use 64-Bit?

The 64-bit version of Objective-C has some compelling advantages: better overall performance, ability to handle large amounts of data, and less code. You can get some benefits by building hybrid apps, but the real fun starts when you can write software built specifically for 64-bit.

So when should you starting doing that? There's no single answer. The conservative view is that breaking 32-bit compatibility limits your potential pool of users. However, there are a few factors to consider:

High-end markets
> If your application addresses a specialized high-end need—such as scientific modeling or video production—modern hardware may be a cost of doing business. In fact, those who don't upgrade are probably less likely to pay for high-end software.

Enthusiast users
> If you're writing software that appeals to "alpha geeks," you can usually assume more modern hardware because they're thinking about upgrades on a regular basis. Many factor new computer purchases into their budgets, particularly if their jobs are focused on technology.

Differentiation
> If you're entering a market with an established product backed by a large company, you might be able to make an impact by doing something the company can't do: target modern hardware. Often big companies do not want to risk cutting existing customers out of their upgrade revenue, but if you're starting from zero, you have nothing to lose. You can create a faster, more streamlined application that is designed for 64-bit.

Platform migration

Snow Leopard runs on Intel Macs only. This will likely be a catalyst that sparks a new upgrade cycle for some users who have PowerPC hardware. When they do upgrade, they will be buying 64-bit machines.

All of that said, there are a lot of computers in use that are not 64-bit capable, particularly those owned by casual users and educational institutions. If that's the type of user you're targeting, you may want to support 32-bit machines as well.

All Further Examples Assume 64-Bit

Because of the simpler syntax, performance improvements, and rapid adoption of 64-bit Macs, the rest of the examples you'll read here assume you're compiling for 64-bit Macs. If you need to write apps for 32-bit Macs or the iPhone, iPad, or iPod touch, the main difference is that you will need to declare instance variables separately from properties.

So if you see an example like this:

```
@interface Bookmark : NSObject
@property (retain) NSString* siteName;
@property (retain) NSString* url;
@end
```

change it to this to make it compatible with 32-bit Macs (and iPhone OS):

```
@interface Bookmark : NSObject {
    NSString* siteName;
    NSString* url;
}
@property (retain) NSString* siteName;
@property (retain) NSString* url;
@end
```

 If you want to use the 64-bit conveniences while still targeting 32-bit Macs, and don't need to share code with other projects, you might be able to use the NS_BUILD_32_LIKE_64 build setting in Xcode. See "Bridge Cocoa and CoreGraphics Geometry" (*http://theocacao.com/document .page/552*) for more.

Categories

Usually when you want to change the way a class works, you create a subclass and override methods. Some classes are difficult to subclass, though; even if you create a custom version of NSString, for example, Cocoa's built-in classes won't know to use it.

Objective-C's solution to this is *categories*, which allow you to add new methods to existing classes without subclassing them. A subclass is a direct descendant of the original, but a category method is sort of "bolted onto" the existing class (see Figure 6-4).

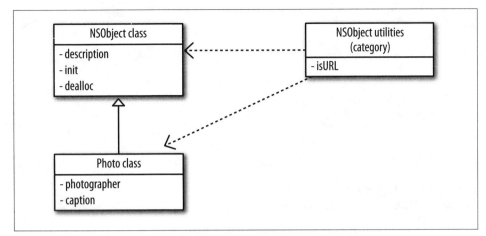

Figure 6-4. Categories are attached to a class, and inherited by the subclasses

If I wanted to add a method to **NSString** to determine if its contents are a URL, I'd use an interface declaration like Example 6-1.

Example 6-1. NSString-Utilities.h

```
#import <Cocoa/Cocoa.h>

@interface NSString (Utilities)
- (BOOL) isURL;
@end
```

This is similar to a class declaration, except there's no section for instance variables. Instead of providing the name of a new subclass, you provide the name of the class you want to add methods to, and then give the category a unique name in the parentheses. The name can be whatever you want, though it should communicate what the methods inside do.

Example 6-2 shows the implementation of the **isURL** category method. This is not a *good* implementation of URL detection; I'm just using it to demonstrate how categories work.

Example 6-2. NSString-Utilities.m

```
#import "NSString-Utilities.h"

@implementation NSString (Utilities)

- (BOOL) isURL {

  if ( [self hasPrefix:@"http://"] )
    return YES;
  else
    return NO;
}
```

```
@end
```

Now you can use this method on any **NSString** object (Example 6-3).

Example 6-3. UseNSStringCategory.m

```
NSString* string1 = @"http://cocoabook.com/";
NSString* string2 = @"Cocoa Book";

if ( [string1 isURL] ) {
  NSLog (@"string1 is a URL");
}

if ( [string2 isURL] ) {
  NSLog (@"string2 is a URL");
}
```

This example would display the following in the console:

```
    string1 is a URL
```

 It's common to include the category name in the filename, so the category files are called *NSString-Utilities.h* and *NSString-Utilities.m*.

Once a category method is added to a class by Objective-C, the method is available to *all* instances of the class, even the ones you didn't specifically create. The main limitation of adding category methods compared to subclassing is that you can't add instance variables to the class.

You can also use categories to *replace* existing methods on classes. This is an extremely powerful feature, but I can't overemphasize how important it is to be careful with this. If you use a category to replace the **NSObject** version of **-init**, for example, your application will probably not run long enough to see the main window show up. Adding methods to existing classes is generally safe; *replacing* them must be done very carefully and only with good reason.

 If two categories implement or override the same method for the same class, it's undefined which one will actually be accepted. You also must be careful not to *accidentally* override a method on a built-in Cocoa class by giving your method the same name—though that applies to subclasses, too.

Categories for Private Methods

Many Cocoa programmers use categories to declare private methods. For example, if you created methods for the **Photo** class to return a default caption (because the default

---

caption affects every Photo instance, it is declared as a class method) and log the photographer to the console, you could declare them using categories, like in Example 6-4.

Example 6-4. Excerpt of Photo.m

```
@interface Photo (Private)
+ (NSString*) defaultCaption;
- (void) logPhotographer;
@end
```

Objective-C does not currently have a formal "private" designation for methods, so the
convention is simply not to put the category declaration in the main header file. A
common way to do this is to declare the category in the actual *Photo.m* file, above the
`@implementation` block (rather than putting the methods in a separate file, as in Example 6-4). The method implementations themselves, though, are mixed in with the rest
of the class. Example 6-5 contains an example.

Example 6-5. Excerpt of Photo.m

```
#import "Photo.h"

@interface Photo (Private)
+ (NSString*) defaultCaption;
- (void) logPhotographer;
@end


@implementation Photo

  @synthesize caption;
  @synthesize photographer;

- (void) dealloc {

    [caption release];
    [photographer release];
    [super dealloc];
}

// private methods.

+ (NSString*) defaultCaption {
    return @"Untitled Photo";
}

- (void) logPhotographer {
    NSLog(@"Photographer: %@", photographer);
}

@end
```

Here's an example of using these methods inside the class:

```
- (id) init {

    if ( self = [super init] ) {

        self.caption = [Photo defaultCaption];
    }
    return self;
}

- (void) setPhotographer: (NSString*)input {

    [photographer autorelease];
    photographer = [input retain];
    [self logPhotographer];
}
```

I used [Photo defaultCaption] here for clarity, but usually it's better to use [[self class] defaultCaption] inside of the class. The reason for this is to ensure that the same code will work for subclasses as well. If you hardcode the class to Photo, you ignore any alternative versions of +defaultCaption that a subclass may provide. This means that the subclass would have to manually set the initial caption *again* in its own version of the -init method. If you use [[self class] defaultCaption], though, any new versions provided by subclasses will be used automatically.

 Declaring a method outside of the main header file discourages you or other programmers on your team from writing code that calls that method incorrectly. By limiting the number of public methods, you make the intent of the class more obvious, while making it easier to change the internal workings later.

Introspection

Sometimes you want to find out details about an object beyond what it offers as properties, such as which class it belongs to or which methods it implements. This is called *introspection*. For example, if you want to know which class an object belongs to, you can use the -isMemberOfClass: method:

```
- (id) currentObject {
    return [Photo photo];
}

- (void) checkObjectType {

    id object = [self currentObject];
    BOOL isPhoto = [object isMemberOfClass: [Photo class]];

    if ( isPhoto )
        NSLog( @"object is an instance of Photo" );
}
```

which results in:

```
object is an instance of Photo
```

 If you are testing this with the PhotoInfo Xcode project from Chapter 5, you can put these methods into *PhotoInfoAppDelegate.m* and add a call to [self checkObjectType]; to the -applicationDidFinishLaunching: method.

This example uses the +class method, which returns a `Class` object (as strange as that sounds). The -isMemberOfClass: method returns YES only if the object is a member of the *exact class* you give it—it doesn't work on subclasses.

If you want to know whether an object is a member of a class or *any of the subclasses of that class*, you can use the -isKindOfClass: method. For example, consider the Movie class, which inherits from the Media class:

```
@interface Media : NSObject
@property (copy) NSString* author;
@end

@interface Movie : Media
@property float framesPerSecond;
@end

@implementation Media
@synthesize author;
@end

@implementation Movie
@synthesize framesPerSecond;
@end
```

Now, here's a possible scenario for these classes:

```
- (id) currentObject {
    return [[[Movie alloc] init] autorelease];
}

- (void) checkObjectType {

    id object = [self currentObject];

    Class mediaClass       = [Media class];
    BOOL  isMedia          = [object isMemberOfClass: mediaClass];
    BOOL  isMediaOrSubclass = [object isKindOfClass: mediaClass];

    if ( isMedia ) {
        NSLog(@"object is an instance of Media");
    }

    if ( isMediaOrSubclass ) {
        NSLog(@"object is an instance of Media or a subclass");
```

```
        }
    }
```

Here's the result in the console:

```
object is an instance of Media or a subclass
```

This is especially important to know about when working with Cocoa's built-in classes. In some cases, you may not get an instance of the exact class you specify, possibly for performance or compatibility reasons. To demonstrate this, I'll use the -className method on an instance of NSString:

```
id object    = [NSString string];
BOOL isString = [object isKindOfClass: [NSString class]];

if ( isString )
    NSLog( @"object is a string: %@", [object className] );
```

You might be surprised by the result:

```
object is a string: NSCFString
```

I'll go into more detail about NSString in Chapter 7, and explain how it relates to this class name. The message here, though, is that you usually want to use -isKindOfClass: unless you are certain you need a specific class.

That said, expert Cocoa programmers usually don't pay much attention to which class an object belongs to. Instead, they just want to know which methods it implements. One way to do this is by using protocols.

Protocols

A protocol allows you to specify that you want an object that responds to a certain group of methods, regardless of which class the object belongs to. This is really helpful when you want to use different kinds of objects together, even though they don't inherit from the same parent. For example, imagine you're creating an application launcher, and want to display both photos and website bookmarks. The classes look like this:

```
@interface Media : NSObject
@property (copy) NSString* author;
@end

@interface Photo : Media
@property (copy) NSString* caption;
@property (copy) NSString* photographer;
@end

@interface Bookmark : NSObject
@property (copy) NSString* siteName;
@property (copy) NSString* url;
@end

@implementation Media
```

```
@synthesize author;
@end

@implementation Photo
@synthesize caption;
@synthesize photographer;
@end

@implementation Bookmark
@synthesize siteName;
@synthesize url;
@end
```

And here's the method to add an item to the application launcher window:

```
- (void) addLauncherItem:(id)newItem;
```

It doesn't make sense to specify a single class, because you want both to work. You can't define a method twice, so this will just generate a build error:

```
// INCORRECT: this will generate an error.
- (void) addLauncherItem: (Photo*)newItem;
- (void) addLauncherItem: (Bookmark*)newItem;
```

Another way to do this is to make both classes inherit from the same superclass, such as LauncherItem, but this is very rigid design, because the Photo and Bookmark classes may do many things besides appearing in the launcher window. It would be like saying a person who buys clothes occasionally is a "clothing buyer," but that's a very restrictive definition. Instead, that person is one who buys clothes *in addition* to many other things.

You could just leave the input type as id, but it might be nice to make sure that the class supports the methods you're trying to call on it ahead of time. The reality is that the class isn't that important. I just need to know that an object will provide me some basic information. This is where *protocols* come in. I can create a list of methods I want an object to implement without specifying any one class:

```
@protocol IconViewInfo <NSObject>
- (NSString*) title;
- (NSString*) fileName;
- (NSString*) summary;
@optional
- (NSString*) author;
- (id) previewData;
@end
```

This protocol definition lists the methods that any class that claims to support the protocol must implement. This protocol inherits from the NSObject protocol (yes, it's both a class *and* a protocol), which allows me to use -respondsToSelector: and other common methods. Most of the methods I added are required, but the two methods below the @optional line are not.

Now I can use this protocol in my method definition:

```
- (void) addLauncherItem:(id <IconViewInfo>)newItem {
    NSLog(@"Title: %@, Filename: %@, Summary: %@",
        [newItem title], [newItem fileName], [newItem summary]);
}
```

I'll also update my class definitions to declare that they conform to the `IconViewInfo` protocol:

```
@interface Media : NSObject
@property (copy) NSString* author;
@end

@interface Photo : Media <IconViewInfo>
@property (copy) NSString* caption;
@property (copy) NSString* photographer;
@end

@interface Bookmark : NSObject <IconViewInfo>
@property (copy) NSString* siteName;
@property (copy) NSString* url;
@end
```

Each class can implement the methods using the data that it already has:

```
@implementation Media
@synthesize author;
@end

@implementation Photo

@synthesize caption;
@synthesize photographer;

-(NSString *) title {
    return self.caption;
}

-(NSString *) fileName {
    return [self.caption stringByAppendingPathExtension:@"jpg"];
}

-(NSString *) summary {
    return [NSString stringWithFormat:
            @"'%@' by %@", self.caption, self.photographer];
}
@end

@implementation Bookmark
@synthesize siteName;
@synthesize url;

-(NSString *) title {
    return self.siteName;
}

-(NSString *) fileName {
```

```
        return [self.siteName stringByAppendingPathExtension:@"webloc"];
}

-(NSString *) summary {
    return [NSString stringWithFormat:
                @"'%@' at %@", self.siteName, self.url];
}
@end
```

This code creates a bookmark and a photo, and passes them both to addLauncherItem::

```
Bookmark *bookmarkItem = [[Bookmark alloc] init];
bookmarkItem.siteName  = @"O'Reilly Media, Inc.";
bookmarkItem.url        = @"http://www.oreilly.com/";
[self addLauncherItem: bookmarkItem];

Photo *photoItem      = [[Photo alloc] init];
photoItem.caption      = @"Big Tree";
photoItem.photographer = @"That dude who borrowed my camera.";
[self addLauncherItem: photoItem];
```

This code would display the following in the Xcode console:

```
Title: O'Reilly Media, Inc., Filename: O'Reilly Media, Inc..webloc,
    Summary: 'O'Reilly Media, Inc.' at http://www.oreilly.com
Title: Big tree, Filename: Big tree.jpg,
    Summary: 'Big tree' by That dude who borrowed my camera
```

One of the most interesting aspects of protocols is that you can take an existing class, like NSString, and add category methods to it so that it conforms to the protocol—all without subclassing. Just declare the required methods in a category and add the protocol definition at the end:

```
@interface NSString (IconView) <IconViewInfo>
- (NSString*) title;
- (NSString*) fileName;
- (NSString*) summary;
@end

@implementation NSString (IconView)

- (NSString*) title {
    return self;
}

- (NSString*) fileName {
    return [self stringByAppendingPathExtension:@"txt"];
}

- (NSString*) summary {
    return [@"Summary: " stringByAppendingString: self];
}

@end
```

This is another way to reduce the number of classes in your project. Remember, less code means that it's easier to understand; easier to understand is easier to improve; and improved software always makes the user happy.

Dynamic Messaging

Because Objective-C is a dynamic language, you can store method names (or, technically, *message* names) as variables and pass them between different objects. In Objective-C, the term for a method name is a *selector*, which is a SEL value type. You can either create a selector using the @selector() syntax, or you can use the NSSelectorFromString() function:

```
SEL homeSelector = @selector( loadHomeScreen: );

NSString* selectorName = @"loadPreviewScreen:";
SEL previewSelector    = NSSelectorFromString( selectorName );
```

 If you've written C programs before, selectors may seem like function pointers. The idea is similar, but selectors are a bit more flexible, because they aren't linked to a specific class or function implementation.

Selectors must include the entire method name, but they do not include the type information. For example, here's a method built into Cocoa:

```
- (NSComparisonResult) compare: (NSString *)string
                       options: (NSStringCompareOptions)mask
                         range: (NSRange)compareRange;
```

A selector for this method looks like this:

```
SEL compareSelector = @selector(compare:options:range:);
```

Of course, you want to include the colon at the end of the selector only if the method actually expects an input value. For example, here's the -caption method and its selector. It doesn't take an input value, so the selector does not have a colon at the end.

```
- (NSString*) caption;

SEL captionSelector = @selector( caption );
```

Selectors open up a world of options for designing the way your code works. For example, if you want to create a text file with a list of methods to call on an object, convert each line of the file into a selector using NSSelectorFromString(). This can help create scripting tools or support plug-ins for your application.

You can also use selectors to see whether an object implements a particular method before calling it. This helps you avoid errors while your program is running, and can make your application design more flexible. Cocoa uses this feature of Objective-C extensively to do things like automatically disable menu items if your application doesn't support certain features and determine which control should respond to a user action.

Using Selectors to Call Methods

Once you have a method selector, you can call that method on an object using -performSelector:. If you're calling the method on *another* object (in other words, not self), you'll often want to use the -respondsToSelector: method first to make sure the object will actually understand it.

For the purpose of this example, let's assume that the Photo and Album classes look like this:

```
@interface Photo : NSObject
- (NSString*) caption;
- (void) setAlbum:(Album*)album;
@end

@interface Album : NSObject
+ (id) defaultAlbum;
@end
```

Here are three examples of using -respondsToSelector: and -performSelector: to see whether an object responds to a method, and then actually calling the method if it does:

```
Photo* myPhoto = [[Photo alloc] init];
Album* myAlbum = [[Album alloc] init];

SEL captionSelector = @selector( caption );
SEL albumSelector   = @selector( setAlbum: );
SEL unknownSelector = @selector( yeahThisMethodDoesntActuallyExist );

if ([myPhoto respondsToSelector: captionSelector]) {

    NSLog (@"Calling '%@'", NSStringFromSelector( captionSelector ));
    NSString* caption = [myPhoto performSelector:captionSelector];
    NSLog (@"Photo caption: '%@'", caption);
}

if ([myPhoto respondsToSelector: albumSelector]) {

    NSLog (@"Calling '%@'", NSStringFromSelector( albumSelector ));
    [myPhoto performSelector:albumSelector withObject:myAlbum];
}

if ([myPhoto respondsToSelector: unknownSelector]) {

    NSLog (@"Calling '%@'", NSStringFromSelector( unknownSelector ));
    [myPhoto performSelector:unknownSelector];
}

[myPhoto release];
[myAlbum release];
```

Here's the result in the Xcode console when I run this code. The method for `unknownSelector` is never called, because the object does not respond to it:

```
Calling 'caption'
Photo caption: 'Untitled Photo'
Calling 'setAlbum:'
```

By the way, `-respondsToSelector:` does not look at which methods the class *declares* in the header. It checks to see which methods are actually *implemented* in the class. This is important, because it means that methods can be added as the program is running, long after you created the header file.

Forwarding Messages

The basic theory behind dynamic languages is that a flexible design is generally better than a rigid one. Instead of manually orchestrating every single piece of the program, you can let the pieces fall into place. One of the ways that Objective-C enables this is through *message forwarding*. Forwarding messages in Objective-C is fairly simple, and requires only the `NSInvocation` and `NSMethodSignature` classes.

The `NSInvocation` class is an object-oriented interface for messages, and `NSMethodSignature` describes the input and output types for a given method that the message eventually resolves to. Each time you call a method on an object, you are effectively creating an invocation. In other words, the `NSInvocation` is the message "in transit," but the `NSMethodSignature` is the destination.

Here's an example of an object receiving a message for a selector it doesn't implement, then forwarding it on to another object that does implement it:

```
@interface Cat : NSObject
- (void) meow;
@end

@interface Dog : NSObject
- (void) woof;
@end


@implementation Cat
- (void) meow {
    NSLog( @"%@: Meow", [self className] );
}
@end

@implementation Dog

- (void) woof {
    NSLog( @"%@: Woof", [self className] );
}

- (NSMethodSignature*) methodSignatureForSelector: (SEL)selector {
```

```
    NSString* name = NSStringFromSelector( selector );
    NSLog( @"-[%@: methodSignatureForSelector: %@]", [self className], name );

    if ([Cat instancesRespondToSelector: selector])
        return [Cat instanceMethodSignatureForSelector: selector];

    return [super methodSignatureForSelector: selector];
}

- (void) forwardInvocation: (NSInvocation*) invocation {

    NSString* name = NSStringFromSelector( invocation.selector );
    NSLog( @"-[%@: forwardInvocation: %@]", [self className], name );

    id theCat = [[Cat alloc] init];
    NSLog( @"Forwarding '%@' to %@", name, theCat );
    [invocation invokeWithTarget: theCat];
    [theCat release];
}

@end
```

Now all I need to do is call -meow on the Dog object, and see what happens. Remember that the Dog class does not implement the method:

```
id dog = [[Dog alloc] init];
[dog woof];
[dog meow];

[dog release];
```

Here's the result in the console:

```
Dog: Woof
-[Dog: methodSignatureForSelector: meow]
-[Dog: forwardInvocation: meow]
Forwarding 'meow' to <Cat: 0x100178260>
Cat: Meow
```

Exceptions

Exceptions are not used as extensively in Cocoa as other frameworks. This is especially important in the sense that they should not be used to send notifications or general errors. The official documentation for Objective-C makes it clear that an exception is "a special condition that interrupts the normal flow of program execution." Exceptions are not used the same way in Cocoa as they are in other programming environments. As soon as an exception is thrown, the application should quit as soon as possible (even when you catch the exceptions). Continuing to run the application after that point is generally not safe.

One way to think of this is to throw an exception when there's a breakdown in the *logic* and the application is no longer in a known good state. A missing user datafile is not a critical error, because you can simply tell the user that the file could not be located, and return to normal flow. Calling a method that does not exist *is* an exception in Cocoa, because that method may have been critical.

Exceptions are usually contained in an **NSException** object. You won't use exceptions frequently while getting started with Cocoa, so I'll just share a few basic examples with you. Here's an example of catching an "unrecognized selector" exception:

```
NSString* myString = [[NSString alloc] init];

@try {

    char firstChar = [myString characterAtIndex:0];
    int  length    = [myString length];
    NSLog( @"Length is: %i", length );
}
@catch (NSException * e) {

    NSLog( @"Caught an NSException, returning." );
    NSLog( @"Name:   %@", e.name );
    NSLog( @"Reason: %@", e.reason );
    return;
}
@finally {

    // will still get called, even if above returns.
    NSLog( @"Releasing string.");
    [myString release];
}
```

Here's the result in the console:

```
Caught an NSException, returning.
Name:   NSRangeException
Reason: *** -[NSCFString characterAtIndex:]: Range or index out of bounds
Releasing string.
```

The **@try** block ended as soon as it encountered an error, and the program flow moved to the **@catch** block. In this case, the exception was that I tried to get the first character of an empty string. The **@finally** block will always run, regardless of what happens in the **@try** block or even if I use the **return** statement. This guarantees that I'll have a chance to clean up whatever data I was working on.

And although you won't be using them often (I did mention exceptions should be used sparingly, right?), here's how you throw an exception from within your own code:

```
int maxDataSize = [self maximumDataSize];
id  dataStorage = [self privateDataStorage];

if ( [dataStorage length] > maxDataSize ) {

    NSException* e;
    e = [NSException exceptionWithName: @"DataSizeException"
                               reason: @"Data size is larger than maximum."
                             userInfo: nil];
```

```
    @throw e;
}
```

Example: DataCollector

Launch Xcode and click "Create a new Xcode project," or choose File → New Project from the menu. In the New Project window, click on Application under the Mac OS X section and select the Cocoa Application icon as shown in Figure 6-5.

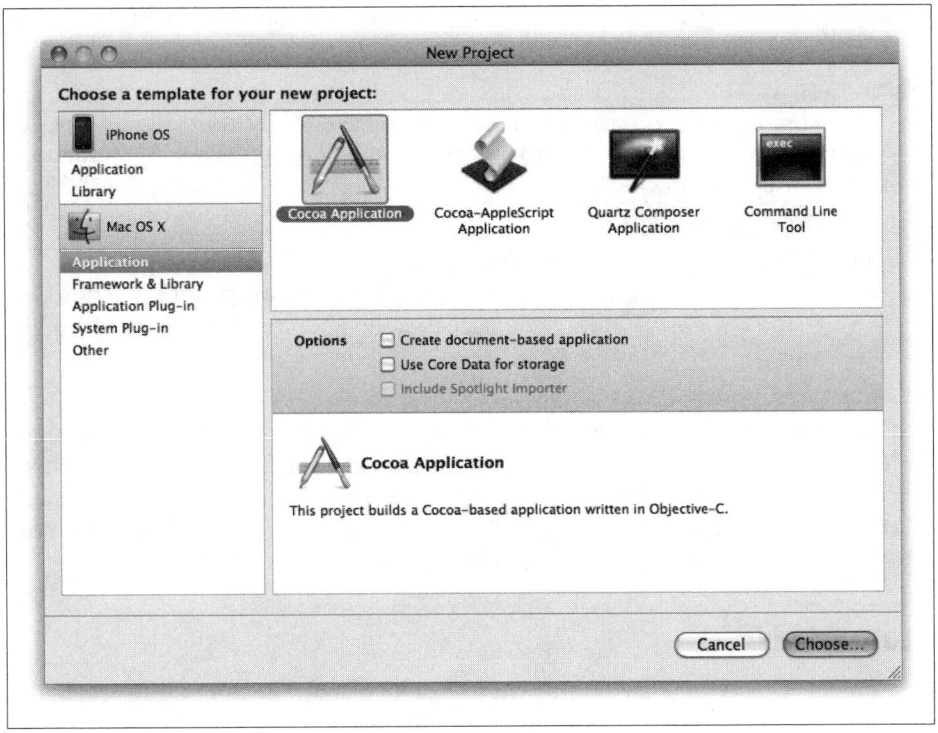

Figure 6-5. The New Project window in Xcode

Click the Choose button, and you'll be asked to select a location for the project. Go to the *CocoaBook* folder you created at the beginning of the book, and create a new sub-folder called *ch06*. Select the *CocoaBook/ch06/* folder as the save location and enter "DataCollector" as the project name. Click Save.

Some New Classes and Methods

To make this example more interesting, I'm going to quickly introduce you to four new classes and two new methods:

NSArray *and* NSMutableArray

Although it supports C-style arrays, Cocoa offers a vastly improved take on the concept with the NSArray and NSMutableArray classes. I'll go into more detail in Chapter 7, but the only two methods you need to know for now are -addObject: and -objectAtIndex:, which allow you to add an object to an array and retrieve it, respectively. An instance of NSArray cannot be changed once it's created, but an instance of its subclass, NSMutableArray, can be changed at any time.

NSWorkspace

The NSWorkspace class gives you a way to find and launch applications, get icons for files, present the contents of folders to the user, and many other common tasks. In this case, I'm going to use it to get a list of running applications.

NSRunningApplication

The -[NSWorkspace runningApplications] method returns an array of NSRunningApplication objects, each of which contains details about one of the apps that the user has launched and is currently running.

+[NSString stringWithFormat:]

The +stringWithFormat: method allows you to create an NSString object using the same format as NSLog(). It's the Cocoa equivalent of the asprintf() function (see "Strings and Dynamic Memory" on page 56), though it returns objects instead of char strings.

-[NSObject description]

The -description method is called on an object anytime the %@ marker is used for a value in a format string, such as for NSLog() or the +stringWithFormat: method. The -description method returns a string that describes the object. The default version just returns the class name and memory address of the object, but most classes override it to provide more helpful information.

Create the Files

Create a new Objective-C class file by choosing File → New File from the menu. In the New File window, select Cocoa Class under the Mac OS X section, then select the "Objective-C class" icon and click Next. Name the file *DCDataGroup.m*, and accept all of the default options. Click Finish.

Open *DCDataGroup.h* by clicking on it in the Xcode sidebar. If you had a group selected when you chose New File, the class files may be in that group. Type the following into *DCDataGroup.h*:

```
#import <Cocoa/Cocoa.h>

// the protocol required by all items in a data group.
@protocol DCDataItem <NSObject>
- (id)        contents;
- (NSString*) typeName;
- (NSString*) title;
```

```
@optional
- (NSString*) author;
@end


// the main data group class.
@interface DCDataGroup : NSObject

@property (copy)            NSString* name;
@property (retain, readonly)  NSMutableArray* items;
@property (assign, readonly)  int itemCount;

+ (id) runningApplicationsDataGroup;
- (void) addItem:(id <DCDataItem>)newItem;

@end
```

 In this and the following examples, be sure to replace the existing code in the file with what you're typing.

Now click *DCDataGroup.m* in the Xcode sidebar to start editing it, and type the following into the file:

```
#import "DCDataGroup.h"
#import "NSRunningApplication-DCDataItem.h"


@interface DCDataGroup ()
// privately redefine properties as writable.
@property (retain, readwrite) NSMutableArray* items;
// private methods.
+ (NSString*) defaultName;
@end


@implementation DCDataGroup

@synthesize name;
@synthesize items;

- (id) init {

    if ( self = [super init] ) {

        self.name  = [[self class] defaultName];
        self.items = [NSMutableArray array];
    }
    return self;
}

- (void) dealloc {
```

```
        self.name  = nil;
        self.items = nil;

        [super dealloc];
    }

    - (int) itemCount {
        return self.items.count;
    }

    + (id) runningApplicationsDataGroup {

        DCDataGroup* newDataGroup = [[DCDataGroup alloc] init];
        newDataGroup.name = @"Application Items";

        // get all running applications.
        NSWorkspace* ws = [NSWorkspace sharedWorkspace];
        NSArray* apps   = [ws runningApplications];

        // add each NSRunningApplication to group.
        for ( int i = 0; i < apps.count; i++ ) {

            NSRunningApplication* app = [apps objectAtIndex:i];
            [newDataGroup addItem:app];
        }

        return [newDataGroup autorelease];
    }

    - (void) addItem:(id <DCDataItem>)newItem {
        [self.items addObject:newItem];
    }

    + (NSString*) defaultName {
        return @"Untitled Group";
    }

    - (NSString*) description {
        return [NSString stringWithFormat:
                @"Data Group: %@ %@", self.name, self.items];
    }

    @end
```

Create another Objective-C class called DCTextItem, using the same options as before.
Type the following into *DCTextItem.h*:

```
#import <Cocoa/Cocoa.h>
#import "DCDataGroup.h"

@interface DCTextItem : NSObject <DCDataItem>

@property (copy)            NSString* contents;
@property (copy, readonly)  NSString* typeName;
@property (copy)            NSString* title;
@property (copy)            NSString* author;
```

```
@end
```

And type this into the implementation file, *DCTextItem.m*:

```objc
#import "DCTextItem.h"

@interface DCTextItem ()
// privately redefine properties as writable.
@property (copy, readwrite) NSString* typeName;
// private methods.
+ (NSString*)  defaultTitle;
+ (NSString *) defaultAuthor;
@end


@implementation DCTextItem

@synthesize contents;
@synthesize title;
@synthesize typeName;
@synthesize author;

- (id) init {

    if ( self = [super init] ) {

        self.contents = nil;
        self.title    = [[self class] defaultTitle];
        self.typeName = @"Text";
        self.author   = [[self class] defaultAuthor];
    }
    return self;
}

- (void) dealloc {

    self.contents  = nil;
    self.title     = nil;
    self.typeName  = nil;
    self.author    = nil;

    [super dealloc];
}

- (NSString*) description {
    return [NSString stringWithFormat:@"%@: %@",
                        self.title, self.contents];
}

+ (NSString *) defaultTitle {
    return @"Untitled";
}

+ (NSString *) defaultAuthor {
    return @"Unattributed";
```

```
    }

    @end
```

The last file you need to create for this project will contain a category for NSRunningApplication. Create a new Objective-C class and name the file *NSRunningApplication-DCDataItem.m*, using the same options as before.

Open the *header* file, *NSRunningApplication-DCDataItem.h*. Type the following code into the file:

```
    #import <Cocoa/Cocoa.h>
    #import "DCDataGroup.h"

    @interface NSRunningApplication (DCDataItemMethods) <DCDataItem>

    // methods to make NSRunningApplication conform to
    // the DCDataItem protocol.
    - (id)          contents;
    - (NSString *) typeName;
    - (NSString *) title;

    @end
```

Now open the implementation file, *NSRunningApplication-DCDataItem.m*. Type the following code into the file:

```
    #import "NSRunningApplication-DCDataItem.h"

    @implementation NSRunningApplication (DCDataItemMethods)

    // methods to make NSRunningApplication conform to
    // the DCDataItem protocol.

    - (id) contents {
        return self.bundleURL;
    }

    - (NSString *) typeName {
        return @"Application";
    }

    - (NSString *) title {
        return self.localizedName;
    }

    - (NSString*) description {
        return [NSString stringWithFormat:
                    @"%@: %@", self.title, self.contents];
    }

    @end
```

Now that all of the project files are in place, type the following code into *DataCollectorAppDelegate.m* (this file was created automatically when you created the new project and can be found in the Classes subdirectory on the Groups & Files pane on the left of the Xcode window):

```
#import "DataCollectorAppDelegate.h"
#import "DCDataGroup.h"
#import "DCTextItem.h"

@implementation DataCollectorAppDelegate
@synthesize window;

- (void)applicationDidFinishLaunching:(NSNotification *)aNotification {

    NSString* q1;
    q1 = @"We are a way for the universe to know itself.";

    NSString* q2;
    q2 = @"Heard melodies are sweet, but those unheard are sweeter.";

    NSString* q3;
    q3 = @"I owe my success to the fact that I never had a clock in my workroom.";


    // create the text data group.
    DCDataGroup* textDataGroup = [[DCDataGroup alloc] init];
    textDataGroup.name = @"Text Items";

    // text item 1.
    DCTextItem* textItem1 = [[DCTextItem alloc] init];
    textItem1.contents = q1;
    textItem1.title    = @"Carl Sagan On the Universe";
    textItem1.author   = @"Carl Sagan";

    [textDataGroup addItem:textItem1];
    [textItem1 release];

    // text item 2.
    DCTextItem* textItem2 = [[DCTextItem alloc] init];
    textItem2.contents = q2;
    textItem2.title    = @"John Keats on What is Heard";
    textItem2.author   = @"John Keats";

    [textDataGroup addItem:textItem2];
    [textItem2 release];

    // text item 3.
    DCTextItem* textItem3 = [[DCTextItem alloc] init];
    textItem3.contents = q3;
    textItem3.title    = @"Thomas Edison on Clocks";
    textItem3.author   = @"Thomas Edison";

    [textDataGroup addItem:textItem3];
    [textItem3 release];


    // create the applications data group.
```

```
        DCDataGroup* appGroup = [DCDataGroup runningApplicationsDataGroup];

        // display the result in the console.
        NSLog ( @"%@", textDataGroup  );
        NSLog ( @"%@", appGroup );

        // all done.
        [textDataGroup release];
    }

    @end
```

Build and Run

Save all of the files, then build and run the project. The window will be blank, but you should see something similar to the following in the console:

```
Data Group: Text Items (
    "Carl Sagan On the Universe:
        We are a way for the universe to know itself.",
    "John Keats on What is Heard:
        Heard melodies are sweet, but those unheard are sweeter.",
    "Thomas Edison on Clocks:
        I owe my success to the fact that I never had a clock in my workroom."
)
Data Group: Application Items (
    "loginwindow: file://localhost/System/Library/CoreServices/loginwindow.app/",
    "Dock: file://localhost/System/Library/CoreServices/Dock.app/",
    "Finder: file://localhost/System/Library/CoreServices/Finder.app/",
    "Versions: file://localhost/Applications/Versions.app/",
    "Safari: file://localhost/Applications/Safari.app/",
    "TextMate: file://localhost/Applications/TextMate.app/",
    "QuickTime Player: file://localhost/Applications/QuickTime%20Player.app/",,
    "Tweetie: file://localhost/Applications/Tweetie.app/",
    "Xcode: file://localhost/Developer/Applications/Xcode.app/",
    "Preview: file://localhost/Applications/Preview.app/",
    "Terminal: file://localhost/Applications/Utilities/Terminal.app/"
)
```

The list will reflect whatever applications you have running. Try launching or quitting some apps and rerunning. You can also try changing the implementation of -description on either DCTextItem or the NSRunningApplication category to display different details in the console.

CHAPTER 7

Foundation Value Classes

Objective-C makes it easy to use standard C types like `int`, `float`, and `char`, but that doesn't mean they're always your best options. Cocoa provides actual classes for storing common types of data like numbers and strings. These are informally called *value classes*, or *Foundation value classes*.

This is a good time for me to explain that "Cocoa" can actually mean two separate things. Most people use it very broadly to describe an overall ecosystem to write apps for Mac, iPhone, iPod touch, and iPad. Some veteran Mac programmers think of Cocoa specifically as an *umbrella framework*, which is a framework that contains other frameworks. Whichever definition you prefer, you should understand what each refers to. The Cocoa framework itself encapsulates three separate frameworks: Foundation, AppKit, and Core Data:

Foundation
> Provides all of the basic building block classes, such as strings, numbers, arrays, file access, and so on. This framework is used on Mac and iPhone OS (which is used by iPhone, iPod touch, and iPad).

AppKit
> Provides everything specifically dealing with user interface elements, such as windows, controls, and fonts. AppKit is the Mac counterpart of UIKit on iPhone OS, and both are built around the same core concepts.

Core Data
> Provides data storage, data modeling, and automatic change tracking (also known as automatic Undo and Redo). You can store data using SQLite, XML, binary storage, or even create your own store type. Core Data is available on both Mac and iPhone OS.

Historically, Cocoa has been *only* AppKit and Foundation—not Core Data. In practice, I think it's all three. For what it's worth, the *Cocoa.h* file actually imports all three frameworks. In the big picture, though, this is just a philosophical detail that doesn't actually change anything you do.

Although low-level C types are fast and use little memory, they offer very little in terms of safeguards or conveniences. Safeguards are increasingly important as more Cocoa apps fetch data from the Internet. Using the Foundation classes instead of C primitives makes it much harder for anyone to get into the guts of your program over a network connection. Foundation classes also make it much easier to work with international text and large numbers, abstracting you from a lot of the tedious details

That said, most Mac apps use a mix of primitive C types and Foundation classes. It will be more clear when to use each by looking at some of the sample code.

NSString

NSString is Cocoa's class for working with text. Text is so common in Mac apps that it might be the class you work with most on a minute-to-minute basis. Here are some simple examples:

```
// combining two strings.
NSString* firstName = @"Albert ";
NSString* lastName  = @"Einstein";
NSString* fullName  = [firstName stringByAppendingString:lastName];
NSLog( @"fullName: %@", fullName );

// combining more than two strings.
NSString* sentence = @"Welcome ";
sentence = [sentence stringByAppendingString:@"to the "];
sentence = [sentence stringByAppendingString:@"future."];
NSLog( @"sentence: %@", sentence );
```

Here's the output:

```
fullName: Albert Einstein
sentence: Welcome to the future.
```

In the second part of the example, I declared only one string variable, but created three separate string *objects*. Using a single variable for all three works out because +stringByAppendingString: returns an autoreleased object. Each line creates a new NSString, adding to the contents of the previous one.

Once you assign a new object to a variable, you've lost the reference to the original object and can't call -release on it, but it's still taking up memory. Reusing variables like this only works when creating autoreleased objects, because you don't need to manually release them later. This would be a problem if the strings were created with +alloc instead:

```
NSString* first  = @"Monday";
NSString* second = @"Tuesday";
NSString* third  = @"Wednesday";

// INCORRECT. this is a memory leak!
// calling -release only once for three +alloc calls!
NSString* dayOfWeek1 = nil;
dayOfWeek1 = [[NSString alloc] initWithString:first];
dayOfWeek1 = [[NSString alloc] initWithString:second];
dayOfWeek1 = [[NSString alloc] initWithString:third];
[dayOfWeek1 release];

// BETTER: doesn't leak, but bad style.
NSString* dayOfWeek2 = nil;
dayOfWeek2 = [[[NSString alloc] initWithString:first] autorelease];
dayOfWeek2 = [[[NSString alloc] initWithString:second] autorelease];
dayOfWeek2 = [[[NSString alloc] initWithString:third] autorelease];

// BEST: when reusing a variable, use a class method
// with built-in autorelease.
NSString* dayOfWeek3 = nil;
dayOfWeek3 = [NSString stringWithString:first];
dayOfWeek3 = [NSString stringWithString:second];
dayOfWeek3 = [NSString stringWithString:third];
```

 The +stringByAppendingString:, -initWithString:, and +stringWith
String: methods all *copy* the contents of the input string, so you don't
need to call -copy manually.

Table 7-1 gives a quick overview of some of the other basic methods in NSString.

Table 7-1. Basic NSString methods

Method	Description
+stringWithFormat:	Creates a string using NSLog() formatting
-length	Returns the length of the string
-characterAtIndex:	Returns the single character at a specific point in the string
-hasPrefix:	Returns YES if the string starts with a specific prefix
-intValue	Returns an int version of the string contents (for example, @"12abc" would result in the integer value 12)
-UTF8String	Returns a char* version of the string for use with C functions
-substringFromIndex:	Returns a substring with all of the characters between a starting point and the end
-substringWithRange:	Returns a substring with a specific starting point and length
-rangeOfSubstring:	Searches for the starting point and length of a substring

Ranges and Substrings

Cocoa uses *ranges* for working with specific sections of a string. Unlike most Cocoa types, NSRange is actually a *struct*, not an object. Because it's just a regular struct, it's not a pointer type so you don't add an asterisk to it. A range has two integer fields: location and length:

```
typedef struct _NSRange {
  NSUInteger location;
  NSUInteger length;
} NSRange;
```

 NSUInteger is simply a way to store unsigned integer values for both 64-bit and 32-bit systems. See "Cocoa Primitive Types" on page 160 for a more detailed explanation.

This struct is part of Cocoa itself, so you don't need to type that code in. The location field specifies a starting point, and the length field contains the "run" of characters from that starting point. You can use NSRange to get the characters in a specific portion of a string:

```
NSString* fullName  = @"Albert Einstein";
NSRange    myRange  = NSMakeRange ( 0, 6 );

NSString* firstName = [fullName substringWithRange: myRange];
NSLog (@"firstName: %@", firstName);
```

Like an array, a range starts at 0, not 1. Here's the result of the above code in the console:

```
firstName: Albert
```

This code is useful only if we already know where the string is that we want. NSString provides another method (-substringFromIndex:) that can search for the substring automatically. In this example, I'll search for a header, and then display all the text that follows the header:

```
NSString* fullName   = @"Last name: Einstein";
NSRange    fieldRange = [fullName rangeOfString:@"Last name: "];

if ( fieldRange.length > 0 ) {

    int start = fieldRange.location;
    int count = fieldRange.length;

    int startOfName = start + count;
    NSString* lastName = [fullName substringFromIndex: startOfName];
    NSLog (@"lastName: %@", lastName);
}
```

I added an `if` statement to check the `length` of the range returned from the `-rangeOfString:` method. The range will have a length of `0` if the string wasn't found. If it is found, it prints the name after the header:

```
lastName: Einstein
```

Using NSString with C Types

Even though Cocoa's value classes are robust and generally easy to use, there are many cases where you want to work with standard C types. Fortunately, it's easy to convert `NSString` objects to and from primitive types. Here are some quick examples:

```
NSString* totalString       = @"10";
NSString* goldenRatioString = @"1.618";
NSString* cityName          = @"Cupertino";

int total = [totalString intValue];
float goldenRatio = [goldenRatioString floatValue];
const char* cityNameCString = [cityName UTF8String];
```

You can also create strings from primitive C types using `+stringWithFormat:` and `+stringWithUTF8String`:

```
int    count    = 100;
float piValue   = 3.1415926;
char* starName = "Vega";

NSString* countString    = [NSString stringWithFormat:@"%i",count];
NSString* piString       = [NSString stringWithFormat:@"%f", piValue];
NSString* starNameString = [NSString stringWithUTF8String:starName];
```

Comparing Strings for Equality

Each `NSString` is an object, and the variables that refer to it are *pointers* to an object. So if you compare two string variables using the == sign, you'll be comparing the pointer address, not characters in the string:

```
NSString* firstString  = [NSString stringWithFormat:@"%i", 10000];
NSString* secondString = [NSString stringWithFormat:@"%i", 10000];

if ( firstString == secondString ) {
    NSLog (@"The strings are the same");
} else {
    NSLog (@"The strings are not the same");
}

NSLog (@"firstString  string: '%@' pointer: %p", firstString, firstString);
NSLog (@"secondString string: '%@' pointer: %p", secondString, secondString);
```

This displays the following in the console:

```
The strings are not the same
firstString  string: '10000' pointer: 0x100429540
secondString string: '10000' pointer: 0x100403630
```

When you use the %p marker to display the string, you can see the exact memory address of the `NSString` it represents. As a result, comparing them for equality using the `==` symbol will not give the correct answer. To compare the string contents, we use the `-isEqualToString:` method:

```
NSString* firstString  = [NSString stringWithFormat:@"%i", 10000];
NSString* secondString = [NSString stringWithFormat:@"%i", 10000];

if ( [firstString isEqualToString:secondString] ) {
    NSLog (@"The strings are the same");
} else {
    NSLog (@"The strings are not the same");
}
```

Now you see this in the console:

```
The strings are the same
```

By the way, the reason I used `+stringWithFormat:` instead of just using the shortcut syntax to create the string is that those *would* actually end up being the same object. For example, here's a case where I compare two literal strings that I created using the string shortcut syntax:

```
NSString* firstCity  = @"Cupertino";
NSString* secondCity = @"Cupertino";

if ( firstCity == secondCity ) {
    NSLog (@"The cities are the same");
} else {
    NSLog (@"The cities are not the same");
}

NSLog (@"firstCity  string: '%@' pointer: %p", firstCity, firstCity);
NSLog (@"secondCity string: '%@' pointer: %p", secondCity, secondCity);
```

This has a surprising result:

```
The cities are the same
firstCity  string: 'Cupertino' pointer: 0x100002068
secondCity string: 'Cupertino' pointer: 0x100002068
```

Even though I had two variables and typed in two separate strings, I ended up with *one object*. The compiler is smart enough not to make a duplicate version of the same string literal, so the objects are actually the same. This means you could end up with a `==` comparison that works in some cases, but would not work consistently. The main thing to take away here is to use `-isEqualToString:` when you want to compare the *contents* of a string, because it will work regardless of how each string was created.

Strings As File Paths

`NSString` includes extensive support for managing paths (see Table 7-2), as well as support for working with files in general. You can refer to files on disk using either traditional Unix-style paths, such as */Volumes/Macintosh HD/Applications*, or using

URLs with a `file:///` prefix. URLs are encouraged more in Snow Leopard, but there is a lot of existing Objective-C code that uses regular file path strings, so let's look at some of the basics.

Table 7-2. Common NSString methods for file paths

Method	Description
-lastPathCompo nent	Returns the last part of a path, such as a filename
-pathExtension	Returns the file extension of the last part of the path, such as *.txt*
-stringByExpan dingTildeInPath	Returns a copy with a Unix-style ~*username* path fully resolved
-stringByDeletin gLastPathCompo nent	Returns a copy with the last path item removed, such as the filename
-stringByDele tingPathExten sion	Returns a copy with just the file extension removed, such as *.html*
-stringByAppen dingPathCompo nent	Returns a copy with an additional path item (you could use this to add a filename to a folder path, for example)
-stringByResol vingSymlinksIn Path	Returns a copy with any symbolic links fully resolved (does not work with aliases created by the Finder's File → Make Alias command)
-isAbsolutePath	Returns YES if the path is referenced from the top of the filesystem (such as */Developer/Applications/ Xcode.app*)

Here's a very basic example of working with file paths:

```
NSString* pathToApp      = @"/Applications/Safari.app";
NSString* fullFileName   = [pathToApp lastPathComponent];
NSString* fileName       = [fullFileName stringByDeletingPathExtension];

if ( [pathToApp isAbsolutePath] ) {
  NSLog(@"The application's path is absolute.");
}

NSLog(@"pathToApp: %@", pathToApp);
NSLog(@"fullFileName: %@", fullFileName);
NSLog(@"fileName: %@", fileName);
```

Here's the output in the console:

```
The application's path is absolute.
pathToApp: /Applications/Safari.app
fullFileName: Safari.app
fileName: Safari
```

Cocoa also provides functions, shown in Table 7-3, to get to commonly used paths and basic user information. These are freestanding C functions that return NSString objects. They're not part of a class.

Table 7-3. Common functions for standard paths

Function	Description
NSUserName()	Returns the Unix-style username
NSFullUserName()	Return the user's full name
NSHomeDirectory()	Returns the user's home directory as a file path
NSTemporaryDirectory()	Returns a path for a place to store temporary files

Here are some examples:

```
NSLog ( @"My user name is: %@",      NSUserName());
NSLog ( @"My full name is: %@",      NSFullUserName());
NSLog ( @"My home directory is: %@", NSHomeDirectory());
```

For me, this displays the following in the console:

```
My user name is: scott
My full name is: Scott Stevenson
My home directory is: /Users/scott
```

This is just a quick look at some of the basic file path functions. There's much more to files and URLs, as you'll see later.

Reading and Writing Files with Strings

As common as it is to work with text files in programming, it's generally somewhat awkward in standard C. Fortunately, Cocoa makes it very easy to work with files. You can ask an NSString to write its contents to a file in just one line of code, and then just as easily read it back in. Here's how you write the file:

```
NSString* lastLine = @"Beauty is truth, truth beauty";
NSString* fileName = @"GrecianUrn.txt";
NSString* homeDir  = NSHomeDirectory();
NSString* fullPath = [homeDir stringByAppendingPathComponent:fileName];

[lastLine writeToFile:fullPath atomically:NO];
```

Now I can go look in my home directory and see that the file is there (see Figures 7-1 and 7-2).

The -writeToFile:atomically: method takes a destination file path and a YES or NO to indicate if the file should be written *atomically*. In this case, "atomically" specifies that the method should write to a temporary file before moving it to the location. This is potentially a more robust way to write to files, but it's overkill for what we're doing here.

scott
DEVICES
PLACES
Desktop
scott
Applications
Documents
code
SEARCH FOR
Name
Desktop
Documents
Downloads
Dropbox
GrecianUrn.txt
Library
Movies
Music
Pictures
Public
Sites
1 of 11 selected, 125.66 GB available

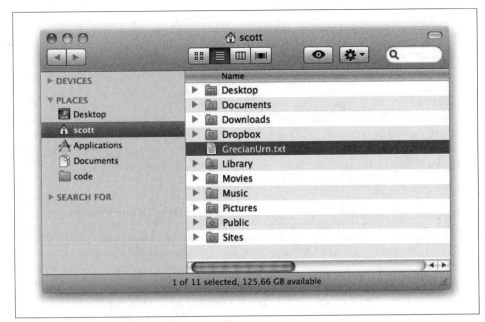

Figure 7-1. The GrecianUrn.txt file in the Finder

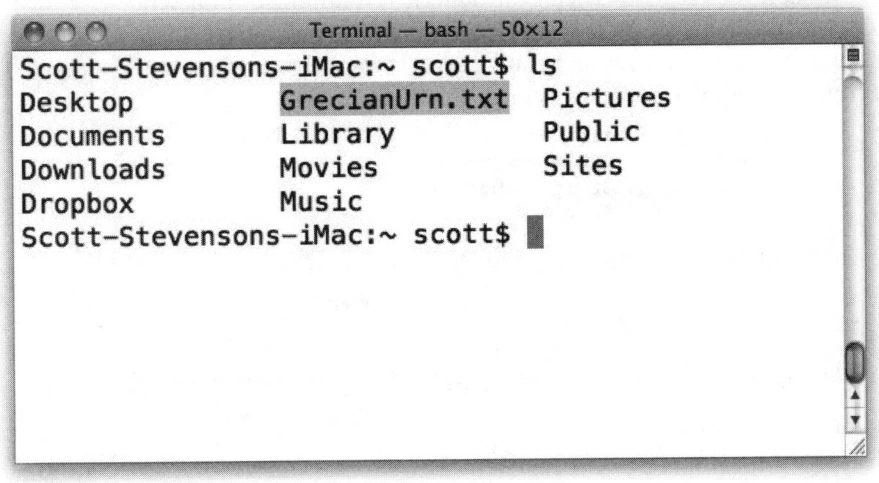

Terminal — bash — 50×12
Scott-Stevensons-iMac:~ scott$ ls
Desktop GrecianUrn.txt Pictures
Documents Library Public
Downloads Movies Sites
Dropbox Music
Scott-Stevensons-iMac:~ scott$

Figure 7-2. The GrecianUrn.txt file on the command line, viewed through the Terminal application

The one other important note about this method is that it was deprecated in Snow Leopard. This means that it will still work, but it will be removed in a future release. There's almost always a better version that replaces a deprecated method though, so you should usually use the newer version. Here's the new version that's recommended for Snow Leopard and later:

```
[lastLine writeToFile: fullPath
         atomically: NO
           encoding: NSASCIIStringEncoding
              error: &error];
```

It's a bit wordier, but all in the name of safer, more predictable behavior. The additional input options allow you to specify the text encoding in the string, as well to opt to receive an error if anything goes wrong. Previously, if the file couldn't be written, the method would just silently fail. This version gives you more control.

 A longer method name may seem like unnecessary complication, but one of the stated goals of Mac OS X 10.6 Snow Leopard was to improve the speed, reliability, or functionality of existing classes. Specifying string encoding and providing error messages allows developers to write more robust software.

The upside of this new method is that you can display a message in a dialog box if the file wasn't written. To do this, create an **NSError** variable and set it to an initial value of **nil**. You pass in a *reference* to that variable using the *address-of* operator (ampersand), and the method will populate the variable if an error occurred.

You probably remember this being introduced as returning by indirection (see "Strings and Dynamic Memory" on page 56). You can usually tell when a value is meant to be returned by indirection, because you'll see an extra asterisk on the type name, such as **NSError****. Here's the declaration for the method:

```
- (BOOL)writeToFile: (NSString *)path
        atomically: (BOOL)useAuxiliaryFile
          encoding: (NSStringEncoding)enc
             error: (NSError **)error;
```

Here's the full version of the code, with error detection:

```
NSString* lastLine = @"Beauty is truth, truth beauty";
NSString* fileName = @"GrecianUrn.txt";
NSString* homeDir  = NSHomeDirectory();
NSString* fullPath = [homeDir stringByAppendingPathComponent:fileName];

NSError* error = nil;
[lastLine writeToFile:fullPath atomically:NO encoding:NSASCIIStringEncoding
 error:&error];

if ( error != nil ) {
  [NSApp presentError:error];
}
```

If the method can't write the file, it creates an **NSError** object and assigns it to the variable you provide. If the file *is* written, the **error** variable stays set as **nil**. I can just add a simple test to see whether the error is nonnil, and use the method -presentError: to display it to the user (see Figure 7-3).

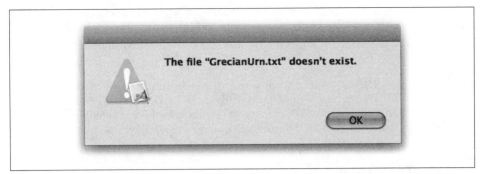

Figure 7-3. An NSError object displayed with the -[NSApplication presentError:] method

If you want to try this out, you can force the display of the error by replacing NSHomeDirectory() with @"/error/" for the homeDir path. You could, of course, do other things with the error, such as write it to a file or display it in a custom dialog box. It's generally better to display a custom error message when possible, as you can give suggestions that apply specifically to your application.

Although it looks like a class, NSApp is actually a special global variable that refers to the one and only instance of NSApplication in each program. It allows you to perform broad, application-wide tasks, such as setting the icon in the Dock or finding the frontmost window.

Reading files is similar to writing them. The main difference is that you generally don't create a string and then read data into it. Instead, you create a new string using the contents of a file. Here's how I create a string with the contents of the file I just created:

```
NSString* fileName = @"GrecianUrn.txt";
NSString* homeDir  = NSHomeDirectory();
NSString* fullPath = [homeDir stringByAppendingPathComponent:fileName];


NSError* error = nil;
NSStringEncoding encoding;

NSString* contents = [NSString stringWithContentsOfFile: fullPath
                                           usedEncoding: &encoding
                                                  error: &error];

if ( error != nil ) {
  [NSApp presentError:error];
}

NSLog(@"Contents of '%@': %@", fileName, contents);
```

Here's the result in the console:

```
Contents of 'GrecianUrn.txt': Beauty is truth, truth beauty
```

Because this method *reads* files, it will *tell you* which string encoding the file used by writing it to the `encoding` variable. As with all values that are returned by indirection, you pass in a reference to the `encoding` variable using the address-of operator (&).

 Both C and Objective-C allow you to span function or method calls across several lines. This is particularly useful for Objective-C's multi-part method names. It's common to split these methods into multiple lines and align them at the colon character for readability.

Mutability

Most of the base Foundation value classes come in two flavors: *mutable* and *immutable*. The word "mutable" means that the value of the object can be changed. You can't change the contents of an `NSString` once you create it, but you *can* change the contents of an `NSMutableString`:

```
NSMutableString* name = [NSMutableString stringWithString:@"Helen"];
[name setString:@"Sarah"];
[name setString:@"Daisy"];
```

The mutable versions of the value classes inherit all of the methods from their immutable superclasses, so methods like `-length` and `-substringWithRange:` work exactly the same. If you have an immutable version of an object, you can get a mutable version with the `-mutableCopy` method:

```
NSString*       originalString = @"Friday";
NSMutableString* editableString = [originalString mutableCopy];

[editableString setString:@"Saturday"];
[editableString release];
```

It's important to know that calling `-copy` on a mutable object *returns an immutable version*. If you want to copy a mutable object and maintain mutability in the new version, you must call `-mutableCopy` on the original. This is useful, though, because if you want to "freeze" a mutable object, you can just call `-copy` on it.

There's a subtle point here, though. A constant variable (see "Constants" on page 23) can refer to a mutable object, which means you can't change the object, but you can change the contents:

```
NSMutableString* const name = [NSMutableString stringWithString:@"Lea"];

// OK: 'const' doesn't effect object mutability.
[name setString:@"Sally"];

// ERROR: can't change the object.
name = @"Sally";
```

Because of this, it's usually useful to declare object variables as const only if they refer to an immutable object. The const keyword is not part of Objective-C directly—it's inherited from C. It's also important to know that the type you declare for an object variable doesn't determine what kind of object it will be. For example, this code will create a regular NSString, not an NSMutableString:

```
NSMutableString* name = @"Jane";
```

Fortunately, Xcode will generally warn you about cases like this when you build your project. To create a mutable string from a literal string (like @"My String"), you must use either the +[NSMutableString stringWithString:] class method, or the -[NSMutableString initWithString:] method:

```
NSMutableString* name1 = [NSMutableString stringWithString:@"Jane"];
NSMutableString* name2 = [[NSMutableString alloc] initWithString:@"Jane"];
[name2 release];
```

All of the general rules about mutability—that is, those that don't directly involve text, such as -mutableCopy—apply to all mutable Foundation classes, not just NSMutableString.

Advantages of Mutability

Using mutable objects can make certain kinds of code much more efficient. Creating objects always takes some CPU power and some memory. If you're appending hundreds or thousands of string objects, it's generally much more efficient to make a single NSMutableString object, and append new text to it directly:

```
// slower to create 1000 separate strings.
NSUInteger count  = 1000;
NSString*  total1 = [NSString string];

for ( NSInteger i = 0; i < count; i++ ) {
    total1 = [total1 stringByAppendingFormat:@"%ld", i];
}

// faster to add a single mutable string.
NSMutableString* total2 = [NSMutableString string];
for ( NSInteger i = 0; i < count; i++ ) {
    [total2 appendFormat:@"%ld", i];
}
```

This is particularly important on highly mobile hardware, such as iPhone and iPad. Highly mobile devices have far less memory and lower-power CPUs. So even though you may never see a performance hit from creating thousands of objects on a desktop machine, the same code can potentially cause a mobile app to slow to a crawl.

Advantages of Immutability

The obvious question here is why Cocoa bothers to separate these two. The most important reason is that immutable NSStrings can save memory, particularly because "copies" of immutable strings are usually the same string:

```
NSString* firstString  = @"Palo Alto";
NSString* secondString = [firstString copy];

NSLog (@"firstString  address: %p", firstString);
NSLog (@"secondString address: %p", secondString);
```

In the console, we can see that even though -copy was used, we were given back the same string because it's immutable. There's no reason to eat up memory for new objects when the originals have the same value:

```
firstString  address: 0x1000020a8
secondString address: 0x1000020a8
```

The other important reason, though, is that you may not want the value of your object to change. For example, here's how it could actually cause a security flaw:

```
CocoaBookSystemUser* guestUser = [CocoaBookSystemUser guestUser];
CocoaBookSystemUser* adminUser = [CocoaBookSystemUser adminUser];

NSMutableString* filePath = [NSMutableString string];

[filePath setString: @"public_file.txt"];
[guestUser grantAccessToFileAtPath:filePath];
[filePath setString: @"super_secret_file.txt"];
[adminUser grantAccessToFileAtPath:filePath];

[guestUser savePrivileges];
[adminUser savePrivileges];
```

It's very likely that the guest user would end up getting access to the secret file. The way to address this is to use the copy option in the @property declaration. This generates a setter method that calls -copy on objects passed in, including mutable objects. Because calling -copy on mutable Foundation classes always returns an immutable copy, an immutable object will always be stored as the property value.

Core Foundation

Foundation provides a set of Objective-C classes like NSString, but many of these classes actually use code in a lower-level C framework called *Core Foundation*. You usually don't have to think about any of this, because Cocoa handles the details for you, but there is code out in the world that refers to this framework directly.

Even if you don't use it every day, it helps to at least understand the basics of Core Foundation, because some other frameworks are based on the same ideas. First, here's a quick test to show you something about the NSString class:

```
NSString* myString = @"The Fighting Mongooses";
NSLog( @"class of myString: %@", [myString className] );
```

Here's the result in the console:

```
class of myString: NSCFString
```

The Core Foundation string type is **CFStringRef**, though many Cocoa developers just refer to it as **CFString** in conversation. The **CF** in the class name **NSCFString** indicates that an **NSString** object in Cocoa is actually based on **CFString**.

Like all of the key Core Foundation data types, **CFString** is not an Objective-C class. It's an *opaque struct*, or *opaque data type*, which means that it's a normal C struct, but you don't write code that directly accesses the fields. Instead, you use a series of functions that are designed specifically for **CFString**. Here are a few of them:

```
CFStringRef myString = CFSTR("Welcome to Core Foundation.");
CFIndex     length   = CFStringGetLength ( myString );

printf( "myString length: %ld\n", length );

if ( CFStringHasPrefix( myString, CFSTR("Welcome") )) {
    printf( "myString starts with 'Welcome'\n" );
}
```

Here's the output:

```
myString length: 27
myString starts with 'Welcome'
```

The **CFSTR("String")** macro is the equivalent of the **@"String"** syntax in Objective-C. And **CFIndex** is essentially the same thing as **NSInteger**. The structural difference is that Core Foundation types aren't objects, so you can't call methods on them. Instead, they are just data containers that you pass into regular C functions. For more context, here's the Foundation and Core Foundation versions of the same program, side by side:

```
- (void) foundationStringTest {

    NSString* myString = @"Welcome to Foundation.";
    NSInteger length   = myString.length;

    NSLog( @"myString length: %ld", length );

    if ( [myString hasPrefix:@"Welcome"] ) {
        NSLog(@"myString starts with 'Welcome'" );
    }
}

void coreFoundationStringTest () {

    CFStringRef myString = CFSTR("Welcome to Core Foundation.");
    CFIndex     length   = CFStringGetLength ( myString );

    printf( "myString length: %ld\n", length );
```

```
        if ( CFStringHasPrefix( myString, CFSTR("Welcome") )) {
            printf( "myString starts with 'Welcome'\n" );
        }
    }
```

 You'd invoke each of these differently; one is an Objective-C method, and the other is a C function:

```
[self foundationStringTest];
coreFoundationStringTest();
```

What this means is that you can effectively use the core of NSString in regular C files, because CFString and all of the associated functions are just plain C. This can be really useful if you want to write a Cocoa app that uses existing C code, such as a C library that's used within your company. You can also use CFString directly in your Cocoa classes because you can use C code anywhere in an Objective-C file.

Memory Management

The memory management system in Core Foundation is heavily based on Objective-C's reference counting system. Instead of +alloc, Core Foundation types are created with functions that have Create in the name:

```
CFStringCreateWithSubstring();
CFStringCreateCopy();
CFStringCreateWithFormatAndArguments();
```

Instead of calling -release on objects that you no longer need, you pass structs into CFRelease():

```
CFStringRef myString1 = CFSTR("Welcome to Core Foundation.");
CFRange     range     = CFRangeMake( 0, 7 );

CFStringRef myString2;
myString2 = CFStringCreateWithSubstring( NULL, myString1, range );

CFShow( myString2 );
CFRelease( myString2 );
```

Because I used a function with Create in the name, I have to pass the string into CFRelease() when I'm done with it. The first input value for the creation function is the CFAllocatorRef that does the actual memory allocation. I used NULL as the value, which will cause it to use the default kCFAllocatorDefault. You rarely need to customize this, so NULL is usually fine.

The CFRange struct is the Core Foundation equivalent of NSRange. The CFShow() method logs the contents of a CF data struct to the console, but this should only be used for testing, not in release versions of your app.

One other important note here is that CFStringRef ends in Ref, but CFRange does not. The reason for this is that CFRange is a regular struct; you can freely access its fields. But CFStringRef is a pointer type, like an Objective-C object. Even though there's no asterisk used when declaring CFStringRef variables, CFStringRef *is* a pointer type. Here's the definition from *CFBase.h*:[*]

```
typedef const struct __CFString * CFStringRef;
```

This typedef statement declares that CFStringRef is a pointer to a private data struct. Like Objective-C objects, Core Foundation reference types are allocated from dynamic memory, and are passed around *by reference*. A few Core Foundation types like CFRange don't end in Ref, and are local variables passed around by value.

Some Core Foundation functions include Get in their name, which means that you are not returning an object that you own. If you want to keep the object around, you need to call CFRetain() on it and then CFRelease() it when you're done with it:

```
CFStringRef encodingName = CFStringGetNameOfEncoding( kCFStringEncodingUTF8 );

CFRetain  ( encodingName );
CFShow    ( encodingName );
CFRelease ( encodingName );
```

The Get naming convention is also used for primitive and generic struct values that you don't need to retain, such as CFIndex and CFRange. So, to sum up, Core Foundation memory management has two main rules:

1. When you receive a Ref data item from a function with Create or Copy in the name, you must CFRelease() the item when you're done with it.

2. When you receive a Ref data item from a function with Get in the name, you must CFRetain() the item if you want it to stay around, then CFRelease() the item when you're done with it.

Core Foundation Mutability

Like the standard Foundation classes, Core Foundation types come in mutable and immutable flavors. For example, you can create a CFMutableStringRef and add to it using the CFStringAppend() function:

```
CFMutableStringRef street = CFStringCreateMutable( NULL, 0 );

CFStringAppend( street, CFSTR("N. ") );
CFStringAppend( street, CFSTR("Wolfe ") );
CFStringAppend( street, CFSTR("Road") );

CFShow    ( street );
CFRelease ( street );
```

[*] */System/Library/Frameworks/CoreFoundation.framework/Headers/CFBase.h.*

The second input value for `CFStringCreateMutable()` is the maximum length for the string. If you pass in 0, there will be no predetermined maximum. Here's the result in the console:

```
N. Wolfe Road
```

Toll-Free Bridging

There are times when you want to use Core Foundation types and Foundation classes in the same app. In fact, you may need to do this a lot if you're incorporating existing C code. Fortunately, there's no conversion necessary for most of the Core Foundation types and their Foundation counterparts. Anywhere you would typically use an `NSString`, you can use a `CFStringRef` instead, or vice versa. This is called *toll-free bridging*. The one catch is that you have to cast the variable to the expected type to avoid compiler warnings:

```
// using an NSMutableString as a CFMutableStringRef.

NSMutableString* street = [[NSMutableString alloc] init];

CFStringAppend( (CFMutableStringRef)street, CFSTR("N. ") );
CFStringAppend( (CFMutableStringRef)street, CFSTR("Wolfe ") );
CFStringAppend( (CFMutableStringRef)street, CFSTR("Road") );

CFShow ( street );
[street release];


// using a CFMutableStringRef as an NSMutableString.
// cast to separate variable for convenience.

CFMutableStringRef colors    = CFStringCreateMutable( NULL, 0 );
NSMutableString*   colorsObj = (NSMutableString*)colors;

[colorsObj appendString:@"Red, "];
[colorsObj appendString:@"Green, "];
[colorsObj appendString:@"and Blue."];

NSLog( @"colors: %@", colors );
CFRelease ( colors );
```

This means that you can and *should* use `NSLog()` to display Core Foundation types instead of `CFShow()` whenever possible. There are some exceptions, because the two frameworks do not have the exact same set of classes, but all of the most common types are supported. In addition to integrating with C, this is also helpful, because Core Foundation and Foundation do not have the exact same feature sets. Sometimes you need to temporarily switch types for a small section of code.

One critical detail here is that you don't need to switch to `CFStringRef` just because you're working in a plain C function:

```
NSString* stringObjectInFunction ( char* string ) {

    NSString* stringObject;
    stringObject = [NSString stringWithUTF8String:string];
    return stringObject;
}

void testStringObject () {

    NSString* country = stringObjectInFunction("New Zealand");
    NSLog( @"country: %@", country );
}
```

You can freely use Objective-C classes inside C code as long the as the file itself is compiled as Objective-C (usually determined by the .*m* file extension).

Core Foundation Types As Properties

You can create @property declarations for any kind of value, including primitive C types and structs. Core Foundation types are structs, but their memory is dynamically allocated and managed by a retain and release scheme. If you just use assign in the property declaration, the memory will never be freed. However, using the retain option will generate a build error (see Figure 7-4).

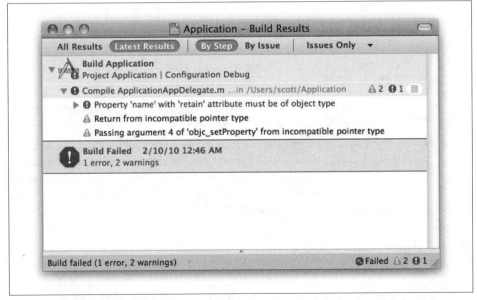

Figure 7-4. Xcode displays a build error if you try to use a Core Foundation type with the retain option in an @property declaration

The way around this is to use the __attribute__ keyword in the declaration to generate code that works as if the value was a regular Objective-C object:

```
@property (retain) __attribute__((NSObject)) CFStringRef name;
```

This usually isn't necessary, because most Core Foundation types are toll-free bridged with their Foundation versions. If you must use a type like `CFStringRef`, just declare the property to be `NSString` and cast it to `CFStringRef` inside of methods when necessary.

Drawbacks of Core Foundation Types

Even though Foundation uses them at a lower level, Core Foundation data types are not Objective-C. If you're using `CFString` directly, you can't declare categories on it or use any of the other special runtime tricks. It's also generally harder to manage memory for Core Foundation types.

You can cast it to an `NSString`, but there's no reason to use `CFString` except when you need pure C. You should use standard Objective-C objects in all other cases, because you have to write less code and you have a much wider set of programming options available to you.

Open Source

The source code of Core Foundation is available at *http://opensource.apple.com*. The exact path changes between releases, but the easiest approach is usually to click on a version of Mac OS X on the site's home page to see all of the open source packages in that release. In the list of packages, click on the "CF" item, which is followed by a version number (see Figure 7-5).

Inside the CF directory, you'll see a list of the *.c* and *.h* files for each of the types in Core Foundation, such as *CFString.h* and *CFString.c* (see Figure 7-6).

You can click on the file to see the contents. The source code is covered by the APSL license, which you can read about at *http://www.opensource.apple.com/license/apsl/*.

The site has source code for many other interesting packages, including the Mac OS X kernel (the "xnu" package), many of the built-in Unix tools and libraries, and the source code for the Objective-C language and runtime. There are also many related open source projects at *http://www.macosforge.org*, including the Calendar and Contacts Server, Grand Central Dispatch, and MacPorts.

NSNumber

Standard C includes several built-in number types, such as `int`, `unsigned int`, `long`, `float`, and `double`. This is a pretty short list, but it would be nice if a single type could encapsulate all of your number-storing needs. Cocoa's `NSNumber` class comes close to doing just that. It will accept nearly any kind of common number data without having to contend with data size issues.

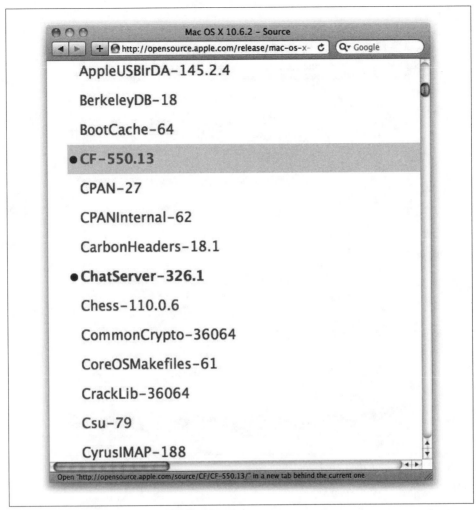

Figure 7-5. Package list for Mac OS X at http://opensource.apple.com

Unlike many Foundation classes, `NSNumber` does not have a mutable subclass.

New Cocoa programmers sometimes assume that because `NSNumber` is a class, it must be too slow to use for common tasks. Though the primitive types *are* faster due to their simplistic nature, `NSNumber` is very efficient and offers substantially more flexibility than the standard C types. Only high-end applications processing large amounts of data very rapidly will see any practical performance difference. Table 7-4 lists some of the most common methods.

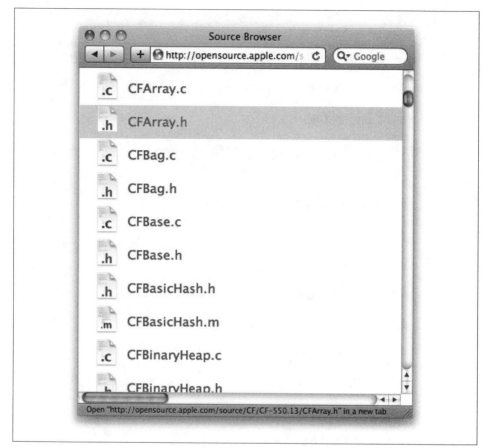

Figure 7-6. The files in the Core Foundation package

Table 7-4. Common NSNumber methods

Method	Description
+numberWithInt:	Creates a number with an int
+numberWithFloat:	Creates a number with a float
+numberWithBool:	Creates a number with a YES or NO value
-intValue	Returns an int version of the number
-floatValue	Returns a float version of the number
-boolValue	Returns an YES or NO version of the value
-stringValue	Returns an NSString with the number as text
-isEqualToNumber:	Compares the equality of another NSNumber instance

Fortunately, there's not much of a learning curve for this class. It pretty much does what you'd expect. You can create an instance using any standard C number type, and get the value back later as the same type, or convert it to another type. Here are some simple examples:

```
NSNumber* secondsInDay = [NSNumber numberWithInt:(60 * 60 * 24)];
NSNumber* scaleFactor  = [NSNumber numberWithFloat:0.865];
NSNumber* enableExtras  = [NSNumber numberWithBool:YES];

NSLog (@"secondsInDay: %@ as int:   %i", secondsInDay, secondsInDay.intValue);
NSLog (@"scaleFactor:  %@ as float: %f", scaleFactor,  scaleFactor.floatValue);
NSLog (@"enableExtras: %@ as BOOL:  %i", enableExtras, enableExtras.boolValue);
```

Here's the result in the console:

```
secondsInDay: 86400 as int:   86400
scaleFactor:  0.865 as float: 0.865000
enableExtras: 1 as BOOL: 1
```

There is a complete set of methods for dealing with all of the built-in C number types, but the naming conventions are consistent enough that you can safely guess what they are, such as using the +numberWithUnsignedInt: method for creating an instance with an unsigned int value. The full list, of course, is spelled out in the developer documentation (Help → Developer Documentation).

CFNumberRef

The CFNumberRef type is fairly simple; it includes only a handful of functions for basic setting and getting of values. Here are two simple examples:

```
NSInteger   intValue  = 2000;
CFNumberRef intNumber  = CFNumberCreate( NULL,
                                         kCFNumberNSIntegerType,
                                         &intValue );

CGFloat     floatValue = 105.3;
CFNumberRef floatNumber = CFNumberCreate( NULL,
                                          kCFNumberCGFloatType,
                                          &floatValue );

NSLog( @"intNumber:   %@", intNumber );
NSLog( @"floatNumber: %@", floatNumber );

CFRelease( intNumber   );
CFRelease( floatNumber );
```

Here's the result in the console:

```
intNumber:   2000
floatNumber: 105.3
```

A related type is `CFBooleanRef`, which you use through one of the two constant instances, `kCFBooleanTrue` and `kCFBooleanFalse`. The advantage of this being a `Ref` type is that it can be stored in a collection, such as an array (see "NSArray" on page 169 for more on arrays). Core Foundation also offers a primitive Boolean type, which is effectively the same as a `BOOL` in Objective-C:

```
CFBooleanRef controlEnabled    = kCFBooleanTrue;
CFBooleanRef resetPreferences = kCFBooleanFalse;

if ( CFBooleanGetValue( controlEnabled ) == true )
    NSLog( @"controlEnabled" );

if ( CFBooleanGetValue( resetPreferences ) == true )
    NSLog( @"resetPreferences" );
```

You probably will not use `CFNumberRef` or `CFBooleanRef` very often, as `NSNumber` can usually do the same work with less code. As with the other Core Foundation types, these are most useful when working a file that will be compiled as plain C. If you need to use `CFNumberRef`, though, you may want to look at `CFNumberFormatterRef` to format values.

Cocoa Primitive Types

Although Cocoa is completely compatible with the standard C types, it also offers its own primitive number types, which are not full-fledged classes (Table 7-5).

Table 7-5. Cocoa primitive number types

Type	Description
NSInteger	Integer values
NSUInteger	Unsigned integer values
CGFloat	Floating-point values

The `NSInteger` and `NSUInteger` types are set up to refer to the appropriate size depending on which architecture you're compiling for: `int` and `unsigned int` in 32-bit applications, and `long` and `unsigned long` in 64-bit applications. You'll see these types anywhere primitive values are used in Cocoa.

For example, instead of using an `int` for an array index, you should use an `NSInteger`:

```
NSInteger myArray[5] = {1,3,5,7,11};
NSInteger arrayIndex = 4;
NSInteger newValue = myArray[arrayIndex];
```

The `CGFloat` provides the same service for floating-point values. Again, you can just use it anywhere you'd use a `float` value:

```
CGFloat scaleFactor = 0.8;
```

You might expect this to be `NSFloat`, but the 64-bit floating-point type is defined by a framework called *CoreGraphics*. Without going into too much detail here, CoreGraphics is the basis for most 2D graphics in Mac OS X.

NSDecimalNumber

`NSNumber` can only *store* numbers of various sizes; you can't use it to do arithmetic. However, you can do mathematical operations with `NSDecimalNumber`, which is a subclass of `NSNumber`. This is invaluable if you're creating financial or scientific applications that need to be precise. You can create instances with a mantissa (significant part of the value) of up to 38 digits and an exponent from –128 through 127—in other words, a very big number.

You can create an `NSDecimalNumber` either from a string value like `@"7e22"` or using structured data. Here's an example of each:

```
NSDecimalNumber* starsInTheSky;
starsInTheSky = [NSDecimalNumber decimalNumberWithMantissa: 7
                                                 exponent: 22
                                               isNegative: NO];

NSLog( @"starsInTheSky: %@", starsInTheSky );

starsInTheSky = [NSDecimalNumber decimalNumberWithString:@"7e22"];

NSLog( @"starsInTheSky: %@", starsInTheSky );
```

Here's the result in the console:

```
starsInTheSky: 70000000000000000000000
starsInTheSky: 70000000000000000000000
```

Both approaches produce the same result, but methods like `+decimalNumberWith String:` that read input strings are generally a bit slower than those that create the objects directly (of course, if you call it thousands of times, you may see a difference). Once you have a few of these objects, you'll probably want to do something interesting with them. Table 7-6 lists some of the most useful methods.

Table 7-6. Common NSDecimalNumber methods

Method	Description
`+decimalNumberWithMantissa:exponent:isNegative:`	Creates a decimal number with structured values
`+decimalNumberWithString:`	Creates a number from a string
`+maximumDecimalNumber`	Returns an instance with the maximum possible value
`+notANumber`	Returns an object that represents a nonnumeric value for error handling
`-decimalNumberByAdding:`	Adds the value of a secondary object, returns the result

Method	Description
-decimalNumberBySubtracting:	Subtracts the value of a secondary object, returns the result
-decimalNumberByMultiplyingBy:	Multiplies the value of a secondary object, returns the result
-decimalNumberByDividingBy:	Divides the value of a secondary object, returns the result

Here's a simple example that calculates the projected world population for 2015:

```
// current population of 6,778,000,000.
// growth rate of 1.14%.

NSDecimalNumber* population   =
  [NSDecimalNumber decimalNumberWithString:@"6.778e9"];
NSDecimalNumber* annualGrowth =
  [NSDecimalNumber decimalNumberWithString:@"0.0114"];

NSDecimalNumber* yearPopulation = population;
NSDecimalNumber* netGain;

NSInteger year;
for ( year = 2009; year < 2016; year++ ) {

  // calculate the net gain for each year using 'annualGrowth'.
  // add the net gain to the current total.

  netGain = [yearPopulation decimalNumberByMultiplyingBy:annualGrowth];
  yearPopulation = [yearPopulation decimalNumberByAdding:netGain];
}

NSLog ( @"Projected population for 2015: %@", yearPopulation );
```

Here's the result in the console:

```
Projected population for 2015: 7337738147.39358592258590608915712
```

To make this number a bit more friendly, you can round the value using the `-decimal NumberByRoundingAccordingToBehavior:` method. It accepts any object that implements the `NSDecimalNumberBehaviors` protocol. You can make your own class or just create an instance of the `NSDecimalNumberHandler` class. The only catch is that the initialization method for the built-in class is extremely verbose, even by Objective-C standards. Here's how to round the value to a whole number:

```
NSDecimalNumberHandler* round;
NSRoundingMode mode = NSRoundPlain;

round = [NSDecimalNumberHandler decimalNumberHandlerWithRoundingMode: mode
                                                                scale: 0
                                                      raiseOnExactness: NO
                                                      raiseOnOverflow: NO
                                                     raiseOnUnderflow: NO
```

```
                                           raiseOnDivideByZero: NO];

    NSDecimalNumber* total;
    total = [yearPopulation decimalNumberByRoundingAccordingToBehavior:round];

    NSLog ( @"Projected population for 2015: %@", total );
```

And the result:

```
    Projected population for 2015: 7337738147
```

 Cocoa also provides a plain C struct called NSDecimal and a collection of associated functions, but I strongly recommend using the NSDecimalNumber class instead, because it's easier to use and integrates better with the rest of Cocoa.

NSNumberFormatter

Cocoa provides the NSNumberFormatter class to format numbers. You can choose from a stock formatting style, such as currency, or provide your own formatting pattern. NSNumberFormatter inherits from the NSFormatter class, which other built-in formatter classes inherit from as well. The API provides a lot of different options, but let's just focus on the simple case of formatting the projected population:

```
    NSDecimalNumber* total;
    total = [yearPopulation decimalNumberByRoundingAccordingToBehavior:round];
    NSLog ( @"Projected population for 2015: %@", total );


    NSString* totalString;
    NSNumberFormatterStyle formatStyle = NSNumberFormatterDecimalStyle;
    totalString = [NSNumberFormatter localizedStringFromNumber: total
                                             numberStyle: formatStyle];

    NSLog ( @"Projected population for 2015 (formatted): %@", totalString );
```

The interesting thing about the +localizedStringFromNumber:numberStyle: class method is the word *localized* in the beginning. It applies the user's preferences for number formatting, which is usually defined by region. Here's the result if my formatting is set for U.S. standards:

```
    Projected population for 2015: 7337738147
    Projected population for 2015 (formatted): 7,337,738,147
```

If I go into System Preferences → Language & Text → Formats and change my Region to Belgium, then rerun the program, the formatting in the console changes (note the different separator character; see Figure 7-7):

```
    Projected population for 2015: 7337738147
    Projected population for 2015 (formatted): 7.337.738.147
```

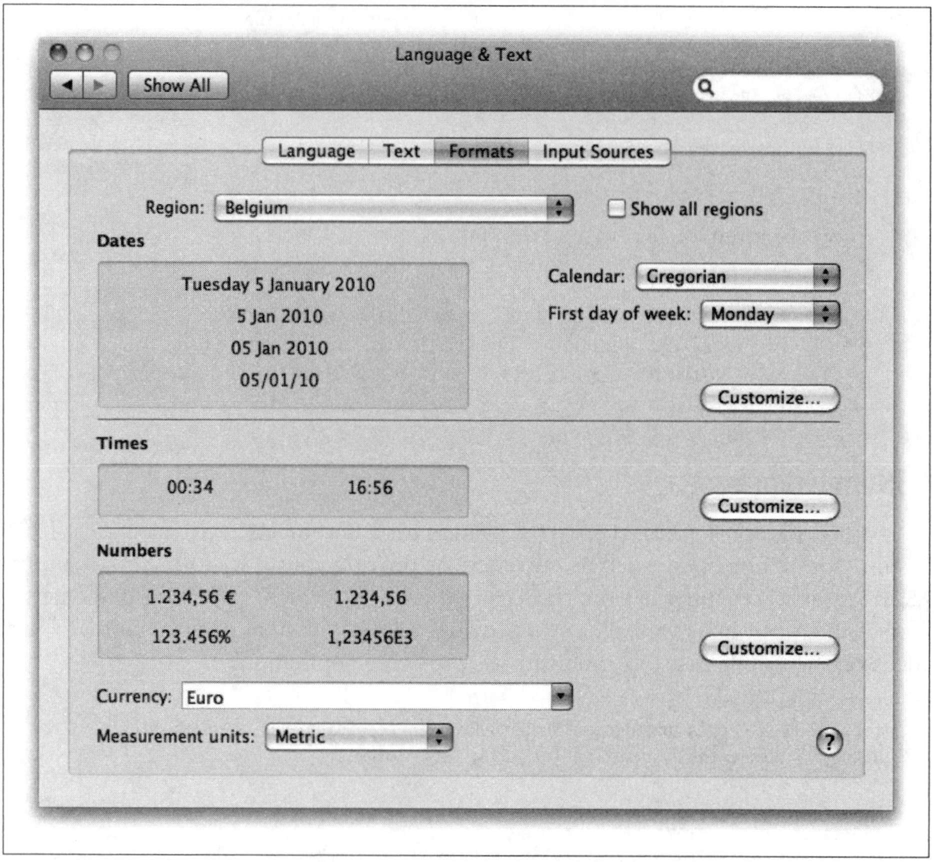

Figure 7-7. You can change the region in System Preferences to test number formatting

> NSNumberFormatter is actually designed to work with NSNumber; it just happens that NSDecimalNumber is a subclass of NSNumber. You can use formatters with either object type.

NSNumberFormatter usually does the most appropriate thing for the situation by default, but you can override that behavior. In the following example, I specify that the asterisk character should be used for the thousand separator:

```
NSNumberFormatter* formatter = [[NSNumberFormatter alloc] init];
[formatter setNumberStyle: NSNumberFormatterDecimalStyle];
[formatter setThousandSeparator:@"*"];
NSString* totalString = [formatter stringFromNumber:total];

NSLog ( @"Projected population for 2015 (formatted): %@", totalString );
[formatter release];
```

Here's the result in the console:

```
Projected population for 2015 (formatted): 7*337*738*147
```

 You can reuse NSNumberFormatter objects any number of times, and they can be somewhat expensive to set up, so it's usually a good idea to keep them around as instance variables if you're going to format a lot of values.

NSNumberFormatter also has a hidden talent that you can trigger with NSNumberFormatterSpellOutStyle. Here's a quick example:

```
NSNumber* secondsInDay = [NSNumber numberWithInt:86400];
NSNumberFormatter* formatter = [[NSNumberFormatter alloc] init];
[formatter setNumberStyle: NSNumberFormatterSpellOutStyle];

NSString* secondsAsString = [formatter stringFromNumber:secondsInDay];
NSLog ( @"Seconds in day (formatted): %@", secondsAsString );
[formatter release];
```

Here's the result:

```
Seconds in day (formatted): eighty-six thousand four hundred
```

The spelled-out style isn't practical for all numbers, but when used in the proper context, it can provide a more friendly experience for the user. If nothing else, though, it's a neat trick.

When to Use Which Number Type

Cocoa provides several different numeric types, so let's run down the list and clarify when to use each one:

NSInteger, NSUInteger, CGFloat
> Use for transient, in-application data, such as an index for an array, a scale factor, or screen coordinates.

NSNumber
> Typically best to use when dealing with persistent user data that will be saved to disk (either integer or floating-point values).

CFNumber
> The Core Foundation number class. You almost always want to use NSNumber instead, the exceptions being when you're writing code in a file that will be compiled as plain C, or if you happen to need a specific behavior in Core Foundation.

NSDecimalNumber
> Use when dealing with vital user data where high-precision math is important, such as bank transactions or scientific measurements.

NSDecimal

Generally works the same as NSDecimalNumber, but is implemented as a plain C struct with companion functions. Unless you know otherwise, it's usually better to use the object-oriented NSDecimalNumber class instead.

NSData

You use NSData to store blocks of raw data. This is useful if your app downloads files over the network, or if you want to save or load data from disk. You can also use NSData to easily deal with raw memory. You can get a lot done with just a handful of methods (Table 7-7).

Table 7-7. Common NSData methods

Method	Description
+dataWithContentsOfURL:	Creates a data object with the contents of a file at a URL
+dataWithContentsOfFile:	Creates a data object with the contents of a file at a path
+dataWithBytes:length:	Creates a data object by copying raw memory
-writeToURL:atomically:	Writes the data to a local file URL
-writeToFile:atomically:	Writes the data to a file path

A lot of other classes can read and write NSData objects too, so it's one of the most widely used object types in Cocoa. Example 7-1 shows some simple examples.

Example 7-1. NSDataBasics.m

```
NSString* moviePath = @"/Users/scott/Movies/trailer.m4v";
NSData*   movieData = [NSData dataWithContentsOfFile:moviePath];

NSInteger byteCount       = 1000;
void*     rawMemory       = malloc ( byteCount );
NSData*   rawMemoryAsData = [NSData dataWithBytes:rawMemory length:byteCount];
```

Data objects are particularly useful with things that can't be reasonably expressed in string form, like images. The NSImage class allows you to load image files from disk or over the network, as well as create images from the contents of a view. Here's an example of loading an image file from disk, and getting the contents as an NSData object:

```
NSString* file      = @"/Library/Desktop Pictures/Plants/Leaf Curl.jpg";
NSImage*  image     = [[NSImage alloc] initWithContentsOfFile:file];
NSData*   imageData = [image TIFFRepresentation];

[image release];
```

See "Images" on page 329 for more on images. You can also convert other Foundation objects into NSData objects, which is sometimes necessary for copying data to the pasteboard, sending it over the network, or storing it in a database. For example, you can convert a string into a data object with the `-dataUsingEncoding:` method, then write it to a file:

```
NSString* streetName = @"Mariani";
NSData*   stringData = [streetName dataUsingEncoding:NSUTF8StringEncoding];
NSString* filePath   =
  [NSHomeDirectory() stringByAppendingPathComponent:@"/streetName.txt"];
[stringData writeToFile:filePath atomically:YES];
```

 NSUTF8StringEncoding is the most common type of *file encoding* in Cocoa. The file encoding determines how the characters in a file or string are interpreted. This is important for supporting international text, but file encodings are not covered in this book. Unless you know otherwise, it's usually best to use NSUTF8StringEncoding when writing files.

There are four main ways to create `NSData` objects from existing memory blocks. Knowing the different options can significantly improve your code:

```
+ (id)data;

+ (id)dataWithBytes: (const void *)bytes
           length: (NSUInteger)length;

+ (id)dataWithBytesNoCopy: (void *)bytes
                 length: (NSUInteger)length;

+ (id)dataWithBytesNoCopy: (void *)bytes
                 length: (NSUInteger)length
           freeWhenDone: (BOOL)b;
```

These are all variations on the same concept. If you create an `NSData` object with the standard +[NSData dataWithBytes:length:] method, the contents of `bytes` will be copied. This can be very useful, because the data object can then be passed around without any concern about the original memory block going away. But some memory blocks are so big that copying them would put too much strain on system resources. If you use one of the methods with `NoCopy` at the beginning, the `NSData` object will just use the existing memory block instead of making its own.

The method that ends with `freeWhenDone` will call `free()` on the memory block when the object goes away. This means you can effectively use Cocoa's memory management conveniences (like autorelease) to manage memory allocated with the `malloc()` function:

```
NSInteger  count        = 4;
NSInteger  byteCount     = (sizeof(NSInteger) * count);
NSInteger* allNumbers    = malloc ( byteCount );
NSInteger* currentNumber = allNumbers;

for ( int i = 0; i < count; i++ ) {

    // advance pointer and set data.
```

```
    currentNumber  =  (allNumbers + i);
    *currentNumber  =  i*100;
}

NSData* data = [NSData dataWithBytesNoCopy: allNumbers
                                   length: byteCount
                              freeWhenDone: YES]];

// no need to call free here. NSData does it.
// free()
```

freeWhenDone exists only for the NoCopy method, because memory is copied by the other variants of dataWithBytes:, and the NSData object will free any memory that it allocates itself.

NSMutableData

NSMutableData is the mutable subclass of NSData. It adds a few key methods that allow you to add or remove data without creating a new NSData object. Here's an example:

```
NSMutableData* data = [NSMutableData data];
[data appendData:[@"First" dataUsingEncoding:NSUTF8StringEncoding]];
[data appendData:[@"Second" dataUsingEncoding:NSUTF8StringEncoding]];
[data appendData:[@"Third" dataUsingEncoding:NSUTF8StringEncoding]];
NSLog(@"data: %@", data);

[data resetBytesInRange: NSMakeRange(0,data.length) ];
NSLog(@"data after resetting contents: %@", data);

// remove all data.
[data setData: [NSData data]];
NSLog(@"data after removing contents: %@", data);

NSInteger  count        = 4;
NSInteger  byteCount     = (sizeof(NSInteger) * count);
NSInteger* allNumbers    = malloc ( byteCount );
NSInteger* currentNumber = allNumbers;

for ( int i = 0; i < count; i++ ) {

    // advance pointer and set data.
    currentNumber  =  (allNumbers + i);
    *currentNumber  =  i*8;
}

[data appendBytes:allNumbers length:byteCount];
NSLog(@"data: %@", data);

[data setData: [NSData data]];
NSLog(@"data after removing contents: %@", data);

free ( allNumbers );
```

This results in the following in the console:

```
data: <46697273 74536563 6f6e6454 68697264>
data after resetting contents: <00000000 00000000 00000000 00000000>
data after removing contents: <>
data: <00000000 00000000 08000000 00000000 10000000 00000000 18000000 00000000>
data after removing contents: <>
```

CFDataRef and CFMutableDataRef

CFDataRef and CFMutableDataRef are the Core Foundation equivalents of NSData and
NSMutableData. They don't offer significant advantages over their Foundation counterparts for most day-to-day tasks, and are toll-free bridged, so they are not covered in
this book. You can find the exact function names in the Xcode documentation.

NSArray

I think you could make the case that arrays are second only to strings in the competition
for the most-used data type in Cocoa apps. The NSArray class is incredibly versatile and
robust. It can store very large quantities of objects, but is also very easy to use. The
mutable subclass is substantially more useful, but let's start with the basics. Here's how
to create an array with three NSString objects:

```
NSArray* array = [NSArray arrayWithObjects:@"One", @"Two", @"Three", nil];
```

This method returns an autoreleased instance of NSArray with the objects you provide.
I used a literal string object here, but you can also just use object variables.

 The +arrayWithObjects: method takes a varying number of arguments.
Always add a nil at the end of the list. If you don't, Xcode will generate
a warning similar to "missing sentinel in function call." If you build and
run without fixing the warning, the app will likely crash when that line
of code is used, because the method will just start loading random
memory.

NSArray objects have some specific behaviors to keep in mind, some of which are different from other programming environments:

- Arrays can contain only objects, not primitive C types, structs, or generic pointers.
  The only exception to this are Core Foundation types, which have a special status.
  See "NSValue" on page 183 for more on wrapping primitive values in objects.

- Arrays can contain objects of mixed types, so a single array can contain some
  NSString objects, some id objects, or instances of any other class, including your
  own.

- You can't store a nil or NULL value in an NSArray, but you can store a special kind
  of object called an NSNull. You should use these sparingly, and instead try to only
  create arrays with valid objects.

- You can store multiple copies of the same object at different slots.

Most of the work you do with arrays is handled by a handful of key methods. Here are some basic examples:

```
NSArray* array = [NSArray arrayWithObjects:@"One", @"Two", @"Three", nil];
NSLog( @"array: %@", array );

id object = [array objectAtIndex:1]; ❶
NSLog( @"object: %@", object );

NSUInteger indexOfObject = [array indexOfObject:@"Three"]; ❷
NSLog( @"indexOfObject: %lu", indexOfObject );

array = [array arrayByAddingObject:@"Four"]; ❸
NSLog( @"array: %@", array );

NSArray* array2 = [[NSArray alloc] initWithObjects:@"Five", @"Six", nil];
array = [array arrayByAddingObjectsFromArray:array2]; ❹
NSLog( @"array: %@", array );
[array2 release];
```

❶ The -objectAtIndex: method returns an object at a specific slot. You shouldn't release an object returned from this method, and if you want to keep the object (for an instance variable, for example), you should retain it first.

❷ The -indexOfObject: method takes an object and returns its position in the array. If the object is not in the array, you will receive the value of NSNotFound instead of the index. This method uses -isEqual: to find the object, so you don't necessarily need to request the exact object, but just an object with the same value.

❸ The -arrayByAddingObject: method returns a new autoreleased array that is the same as the original, but with the additional object added to the end.

❹ The -arrayByAddingObjectsFromArray: method returns a new autoreleased array that combines all of the objects from the original and the second array you pass in.

Here's the result in the console (I reformatted this slightly to make it easier to read):

```
array: ( One, Two, Three )
object: Two
indexOfObject: 2
array: ( One, Two, Three, Four )
array: ( One, Two, Three, Four, Five, Six )
```

You can also create a formatted string from an array, or vice versa:

```
// string from array.
NSArray* array1 = [NSArray arrayWithObjects:
                    @"One", @"Two", @"Three", nil];

NSString* formatted = [array1 componentsJoinedByString:@" -- "];
NSLog( @"formatted: %@", formatted );

// array from string.
NSString* list   = @"Red * Green * Blue";
```

```
NSArray*  array2 = [list componentsSeparatedByString:@" * "];
NSLog( @"array2: %@", array2 );
```

Here's the result in the console:

```
formatted: One -- Two -- Three
array2: ( Red, Green, Blue )
```

Of course, you don't have to use commas or asterisks. You can specify whatever separator you like, and it's not limited to a single character.

Fast Enumeration

Objective-C has a built-in syntax for looping through collection objects such as NSArray. Here's what it looks like:

```
NSArray* weekendDays = [NSArray arrayWithObjects:
                        @"Friday", @"Saturday", @"Sunday", nil];

for (id object in weekendDays) {
    NSLog( @"day: %@", object );
}
```

This is generally much faster and simpler than using the standard C-style for loop in combination with the -objectAtIndex: method, though there are sometimes cases when that approach is useful, too. The fast enumeration feature is available to any classes that support the NSFastEnumeration protocol.

Blocks

When you want to run code against every item in an array, you can use fast enumeration to loop through it, but there's another option in Objective-C called *blocks*. This is a fairly advanced topic that applies to many classes, but the value is immediately clear with arrays.

This is an optional topic, and is not required for the rest of the book. If the concept is a bit hard to wrap your head around now, feel free to skim it now and come back to it later. I'm including it here only because a lot of Cocoa apps are starting to use it.

Blocks are nameless inline functions. If you've written software in other languages, you might also know blocks as *anonymous functions* or *closures*. They're a very compact way to use snippets of code with other methods. Blocks can also be stored as variables and passed between methods. The syntax takes a bit of explanation. First, here's one method from NSArray that takes a block (don't type this into your code; you'll see a complete version of this shortly):

```
- (void)enumerateObjectsUsingBlock: (
        void (^) (id obj, NSUInteger idx, BOOL *stop)
) block;
```

The thing that takes a bit of work to get your head around is that -enumer
ateObjectsUsingBlock: is an Objective-C method, but the method itself takes another
function (a block) as input. That function will be used on every single item in the array.

You declare a block variable with the caret (^) symbol, which is similar to using the
asterisk for declaring pointers. The void at the beginning states that the block won't
return a value. The obj variable is a single item from the array; the idx value is the index
of that item; and the stop variable is a pointer to a BOOL. If you want to stop the loop,
resolve the pointer and set the value to YES, as in *stop = YES.

 The word block in this declaration is just the name of the variable—it's
not part of the syntax. The caret (^) is the block declaration symbol.

To use this method, create a block *implementation* that matches the block *signature*
that the method provides. The signature declares which input and output items your
block implementation must contain, and what their types should be. Here's an example
of creating a block implementation for the -enumerateObjectsUsingBlock: method:

```
NSArray* colors = [NSArray arrayWithObjects:
                   @"Red", @"Green", @"Blue", nil];

// enumeration using a block.
[colors enumerateObjectsUsingBlock:

    // beginning of block.
    ^(id obj, NSUInteger idx, BOOL *stop) {
        NSLog( @"%@ at %lu", obj, idx );

        if ( idx == 1 ) {
            NSLog( @"Found index 1, stopping" );
            *stop = YES;
        }
    } // end of block.
];
```

Here's the result in the console:

```
Red at 0
Green at 1
Found index 1, stopping
```

The stop variable is necessary here because using a return statement would end only
the *current* iteration of the block. The method will call the block once for each item in
the array, so return would just move to the next item in the array. To stop the whole

thing, you have to set the value of stop to YES. This isn't a universal rule of blocks (as not all blocks are attached to loops)—it's just how it happens to work for this method.

Here are two versions of the same code, side by side. The first uses a block, the second uses fast enumeration:

```
NSArray* colors = [NSArray arrayWithObjects:
                          @"Red", @"Green", @"Blue", nil];


// enumeration using a block.
[colors enumerateObjectsUsingBlock:

    // beginning of block.
    ^(id obj, NSUInteger idx, BOOL *stop) {
        NSLog( @"%@ at %lu", obj, idx );

        if ( idx == 1 ) {
            NSLog( @"Found index 1, stopping" );
            *stop = YES;
        }
    } // end of block.
];


// standard enumeration.
for ( id obj in colors ) {

    NSUInteger idx = [colors indexOfObject:obj];
    NSLog( @"%@ at %lu", obj, idx );

    if ( idx == 1 ) {
        NSLog( @"Found index 1, stopping" );
        break;
    }
}
```

NSMutableArray

The joy of using object-oriented arrays increases significantly when you can change them on the fly without having to create new objects. The NSMutableArray class, of course, does just that. It works pretty much as you'd expect, adding methods that add, remove, and replace objects. You can work with individual objects, ranges of objects, or all of the objects at once. Here are examples of the methods you'll probably use most often:

```
// add objects, then empty the array.
NSMutableArray* painters = [NSMutableArray array];
[painters addObject:@"Leonardo"];
[painters addObject:@"Michelangelo"];
[painters addObject:@"Donatello"];
[painters addObject:@"Raphael"];
NSLog(@"painters: %@", painters);
```

```
[painters removeAllObjects];
NSLog(@"painters: %@", painters);


// combine arrays, replace items.
NSMutableArray* allMembers = [NSMutableArray array];
NSArray* members1 = [NSArray arrayWithObjects:@"Paul", @"John", nil];
NSArray* members2 = [NSArray arrayWithObjects:@"George", @"Pete", nil];
[allMembers addObjectsFromArray:members1];
[allMembers addObjectsFromArray:members2];

NSUInteger index = [allMembers indexOfObject:@"Pete"];
[allMembers replaceObjectAtIndex:index withObject:@"Ringo"];
NSLog(@"allMembers: %@", allMembers);
```

Here's the result in the console:

```
painters: ( Leonardo, Michelangelo, Donatello, Raphael )
painters: ( )
allMembers: ( Paul, John, George, Ringo )
```

Fortunately, this class is easy to use. When used in conjunction with the methods inherited from NSArray, the previous example almost certainly covers nearly all of the methods you'll need on a day-to-day basis.

 You should never change an array while you are looping through it; doing so breaks the logic of the loop, possibly causing a crash.

CFArrayRef

In most cases, you should use NSArray and NSMutableArray in Cocoa apps, but the Core Foundation counterparts, CFArrayRef and CFMutableArrayRef, have a few tricks that might be helpful. For example, you can ask the array to use your own custom retain, copy, and release functions as items are added and removed. This may be essential in certain advanced cases, but it can also be helpful for debugging:

```
const void* CBRetainValue (CFAllocatorRef allocator, const void *ptr) {

    CFTypeRef cf = (CFTypeRef)ptr;
    CFRetain( cf );

    NSLog( @"CBRetainValue: %@", cf );
    return cf;
}

- (void) retainCallbacksForArray {

    CFArrayCallBacks callbacks = kCFTypeArrayCallBacks;
    callbacks.retain = CBRetainValue;

    CFIndex capacity = 0; // no limit.
    CFMutableArrayRef array;
```

```
    array = CFArrayCreateMutable( NULL, capacity, &callbacks );

    // items are retained as they are added.
    CFArrayAppendValue( array, @"De Anza Blvd" );
    CFArrayAppendValue( array, @"Homestead Rd" );

    // works when cast to NSMutableArray as well.
    NSMutableArray* arrayObj = (NSMutableArray*)array;
    [arrayObj addObject: @"Sunnyvale Saratoga Rd"];
    [arrayObj addObject: @"Fremont Ave"];
    [arrayObj addObject: @"Stelling Rd"];

    NSLog( @"array: %@", array );
}
```

Here's the result of calling [self retainCallbacksForArray] in the console:

```
CBRetainValue: De Anza Blvd
CBRetainValue: Homestead Rd
CBRetainValue: Sunnyvale Saratoga Rd
CBRetainValue: Fremont Ave
CBRetainValue: Stelling Rd
array: (
    "De Anza Blvd",
    "Homestead Rd",
    "Sunnyvale Saratoga Rd",
    "Fremont Ave",
    "Stelling Rd"
)
```

This isn't something you should need to do on a regular basis, but if you *do* need it, it's invaluable.

NSIndexSet

It's not always convenient to deal with arrays one index at a time. This is where NSIndexSet and NSMutableIndexSet come in: they allow you to create collections of indexes inside of arrays. Some Cocoa UI classes use index sets to describe the selection in controls like table views, where the user can select multiple items at the same time. For example, you can use this to copy out slices of arrays or remove items from an array:

```
NSMutableArray* ninjas = [NSMutableArray array];
[ninjas addObject:@"Leonardo"];
[ninjas addObject:@"Michelangelo"];
[ninjas addObject:@"Donatello"];
[ninjas addObject:@"Raphael"];
NSLog( @"ninjas: %@", ninjas );

NSMutableIndexSet* indexSet;
indexSet = [NSMutableIndexSet indexSet];
[indexSet addIndex:1];
[indexSet addIndex:3];

NSArray* someNinjas;
```

```
someNinjas = [ninjas objectsAtIndexes:indexSet];
NSLog( @"someNinjas: %@", someNinjas );

[ninjas removeObjectsAtIndexes:indexSet];
NSLog( @"ninjas: %@", ninjas );
```

Here's the result:

```
ninjas: ( Leonardo, Michelangelo, Donatello, Raphael )
someNinjas: ( Michelangelo, Raphael )
ninjas: ( Leonardo, Donatello )
```

You can also use them to filter objects based on the code in the block:

```
NSMutableArray* streets = [NSMutableArray array];
[streets addObject:@"De Anza Blvd"];
[streets addObject:@"Homestead Rd"];
[streets addObject:@"Sunnyvale Saratoga Rd"];
[streets addObject:@"Fremont Ave"];
[streets addObject:@"Stelling Rd"];
NSLog( @"All streets: %@", streets );

NSIndexSet* roadsIndexes;
roadsIndexes = [streets indexesOfObjectsPassingTest:

                ^( id obj, NSUInteger idx, BOOL *stop ) {
                    return [obj hasSuffix:@"Rd"];
                }];

NSLog( @"roadIndexes: %lu", roadsIndexes.count );

NSArray* roads = [streets objectsAtIndexes:roadsIndexes];
NSLog( @"roads: %@", roads );
```

Here's the result in the console:

```
All streets: (
    "De Anza Blvd",
    "Homestead Rd",
    "Sunnyvale Saratoga Rd",
    "Fremont Ave",
    "Stelling Rd"
)
roadIndexes: 3
roads: (
    "Homestead Rd",
    "Sunnyvale Saratoga Rd",
    "Stelling Rd"
)
```

Although it's not shown in this example, you can also insert objects at all of the indexes described by an index set, or replace all of the objects at given indexes. This makes it possible to work with large arrays with many selections very efficiently.

NSDictionary

Arrays are used for storing ordered collections of objects, but NSDictionary allows you to store *keyed collections* of objects. Each entry in an NSDictionary has a key and a value. The keys have to be unique within each dictionary, but the values do not. All of the basic rules for NSArray in terms of mixed types and nil values apply here, too.

Like the other Foundation classes, NSDictionary is both robust and easy to use. Here are some basic examples of creating dictionaries and retrieving values:

```
NSString* const CBCityKey    = @"city";
NSString* const CBStateKey   = @"state";
NSString* const CBZipcodeKey = @"zipcode";

NSArray* values = [NSArray arrayWithObjects:
                    @"Cupertino", @"California", @"95014", nil];

NSArray* keys   = [NSArray arrayWithObjects:
                    CBCityKey, CBStateKey, CBZipcodeKey, nil];

NSDictionary* info;
info = [NSDictionary dictionaryWithObjects:values forKeys:keys];
NSLog( @"info dictionary: %@", info );
NSLog( @"info keys: %@", info.allKeys );
NSLog( @"info values: %@", info.allValues );

NSString* city = [info objectForKey:CBCityKey];
NSLog( @"city value: %@", city );
```

 Technically, keys don't have to be NSString objects—you could use NSNumber objects instead—but strings are the most common and generally the most practical.

You can also create a dictionary by using a variable number of arguments instead of arrays. The +dictionaryWithObjectsAndKeys: method takes objects and keys in an alternating pattern, ending with a nil:

```
NSDictionary* info;
info = [NSDictionary dictionaryWithObjectsAndKeys:
                        @"Cupertino", CBCityKey,
                        @"California", CBStateKey,
                        @"95014", CBZipcodeKey,
                        nil];
```

NSDictionary supports both fast enumeration and block enumeration:

```
NSString* const CBCityKey    = @"city";
NSString* const CBStateKey   = @"state";
NSString* const CBZipcodeKey = @"zipcode";

NSDictionary* info;
info = [NSDictionary dictionaryWithObjectsAndKeys:
```

```
                            @"Sunnyvale", CBCityKey,
                            @"California", CBStateKey,
                            @"94086", CBZipcodeKey,
                            nil];

    for ( id key in info ) {
        NSLog( @"%@: %@", key, [info objectForKey:key] );
    }

    [info enumerateKeysAndObjectsUsingBlock:

        ^( id key, id obj, BOOL *stop ) {
            NSLog( @"%@: %@", key, obj );
        }
    ];
```

In these examples, I used string constants for the keys. This isn't required, but I think it's usually a good idea, because it enables the compiler to help you prevent typos. If you just type literal strings everywhere, it's really easy for one line of code to say @"city" and the next line to say @"cityy", which means your program has a bug. Trying to use a constant that doesn't exist will generate a build error, which gives you a chance to fix the mistake before you run the app.

Dictionaries are sometimes useful as a way to try out ideas quickly, without having to create a bunch of classes. When prototyping, you can treat each key-value pair effectively as an instance variable. Once you've decided on a design, though, it's easier to make actual classes, because you can take advantage of class-specific categories, override setters and getters, and so on.

NSMutableDictionary

The NSMutableDictionary class adds methods to NSDictionary that allow you to make changes on the fly. This makes programming with dictionaries vastly easier. Here are some examples of the most important methods:

```
    NSMutableDictionary* info1 = [NSMutableDictionary dictionary];

    [info1 setObject: @"Looking up at the stars."
            forKey: @"title"];
    [info1 setObject: [NSNumber numberWithFloat:1.8]
            forKey: @"focalDistance"];
    [info1 setObject: [NSDate date]
            forKey: @"creationDate"];
    [info1 setObject: [NSNumber numberWithFloat:1.2]
            forKey: @"exposure"];

    NSLog( @"info1: %@", info1 );

    NSMutableDictionary* info2 = [NSMutableDictionary dictionary];

    [info2 setObject: [NSNumber numberWithInteger:500]
            forKey: @"width"];
```

```
[info2 setObject: [NSNumber numberWithInteger:450]
        forKey: @"height"];
[info2 setObject: [NSNumber numberWithInteger:300]
        forKey: @"dpi"];

[info1 addEntriesFromDictionary:info2];
NSLog( @"info1: %@", info1 );

NSArray* keys = [NSArray arrayWithObjects:@"width", @"height", nil];
[info1 removeObjectsForKeys:keys];
NSLog( @"info1: %@", info1 );
```

Here's the result in the console:

```
info1: {
    creationDate = "2010-02-10 05:09:43 -0800";
    exposure = "1.2";
    focalDistance = "1.8";
    title = "Looking up at the stars.";
}
info1: {
    creationDate = "2010-02-10 05:09:43 -0800";
    dpi = 300;
    exposure = "1.2";
    focalDistance = "1.8";
    height = 450;
    title = "Looking up at the stars.";
    width = 500;
}
info1: {
    creationDate = "2010-02-10 05:09:43 -0800";
    dpi = 300;
    exposure = "1.2";
    focalDistance = "1.8";
    title = "Looking up at the stars.";
}
```

This example is pretty simple, but that's because `NSMutableDictionary` is a very straight-forward class. In the vast majority of cases, it just works the way you'd expect.

CFDictionaryRef

The Core Foundation dictionary types are `CFDictionaryRef` and `CFMutableDictionaryRef`. In most cases, you should just use the Foundation classes instead, but `CFDictionaryRef` does offer a few more options for advanced cases. If `NSDictionary` doesn't quite do what you want, `CFDictionaryRef` might be able to. For example, you can choose to retain keys instead of copying them:

```
const void* CBRetainValue (CFAllocatorRef alloc, const void *ptr) {

    CFTypeRef cf = (CFTypeRef)ptr;
    CFRetain(cf);
    NSLog(@"CBRetainValue: %@", cf);
    return cf;
```

```
    }

- (void) dictionaryWithRetainedKeys {

    // start with standard callbacks, add custom retain option.
    // this will cause the keys to be retained instead of copied.
    CFDictionaryKeyCallBacks keyCallbacks;

    keyCallbacks        = kCFCopyStringDictionaryKeyCallBacks;
    keyCallbacks.retain = CBRetainValue;

    CFMutableDictionaryRef dict;
    CFIndex capacity = 0;
    dict = CFDictionaryCreateMutable( NULL,
                                      capacity,
                                      &keyCallbacks,
                                      &kCFTypeDictionaryValueCallBacks );

    CFDictionarySetValue( dict, @"city", @"Palo Alto" );
}
```

You can actually use C types as keys for `CFDictionaryRef`, but it's almost always better to use standard strings. Another option that `CFMutableDictionaryRef` provides is the ability to add, replace, or remove a value for a key only if that key doesn't already exist:

```
CFStringRef const CBCityKey    = CFSTR("city");
CFStringRef const CBStateKey   = CFSTR("state");
CFStringRef const CBZipcodeKey = CFSTR("zipcode");

CFIndex capacity = 0;
CFMutableDictionaryRef dict;
dict = CFDictionaryCreateMutable( NULL,
                                  capacity,
                                  &kCFCopyStringDictionaryKeyCallBacks,
                                  &kCFTypeDictionaryValueCallBacks );

CFDictionaryAddValue ( dict, CBCityKey, @"San Francisco" );
CFDictionaryAddValue ( dict, CBCityKey, @"Mountain View" );

// will not cause exceptions.
CFDictionaryRemoveValue ( dict, CBStateKey );
CFDictionaryReplaceValue ( dict, CBZipcodeKey, @"95014" );
NSLog( @"dict: %@", dict );

CFDictionaryReplaceValue ( dict, CBCityKey, @"Cupertino" );
NSLog( @"dict: %@", dict );

CFRelease( dict );
```

Here's the result in the console:

```
dict: {
    city = "San Francisco";
}
dict: {
```

```
        city = Cupertino;
    }
```

You can do these same things with NSDictionary by checking for an existing key first, but this does it in one step. I suggest you stick with NSDictionary. In my opinion, it's better to have an extra line of code than to switch back and forth between NSDictionary and CFDictionaryRef.

NSSet

An NSArray is an ordered collections of values; an NSDictionary is an unordered collections of values and keys; and an NSSet is an unordered collection of values (without keys). Unlike arrays and dictionaries, all of the items in an NSSet are unique, which is important for certain cases in Cocoa. You will probably not use sets nearly as much as you use arrays, but it is very helpful to have a few basic ideas about how they work:

```
// manually created set.
NSSet* days;
days = [NSSet setWithObjects: @"Friday", @"Saturday",nil];
days = [days setByAddingObject:@"Sunday"];
NSLog( @"days: %@", days );

// set from array.
NSMutableArray* planets = [NSMutableArray array];
[planets addObject:@"Earth"];
[planets addObject:@"Mercury"];
[planets addObject:@"Mars"];
[planets addObject:@"Jupiter"];
[planets addObject:@"Jupiter"];
[planets addObject:@"Jupiter"];

NSSet* planetsSet = [NSSet setWithArray:planets];
NSLog( @"planetsSet: %@", planetsSet );

// add an object.
NSSet* morePlanets = [planetsSet setByAddingObject:@"Venus"];
if ([planetsSet isSubsetOfSet:morePlanets])
    NSLog( @"morePlanets is a superset of planetsSet" );

// loop through with fast enumeration.
for ( id planet in planetsSet ) {
    if ([planet isEqual:@"Earth"]) {
        NSLog ( @"Found home!" );
    }
}

// filter objects with a block.
NSSet* mPlanets = [morePlanets objectsPassingTest:
                    ^(id obj, BOOL *stop) {
                        return [obj hasPrefix:@"M"];
                    }];
```

```
NSLog( @"mPlanets: %@", mPlanets );
```

Here's the result in the console:

```
days: {( Friday, Saturday, Sunday )}
planetsSet: {( Mercury, Jupiter, Mars, Earth )}
morePlanets is a superset of planetsSet
Found home!
mPlanets: {( Mars, Mercury )}
```

The two most import things to notice in this example are:

- If you create an NSSet from an NSArray, and the array has duplicate items, the set will not.

- The items in the set can end up in a different order than in the array. There's no inherent order to the items in a set.

NSMutableSet

NSMutableSet, of course, adds the ability to change the set of objects on the fly, but the methods have a slightly different naming scheme than NSMutableArray or NSMutableDictionary. Here are some basic examples:

```
NSMutableSet* planets1 = [NSMutableSet set];
[planets1 addObject:@"Earth"];
[planets1 addObject:@"Mercury"];
[planets1 addObject:@"Pluto"];

NSMutableSet* planets2 = [NSMutableSet set];
[planets2 addObject:@"Mars"];
[planets2 addObject:@"Jupiter"];

NSMutableSet* allPlanets = [NSMutableSet set];
[allPlanets unionSet:planets1];
[allPlanets unionSet:planets2];
NSLog( @"allPlanets: %@", allPlanets );

NSMutableSet* notPlanets = [NSSet setWithObject:@"Pluto"];
[allPlanets minusSet:notPlanets];
NSLog( @"allPlanets: %@", allPlanets );

NSMutableSet* overlap = [[allPlanets mutableCopy] autorelease];
[overlap intersectSet:planets1];
NSLog( @"overlap: %@", overlap );
```

Heres's the result in the console:

```
allPlanets: {(
    Mercury, Pluto, Mars, Jupiter, Earth
)}
allPlanets: {(
    Mercury, Mars, Jupiter, Earth
)}
```

```
overlap: {(
    Mercury, Earth
)}
```

Although they're not as widely used as arrays, sets can be very useful when you want unique collections of objects.

NSValue

NSValue is used to wrap primitive C values in Objective-C objects. In addition to providing some basic infrastructure for its subclass, NSNumber, it also provides a way to store raw pointers, or even nonretained references to other Objective-C objects. Unlike NSData, it stores the primitive type along with the actual data. Here are some basic examples:

```
typedef struct {
    NSInteger lengthInSeconds;
    NSInteger yearRecorded;
} Song;


- (NSValue*) structObjectValue {

    Song mySong;
    mySong.lengthInSeconds =  243;
    mySong.yearRecorded    = 1970;

    NSValue* item = [NSValue valueWithBytes: &mySong
                                   objCType: @encode(Song)];
    return item;
}


- (NSValue*) stringObjectValue {

    char* itemName = "Hey Jude";
    NSValue* item = [NSValue valueWithBytes: &itemName
                                   objCType: @encode(char**)];
    return item;
}

- (void) testValue {

    // value object with a C string.
    NSValue* stringObject = self.stringObjectValue;

    char* stringValue = NULL;
    [stringObject getValue: &stringValue];
    NSLog( @"stringValue: %s", stringValue );

    // value object with a struct.
    NSValue* structObject = self.structObjectValue;
```

```
    Song mySong;
    [structObject getValue: &mySong];
    NSLog( @"structValue: %ld, %ld",
                mySong.lengthInSeconds, mySong.yearRecorded );

    NSMutableDictionary* songInfo = [NSMutableDictionary dictionary];
    [songInfo setObject:stringObject forKey:@"name"];
    [songInfo setObject:structObject forKey:@"details"];
}
```

Here's the result in the console:

```
stringValue: Hey Jude
structValue: 243, 1970
```

As you can see, wrapping primitive values and structs in NSValue objects allows you to store them in arrays, dictionaries, or sets. You can also wrap regular Objective-C objects in NSValue instances to prevent them from being retained by the collection:

```
NSMutableString* string1 = [[NSMutableString alloc] init];
[string1 appendFormat:@"Item %ld", 1];
[string1 appendFormat:@"Item %ld", 2];
[string1 appendFormat:@"Item %ld", 3];

NSMutableString* string2 = [string1 mutableCopy];
NSLog( @"string 1 retain count: %lu", string1.retainCount );
NSLog( @"string 2 retain count: %lu", string2.retainCount );

NSValue* stringWrapper = [NSValue valueWithNonretainedObject:string2];
NSMutableArray* array  = [NSMutableArray array];
[array addObject:string1];
[array addObject:stringWrapper];

NSLog( @"string 1 retain count: %lu", string1.retainCount );
NSLog( @"string 2 retain count: %lu", string2.retainCount );
```

Here's the result in the console:

```
string 1 retain count: 1
string 2 retain count: 1
string 1 retain count: 2
string 2 retain count: 1
```

You can also prevent retains on objects added to arrays and dictionaries by using custom callbacks with CFArrayRef and CFDictionaryRef, but this allows you to achieve the same end result with less complication.

NSDate

NSDate allows you to calculate points in time as seconds since an event. For example, here's how to calculate one full year since the "reference date," which is January 1, 2001:

```
NSTimeZone* timeZone = [NSTimeZone systemTimeZone];
NSInteger   offset   = [timeZone secondsFromGMTForDate:[NSDate date]];
NSInteger   seconds  = (( 60 * 60 * 24 * 365 ) - offset);
```

```
NSDate* reference;
reference  = [NSDate dateWithTimeIntervalSinceReferenceDate:(-offset)];

NSDate* targetDate;
targetDate = [NSDate dateWithTimeIntervalSinceReferenceDate:seconds];

NSLog( @"reference:  %@", reference );
NSLog( @"targetDate: %@", targetDate );
```

Here's the result in the console:

```
reference:  2001-01-01 00:00:00 -0800
targetDate: 2002-01-01 00:00:00 -0800
```

The reference date is based on the GMT time zone, so I use NSTimeZone to adjust it for the local machine. Dates are much more useful when paired with NSDateFormatter, which does the formatting in both directions. You can either convert a regular date object to a formatted string, or you can create a date object from text.

```
// standard formatting.
NSDateFormatter* formatter1 = [[NSDateFormatter alloc] init];
[formatter1 setLenient: YES];
[formatter1 setDateStyle: NSDateFormatterShortStyle];
[formatter1 setTimeStyle: NSDateFormatterShortStyle];

NSString* dateString    = @"March 24 2001 10:00am";
NSDate*   basicDate     = [formatter1 dateFromString:dateString];
NSString* formattedDate = [formatter1 stringFromDate:basicDate];
NSLog( @"date only:      %@", basicDate );
NSLog( @"short formatted: %@", formattedDate );

NSDateFormatter* formatter2 = [[NSDateFormatter alloc] init];
[formatter2 setLenient: YES];
[formatter2 setDateStyle: NSDateFormatterLongStyle];
[formatter2 setTimeStyle: NSDateFormatterLongStyle];
formattedDate = [formatter2 stringFromDate: basicDate];
NSLog( @"long formatted: %@", formattedDate );

// relative formatting.
NSDateFormatter* formatter3 = [[NSDateFormatter alloc] init];
[formatter3 setLenient: YES];
[formatter3 setDoesRelativeDateFormatting: YES];
[formatter3 setDateStyle: NSDateFormatterShortStyle];
[formatter3 setTimeStyle: NSDateFormatterShortStyle];

NSTimeInterval oneDay = (60*60*24);
NSDate* startDate = [NSDate date];
NSDate* prevDate  = [startDate dateByAddingTimeInterval: -oneDay];
NSDate* nextDate  = [startDate dateByAddingTimeInterval: oneDay];

NSString* startFormatted = [formatter3 stringFromDate: startDate];
NSString* prevFormatted  = [formatter3 stringFromDate: prevDate];
NSString* nextFormatted  = [formatter3 stringFromDate: nextDate];
NSLog( @"relative start:  %@", startFormatted );
NSLog( @"relative prev:   %@", prevFormatted );
```

```
NSLog( @"relative next:    %@", nextFormatted );

[formatter1 release];
[formatter2 release];
[formatter3 release];
```

Here's the result in the console:

```
date only:        2001-03-24 10:00:00 -0800
short formatted:  3/24/01 10:00 AM
long formatted:   March 24, 2001 10:00:00 AM PST
relative start:   Today 4:18 AM
relative prev:    Yesterday 4:18 AM
relative next:    Tomorrow 4:18 AM
```

The most important thing to be aware of is that NSDateFormatter is fairly strict about how it interprets input strings as dates. For example, don't set a time style unless an input string will contain a time. In general, try to be as specific as possible about the format. You can also provide your own custom format strings. Search for NSDateFormatter in the Xcode documentation for more details about the format markers.

There are additional date features available in Cocoa through NSCalendar, CFCalendarRef, and CFGregorianDate, but they are not covered in this book. The methods and functions for each are generally easy to understand and you should be able to get up and running just by viewing the header files.

CFDateRef

The functionality of Core Foundation's CFDate is nearly identical to NSDate, to the point that you can practically guess the method names if you're familiar with their Foundation counterparts:

```
CFTimeZoneRef  timeZone = CFTimeZoneCopyDefault();
CFAbsoluteTime current  = CFAbsoluteTimeGetCurrent();

CFTimeInterval offset   = CFTimeZoneGetSecondsFromGMT( timeZone, current );
CFIndex        seconds  = (( 60 * 60 * 24 * 365 ) - offset);

CFDateRef reference;
reference = CFDateCreate( NULL, -offset );

CFDateRef targetDate;
targetDate = CFDateCreate( NULL, seconds );

NSLog( @"reference: %@", reference );
NSLog( @"targetDate: %@", targetDate );

CFRelease( timeZone   );
CFRelease( reference  );
CFRelease( targetDate );
```

The net result of this is practically identical to the NSDate version. In addition to the CFDateRef type, this example uses the CFTimeZoneRef and CFTimeInterval, which are equivalent to NSTimeZone and NSTimeInterval, respectively. The CFAbsoluteTime type is similar to the "reference date" in Foundation; it's a version of CFTimeInterval that starts counting at January 1, 2001.

If you're using CFDateRef and can't use toll-free bridging with NSDate and NSDateFormatter, you can use CFDateFormatterRef. Although it's not covered in this book, the functionality is very similar to Foundation.

CHAPTER 8

Basic Controls

You've learned Objective-C and the Foundation classes. Now you get to work with the real power of Cocoa: the AppKit user interface layer. There are three ways to use AppKit:

Built-in controls
There's a vast library of built-in controls that you can start using right away, many of which can be added through Interface Builder. This is great for prototyping, and sometimes you can ship an app using only these stock controls.

Customized versions of built-in controls
You can customize many of the built-in controls using properties, delegate methods, or for more direct customization, subclassing.

Brand-new controls from scratch
Many Mac apps use completely custom views that are tuned for features that are not general enough to be built into Cocoa. For example, the music timeline is something very few apps need, but is absolutely essential for music production software. AppKit provides a comprehensive set of building blocks to help you create custom views for your app.

This chapter focuses on basic concepts using built-in controls. While you're learning how to use text fields, buttons, and other standard classes, you'll also be learning about the overall design of AppKit so that you can apply it to your own custom views later.

How to Use This Chapter

Now that you've learned the basics of Objective-C and the Foundation classes, you're probably feeling more confident about trying things out. There are quite a few examples in this chapter. The quickest way to learn about Cocoa's standard controls is to try out each example as you encounter it. You can create a single Cocoa project in Xcode and add controls and code as you go. You can also simply read through the chapter to expose yourself to the concepts, and come back later to try out the examples by hand.

Windows and Views

In a Cocoa user interface (UI), everything starts with an instance of NSWindow. You're already familiar with the standard Mac OS X windows, which have a title bar and resize controls, but windows come in many different forms. Not all of them have a title or a rectangular appearance, and not all of them are even directly visible.

A window is a container for NSView objects (Figure 8-1). A *view* is an item on the screen that you can interact with, such as a text field or a button. A view draws itself into the window, receives user input, and then draws again. Cocoa is an *event-based* framework, which means you don't have to (and shouldn't) constantly check for user input. Instead, Cocoa notifies views when something has happened.

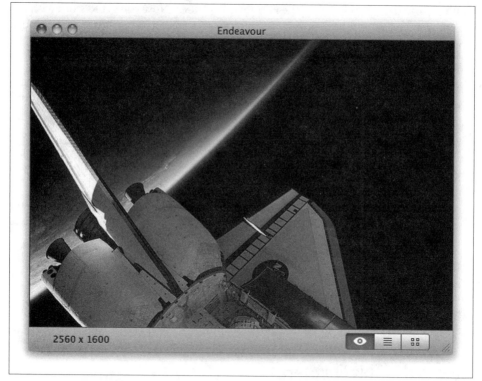

Figure 8-1. An NSWindow instance with NSView objects inside

All views and windows inherit support for mouse, keyboard, and multitouch events from the NSResponder superclass. One important point here is that NSView and NSWindow are peers—they *both* inherit directly from NSResponder, as shown in Figure 8-2. In other words, in AppKit, a window is not a view.

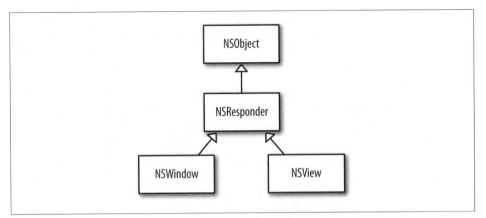

Figure 8-2. The relationships between NSWindow, NSView, and NSResponder

 The UIKit framework for iPhone, iPad, and iPod touch handles this differently. The inheritance path is UIResponder → UIView → UIWindow. In AppKit, though, NSView and NSWindow are peers.

There's also a subclass of NSView called NSControl. A lot of text fields and buttons are based on this class. Each NSControl object has one or more NSCell objects. Cells are not views or responders—NSCell inherits directly from NSObject (see Figure 8-3).

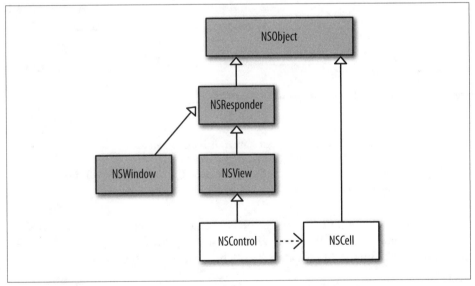

Figure 8-3. How NSControl and NSCell fit into the world of responders and views

For example, in a spreadsheet application, each row of the table could be managed by a cell. In that scenario, a spreadsheet cell is literally an NSCell object, though many simpler controls have cells as well. If you're a curious about this, you can launch Interface Builder now and choose Window → Library, then type "cell" in the search field to see some of the standard NSCell subclasses, as shown in Figure 8-4.

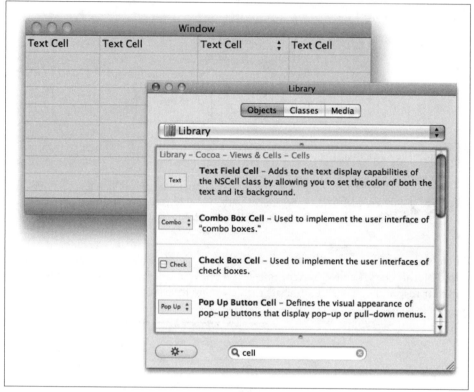

Figure 8-4. Using NSCell classes in Interface Builder

> The iPhone's UIKit does not have a direct counterpart to NSCell, but there is a UITableViewCell class that is designed specifically for tables. The main difference is that UITableViewCell is a subclass of UIView, whereas NSCell is a subclass of NSObject.

As with most of the other concepts in the book, I don't expect you to memorize everything the first time you read it. The idea is just to introduce you to the five basic classes that make up the AppKit class hierarchy. In fact, let's review that now:

NSResponder: *inherits from* NSObject

A superclass that provides basic support for user interaction with mouse, keyboard, and multitouch to windows and views.

NSWindow: *inherits from* **NSResponder**, *contains multiple* **NSView** *instances*

Provides a canvas for views to draw into. Some types of windows have title bars and resize controls, but some are not directly visible.

NSView: *inherits from* **NSResponder**

The most common superclass for custom views in Cocoa apps. Provides support for geometry and drawing, and mouse tracking (for example, for mouseover-style events).

NSControl: *inherits from* **NSView**, **NSResponder**

A view subclass that many standard controls are based on, such as text fields, buttons, and table views. Drawing is usually done by one or more **NSCell** instances.

NSCell: *inherits from* **NSObject**, *owned by an* **NSControl**

Usually does the drawing for **NSControl** classes. The same cell class can be used across multiple controls. For example, a text field cell can be used in either a text field or a table view.

Nearly everything I'll introduce you to in this chapter inherits from one of these classes. When you're using built-in classes, most of this is automatic. In fact, you saw this in Chapter 1 when you created a text editor without any code.

This is one of the most rewarding parts of Cocoa—you don't need to understand how all of the details work to take advantage of the features. Do you know how to handle characters from a foreign alphabet as input? Probably not, but you don't need to, because Cocoa does it for you. That frees you up to focus on what makes your app unique.

Targets and Actions

At first, Cocoa may seem overwhelmingly complex, but that's mostly just because it's new. It's true that there are *parts* of Cocoa that are very complex—sometimes because the subject matter itself is complex, like multilingual text—and writing software inherently demands a lot of your attention, but there's good news about this, too. By design, Cocoa uses the same simple building blocks over and over again.

Even the most complex parts of Cocoa are really just layers of simple things stacked on top of each other. And if you can figure out one layer of simple things, you can figure out the next. If you stay dedicated to learning each piece, eventually it all starts to make sense. One of these layers is called *targets and actions*.

An *action* is a placeholder for a method, or more specifically a selector (see more about selectors in the section "Dynamic Messaging" on page 124). **NSControl** objects use actions to tell other objects that something has happened (see Figure 8-5). For example, you'd probably like to know when the user clicks a button on the screen so your app can perform some task, such as saving a file or opening a web page.

Setting an action for a button is, literally, telling it *which* method to call when it's clicked. It's the Cocoa equivalent of "Call me at this number when you hear anything."

Figure 8-5. A control sending an action message to a target

When that method is called, you can react by running other code in your app to actually perform the task the user is requesting.

Buttons

Buttons are a convenient starting place for learning about actions, because the flow is very easy to understand. The user clicks on the button and the action is sent to another object, called the *target*. There are more complex buttons with toggle states and other variations, but the most common version is the standard push button.

Almost all push buttons are instances of the NSButton class,[*] which inherits from NSControl. Although there are many built-in visual styles for buttons in AppKit, most of them are not subclasses. Instead, the visual styles are defined through properties on the base NSButton class. All of the items in Figure 8-6 are stock NSButton instances with different styles applied.

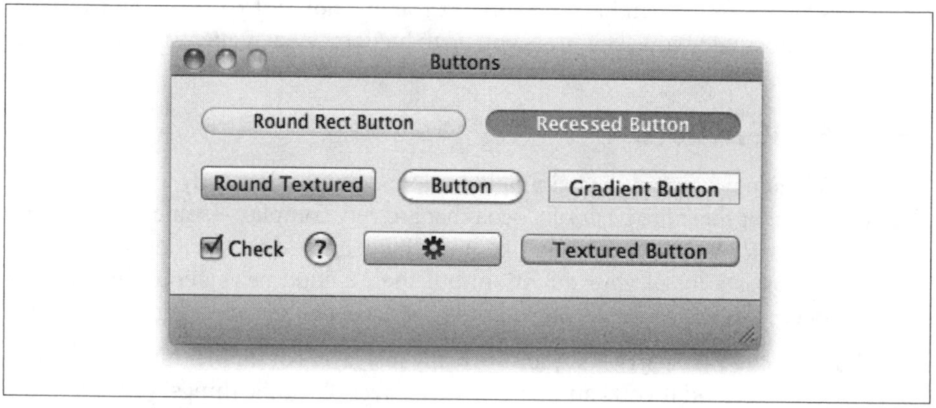

Figure 8-6. The many faces of NSButton

There *are* NSButton subclasses in Cocoa, though. They are mostly used in the cases where the behavior is fundamentally different than a standard push button. NSPopUpButton is probably the most prominent example. It displays a list of items that the user can select from. When an item is selected, it sends the action message to whichever object is the target. Although it's a different class with a different behavior, it still inherits many style options from NSButton. Figure 8-7 shows some of the styles.

---

[*] */System/Library/Frameworks/AppKit.framework/Headers/NSButton.h.*

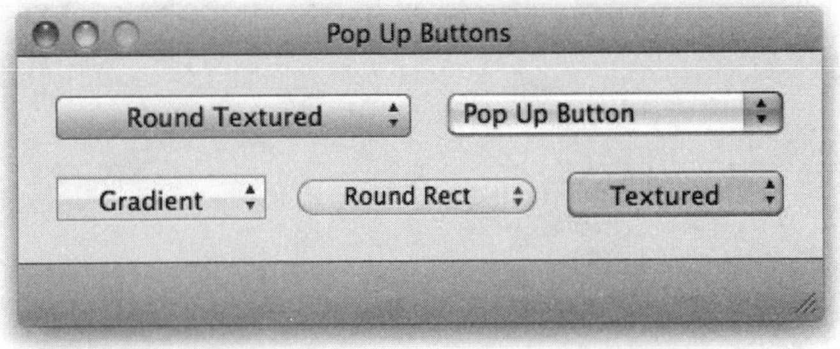

Figure 8-7 shows a window titled "Pop Up Buttons" containing buttons labeled "Round Textured", "Pop Up Button", "Gradient", "Round Rect", and "Textured".

Figure 8-7. Various styles of NSPopUpButton, a subclass of NSButton

Creating a button is as easy as dragging it out from the Library window in Interface Builder right onto your prototype window. This is a good time to try out the various button styles. Launch Interface Builder and create a new file using the Application template found under the Cocoa section of the Choose a Template dialog that appears. Next, choose Tools → Library to open the object library, then type "push button" in the search field and drag the push button out from the Library window onto the prototype window (this is the blank window labeled "Window") as shown in Figure 8-8.

 You will rarely, if ever, create a new file from within Interface Builder. That's because the Xcode project templates include the appropriate Interface Builder files (*.xib* files or *XIBs*) needed for your application. You can add more by right-clicking the Resources folder on the left side of the Xcode window, choosing Add → New File, and choosing one of the XIB templates from under Mac OS X → User Interface or iPhone OS → User Interface.

Select the button and choose Tools → Attributes Inspector (or type Command-1). In the Inspector, try selecting different options from the "Bezel" list, as shown in Figure 8-9.

In particular, try Round Textured, Round Rect, and Gradient. You can try the same thing with NSPopUpButton by searching for "pop up" in the search field. Like other classes based on NSControl, each NSButton has an NSCell. For most buttons, the cell class is NSButtonCell. For pop-up buttons, the cell is NSPopUpButtonCell. Figure 8-10 shows the relationships between all of these.

Declaring Action Methods

A control can tell you when the user does something, but you have to have an action method set up to receive that message. These are called *IBAction* methods, or simply *action methods*. Here are some possible names for action methods. You can name the

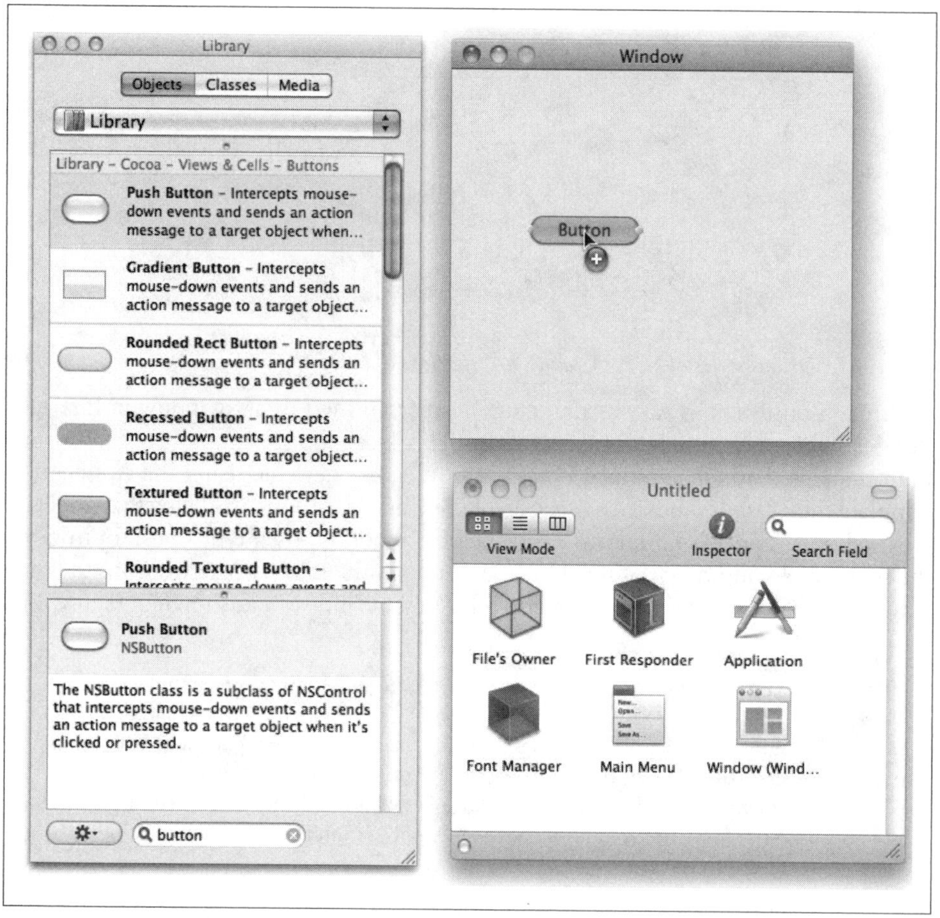

Figure 8-8. Adding a standard button to the prototype window

method anything you want, as long as the signature matches the pattern shown in the examples:

```
- (IBAction) locationFieldUpdated: (id)sender;
- (IBAction) insertObject: (id)sender;
- (IBAction) saveCurrentRecord: (id)sender;
- (IBAction) reload: (id)sender;
- (IBAction) print: (id)sender;
```

The IBAction return type is actually an alias for void. Either one will work, but using IBAction usually lets Xcode and Interface Builder know that it is a valid action method. As you'll see shortly, your IBActions will appear in a pop-up menu when you connect controls to actions. An action method also must take a single id value as input, usually called sender. In most cases, the sender variable refers to the control that the user interacted with.

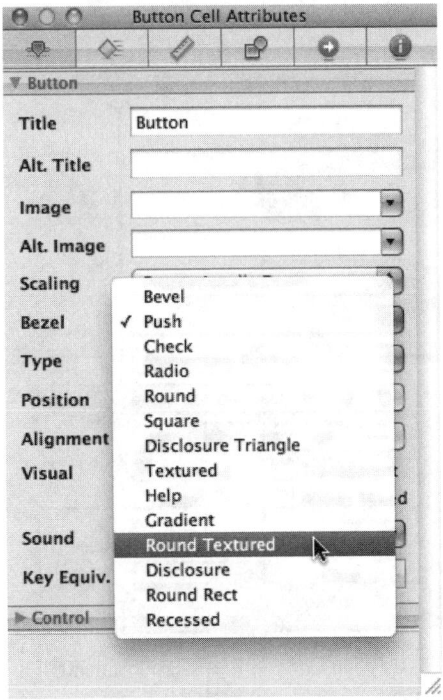

Figure 8-9. The different options for a button's appearance under "Bezel"

There's risk of confusion here, because so many of the terms for actions are similar. Let's step back and review some key items from the phrase book:

Action
> The message that a control *sends* to another object when the user interacts with it, such as when a button is clicked. Technically, you could say that an action is an instance variable that stores an Objective-C selector (a SEL variable).

Target
> The object the action is sent to. In many cases, it's an instance of one of your own classes. The target may not be the final object that receives the message—it's just the starting point.

Action method
> A method in the target's class that *receives* the action message. It must have a return type of IBAction (or void) and accept a single id object as input. The input object will usually be the control that the user interacted with. In many cases, you create the action method in one of your own classes, though some are built into standard Cocoa classes.

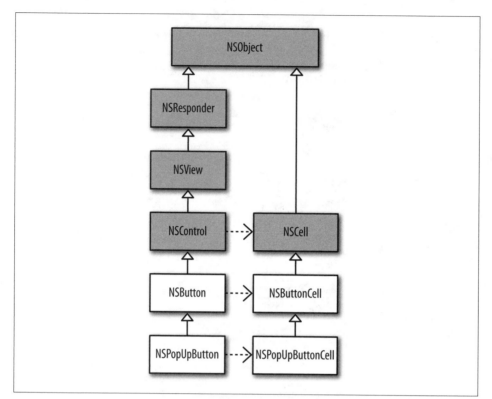

Figure 8-10. The relationship between various control and cell classes

 In AppKit, a control can send only *one* kind of action message. In iPhone's UIKit, a control can send *multiple* kinds of action message.

Connecting Actions

You can connect actions in Interface Builder by holding down the Control key and dragging from the user interface item *toward* the object that should receive the message (you are dragging in the direction of the message). The target must declare at least one IBAction method for this to work. In simple cases, the target is often your application delegate.

To help you better understand how all of this fits together, I'm going to have you put together a simple prototype project so you can learn the concepts by doing them. If you started Interface Builder earlier, quit it now (you don't need to save your work on the view you created back in "Buttons" on page 194). Then, do the following:

1. Open Xcode and create a new project based on the Cocoa Application template (under the Mac OS X template group). Name it "Application".

2. In Xcode, expand the Classes folder, open the *ApplicationAppDelegate.h* interface file, and add the following line just below the @property declaration for the window. This is the action method:

```
@interface ApplicationAppDelegate : NSObject <NSApplicationDelegate>
@property (assign) IBOutlet NSWindow *window;
- (IBAction) buttonClicked:(id)sender;
@end
```

3. Open the *ApplicationAppDelegate.m* class implementation file and add the following method just before the applicationDidFinishLaunching: method:

```
@synthesize window;

- (IBAction) buttonClicked:(id)sender {
    NSLog( @"Please do not press this button again." );
}

- (void)applicationDidFinishLaunching:(NSNotification *)note
```

4. Save both the header and implementation files.

5. Expand the Resources folder and double-click *MainMenu.xib* to open the main XIB file in Interface Builder.

6. Drag a push button from the Library to the prototype window (the window titled "Application").

Now you're ready to connect the button to an action. Control-drag from the button to the application delegate as shown in Figure 8-11. The full name of the object is truncated in the figure, but it is "Application App Delegate." This icon represents the ApplicationAppDelegate class you just edited in the Xcode project.

When you release the mouse button, a pop-up window allows you to select a method. You should see only the -buttonClicked: action method you created back in Xcode (see Figure 8-12).

Once you select an item from the list, the connection is complete, and the button will call that method whenever it's clicked. Save your work in Interface Builder, quit Interface Builder, and return to Xcode. Open the Console (Shift-Command-R), then build and run the Xcode project. When you click the button, you'll see this message in the Console:

```
Please do not press this button again.
```

You can use the same steps to try out the examples throughout this chapter, although you'll be working with different controls and different actions each time.

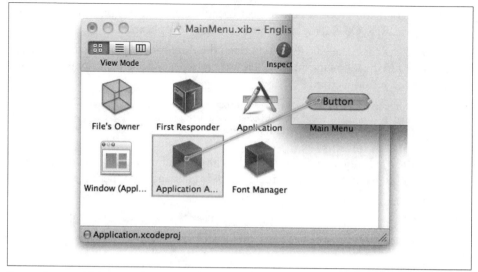

Figure 8-11. Hold down the Control key and drag from the button toward an object to connect an action

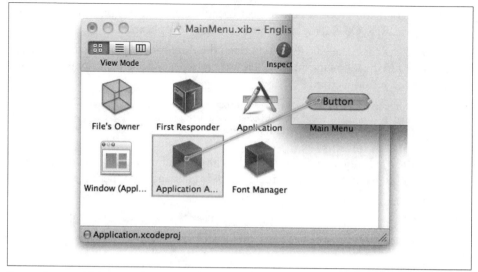

Figure 8-12. Select the method that the button should use for the action

Connecting actions from the HUD

Another way to connect actions is to right-click (or hold Control and click) on an interface item to bring up a HUD window (see Figure 8-13).†

---

† HUD is short for Heads Up Display.

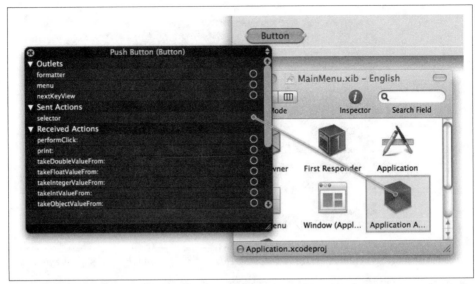

Figure 8-13. Right-click to bring up the HUD window, then drag a connection from "selector" (in the Sent Actions group) toward the target object

There are a lot of items listed in this window, including any *incoming* actions that other controls send to this button. Each can be connected to a target using the circular connection widget at the end of the row.

To connect the button's click action, you only need to use the "selector" item in the Sent Actions group. Drag a line from the *selector* connection widget *toward* the object that should receive the message (you don't need to hold the Control key when you do this). You'll be asked to select a method to complete the connection. Once the action is set, the connection widget will be filled in and the row will be highlighted (see Figure 8-14).

If you want to connect the action to a different target or method, you can just drag a new connection using the connection widget. If you want to *clear* the connection, click the small "x" icon next to the left of the target name.

Connecting actions in code

You can also connect actions in code. Usually it's better to do this in Interface Builder, because it's much easier to visualize the results, and Interface Builder will make sure you don't do something that's wildly incorrect. But if nothing else, seeing how to wire up actions in code helps you understand what happens when you drag connections between objects.

To connect an action on a control, all you need to do is set the `target` and the `action` properties. You can test the results by simulating a click in code with the

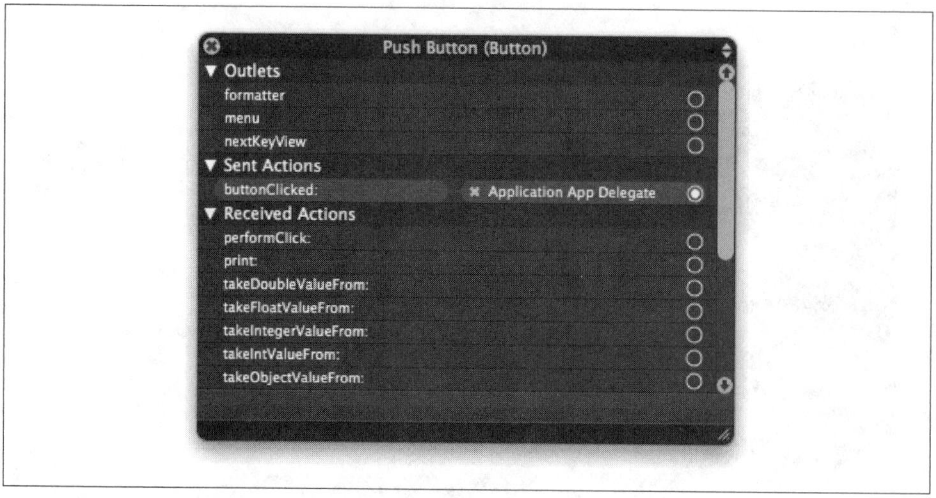

Figure 8-14. Once the action is set, the connection widget is filled in and the row is highlighted

-performClick: method. This example creates a button, adds it to the window, connects an action, and simulates a click.

To try it out yourself, add the code shown to your existing -applicationDidFinish Launching: method and add the entire -reloadDocument: method to the file as well:

```
- (void) applicationDidFinishLaunching: (NSNotification *)note {

    NSRect frame = NSMakeRect(10, 40, 90, 40);
    NSButton* pushButton = [[NSButton alloc] initWithFrame: frame];
    pushButton.bezelStyle = NSRoundedBezelStyle;
    [self.window.contentView addSubview:pushButton];

    pushButton.target = self;
    pushButton.action = @selector(reloadDocument:);

    [pushButton performClick:self];
    [pushButton release];
}


- (IBAction) reloadDocument: (id)sender {

    NSLog( @"Calling -reloadDocument: with sender: %@", sender );
}
```

> See "Basic Geometry" on page 308 for more information on NSMakeRect.

The -performClick: method itself is an action method, so it takes a sender object as input. The normal Cocoa convention when calling an action method directly is to pass in self, though some developers also use nil. Here's the result in the console:

```
Calling -reloadDocument: with sender: <NSButton: 0x100194da0>
```

Menus

The Cocoa menu system is based on the NSMenu and NSMenuItem classes. The classes are not *conceptually* complex, but they do have quite a few methods. An NSMenu is a container for NSMenuItem objects, and a menu can contain submenus. So each menu can be a *tree* of items and other submenus.

All of the basic Cocoa application templates in Xcode come with a *MainMenu.xib* file, with built-in common menus like File, Edit, Window, and so on. You can double-click the Main Menu icon in the document window to display it. Click on a menu name to open the menu, and select a menu item to display its properties in the Attributes Inspector (of course, the Attributes Inspector has to be open; if it is not, press Command-1). See Figure 8-15.

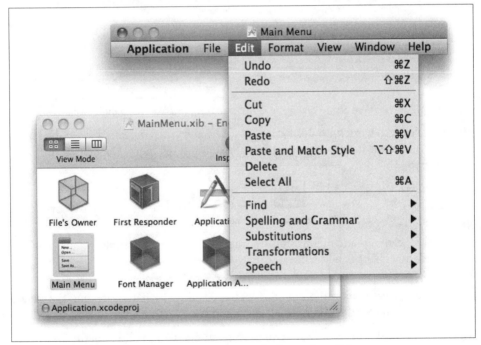

Figure 8-15. Double-click on the Main Menu icon to display it, then click on a menu name

You can add menus or menu items by dragging them out of the Library window. Just type "menu" in the search box to see all of your options, then drag one over to the menu bar (see Figure 8-16).

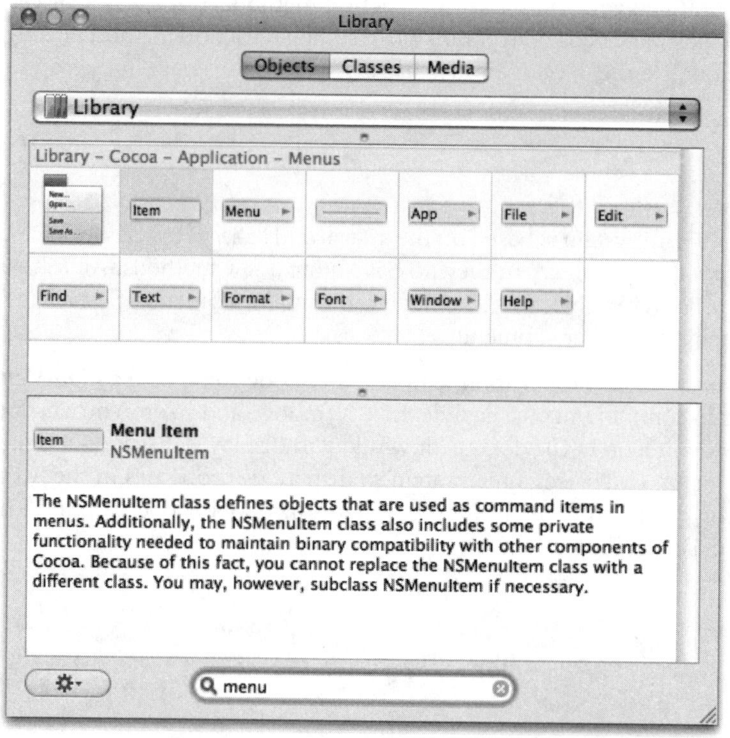

Figure 8-16. You can drag menus and menu items from the Library window into the menu bar

Menus are easy to work with in Interface Builder, and you can learn a lot of the basics just by adding some items to the menu bar and rearranging them. Here are some things you can try:

Rename items

Rename menu and menu items by double-clicking them and typing in a new name.

Rearrange items

Rearrange menus and menu items by dragging them to different locations. You can reverse any changes with Undo.

Remove items

You can delete menus and menu items by selecting them and pressing the Delete key. You can also drag them off of the menu bar to remove them.

Menus have built-in support for key equivalents, such as Command-S for the Save menu item. Setting the equivalents is simple. Just select a menu item and bring up the Attributes tab of the Inspector (Command-1). Select the Key Equivalent box and type a key shortcut that you want to use for the menu (see Figure 8-17).

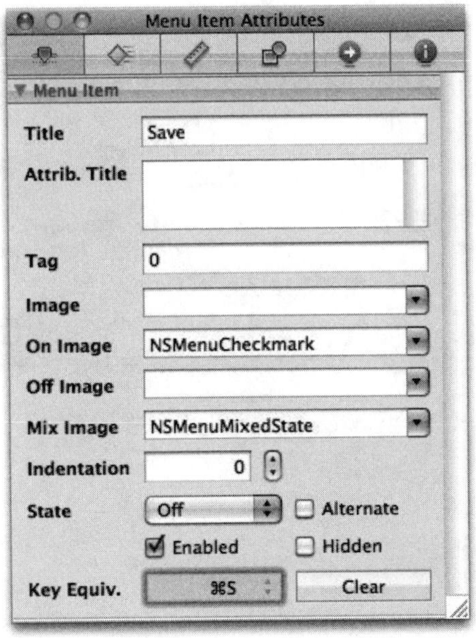

Figure 8-17. Click the Key Equivalent box and type a key shortcut for the menu item

The easiest way to set up a key shortcut for your application is to create a menu item and assign a key equivalent to it. You don't need to write any code to do it, and Cocoa will handle all of the details for you.

Menu items work like buttons, but they're not actually views—both `NSMenu` and `NSMenuItem` inherit directly from `NSObject`.‡ Just like with buttons, you can assign actions for menu items by holding Control and dragging from the item toward the target, or you can right-click on the menu item to bring up the HUD window (see Figure 8-18).

> Even though `NSMenu` and `NSMenuItem` are not views, a menu item can *contain* a view. This allows you to embed specialized controls in your menus, similar to the Label color control in the Finder's contextual menus.

However, there's one key difference. The actions in menus have to be sent to different places, depending on what the user is doing. Cocoa's solution to this is the responder chain.

---

‡ This is a great example of Cocoa's "shallow class hierarchy" in action. You don't have to climb up an inheritance tree to figure out how the class works.

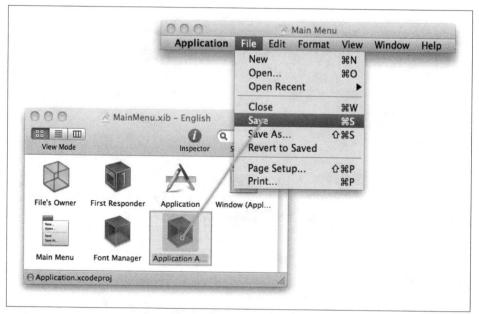

Figure 8-18. Drag a connection from the menu item to a target

Responder Chain

Some actions need to be sent to different targets based on what the user is doing at the moment. If the application has three text fields in two separate windows, and they all implement the -copy: action method, which one do you connect the Copy menu item to? If you send the action to the *responder chain*, Cocoa will figure that out for you as the program is running.

The responder chain itself isn't an actual class but a convention (see Figure 8-19). When an action message is sent into the chain, Cocoa checks with a series of objects (following a specific search path) to see if they implement the method. The first object that *does* implement the method receives the message.

The first object in the chain is the called the *first responder*, and it's usually the last control that the user clicked on and that currently has focus. Each window has its own first responder so that focus is maintained even when switching between windows and applications. Many controls draw a colored border—called a *focus ring*—when they're the first responder (see Figure 8-20).

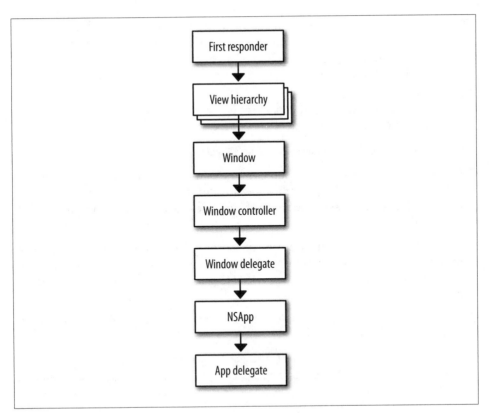

Figure 8-19. The responder chain

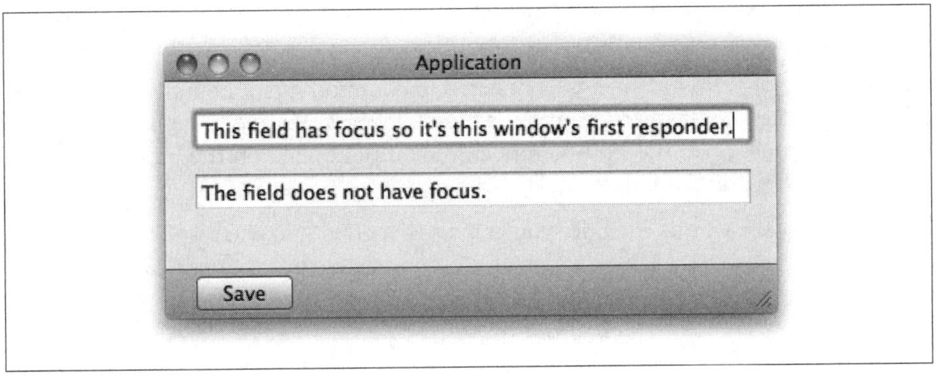

Figure 8-20. The text field with focus is the current "first responder" in this window

`NSResponder` has a few methods that make all of this work. Keep in mind that these are not steps in the search, just a list of methods related to the responder chain:

```
- (BOOL) acceptsFirstResponder; ❶
- (BOOL) becomeFirstResponder;
- (BOOL) resignFirstResponder;

- (NSResponder *) nextResponder; ❷
- (void) setNextResponder:(NSResponder *)aResponder;

- (BOOL) tryToPerform:(SEL)anAction with:(id)anObject; ❸
```

❶ Cocoa will ask a control if it's willing to be the first responder. The control returns YES from -`acceptsFirstResponder` if it's *ever* willing to be first responder. If so, Cocoa will call -`becomeFirstResponder` when the user selects the control, and the control will return YES to confirm.

When the user clicks on another control, Cocoa will call -`resignFirstResponder` on the previous control, which returns YES if it's ready to resign first responder status. The control can return NO if the user needs to provide a critical piece of data before doing something else.

❷ Each responder object in the chain knows what the *next* responder is. You usually don't have to set this manually.

❸ Each object in the chain calls -[`NSResponder tryToPerform:with:`] on the next responder to see if it implements the selector. If it does, the method is called and the search is complete. Otherwise, the action message is relayed to the next object in the chain and -`tryToPerform:with:` is called again.

If you want to send an action to the responder chain, drag a connection from the control or menu item to the First Responder icon in the Interface Builder document window.

If you right-click on the First Responder icon, you'll see a very long list of built-in actions. Many of them are already connected to common menu items by default. For example, you can hover over the -`copy:` action and the Copy menu item will be highlighted (you must open the Edit menu before you right-click on the First Responder icon for this to work; see Figure 8-21).

If you need to set actions in code, you can send actions into the responder chain by setting the target to `nil`. This code creates a menu item, but it doesn't add it to any menu, so it remains invisible (but still active):

```
NSMenuItem* menuItem = [[NSMenuItem alloc] init];

menuItem.title  = @"Copy";
menuItem.target = nil;
menuItem.action = @selector(copy:);

[menuItem release];
```

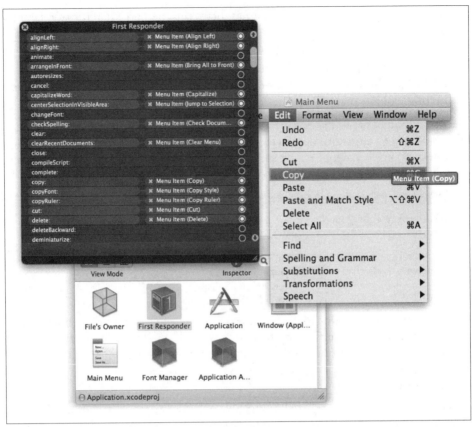

Figure 8-21. The long list of built-in actions for First Responder; hover over the -copy: action to highlight the Copy menu item

 Knowing how to create menus in code can be useful if you want to populate items as the program is running. For example, a plug-in may be able to provide additional menu items once it's loaded.

Two meanings of first responder

There's a subtle but important point here. The NSWindow class and Interface Builder use the term "first responder" slightly differently. In addition to the methods it inherits from the NSResponder superclass, NSWindow adds two of its own responder methods:

```
- (NSResponder *)firstResponder;
- (BOOL)makeFirstResponder:(NSResponder *)aResponder;
```

1. In code, calling -[NSWindow firstResponder] always returns the NSResponder object in the window that currently has focus, which means it's the first object *that has a chance to respond* to an action *at the time you call the* -firstResponder *method.* If

there's a control in the window that has focus, this method will return a reference to it.

2. In Interface Builder, the First Responder *icon* represents the responder chain. In other words, it is the object in the chain *that will respond* to an action *whenever that action is sent*. This icon does not represent a specific class or object; it's a stand-in for the object that will be selected from the responder chain.

The distinction between the two is razor-thin. The difference is that if you try to set a menu or control's target (in code) to the result of -firstResponder, you will end up with some very strange behavior because the action will *always* go to that object, even when it no longer has focus. I can't think of a reason you would ever want to do this:

```
NSMenuItem* menuItem = [[NSMenuItem alloc] init];

menuItem.title  = @"Save";
menuItem.action = @selector(save:);

// INCORRECT. does not use the responder chain.  :(
menuItem.target = self.window.firstResponder;

[menuItem release];
```

If you connect a menu action to the First Responder *icon* in Interface Builder (or set the target to nil in code), the action will be sent into the responder chain, *starting with the object that has focus at the time the menu is clicked*. This is what you should do:

```
// CORRECT! will use the responder chain.  :)
menuItem.target = nil;
```

One interesting point is that not all of the objects in the responder chain inherit from NSResponder. As strange as it sounds, that's actually what you want, because action methods are usually not sent to other controls. This might be the most important thing you will read in this chapter, so I'm going to repeat it with slightly different wording to make sure you really have it.

Take-away point: The -[NSWindow firstResponder] method returns the NSResponder object that currently has focus, usually an NSView, NSControl, or NSWindow. The First Responder *icon* in Interface Builder allows you to send actions to objects in the responder chain, and not all of the objects in the chain are NSResponder objects. This is important, because action methods are usually not sent from one control to another.

Here's an example of how the -[NSWindow firstResponder] method works. The contentView property is the root view in a window. All of the views in a window are in the content view or one of its subviews. You can add this code to any method in your application, such as in the application delegate's -applicationDidFinishLaunching: method:

```
NSWindow* myWindow = [[NSWindow alloc] init];
NSButton* myButton = [[NSButton alloc] init];
[myWindow.contentView addSubview:myButton];
[myButton release];
```

```
NSLog (@"firstResponder: %@", myWindow.firstResponder);

[myWindow makeFirstResponder:myButton];
NSLog (@"firstResponder: %@", myWindow.firstResponder);

[myWindow makeFirstResponder:nil];
NSLog (@"firstResponder: %@", myWindow.firstResponder);

[myWindow release];
```

Here's the console output:

```
firstResponder: <NSWindow: 0x100123a90>
firstResponder: <NSButton: 0x10016b870>
firstResponder: <NSWindow: 0x100123a90>
```

The first responder for a window is initially the NSWindow object itself. You can make a control the first responder by passing it into -[NSWindow makeFirstResponder:], and you can set it back to the window by passing in nil instead.

Cocoa usually handles this whole process automatically, but there some cases where you may want to do it in code. Setting the first responder to nil will commit any pending changes in a text field, which is especially important to do before saving a document or when switching between panes in a tab view. You want to make sure all of the user's typing has been "locked in" before saving or switching to another tab.

Pop-up Buttons

NSPopUpButton behaves like a cross between a button and a menu, but it's technically a subclass of NSButton. You can work with pop-up items purely as title strings, or you can use the actual NSMenuItem objects.

To add an item to a pop-up button in Interface Builder, double-click the button to display the menu, then drag in an NSMenuItem from the Library window. You can also select an existing item and press Command-D to duplicate it. Once you've added an item, double-click it to set the name. You connect a pop-up button action the same way you do for other buttons, using Control-drag or by bringing up the HUD window by right-clicking the button.

When the user selects an item, the pop up sends its action message to the target. You can then ask the pop up for the -selectedItem, -indexOfSelectedItem, or -titleOfSelectedItem to know which one the user chose. Here's the code for a method that responds to a pop-up button action, which you can add to your application delegate's implementation (.m) file:

```
- (IBAction) imageFormatPopUpDidChange: (id)sender {

    NSLog( @"selected item:  %@", [sender selectedItem] );
    NSLog( @"selected index: %i", [sender indexOfSelectedItem] );
    NSLog( @"selected title: %@", [sender titleOfSelectedItem] );
}
```

You'll also need to add the declaration to your application delegate's interface (*.h*) file:

```
- (IBAction) imageFormatPopUpDidChange: (id)sender;
```

 For the rest of the examples in this chapter, I'll just show you the method implementation. You can derive the declaration needed for the interface file from the first line of the method implementation.

Then I just need to connect the pop-up button's action to the class that implements the action method (see Figure 8-22).

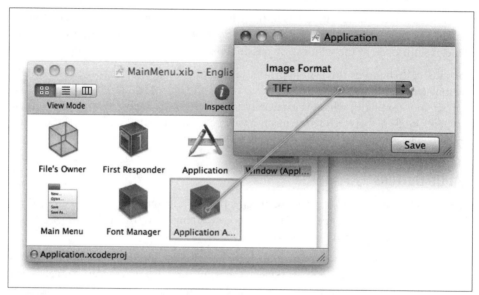

Figure 8-22. Connecting the pop-up button's action to a target

 When adding a new action method, you must add the method declaration and implementation and save both files in Xcode first. Once you've done that, you can switch back to Interface Builder to connect a control to the action method in the XIB file (in this case, *MainMenu.xib*). Interface Builder automatically reloads the list of methods when you save the files in Xcode.

When I run the application, I select an item from the pop up (see Figure 8-23).

In the console, I see this result:

```
selected item:   <NSMenuItem: 0x10012aa90 PNG>
selected index: 0
selected title: PNG
```

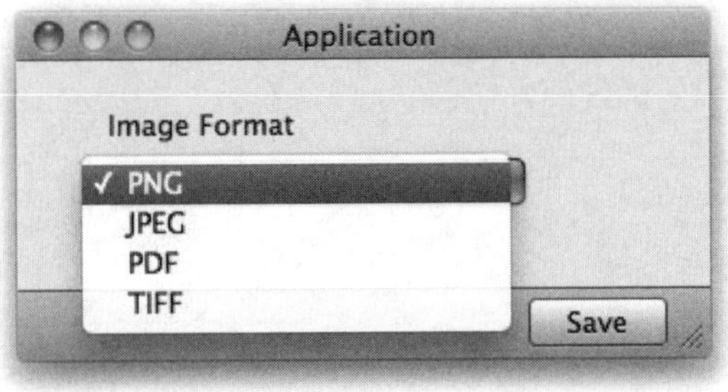

Figure 8-23. Selecting an item from the pop-up button

You can also add, remove, and edit pop-up button items directly in code. Here's an example of creating the same pop up in code, making several changes to it. Notice the difference between -[NSPopUpButton itemArray], which returns an array of NSMenuItem objects and -[NSPopUpButton itemTitles], which returns NSString objects. You won't be able to interact with this pop up, because I remove all of its items at the end of this program:

```
NSRect frame = NSMakeRect(10, 40, 120, 40);
NSPopUpButton* popUpButton = [[NSPopUpButton alloc] initWithFrame:frame];
[self.window.contentView addSubview:popUpButton];

[popUpButton addItemWithTitle: @"PNG"];
[popUpButton addItemWithTitle: @"JPEG"];
[popUpButton addItemWithTitle: @"PDF"];
[popUpButton addItemWithTitle: @"TIFF"];
NSLog(@"popUpButton itemArray:  %@", popUpButton.itemArray);
NSLog(@"popUpButton itemTitles: %@", popUpButton.itemTitles);

[popUpButton removeItemWithTitle: @"JPEG"];
NSLog(@"popUpButton itemTitles: %@", popUpButton.itemTitles);

[[popUpButton itemWithTitle: @"TIFF"] setTitle:@"M4V"];
NSLog(@"popUpButton itemTitles: %@", popUpButton.itemTitles);

[popUpButton removeAllItems];
NSLog(@"popUpButton itemTitles: %@", popUpButton.itemTitles);

[popUpButton release];
```

Here's the output in the console:

```
popUpButton itemArray:  (
    "<NSMenuItem: 0x1001628c0 PNG>",
    "<NSMenuItem: 0x100162b10 JPEG>",
    "<NSMenuItem: 0x100162bd0 PDF>",
    "<NSMenuItem: 0x100162d70 TIFF>"
)
popUpButton itemTitles: (
    PNG,
    JPEG,
```

```
            PDF,
            TIFF
    )
    popUpButton itemTitles: (
            PNG,
            PDF,
            TIFF
    )
    popUpButton itemTitles: (
            PNG,
            PDF,
            M4V
    )
    popUpButton itemTitles: (
    )
```

Sliders

Like buttons, sliders send action messages when the user interacts with them. Once the action message is sent, the target object usually asks the slider for its `floatValue`, which represents the current position of the knob. You can create a slider by opening Interface Builder and searching for "slider" in the Library window (see Figure 8-24).

Once you've added the slider to the window, you can select it and bring up the Attributes Inspector. This allows you to set the minimum and maximum values (see Figure 8-25).

When the slider knob is all the way to the right, the `-[NSSlider floatValue]` method will return the maximum value. When the knob is all the way to the left, `-[NSSlider floatValue]` will return the minimum value. You can also set the values in code with the `-setMinValue:` and `-setMaxValue:` methods. In general, though, it's better to just do this in Interface Builder. Here's a sample action method implementation:

```
- (IBAction) sliderDidChange:(id)sender {

    NSLog( @"sender: %@", sender );
    NSLog( @"sender value: %2.f%%", [sender floatValue] );
}
```

Switch back to Xcode and add that method to the app delegate implementation file (and the corresponding declaration to its interface file). Don't forget to save your work in Xcode before you Control-drag from the slider to the application delegate. When I drag the slider knob around, I see output like this in the console:

```
sender: <NSSlider: 0x100416e60>
sender value: 73.97%
sender: <NSSlider: 0x100416e60>
sender value: 100.00%
sender: <NSSlider: 0x100416e60>
sender value: 0.00%
sender: <NSSlider: 0x100416e60>
sender value: 24.48%
```

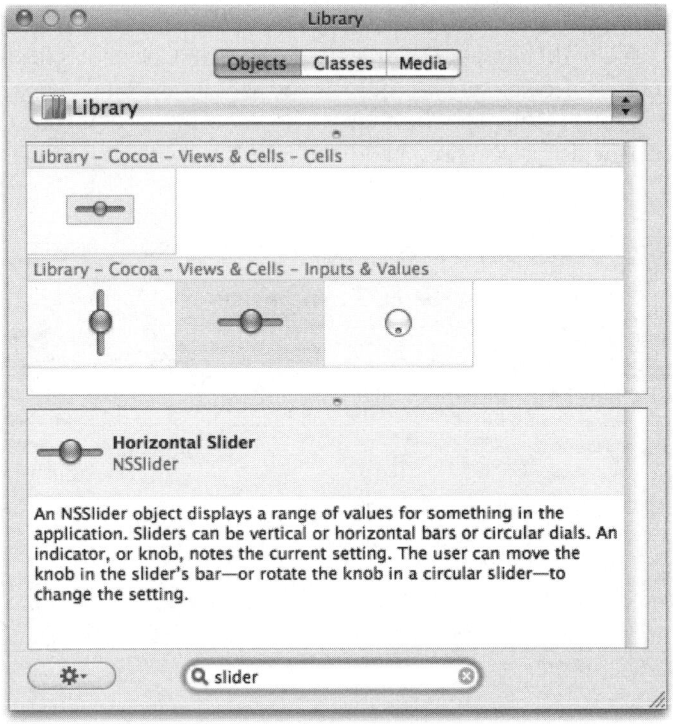

Figure 8-24. Search for "slider" in the Interface Builder Library window

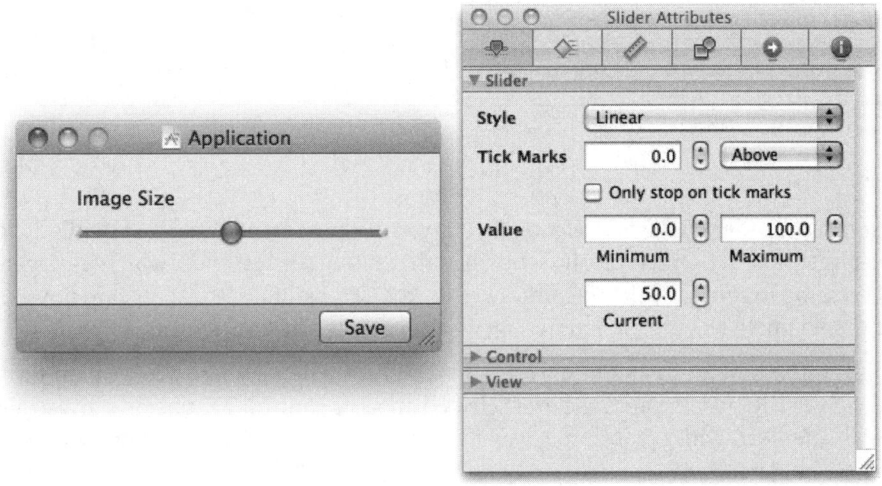

Figure 8-25. Use the Attributes Inspector to set the minimum and maximum values

Text Fields

NSTextField is one of the most commonly used classes in Cocoa. It's flexible and easy to use, so you rarely need to subclass it. It can be used as an editable text field, or just as a label for another control. The drawing is done by an embedded instance of NSTextFieldCell (which is also used in other controls; see Figure 8-26).

Figure 8-26. Search for "text field" in the Interface Builder Library window

Just like the other controls I've shown you, you connect an editable text field's action to a target. The action is typically sent when the editing session ends, which is triggered by pressing Return, or selecting another control (see Figure 8-27). You can, however, set the text field to send an action *only* when the user presses Return.

This is important for cases like a web browser location field, where you wouldn't want to load the URL just because the user selected another control. Text fields can also have *placeholder text*, which is a simple way to communicate the purpose of the field to the user (see Figure 8-28).

I can just add a text field to the window and connect its action to a target. Here's the method on the target side:

```
- (IBAction) textFieldChanged:(id)sender {

    NSLog( @"sender: %@", sender );
    NSLog( @"sender text: %@", [sender stringValue] );
}
```

Switch back to Xcode and add that method to the app delegate implementation file (and the corresponding declaration to its interface file). Don't forget to save your work in Xcode before you Control-drag from the text field to the application delegate. When I type text in the text field and press Return, I see this in the console:

```
sender: <NSTextField: 0x10011ffe0>
sender text: I'm stuck in a text field.
```

Figure 8-27. By default, leaving the text field or pressing Return causes a text field to send its action message, but you can choose to have the action message sent only when Return is pressed

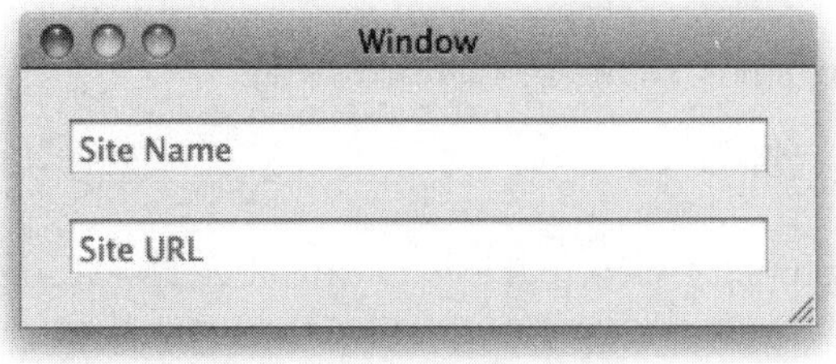

Figure 8-28. Placeholder text indicates the purpose of a text field to the user

Outlets

All of the previous examples in this chapter rely on the **sender** input variable of an action method. That is, you can call methods only on the control that the user clicked on. However, there are many cases where you want to keep a persistent reference to a control. For example, you may want to allow the user to click a button that changes the contents of a text field. You couldn't set the value of the text field using **sender** in that case, because it would refer to the button.

To keep a reference to something, you usually allocate an object and assign it to an instance variable. But when you add user interface elements to your application using Interface Builder, the objects are loaded automatically when the application starts up. You can create references to those objects in code using *outlets*. Outlets are simply variables that are assigned values by Cocoa at runtime. You start by defining an IBOutlet property in your class header (such as your application delegate):

```
@property (retain) IBOutlet NSTextField* mainTextField;
```

Then add a **synthesize** statement in the implementation file:

```
@synthesize mainTextField;
```

In Interface Builder, right-click on the object (such as the application delegate) with the IBOutlet to bring up its HUD window. The IBOutlet properties are listed under the Outlets section in the HUD. Drag a connection *from the outlet toward the view it should be connected to* (see Figure 8-29).

Now you can call methods on the outlet in your code, even if it wasn't the one that sent the action message. For example, I'll add this action method to my class header:

```
- (IBAction) populateTextField:(id)sender;
```

I'll use this method body in the class implementation file:

```
- (IBAction) populateTextField:(id)sender {

    NSDateFormatter* formatter = [[NSDateFormatter alloc] init];
    [formatter setDoesRelativeDateFormatting: YES];
    [formatter setDateStyle: NSDateFormatterLongStyle];
    [formatter setTimeStyle: NSDateFormatterShortStyle];

    NSDate* now = [NSDate date];
    NSString* formattedDate = [formatter stringFromDate:now];
    self.mainTextField.stringValue = formattedDate;

    [formatter release];
}
```

The **mainTextField** property refers to the text field outlet, and **stringValue** is a property on **NSTextField**. This method assigns a formatted version of the current date to the text field. Finally, I connect the button's action to the **-populateTextField:** method (see Figure 8-30).

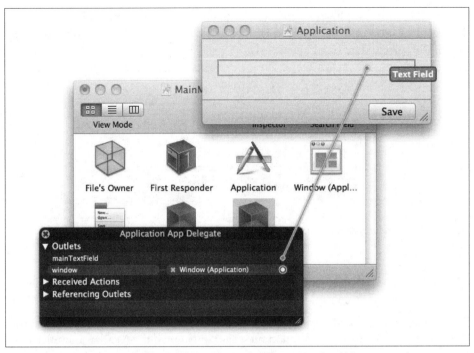

Figure 8-29. Drag a connection from the outlet toward the view it should be connected to

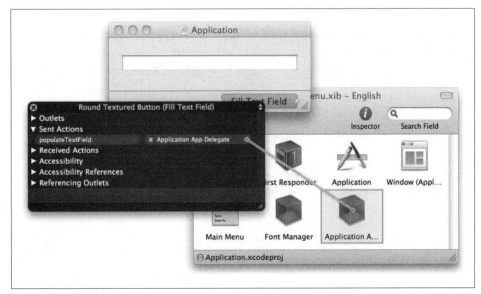

Figure 8-30. Connect the button's action to the target's action method

I build and run the application, then click the button in the main window. This calls the -populateTextField: method, which populates the text field with a formatted version of the current date (see Figure 8-31).

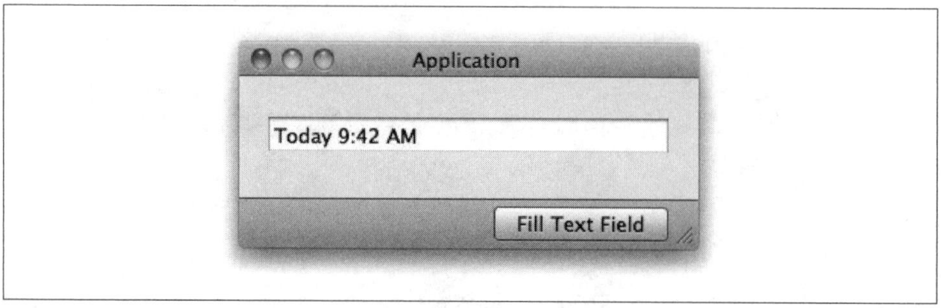

Figure 8-31. The date appears in the text field after I click the button

Outlets can refer to any object, though they're most useful for onscreen controls or other items in the XIB file. Sometimes it's helpful to use the value of the sender to decide what value to set on a control referenced by an outlet.

For this example, I've added a slider control and two text labels to a standard window. By default, most controls send action messages only when the user has completed an action, such as releasing the mouse button. In this case, I want the slider to continuously send action messages as the user is dragging the knob in the slider. I select the slider in the window and open the Attributes Inspector. I click the Continuous checkbox under the Control section in the Inspector (see Figure 8-32).

I then add an IBOutlet property for the text field on the right side of the window, as well as the declaration for the slider's action method:

```
@interface ApplicationAppDelegate : NSObject <NSApplicationDelegate>

@property (assign) IBOutlet NSWindow *window;
@property (retain) IBOutlet NSTextField* sliderCompanionField;

- (IBAction) sliderDidChange:(id)sender;
```

> This interface declaration uses the 64-bit style described in "All Further Examples Assume 64-Bit" on page 114.

I then add a synthesize statement in the implementation file, along with the implementation of the action method:

```
@implementation ApplicationAppDelegate

@synthesize window;
@synthesize sliderCompanionField;
```

```
- (IBAction) sliderDidChange:(id)sender {

    NSInteger amount = [sender integerValue];
    NSString* label  = @"";

    if ( amount < 20 ) {
        label = @"Nano";
    } else if ( amount < 40 ) {
        label = @"Small";
    } else if ( amount < 60 ) {
        label = @"Regular";
    } else if ( amount < 80 ) {
        label = @"Largish";
    } else {
        label = @"Massive";
    }

    self.sliderCompanionField.stringValue = label;
}
```

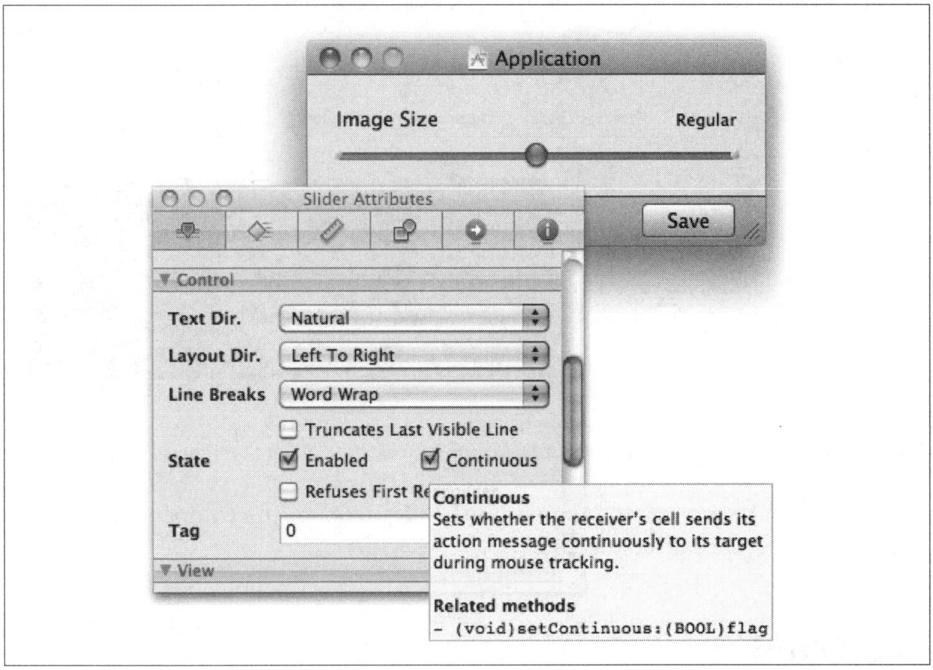

Figure 8-32. The Continuous checkbox in the Attributes Inspector instructs the control to send action messages while the user is moving the knob in the slider control

I used `integerValue` in this example because I don't need the level of precision that `floatValue` offers, and the code is slightly simpler when dealing with only whole numbers.

Finally I save all my changes in Xcode, return to Interface Builder, and connect the `sliderCompanionField` outlet to the text field, and the slider's action to the `-sliderDidChange:` action method as shown in Figures 8-33 and 8-34.

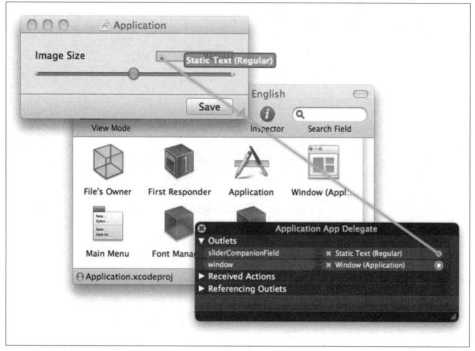

Figure 8-33. Connect the sliderCompanionField outlet to the text field at the right side of the window

Now I build and run the app. As I drag the slider around, the companion text field updates to reflect the current position (see Figure 8-35).

Datasources

Simple controls like text fields and pop-up buttons work by explicitly getting and setting values. Unless you set a new string for the text field, it won't change. Some of the more complex controls in Cocoa use a different technique: they load their data from a *datasource*.

In most cases, a datasource object can be a member of any class; often it's declared as an `id` type. It has to implement a few key methods that the view can call to load data.

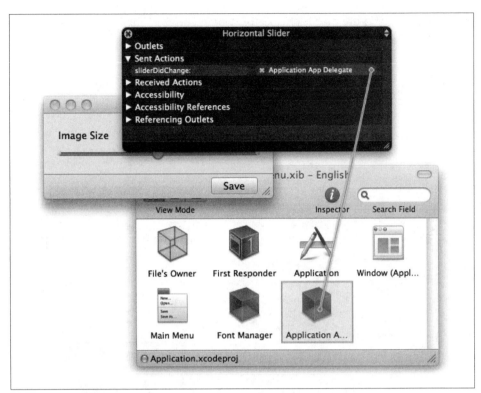

Figure 8-34. Connect the slider's action to the -sliderDidChange: action method

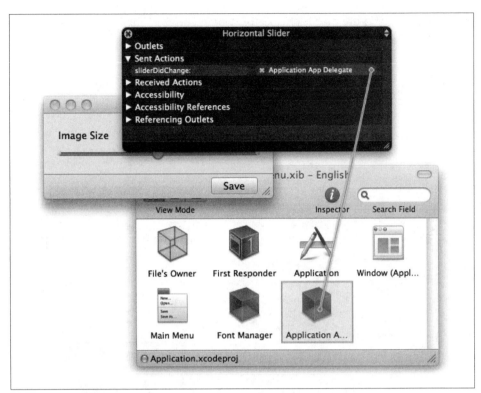

Figure 8-35. The value of the companion text field updates as you adjust the slider

In some cases, the methods are declared in a formal @protocol declaration, but sometimes they're just included as part of a category in the view's header file.

For this example, I'm going to make a mock guestbook application. If you'd like to follow along, create an Xcode project named GuestBook as described in "Connecting Actions" on page 198 and then open the *MainMenu.xib* in Interface Builder. First, I search for "table view" in the Interface Builder Library window to find the icon for NSTableView, then I drag it out onto the prototype window. I resize it so that it fills most of the window, and I use the Size Inspector (Command-3) to make sure it resizes with the window, as shown in Figure 8-36.

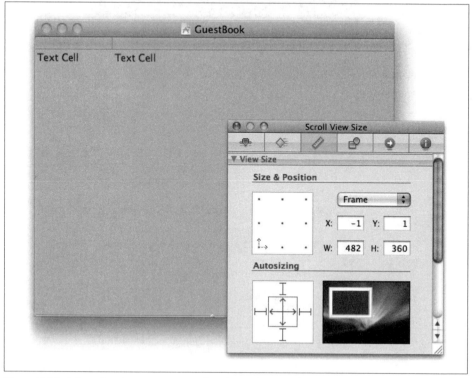

Figure 8-36. Adjust the view properties so that the application fills the window

Using the Attributes Inspector, I specify that the table should have two columns. I can double-click the column headers to set the titles: Name and Date, as shown in Figure 8-37.

I then click on the columns themselves so I can view their properties in the Attributes Inspector. I set an identifier for each column. These don't have to have the same names as the titles, but it's usually good if they're as similar as possible. Identifiers are usually lowercase, though.

 It's not always easy to select the exact view you want. To see a list of all of the views under the mouse, hold Command and Shift and right-click (or Command-Shift-Control-click) above a view. This will allow you to, for example, select the table column that is embedded in a table. You can also click on a view to select it, then hold down Command and Control and use the up or down arrow keys to go higher or lower in the view hierarchy.

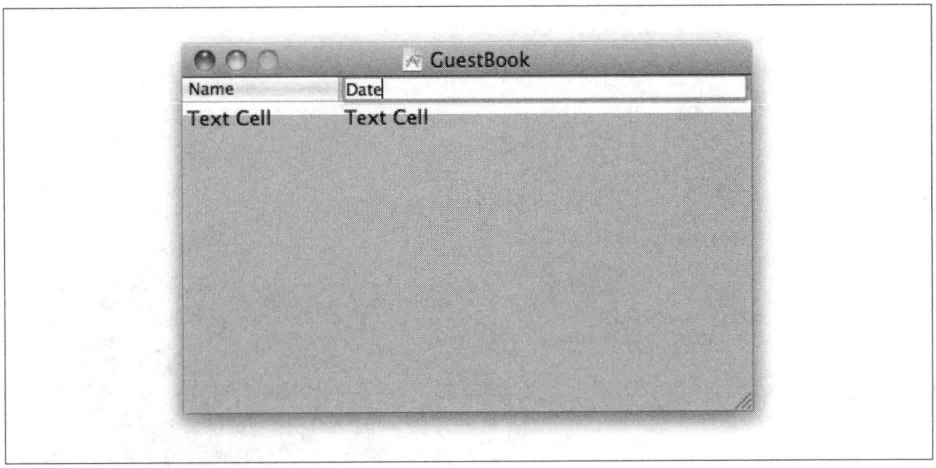

Figure 8-37. Set the table column titles

For this example, I set them to name and date. For the Date column, uncheck the Editable checkbox as shown in Figure 8-38, so that the user cannot provide his own value.

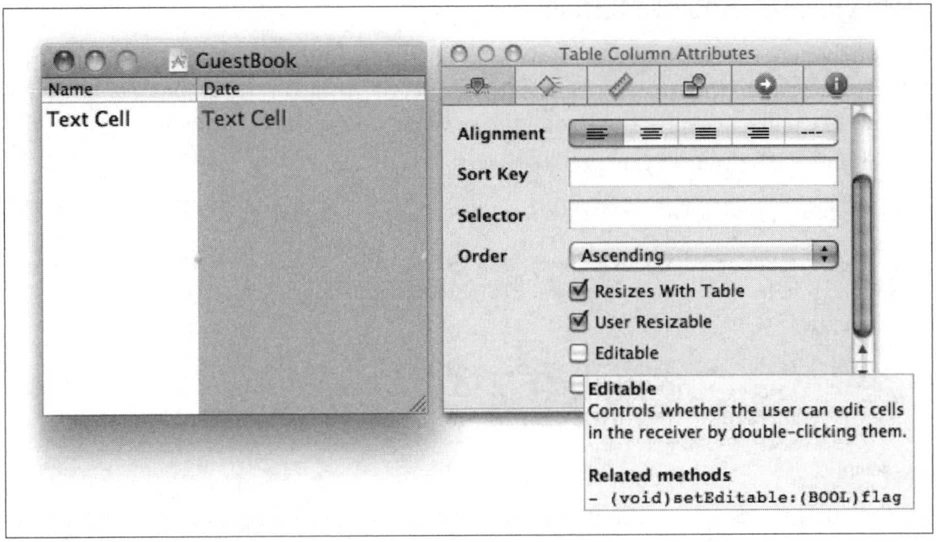

Figure 8-38. Uncheck the Editable checkbox

I then connect the table view's (Command-Shift-Control-click and choose the Table View first) datasource outlet to my application delegate (see Figure 8-39). I'm using this as the example because it's the standard class that's provided in most Cocoa project templates, but you can use any object that implements the datasource methods.

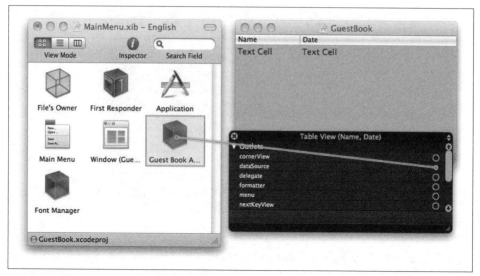

Figure 8-39. Connect the table's dataSource outlet to the Guest Book App Delegate icon

Table View Datasource Methods

The datasource methods for NSTableView are described by the NSTableViewDataSource protocol. I've taken the following methods directly from the *NSTableView.h* header file, but I've chosen a subset of the methods to introduce to you initially:

```
@protocol NSTableViewDataSource <NSObject>

- (NSInteger) numberOfRowsInTableView: (NSTableView *)table; ❶

- (id)    tableView: (NSTableView *)table ❷
          objectValueForTableColumn: (NSTableColumn *)column
          row: (NSInteger)row;

- (void) tableView: (NSTableView *)table ❸
          setObjectValue: (id)object
          forTableColumn: (NSTableColumn *)column
          row: (NSInteger)row;
@end
```

For each of these datasource methods, you're expected to either get or set a value based on the input value passed into the method. For this to work, you need some source data, but we'll get to that shortly. The table view itself is passed into each method so that a single datasource object can provide data for multiple tables. If you only have one table for each data source, you can ignore the table variable.

❶ This method returns the number of rows the table should have. For example, if you want to display a week view and have one row for each day of the week, you would return **7** here. Usually, though, you return the **count** of an array that you want to use as source data.

❷ In this method, you return a specific attribute for an object in an array. You figure out which object to use by using the value of **row** as the array index. You can determine the attribute to use by using the `-[NSTableColumn identifier]` method. This method uses the identifiers you specified in your XIB file in Interface Builder.

❸ Finally, this method receives an input value that the user typed in to save in your application's source data. For example, you might use the **row** value to find an object in an array, and then call a setter method on that object that matches the identifier, such as `person.name = object`.

The key with these methods is that you never call them directly. Instead, you wait until the table view needs the data and calls these methods. This is important, because the views that are built into Cocoa are highly optimized for the design of the framework, and can provide a much better experience for the user if she has control over when these methods are used.

The only thing you do have to do in your code is to call `-[NSTableView reloadData]` whenever the source data changes without the user's intervention. Shortly after that, the table will call the datasource methods to repopulate the rows with fresh data. You should *not* do this when the datasource methods are called.

In my experience, the most common reason a table view doesn't work is that the datasource outlet has not been connected, or it's connected to the wrong object. Make sure you connect the outlet to an object that implements these methods, and that you save the XIB file when you're done.

 Although there are many things that are similar about writing apps for Mac and apps for iPhone, iPad, and iPod touch, table views are not among them. NSTableView is a fundamentally different design than UITableView, so many of the concepts will not translate across directly.

Implementing Datasource Methods

The list of guests for the guestbook will be managed by an **NSMutableArray** and each entry in the array will be an **NSMutableDictionary**. The datasource methods will use the combination of these to provide values to the table view.

 The basic Foundation classes are great for prototyping. If I decided I wanted to make this a real shipping application with more features, I would probably create a dedicated class to represent an entry in the guestbook.

First I'll add properties for the guests array and the guestsTableView outlet. I'm also declaring an action method called -signIn: that will accept button clicks to add new guests. Add the lines shown in bold to *GuestBookAppDelegate.h*:

```
#import <Cocoa/Cocoa.h>

@interface GuestBookAppDelegate : NSObject <NSApplicationDelegate>

// outlets.
@property (assign) IBOutlet NSWindow* window;
@property (retain) IBOutlet NSTableView* guestsTableView;

// data.
@property (retain) NSMutableArray* guests;

// action methods.
- (IBAction)signIn:(id)sender;

@end
```

Save your changes to *GuestBookAppDelegate.h* and open *MainMenu.xib* in Interface Builder. Control-drag from the Guest Book App Delegate to the table view, release the mouse, and select guestsTableView from the menu.

Now I'll create a basic implementation that synthesizes the properties and provides a basic set of data. Replace the entire contents of your application delegate implementation (*GuestBookAppDelegate.m*) file with the following:

```
#import "GuestBookAppDelegate.h"

NSString* const CBNameIdentifier = @"name";
NSString* const CBDateIdentifier = @"date";

@interface GuestBookAppDelegate (Private)
+ (id) guestWithName:(NSString*)name;
- (void) setupDefaultGuests;
@end


@implementation GuestBookAppDelegate

@synthesize window;
@synthesize guestsTableView;
@synthesize guests;

- (void)applicationDidFinishLaunching:(NSNotification *)aNotification {
    [self setupDefaultGuests];
}

- (void) dealloc {
    self.guestsTableView = nil;
    self.guests = nil;
    [super dealloc];
}
```

```
// action methods.

- (IBAction)signIn:(id)sender {

    id guest = [[self class] guestWithName:nil];
    [self.guests addObject:guest];
    [self.guestsTableView reloadData];

    // edit the item we just added.
    NSInteger columnIndex = [self.guestsTableView columnWithIdentifier:@"name"];

    [self.guestsTableView editColumn: columnIndex
                                 row: [self.guests indexOfObject:guest]
                           withEvent: nil
                              select: YES];
}

// private methods.

+ (id) guestWithName:(NSString*)name {

    if ( name == nil )
        name = @"New Guest";

    NSMutableDictionary* guest = [NSMutableDictionary dictionary];
    [guest setObject: name
              forKey: CBNameIdentifier];
    [guest setObject: [NSDate date]
              forKey: CBDateIdentifier];

    return guest;
}

- (void) setupDefaultGuests {

    id guest = [[self class] guestWithName:@"Bruce Wayne"];

    NSMutableArray* newGuests = [NSMutableArray array];
    [newGuests addObject: guest];
    self.guests = newGuests;
    [self.guestsTableView reloadData];
}

@end
```

Now I need to add the datasource methods to the implementation file (*GuestBookApp-Delegate.m*):

```
// datasource methods.

- (NSInteger) numberOfRowsInTableView:(NSTableView *)table {

    return self.guests.count;
}

- (id) tableView: (NSTableView *)table
```

```
        objectValueForTableColumn: (NSTableColumn *)column
        row: (NSInteger)row {

    NSDictionary* guest = [self.guests objectAtIndex:row];
    NSString* identifier = column.identifier;

    return [guest objectForKey:identifier];
}

- (void) tableView: (NSTableView *)table
        setObjectValue: (id)object
        forTableColumn: (NSTableColumn *)column
        row: (NSInteger)row {

    NSMutableDictionary* guest = [self.guests objectAtIndex:row];
    NSString* identifier = column.identifier;

    [guest setObject:object forKey:identifier];
}
```

The datasource methods never explicitly check what the identifier is; they just pass it directly into the dictionary as a key. The reason this works is that the values of CBNameIdentifier and CBDateIdentifier match the identifiers in the XIB file. If those don't match exactly (including the case of each letter), then the methods won't work.

All I need to do now is add a button labeled "Sign In" and connect it to the action method, as shown in Figure 8-40.

Now I build and run the application. Each time I click Sign In, a new row is added to the guestbook and I can enter the name, as shown in Figure 8-41.

The one thing that could better here is the appearance of the date column. It's a very verbose description of the date. You can improve that with an NSDateFormatter. Although you used the class in code in Chapter 7, you can also apply a formatter inside of Interface Builder. Open the Library window in Interface Builder and type "formatter" in the search box. Drag the date formatter directly onto the first text field cell in the Date column, as shown in Figure 8-42.

With the date formatter still selected, open the Attributes Inspector and set the Date and Time styles to Medium. Save the file and rerun the project. The Date column now looks much nicer (see Figure 8-43).

Bindings

Using actions and outlets works fine in many cases, but the more data and controls you have in your application, the more code you need to keep everything wired together. The more complex the interactions become, the harder it is to keep everything working properly. One way to simplify all of this is to use *Cocoa bindings*.

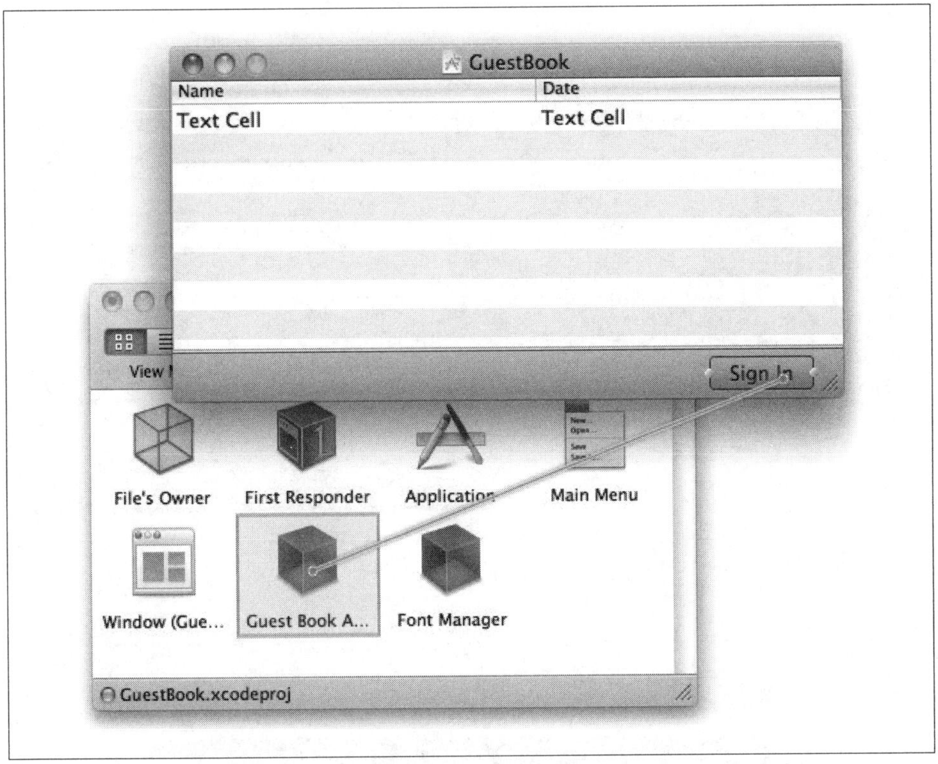

Figure 8-40. Connecting the Sign In button to the -signIn: action method

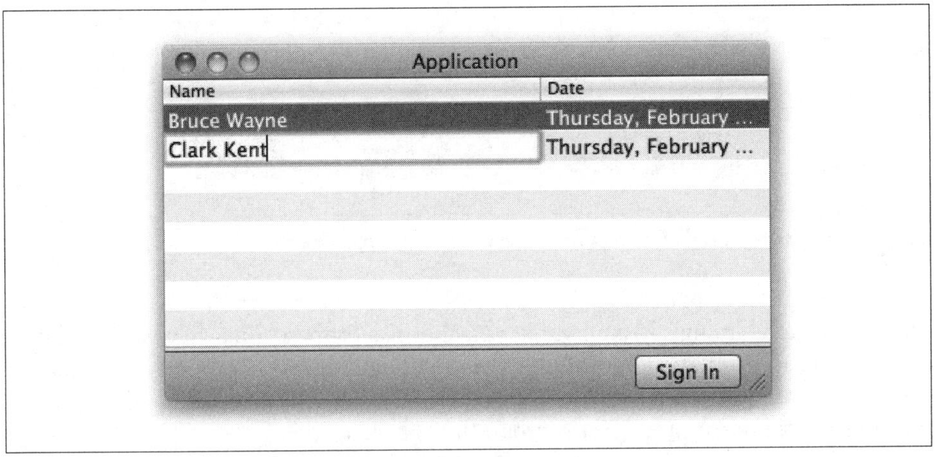

Figure 8-41. Adding a new row in the GuestBook application

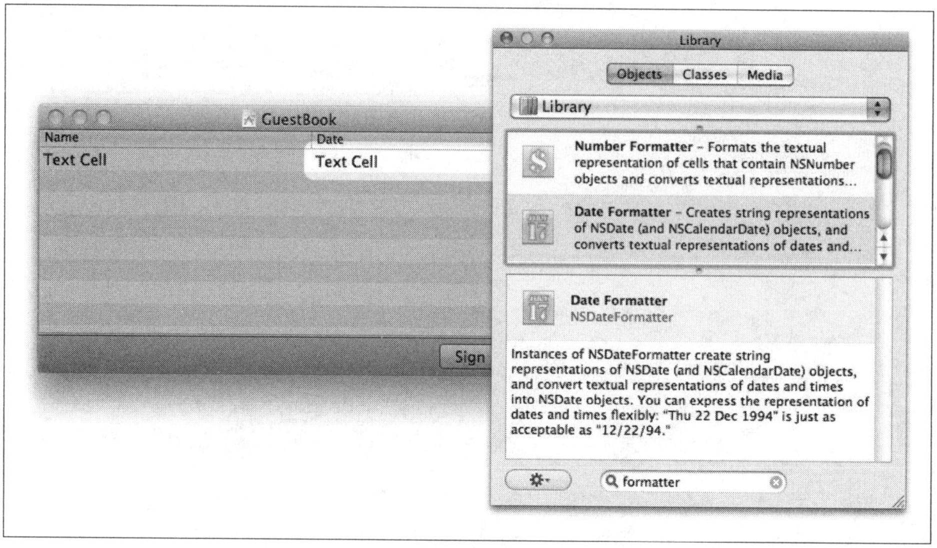

Figure 8-42. Adding an NSDateFormatter to the Date column

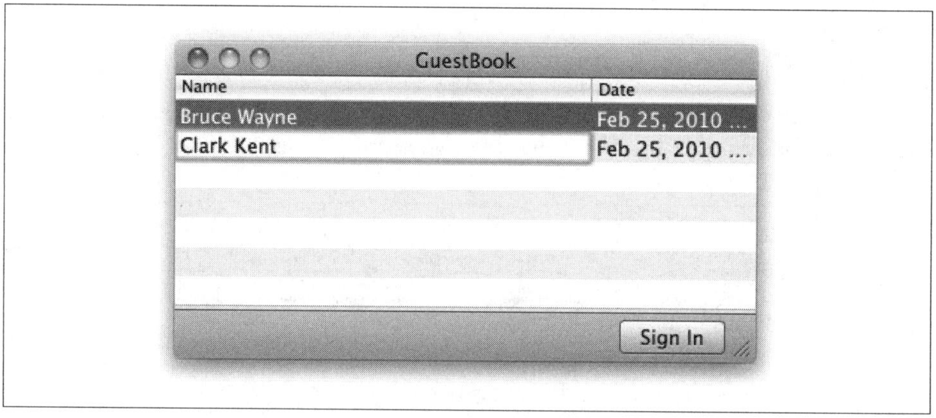

Figure 8-43. The improved Date column in the GuestBook application

The idea behind bindings is simply that you choose a property on a view and bind it to another object's property. For example, you could bind the `title` property of a window to a `documentName` property on your application delegate. Once you make this connection, Cocoa will make sure the two properties stay in sync.

You can configure bindings entirely in code, but it's more common to set them up in Interface Builder using the various subclasses of `NSController`. You can see them by opening the Library window in Interface Builder and searching for "controller" (see Figure 8-44).

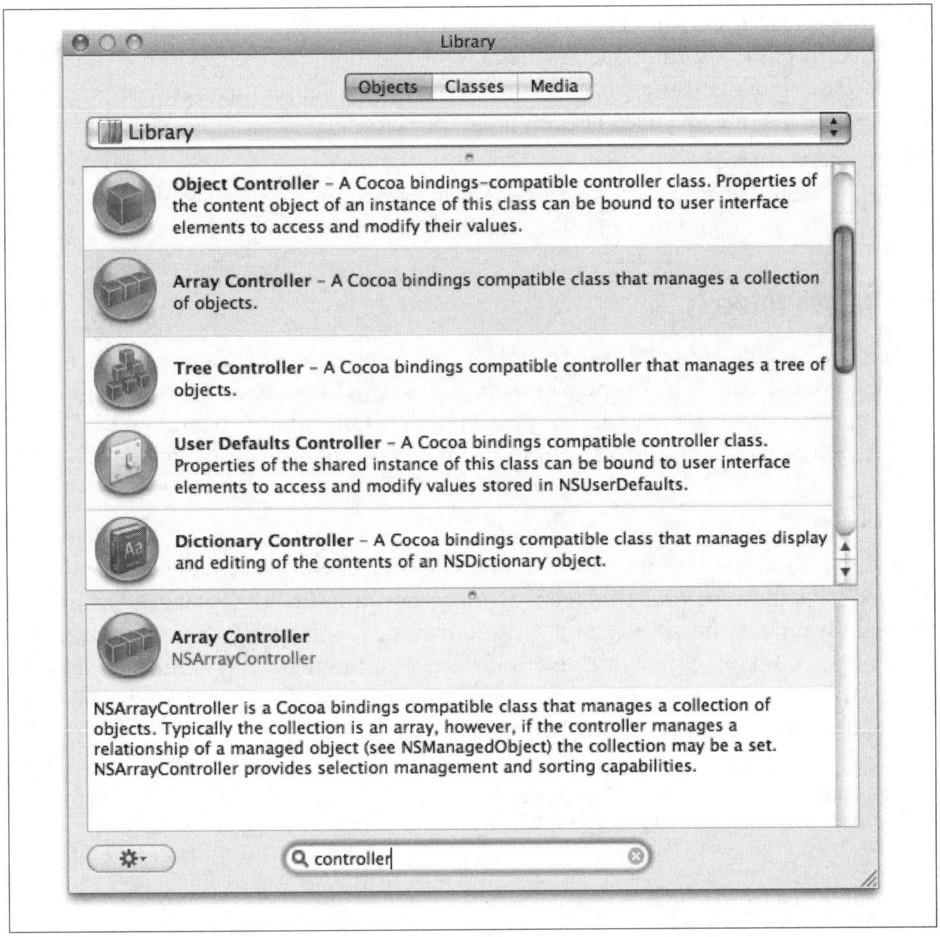

Figure 8-44. The classes that inherit from NSController

NSObjectController

> The basic controller class, which is appropriate for binding a view to a single object. For example, you could use this to bind a text field to the firstName property of a Person object.

NSArrayController

> Used for setting up bindings for views that display collections of objects, such as an NSTableView. It provides methods for adding and removing objects, managing selections, sorting, and more. You'll probably use this controller class most frequently.

NSTreeController

> Used for views that need to bind to trees of objects, such as an outline view. Use this class when you want to manage arrays of objects with parent/child relationships.

NSUserDefaultsController

> Used to bind user interface elements to application preferences. This should be used for data that is not vital to preserve, such as whether the user wishes to see a simplified or an advanced version of an interface.

NSDictionaryController

> Used to bind views to a series of key-value pairs supplied by an NSDictionary. For example, you could use this class to display a series of properties for an image.

Key-Value Protocols

The Cocoa Bindings system is supported by three protocols: *Key-Value Coding* (KVC), *Key-Value Observing* (KVO), and *Key-Value Binding* (KVB). Because this is a high-level introduction, I'm not going to describe each one in detail, but understanding Key-Value Coding will helping you in all of your Cocoa projects, not just those that use bindings.

Key-Value Coding

Although it sounds like a complex system, Key-Value Coding is actually a fairly simple protocol, at least from your perspective. In practice, it means that you can get and set values indirectly. Instead of calling specific methods, you *specify keys by name*, and Cocoa figures out *on the fly* which methods or properties match up to those keys. Key-Value Coding works with almost any class in Cocoa. It also works with your own classes. Imagine a class that looks like this:

```
@interface Person : NSObject
@property (copy) NSString* firstName;
@property (copy) NSString* lastName;
@end

@implementation Person
@synthesize firstName;
@synthesize lastName;

- (NSString*) firstName {
    NSLog( @"calling -firstName");
    return firstName;
}

- (void) setFirstName:(NSString *)newName {
    NSLog(@"calling -setFirstName:");
    [firstName autorelease];
    firstName = [newName copy];
}

- (NSString*) lastName {
    NSLog( @"calling -lastName");
    return lastName;
}

- (void) setLastName:(NSString *)newName {
```

```
        NSLog(@"calling -setLastName:");
        [lastName autorelease];
        lastName = [newName copy];
    }

    - (void) dealloc {
        [firstName release];
        [lastName release];
        [super dealloc];
    }
    @end
```

Given this class, I can now use the -setValue:forKey: and -valueForKey: methods:

```
- (void)applicationDidFinishLaunching:(NSNotification *)note {

    Person* myPerson = [[Person alloc] init];

    [myPerson setValue:@"Bob"   forKey:@"firstName"];
    [myPerson setValue:@"Smith" forKey:@"lastName"];

    // get value using KVC.
    NSLog(@"myPerson firstName: %@", [myPerson valueForKey:@"firstName"]);
    // get value using normal accessor.
    NSLog(@"myPerson lastName: %@",  myPerson.lastName);

    [myPerson release];
}
```

Here's the result in the console:

```
calling -setFirstName:
calling -setLastName:
calling -firstName
myPerson firstName: Bob
calling -lastName
myPerson lastName: Smith
```

Using KVC causes Cocoa to dynamically search for a method that matches the key you provide. In effect, this means that you can write code that's very generic, just as if your class were a dictionary. But you can still call methods directly, as well. To make the value of this more clear, let me show you what happens when I store objects in an array and use KVC methods to get values out:

```
Person* myPerson1 = [[[Person alloc] init] autorelease];
[myPerson1 setValue:@"Paul" forKey:@"firstName"];

Person* myPerson2 = [[[Person alloc] init] autorelease];
[myPerson2 setValue:@"John" forKey:@"firstName"];

Person* myPerson3 = [[[Person alloc] init] autorelease];
[myPerson3 setValue:@"George" forKey:@"firstName"];

Person* myPerson4 = [[[Person alloc] init] autorelease];
[myPerson4 setValue:@"Ringo" forKey:@"firstName"];
```

```
NSMutableArray* array = [NSMutableArray array];
[array addObject:myPerson1];
[array addObject:myPerson2];
[array addObject:myPerson3];
[array addObject:myPerson4];

NSLog( @"Names %@", [array valueForKey:@"firstName"] );
```

Here's the result in the console:

```
calling -setFirstName:
calling -setFirstName:
calling -setFirstName:
calling -setFirstName:
calling -firstName
calling -firstName
calling -firstName
calling -firstName
Names (
    Paul, John, George, Ringo
)
```

The NSArray versions of -valueForKey: and -setValue:forKey: actually call the same methods *on each item in the array*. In the case of -valueForKey:, it actually bundles up all of the returned values into a new array. This works even if the objects in the array are not all members of the same class.

Key-Value Coding is useful in many parts of Cocoa, but it's essential with Cocoa bindings. The fact that it isn't tied to a particular class means that a view can bind to the properties of any kind of object. This kind of design is called *generic programming*, and it allows you a lot more flexibility when designing your application. Generic programming means there's less tedious code, which means that your project is simpler and easier to improve.

 Key-Value Coding automatically wraps primitive values as NSNumber objects. So you can even use -valueForKey: to retrieve values from properties defined as CGFloat, NSInteger, or NSUInteger (or their standard C counterparts).

Bindings for Simple Controls

Let's put this into action. Create a new Cocoa project in Xcode called BasicBindings. Type the code from Example 8-1 into *BasicBindingsAppDelegate.h*.

Example 8-1. BasicBindingsAppDelegate.h

```
#import <Cocoa/Cocoa.h>

@interface BasicBindingsAppDelegate : NSObject <NSApplicationDelegate>

@property (assign) IBOutlet  NSWindow *window;
```

```
@property (copy)   NSString* imageTitle;
@property (assign) NSInteger imageScale;

- (IBAction) resetAllValues:(id)sender;

@end
```

 This interface declaration uses the 64-bit style described in "All Further Examples Assume 64-Bit" on page 114.

Note that there's only one action method and no outlets. You're about to see some Cocoa magic. Type the code from Example 8-2 into *BasicBindingsAppDelegate.m*.

Example 8-2. BasicBindingsAppDelegate.m

```
#import "BasicBindingsAppDelegate.h"

NSString* const CBDefaultTitle = @"New Image";
NSInteger const CBDefaultScale = 50;

@implementation BasicBindingsAppDelegate

@synthesize window;
@synthesize imageTitle;
@synthesize imageScale;

// startup and shutdown.
- (void)applicationDidFinishLaunching:(NSNotification *)note {
    [self resetAllValues:self];
}

- (void) dealloc {
    self.imageTitle = nil;
    [super dealloc];
}

// accessors (only implemented for bindings testing).
- (NSString *) imageTitle {
    NSLog( @"-imageTitle %@", imageTitle );
    return imageTitle;
}

- (void) setImageTitle:(NSString *)newTitle {
    NSLog( @"-setImageTitle: %@", newTitle );
    [imageTitle autorelease];
    imageTitle = [newTitle copy];
}

- (NSInteger) imageScale {
    NSLog( @"-imageScale %i", imageScale );
    return imageScale;
```

```
}

- (void) setImageScale:(NSInteger)newScale {
    NSLog( @"-setImageScale: %i", newScale );
    imageScale = newScale;
}


// action methods.
- (IBAction) resetAllValues:(id)sender {
    self.imageTitle = CBDefaultTitle;
    self.imageScale = CBDefaultScale;
}

@end
```

Save the files and press Command-B to make sure that everything builds correctly. Now double-click *MainMenu.xib* (as with the other projects, it's in the *Resources* folder in the Xcode project) to open it in Interface Builder. Double-click the window icon to display it, then use items from the Library to create a user interface like the one shown in Figure 8-45.

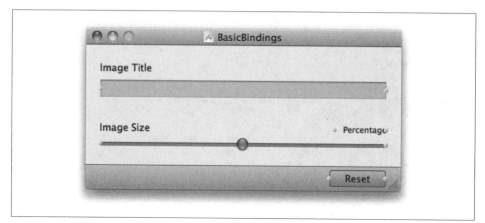

Figure 8-45. Add controls from the Library to create a window as shown here

The key pieces are an NSTextField (text field), an NSSlider (horizontal slider), and an NSButton (push button). You'll also need three uneditable label text fields. The only essential label is the one titled "Percentage." The other two are optional. You need to connect only one action. Control-drag from the Reset button to Basic Bindings App Delegate, and connect it to the -resetAllValues: action method. (To get the gray border at the bottom, click on Window in the *MainMenu.xib* window, open the Size Inspector with Command-3, and select Large Bottom Border from the Content Border pop-up menu.)

If you need additional help adding these controls to the window, go back to the earlier parts of the chapters that introduced NSButton, NSSlider, and NSTextField. Be sure to set the slider to "Continuous" for maximum enjoyment from this example.

Connect the bindings

In the window titled *MainMenu.xib*, Select the Window icon and bring up the Bindings Inspector (Command-4). This panel may look a bit overwhelming, but you can handle it. Each of the items in this panel represents a different window property that you can set up a binding for. Click the disclosure triangle for Title to show the options for the Title binding.

Click the "Bind to" checkbox, and select Basic Bindings App Delegate from the "Bind to" pop-up menu. Then type imageTitle into the Model Key Path field. Figure 8-46 shows how the Inspector should look when you are done.

Figure 8-46. Setting the Title binding for the window

This establishes a binding for the window's title to the app delegate's imageTitle property. Whenever one changes, the other will get the new value. Now select the editable text field you added to the prototype window and open the Bindings Inspector with Command-4. Use the exact same settings for the text field's Value binding as you did for the window's Title binding: check the "Bind to" box, select Basic Bindings App Delegate from the "Bind to" pop-up menu, and use imageTitle for the Model Key Path.

Both the window's Title binding and the text field's Value binding are bound to the application delegate's imageTitle property. All three will stay in sync. Now, select the slider control and open the Bindings Inspector. Open the Value binding. Just as before, check the "Bind to" checkbox, and select Basic Bindings App Delegate from the pop up. This time, however, type `imageScale` in the Model Key Path field. Figure 8-47 shows how the Inspector will look when you are done.

 Make sure you use the Value binding for the slider, not Max Value or Min Value.

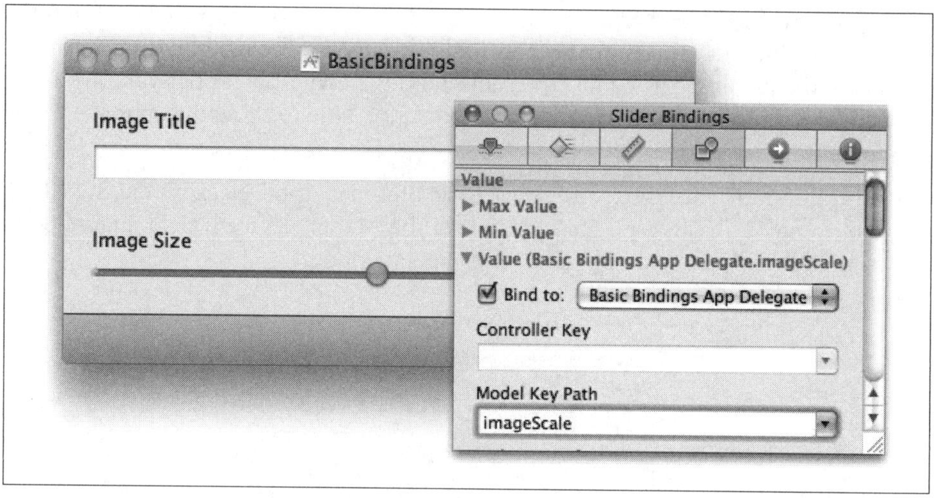

Figure 8-47. *Associate the Value binding for the slider with the application delegate's imageScale property*

There's one last binding to set up. Select the Percentage label text field and open the Bindings Inspector. This time, instead of using the Value binding, open the section in the Inspector called Value With Pattern. Open Display Pattern Value1. Check the "Bind to" checkbox as before, and select Basic Bindings App Delegate from the pop up. Type in `imageScale` for the Model Key Path. As a last step, type `%{value1}@%` in the field titled Display Pattern. This will take the value of `imageScale` and format it with a percentage sign. It's similar to the way `NSLog()` formats strings.

When you're done, right-click (or Control-click) on the blue Basic Bindings App Delegate in the *MainMenu.xib* window, and open the Referencing Bindings section. Click on the Multiple arrows to show their contents. Their contents should look like Figure 8-48.

You probably noticed that I didn't use the `NSController` classes in this example. For simple cases, it's fine to just bind directly to the application delegate or most of the other items in the XIB document window.

Figure 8-48. The active bindings in the HUD window

Run the application

Save the XIB file and switch back to Xcode. Press Command-R to build and run the application. Try typing a name into the text field and press Return. It will appear as the window's title. Drag the slider around and you'll see the Percentage field update. If you click Reset, all of the controls will go back to their default values, including the window title (see Figure 8-49).

If you take a look at the console, you'll see that the accessor methods are getting called. In effect, the views are using Key-Value Coding to get and set values for keys, which translate into calls for the accessor methods:

```
-setImageScale: 80
-imageScale 80
-setImageTitle: Sunnyvale, CA
-imageTitle Sunnyvale, CA
-setImageTitle: New Image
-imageTitle New Image
-imageTitle New Image
-setImageScale: 50
-imageScale 50
-imageScale 50
```

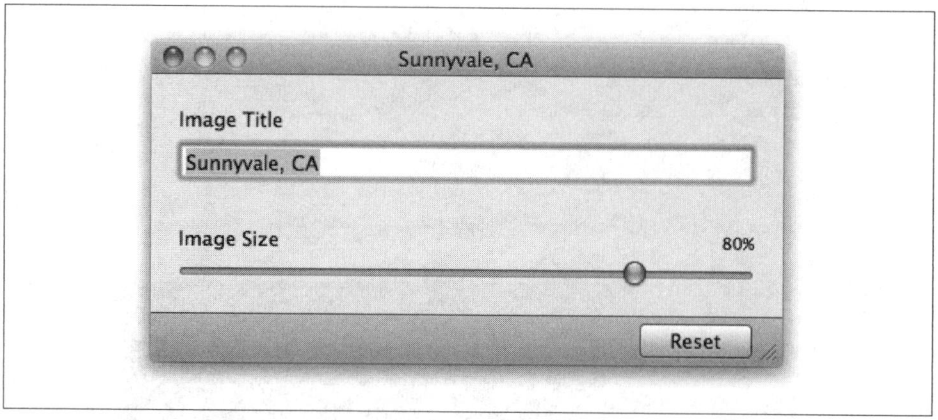

Figure 8-49. Run the application and try out the controls

Notice that all of this happened with only two properties and no outlets. There are still many cases in which you want to use outlets, but using bindings means that you can drastically simplify your code base.

You don't need to implement accessor methods to use Key-Value Coding or bindings; I just added them to help you understand how things work. You can use the versions provided by @synthesize instead. In fact, go ahead and delete the methods and rebuild the project to see whether the result is the same.

Bindings for Complex Controls

For more complex controls like NSTableView, which displays collections of objects, use the NSArrayController to set up bindings. In general, using bindings means that the datasource methods are not used. This isn't true in all cases, but conceptually an NSArrayController becomes the datasource when bindings are used for a table view.

To demonstrate this, I'm going to update the GuestBook application that I created earlier in the chapter. Reopen the project in Xcode now if you'd like to follow along. First, open *GuestBookAppDelegate.m* and delete or comment out all of the datasource methods listed in "Table View Datasource Methods" on page 226. This is optional, but I just want to prove to you that they're not needed with bindings.

Next, make the changes shown in bold to the -signIn: method. This replaces [self.guests addObject:guest] with [[self mutableArrayValueForKey:@"guests"] addObject:guest] and comments out [self.guestsTableView reloadData]:

```
- (IBAction)signIn:(id)sender {

    id guest = [[self class] guestWithName:nil];
    [[self mutableArrayValueForKey:@"guests"] addObject:guest];
    // [self.guestsTableView reloadData];
```

Comment out the same line in the -setupDefaultGuests: method:

```
- (void) setupDefaultGuests {

    id guest = [[self class] guestWithName:@"Bruce Wayne"];

    NSMutableArray* newGuests = [NSMutableArray array];
    [newGuests addObject: guest];
    self.guests = newGuests;
    //[self.guestsTableView reloadData];
```

 If you make changes directly to a mutable array, any views bound to the array will not see the changes. Instead, use the -mutableArrayValueFor Key: method, which returns an array proxy object that is bindings-aware. Any changes to this proxy object will be sent to the bound views.

Now open the *MainMenu.xib* file in Interface Builder. Bring up the HUD for the table view by Shift-Command-Control-clicking on it, selecting the Table View, then right-clicking on it. Under Outlets, click the "x" icon in the row for the dataSource property to disconnect the outlet. This step is important.

Open the Library window and search for "array controller". Drag an instance of NSArrayController to the XIB document window (the one labeled *MainMenu.xib*, not your prototype window). Select it and bring up the Bindings Inspector with Command-4. Bind the array controller's Content Array to Guest Book App Delegate with a Model Key Path of guests (see Figure 8-50).

![Array Controller Bindings inspector window showing Content Array bound to Guest Book App Delegate with Model Key Path guests]

Figure 8-50. Bind the Content Array to the application delegate's guests array property

Next, select the Name table column and bring up the Bindings Inspector. (You can Shift-Command-Control-click on the table to select a specific column.) Bind the column's Value to Array Controller with a Model Key Path of name (see Figure 8-51).

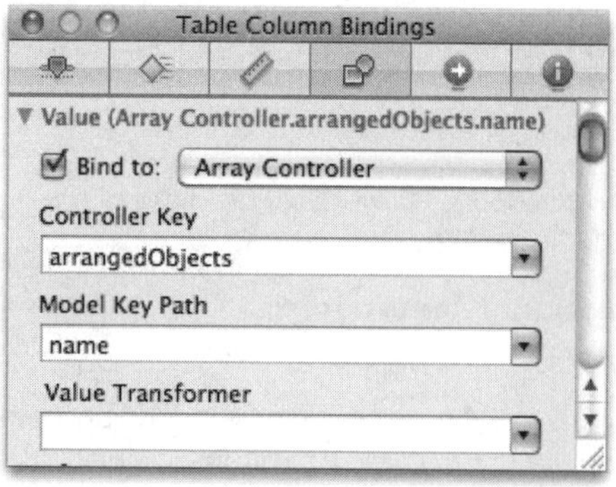

Figure 8-51. Bind the table column's value to the arrangedObjects property of the array controller, and use "name" for the Model Key Path

Do the same for the Date column, but use the Model Key Path of `date`. Save the XIB file and switch back to Xcode. You should see that the application runs the same but with half the code.

Tips for Debugging Bindings

Before we move on from bindings, I want to share with you a few key things to remember if anything doesn't work the way you intended.

Always use accessors

Bindings is based on Objective-C runtime magic that depends on you using accessor methods, especially when setting values. The setter method is what tells observers that a bound value has changed. If you change an instance variable directly, the views that are bound to that value will not get updated.

This is the single most important thing you will ever learn about debugging bindings. If something isn't working, make sure that the setter method is being used.

Method names matter

If you're implementing custom accessor methods, make sure your methods match the pattern -set<Key>: for the setter and -<Key> for the getter. So if the property is firstName, the methods *must* be called -setFirstName: and -firstName. There are some exceptions to this, but keep things simple and just use this style. If you use @synthesize to generate accessors, this is done for you automatically.

Override setters and getters to debug

Bindings uses Key-Value Coding to get and set values. If a value isn't showing up where it should, implement the getter and setter for the property and add an NSLog() statement to each. If they're not getting called, a property may be mistyped somewhere.

Always remember the Model Key Path

A very common mistake when setting up bindings is to forget to specify a Model Key Path in the Bindings Inspector. This will usually generate errors like:

```
-[BasicBindingsAppDelegate copyWithZone:]: unrecognized selector sent to instance
```

This error shows up because the binding is expecting a value that can be copied, but as no Model Key Path is specified, it tries to bind the *entire object*. In this case, the object is the application delegate, so it tries to copy the application delegate itself, which generates the `-copyWithZone:` exception.

CHAPTER 9

Designing Applications Using MVC

New Mac and iPhone programmers seem to have a set life cycle. The early part of the learning process is getting used to Objective-C and maybe some basic memory management. But that's just learning how to use your tools. The next step is figuring out how to arrange your classes and get them to talk to each other.

The first question new Cocoa programmers ask me when they get to this stage is: "How do I send data between classes?" There's no magic `sendDataToClass` method or anything like that. Instead, you use *Model-View-Controller*, or, more commonly, *MVC*. This isn't a class—it's a mindset.

In a nutshell, MVC says that there are three kinds of objects: *model* objects, which hold raw data; *view* objects, which the user can see and click on; and *controller* objects, which keep the model and view objects in sync.

 If you're into science fiction, you can think of MVC as *the force*. It has no physical form, but it is interwoven into every part of Cocoa. It's how Mac and iPhone programmers know how to structure classes.

To see how MVC works, you're going to create a photo gallery application. This will be your biggest project so far in the book, but you can definitely handle it. Here are some of the topics you'll learn about:

Core Data
> As I described in Chapter 7, Core Data is Cocoa's persistence framework. It's what most Cocoa applications use to save and load the data between launches of the application. This is a fairly advanced topic, but we're just going to look at a few high-level concepts.

ImageKit
> ImageKit is one of the more impressive frameworks in Mac OS X. It provides many high-end features like photo grid display, thumbnail scaling, rotation, photo editing, and much more.

Window controllers

So far you've only used project templates with default window configurations. I'm going to show you how to create custom *window controllers*, because using them is an essential skill for Cocoa programmers. Window controllers manage all of the activity within a single window. Typically, each one has its own XIB file.

View controllers

Just as window controllers manage windows, *view controllers* manage the activity within views. These are used in many Mac applications, but they're ubiquitous in UIKit on iPhone, iPad, and iPod touch. Like window controllers, view controllers work best when each one has its own XIB file.

About This Project

This application, shown in Figure 9-1, will be structured a lot differently than the other examples. It's much more aligned with a "real" Cocoa application. One key difference is that different parts of the application are sectioned off. This makes it much easier to change things without breaking the entire project. The key parts are self-sufficient, and can be freely moved around.

Figure 9-1. The gallery application

Window Controllers

Examples in earlier chapters used the stock application delegate class to manage the guts of the application. In big applications, putting everything in a single class leaves you with a big mess. One way to address this is to use window controllers, which are instances of `NSWindowController`. Figure 9-2 shows an example of this.

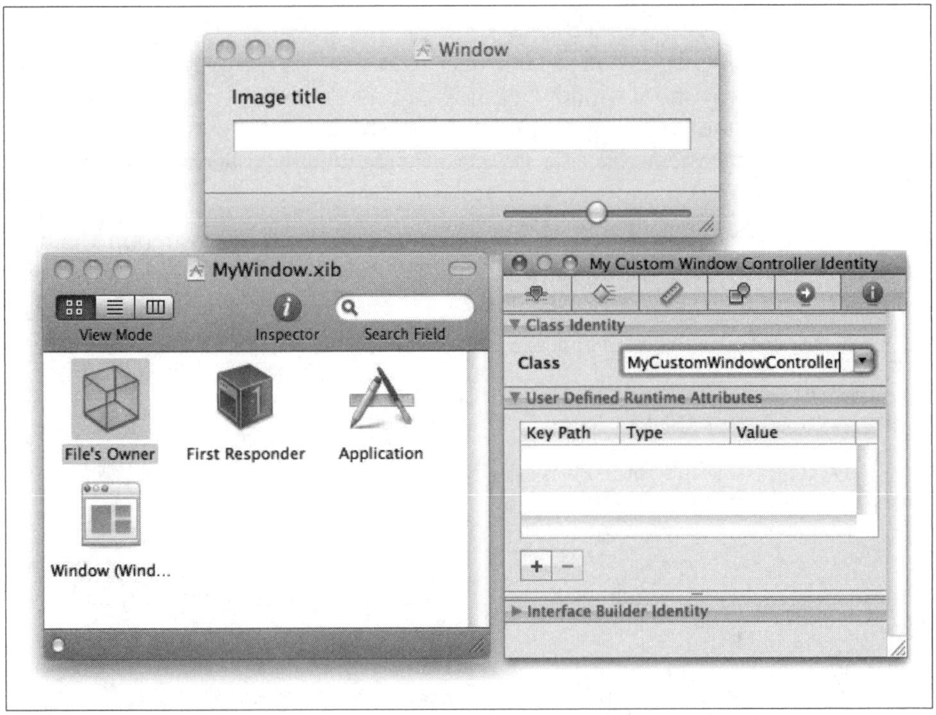

Figure 9-2. A window XIB with a subclass of NSWindowController set as File's Owner

A window controller sounds like a big, complex class, but it's actually very generic. You almost always subclass the base class and extend it with properties and methods specific to your custom window. These are the most important methods:

```
- (id) initWithWindowNibName: (NSString *)windowNibName; ❶
- (void) loadWindow; ❷
- (NSWindow *) window; ❸
- (IBAction) showWindow: (id)sender; ❹
```

❶ Most windows in Cocoa applications have their own XIB file and associated window controller. The window controller "owns" both the XIB file and its window, and this role is actually referred to as *File's Owner* in Interface Builder. The `-[NSWindowController initWithWindowNibName:]` method creates the window controller and loads the contents of the named XIB file.

❷ The -[NSWindowController loadWindow] method actually initializes the window and loads the contents of the XIB. You can override this method (be sure to call [super loadWindow] first), and do your own initialization.

❸ You can use the -[NSWindowController window] to get a reference to the NSWindow instance for any window controller.

❹ The -[NSWindowController showWindow:] method is an action method that simply displays the window onscreen.

With these base methods, a window controller acts like a "carrying case" for a window. A window controller isn't a window itself; it's a way to manipulate the window and the items inside without making a big mess. This extra layer of abstraction also means that you can change the actual window class inside the controller without affecting other parts of the app.

On top of these base methods, you add properties and actions to support the user interface. For example, if the window has a slider control and a text field, your view controller might look like this:

```
@interface MyCustomWindowController : NSWindowController

@property (retain) IBOutlet NSSlider*    slider;
@property (retain) IBOutlet NSTextField* textField;

- (IBAction) sliderDidChange:(id)sender;
- (IBAction) textDidChange:(id)sender;

@end
```

A line of code to create a window controller and display its window typically looks like this:

```
MyWindowController* controller;
controller = [[MyWindowController alloc] initWithWindowNibName:@"Window"];
[controller showWindow:self];
```

When a window controller is deallocated, it also releases the other items in the XIB. This vastly simplifies maintenance for each window.

View Controllers

Views can contain main subviews, and can get very complex. This means they're harder to manage and also take more memory. Splitting them off into their own XIB files means that they're much easier to use, and as a bonus, they are getting loaded into memory only when they're needed. Just as window XIBs have windows controllers, view XIBs have *view controllers*. View controllers are instances of the NSViewController class (see Figure 9-3).

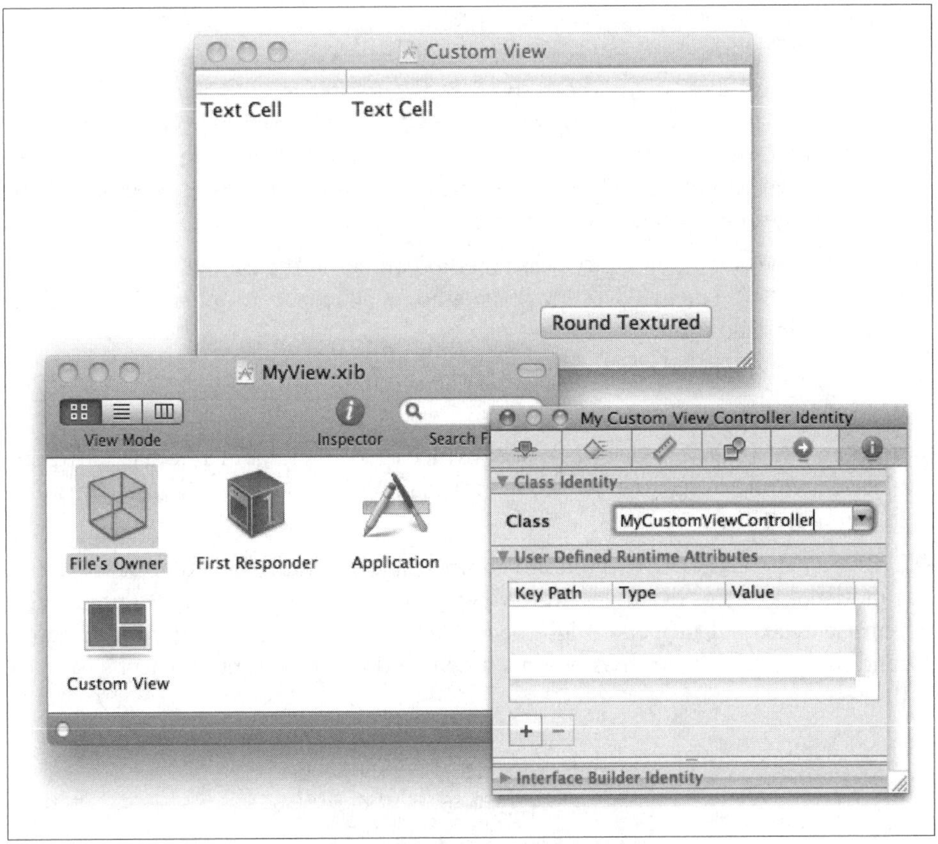

Figure 9-3. A view XIB with a subclass of NSViewController set as File's Owner

View controllers work on all of the same principles as window controllers, but at a finer-grained level. A window might be made of a single window controller and a window XIB file that references the many other view XIB files along with their own view controllers. You can potentially build an application of any level of complexity with these very basic building blocks, as shown in Figure 9-4.

You usually subclass `NSViewController` and add your own properties and methods. Here are the key methods:

```
- (id)initWithNibName:(NSString *)name bundle:(NSBundle *)bundle; ❶
```

```
- (void) loadView; ❷
```

```
- (NSView *) view; ❸
```

```
- (void)setTitle:(NSString *)title; ❹
- (NSString *)title;
```

```
- (void)setRepresentedObject:(id)object; ❺
- (id)representedObject;
```

❶ The view controller "owns" both the XIB file and its view. As with window controllers, this is called *File's Owner* in Interface Builder. The -[NSViewController initWithNibName:bundle:] method creates the view controller and loads the contents of the named XIB file. The bundle variable is used for more advanced cases where your application is built from components or plug-ins.

❷ The -[NSViewController loadWindow] method initializes the view and loads the contents of the XIB. You can override this method (call [super loadView] first), and do your own initialization.

❸ You can use the -[NSViewController view] to get a reference to the view instance for any view controller.

❹ You can give a title to a view controller, which can be helpful in automatically populating user interface items. You could, for example, use the title of a view controller in a pop-up button.

❺ This is a generic property to refer to another object that the view describes—often a model object. For example, if the view displays information about a photo, the representedObject property might be a Photo object. This is helpful for setting up bindings in the view, such as binding a text field to a represented object's caption property.

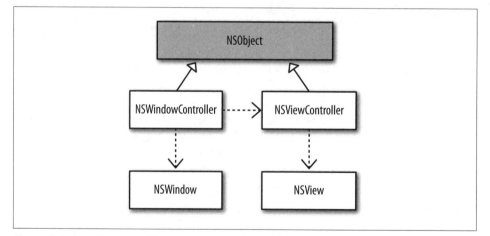

Figure 9-4. A window controller manages a window, and has one or more view controllers; a view controller manages a view

View controllers are fairly popular on the Mac, but they were only officially added in Mac OS X 10.5 Leopard. With UIKit on iPhone and iPad, view controllers are a way of life. In fact, it would be nearly impossible to get any work done without them.

Core Data

Core Data is Cocoa's *persistence framework*, which means it's the way most Cocoa applications store their data. It's an extremely scalable, flexible framework, but can even help in simpler applications. It also offers *change tracking*, which means the Core Data classes are aware of when you've made changes to data in your application, and can undo or redo those changes with little effort on your part.

Core Data offers several built-in storage types: XML, binary, and SQL. All three store data according to a design that you provide. That is, you define the types of data you'd like to store and the relationships between them, and the framework figures out the details. The SQL storage option is based on the SQLite open source library, which is especially interesting because of its incredible scaling power (you can learn more about SQLite at *http://sqlite.org*). You can also provide your own store type by subclassing the NSAtomicStore class. This is an advanced feature, but it's very useful if you have a custom file format you want to use.

This is a high-level introduction to Core Data, so you won't use all of its classes in this chapter, but I want to introduce to a few of the most important ones:

NSManagedObjectModel

> The NSManagedObjectModel class describes the different kinds of data you want your app to store. You're going to build a photo application in this chapter, so you'll create a model that describes photos and albums. You can create models in code, but it's usually much easier to create them using Xcode's built-in graphical modeling tool. A project can contain multiple models, but you're going to use only one in this chapter. You don't need to subclass NSManagedObjectModel.

NSEntityDescription

> The NSEntityDescription class describes a single type of data, and belongs to an NSManagedObjectModel. You're used to creating classes to describe a kind of data, but an entity is more abstract than that. It doesn't have any concept of methods or implementation. An entity is *only* a description of data. In this chapter, you'll create an entity called Photo and another called Album.

> An entity owns multiple instances of NSAttributeDescription and NSRelationship Description. An *attribute* is a simple value, like a string, number, or date. A *relationship* is a reference to one or more instances of another entity. A Photo might have a caption attribute, and a relationship to an Album.

> As with NSManagedObjectModel, you can create entities, attributes, and relationships in code, but usually it's easier to create them visually in Xcode.

NSManagedObject

The NSManagedObject class is Core Data's base data class. Each managed object is linked to an instance of NSEntityDescription. The entity defines the attributes and relationships of the managed object. Unlike NSObject, the generic NSManagedObject class can be used as-is; you're not required to subclass it, because it provides its own storage. In most cases, you will create a subclass for each data type to add code to support the other parts of the app.

A managed object holds onto its values until the app saves its data to a file on disk. A generic NSManagedObject instance can act like either a Photo or an Album, depending on the entity it's using.

NSManagedObjectContext

The NSManagedObjectContext manages NSManagedObject instances. Any time you need to load or save data, you use the managed object context. It tracks all of the managed object changes; requests the loading of their data from disk; and handles Undo, Redo, and Save. You may have many managed object contexts active in an application at the same time, or you may only have one.

NSPersistentStoreCoordinator

Each individual file that Core Data saves to is called a *persistent store*. Your application can have multiple persistent stores open at the same time and work with all of the objects in a shared space. NSPersistentStoreCoordinator sets up and manages the persistent stores. Much of this happens automatically, but you can use the persistent store coordinator directly if you want to.

Although these are the most commonly used classes in Core Data, these descriptions only scratch the surface of what the framework can do. Once you learn the basics of how to use it, you should start all new projects with Core Data included. If nothing else, you'll get basic saving, loading, and Undo/Redo support for free.

Create the Project Files

Let's start putting the project together. Open Xcode and create a new Cocoa Application project called "Gallery". Make sure to check the box labeled "Use Core Data for Storage." See Figure 9-5.

Create the Entities

Open the Models group in the Xcode sidebar and click on *Gallery_DataModel.xcdatamodel* to open the model editor (see Figure 9-6). This editor allows you to visually edit the NSManagedObjectModel for your project. The top-left panel lists entities. Click the small plus button at the bottom of the entity table to create a new entity instance.

Double-click the word "Entity" to edit the name, and type in "Photo" (see Figure 9-7).

Now add another entity and name it "Album" (see Figure 9-8).

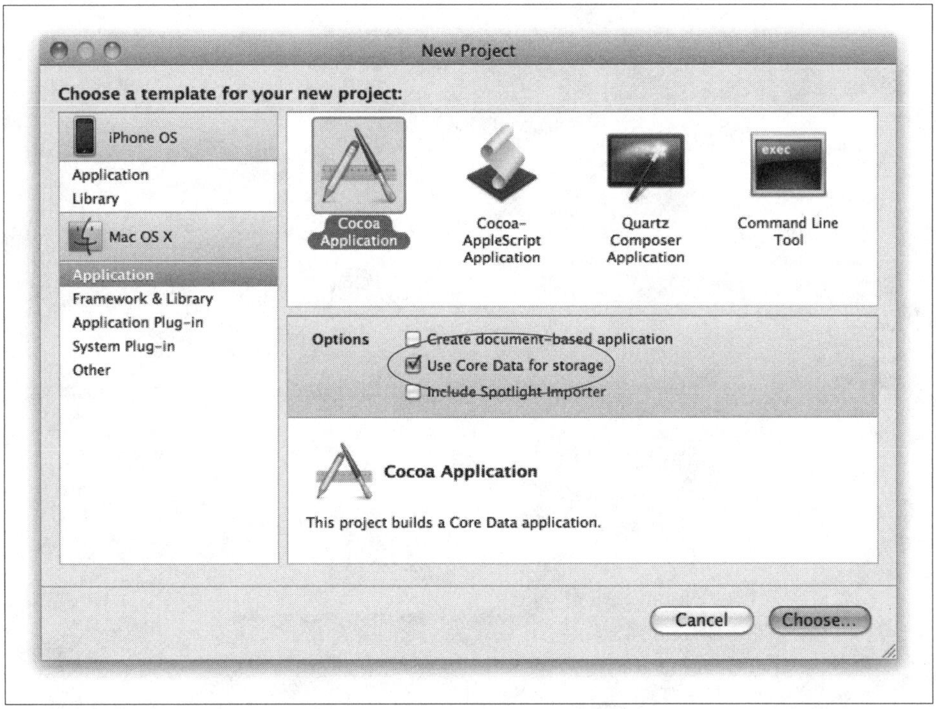

Figure 9-5. Create a new Cocoa project, and check the box labeled Use Core Data for storage

Each row in the entity table has an entry for the Class column. This indicates the `NSManagedObject` subclass that will be used for this entity. Double-click the Class entry for Photo and enter the class name `CBPhoto`. Set the class name for Album to `CBAlbum`. The table should look like Figure 9-9 when you're done.

As you're making these changes, you'll see the graphical grid view change to reflect what you've done. You can arrange the entity graphics any way you like. The graphics are there to help you understand your application's data; their actual position doesn't affect how the program runs.

Add Attributes and Relationships

Just to the right of the entities table is the properties table. Each entry in here describes one piece of data for the selected entity. Select the Photo entity in the lefthand table, then click the plus button in the properties table to the right. Choose Add Attribute from the pop-up menu (see Figure 9-10).

Once you've created the attribute, you'll see some options for it in the view at the far right of the window. Type in `filePath` for the Name field, uncheck Optional, and choose String from the Type drop-down. You can leave all of the other settings empty, as shown in Figure 9-11.

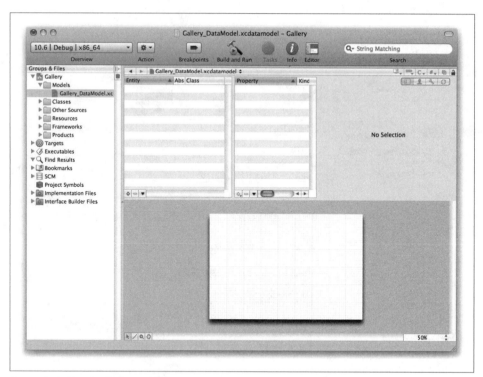

Figure 9-6. The Xcode data modeler

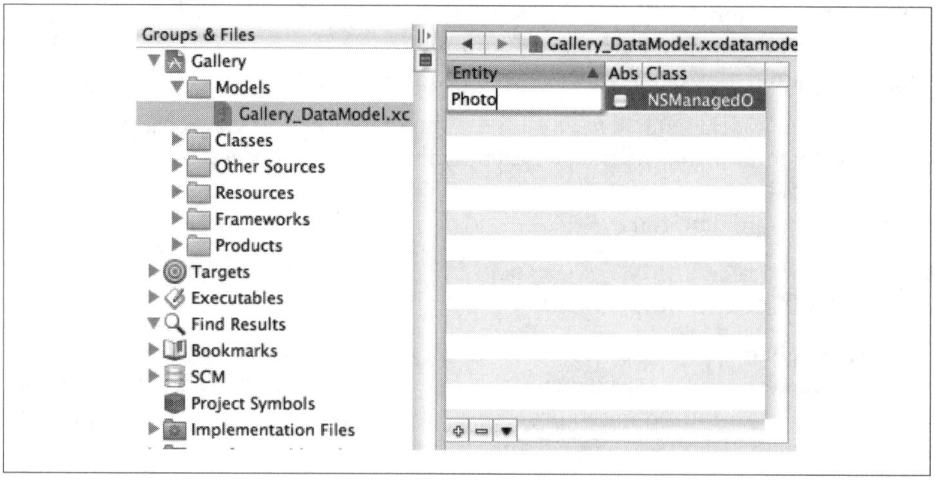

Figure 9-7. Double-click the Entity title and name it "Photo"

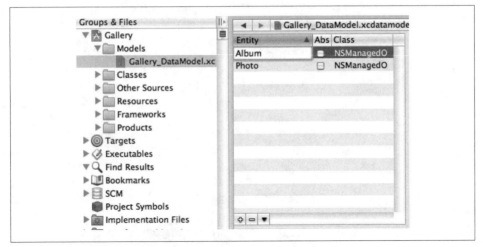

Figure 9-8. Create an entity named "Album"

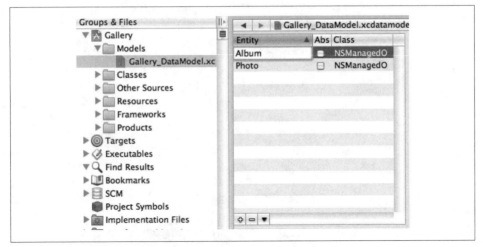

Figure 9-9. The completed entity table

Create another attribute called `uniqueID` with the exact same settings: uncheck Optional, and choose String for the type. Finally, create a nonoptional attribute called `orderIndex` with a type of Int 32 (which is a 32-bit integer value). When you're done, the attribute list for Photo should look like Figure 9-12.

Click the plus button below the properties table to add another property, but this time choose Add Relationship from the pop up (see Figure 9-13).

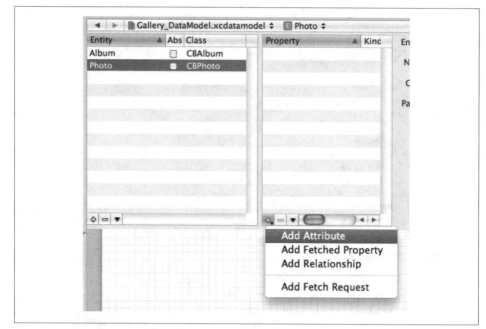

Figure 9-10. Add a new attribute to the Photo entity

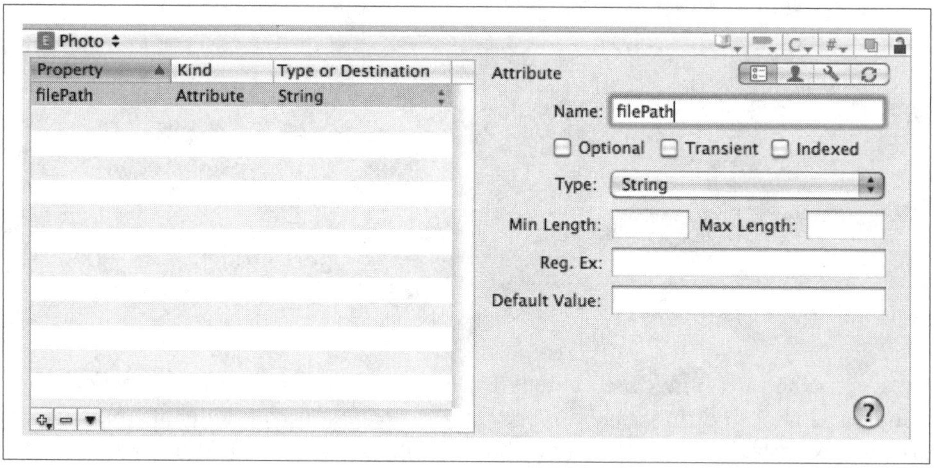

Figure 9-11. Configure the filePath attribute

Name the relationship `album`, and make it nonoptional. Choose Album from the Destination pop up. You can leave the other options at their default values, as shown in Figure 9-14.

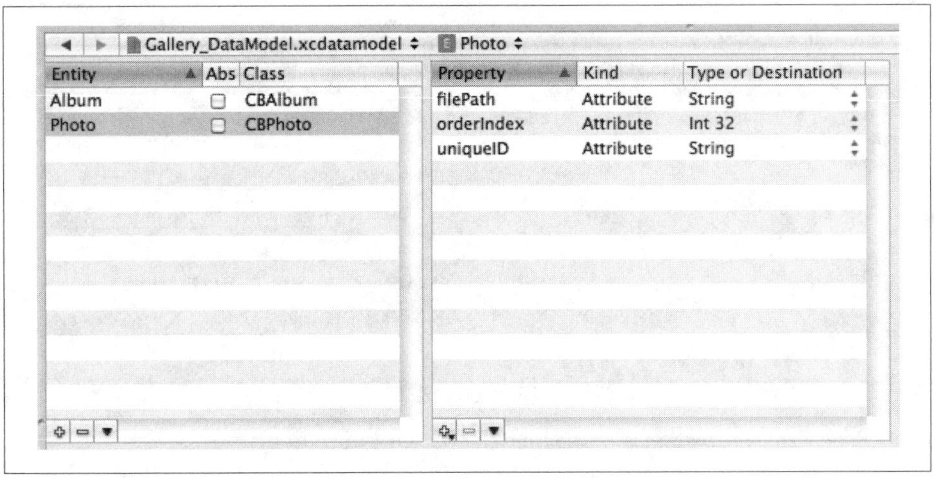

Figure 9-12. The completed attribute list for the Photo entity

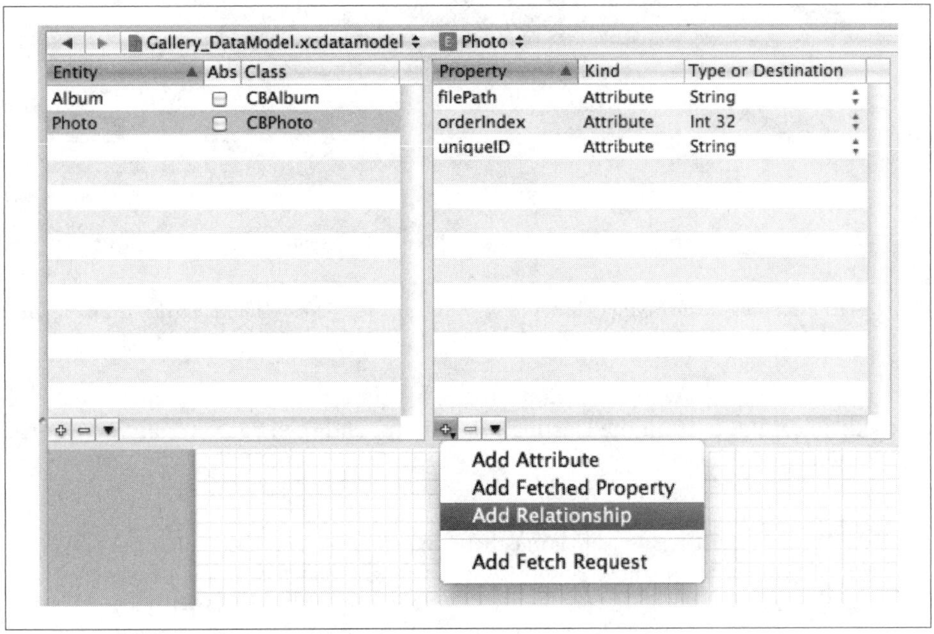

Figure 9-13. Add a new relationship to the Photo entity

Now select the Album entity in the entities table in the far left. You can also click on the Album graphic in the grid view; it has the same effect. Add a nonoptional attribute to Album called `title`, and make it type String. In the Default Value field, type in the text "New Album" (see Figure 9-15).

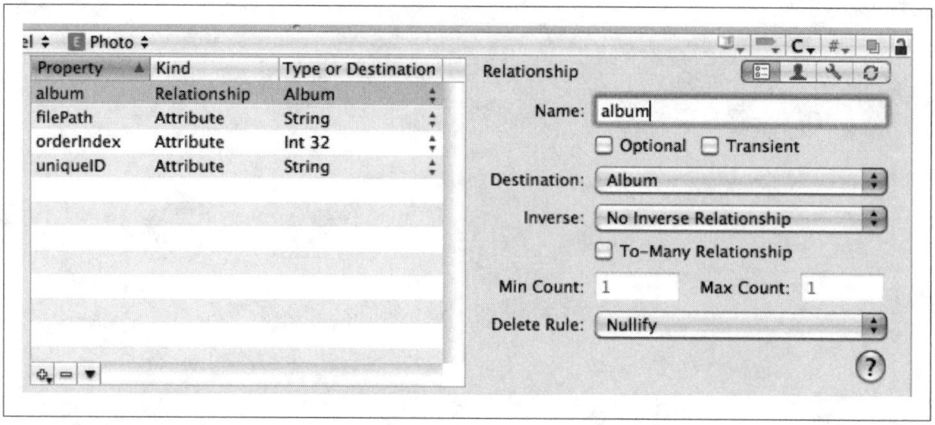

Figure 9-14. Configure the album relationship

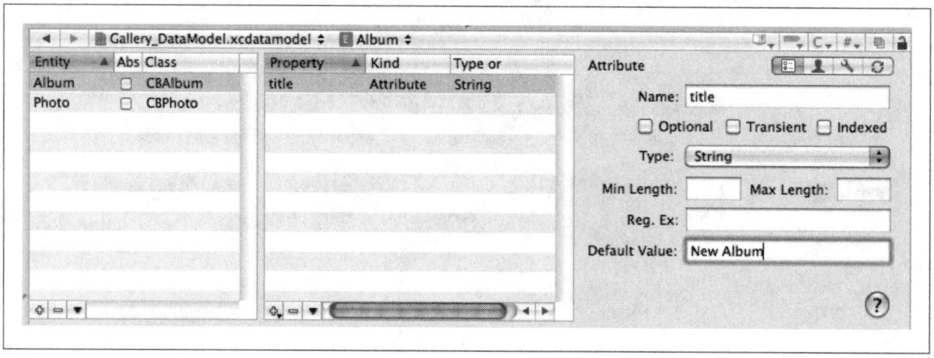

Figure 9-15. Add the title attribute to the Album entity, and use "New Album" as the default value

Add a relationship to Album called photos. This time, leave the Optional checkbox enabled. Select Photo from the Destination pop up, and select album from the Inverse drop-down.

> An *inverse* relationship is one that is maintained on both sides. For example, when you set an object for a Photo's album relationship, Core Data will automatically update the Album's to-many photos relationship, too. This keeps everything in sync without you specifically writing code to do so.

Now check the To-Many Relationship checkbox, which indicates that each Album can have multiple Photo items. Finally, select Cascade from the Delete Rule pop up, which means that when an Album is deleted, all of the Photo objects will be deleted, too. When you're done, the relationship should look like Figure 9-16.

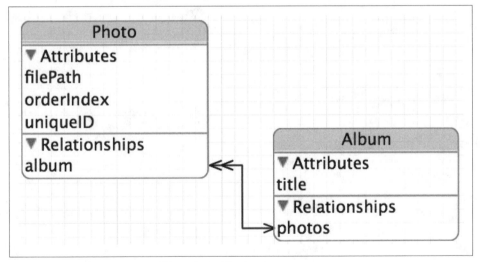

Figure 9-16. Create the photos relationship for the Album entity

Take a moment and verify that your model looks like the grid view in Figure 9-17. It's absolutely critical that each setting is exactly as I described, because Core Data will use this information to save your application data to disk.

When you're done, save the model file.

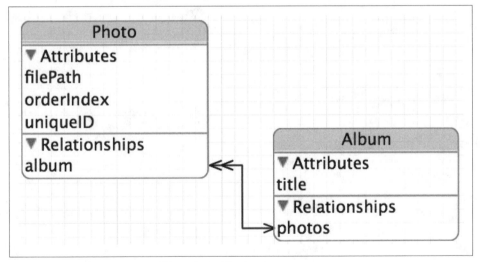

Figure 9-17. Make sure your grid view looks like this

Update the App Delegate

Open the Classes group in the Xcode sidebar, and click on *Gallery_AppDelegate.m*. The Xcode template for Core Data applications provides a handful of methods to support basic loading and saving of data. You can look through these if you're curious, but you don't need to actually change them, except for one small detail.

In the implementation of the `-applicationSupportDirectory:` method, there's one line that returns the file path:

```
return [basePath stringByAppendingPathComponent:@"Gallery"];
```

Replace that line with:

```
return [basePath stringByAppendingPathComponent:@"CocoaBookGallery"];
```

The term "gallery" is generic enough that you may have another application that stores data at the same location. Changing the file path is a way to prevent the data from being overwritten. You can leave the rest of the methods as-is. In fact, add several line breaks and a comment above the implementation of the `-applicationSupportDirectory:` method to indicate where the built-in methods begin:

```
// all of these methods are provided by the template.

- (NSString *)applicationSupportDirectory {
```

Whenever I ask you to add new methods to this class in the chapter, add them above this line for clarity. Replace everything above the first built-in method with the following code:

```
#import "Gallery_AppDelegate.h"
#import "CBMainWindow.h"
#import "CBBrowserView.h"
#import "CBAlbum.h"
#import "CBPhoto.h"

@implementation Gallery_AppDelegate

@synthesize mainWindow;
@synthesize mainWindowController;
@synthesize selectedAlbum;

@synthesize window;
@synthesize managedObjectModel;
@synthesize persistentStoreCoordinator;
@synthesize managedObjectContext;

- (IBAction) newAlbum: (id)sender {
    [CBAlbum albumInDefaultContext];
}

- (BOOL)applicationShouldTerminateAfterLastWindowClosed:
                              (NSApplication *)sender {
    return YES;
}
```

The `-newAlbum:` action method will be used by a menu item you'll add later in the chapter. The second method is a method that `NSApplication` calls on its delegate. Returning `YES` from the method means that the application will quit when the main window closes.

Now switch over to the *Gallery_AppDelegate.h* header file. Remove the curly braces and all of the literal instance variable definitions inside of them, leaving only the `@property` declarations intact. Add a comment to call out which properties are provided by the template.

Add the following properties, class declarations, and action method to the file. Make sure all of them are above the properties provided by the template (the first two lines go above the existing line that reads `@interface Gallery_AppDelegate : NSObject`, the last three below it):

```
@class CBMainWindow;
@class CBAlbum;

@interface Gallery_AppDelegate : NSObject

@property (retain) CBMainWindow* mainWindowController;
@property (retain) CBAlbum*       selectedAlbum;

- (IBAction) newAlbum: (id)sender;
```

When you're done, the file should match the code in Example 9-1. I've put each properties on two lines for formatting reasons, but you can put each one on a single line.

Example 9-1. The reformatted version of Gallery_AppDelegate.h

```
#import <Cocoa/Cocoa.h>

@class CBMainWindow;
@class CBAlbum;

@interface Gallery_AppDelegate : NSObject

@property (retain) CBMainWindow* mainWindowController;
@property (retain) CBAlbum*       selectedAlbum;

- (IBAction) newAlbum: (id)sender;


// provided by template.
@property (nonatomic, retain) IBOutlet NSWindow *window;

@property (nonatomic, retain, readonly)
    NSPersistentStoreCoordinator *persistentStoreCoordinator;
@property (nonatomic, retain, readonly)
    NSManagedObjectModel *managedObjectModel;
@property (nonatomic, retain, readonly)
    NSManagedObjectContext *managedObjectContext;
- (IBAction)saveAction:sender;

@end
```

Add the Quartz Framework

This project will use a class from Mac OS X's ImageKit framework called `IKImageBrowserView`. You need to add the ImageKit framework to the project before you can use the class. The ImageKit framework is actually a subframework in the larger Quartz framework.

Right-click (or Control-click) on the Frameworks → Linked Frameworks group in your project, and choose Add → Existing Frameworks. Choose Quartz.framework from the list and click Add (see Figure 9-18).

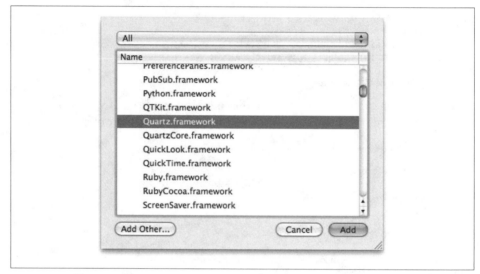

Figure 9-18. The Quartz.framework item in the frameworks sheet

You can now use any classes in the Quartz framework (including those in ImageKit) by including the *Quartz.h* file in any of your header or implementation files.

Create the Window Controller

The window controller class will manage all of the view controllers for the projects, and each view controller will contain a different part of the user interface. There will be one window controller class with its own XIB file (Figure 9-19), and three view controller classes, each with its own XIB file.

Create a new Cocoa class (right-click Classes, choose Add → New File, the choose Objective-C Class from the Cocoa Class section, as shown in Figure 9-20) with a superclass of `NSWindowController`. Name the class *CBMainWindow.m*.

Figure 9-19. The Gallery main window XIB

Replace the contents of the *CBMainWindow.h* header file with the code from
Example 9-2.

Example 9-2. CBMainWindow.h

```
#import <Cocoa/Cocoa.h>
#import <Quartz/Quartz.h>

@interface CBMainWindow : NSWindowController

// outlets.
@property (retain) IBOutlet NSSegmentedControl*  viewSelectionControl;

// view management properties.
@property (retain) NSMutableDictionary* viewControllers;
@property (assign) NSViewController*     currentViewController;
@property (copy)   NSArray*              controllerNamesByIndex;

// view management methods.
- (IBAction) viewSelectionDidChange:(id)sender;
- (void) activateViewController: (NSViewController*)controller;
- (NSViewController*) viewControllerForName: (NSString*)name;

@end
```

Open the *CBMainWindow.m* implementation file and enter the code from Example 9-3.

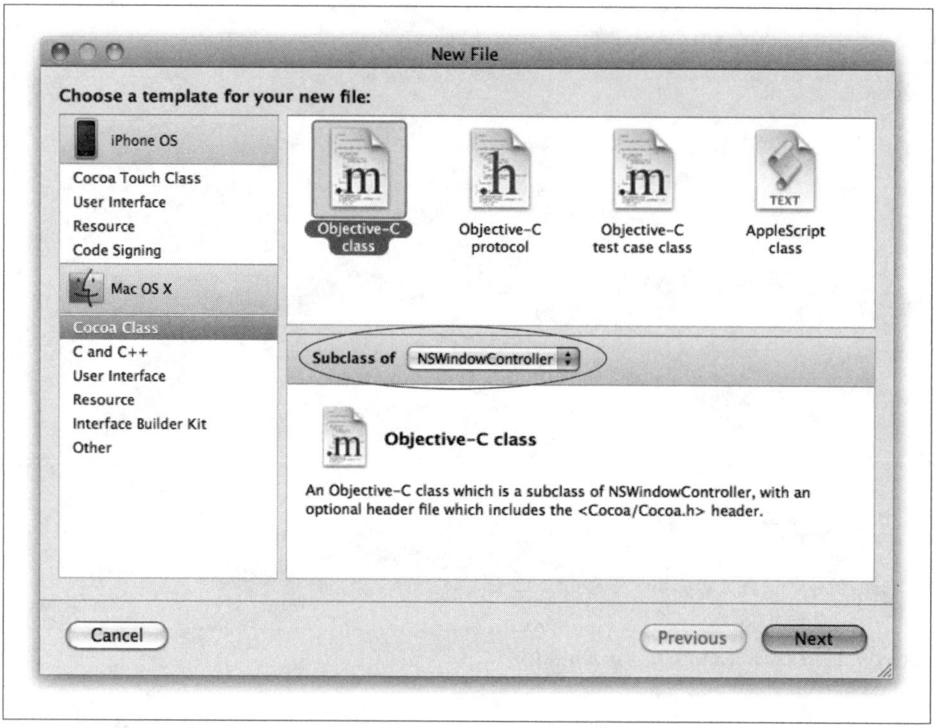

Figure 9-20. Create the CBMainWindow window controller class

Example 9-3. CBMainWindow.m

```
#import "CBMainWindow.h"

// the 'static' means these are only visible in this file.
static const NSInteger BrowserViewIndex = 0;
static const NSInteger EditorViewIndex  = 1;
static const NSInteger ListViewIndex    = 2;

// names for each view.
static NSString* const CBBrowserViewName = @"CBBrowserView";
static NSString* const CBEditorViewName  = @"CBEditorView";
static NSString* const CBListViewName     = @"CBListView";

@implementation CBMainWindow

// view modes.
@synthesize viewSelectionControl;
@synthesize viewControllers;
@synthesize currentViewController;
@synthesize controllerNamesByIndex;


- (void) loadWindow {
```

```
    [super loadWindow];
    self.viewControllers = [NSMutableDictionary dictionary];

    // match up indexes to names.
    NSMutableArray* names = [NSMutableArray array];
    [names insertObject:CBBrowserViewName atIndex:BrowserViewIndex];
    [names insertObject:CBEditorViewName  atIndex:EditorViewIndex];
    [names insertObject:CBListViewName    atIndex:ListViewIndex];
    self.controllerNamesByIndex = names;

    // start on browser mode.
    NSViewController* initial;
    initial = [self viewControllerForName:CBBrowserViewName];
    [self activateViewController:initial];
}

- (IBAction) viewSelectionDidChange:(id)sender {

    // find requested view controller.
    NSInteger selection      = [sender selectedSegment];
    NSArray*  names          = self.controllerNamesByIndex;
    NSString* controllerName = [names objectAtIndex:selection];

    // load view controller.
    NSViewController* controller;
    controller = [self viewControllerForName:controllerName];
    [self activateViewController:controller];
}

- (void) activateViewController: (NSViewController*)controller {

    NSArray*  names     = self.controllerNamesByIndex;
    NSInteger segment   = self.viewSelectionControl.selectedSegment;

    NSString* targetName  = [controller className];
    NSInteger targetIndex = [names indexOfObject:targetName];

    // update segmented control.
    if ( segment != targetIndex )
        [self.viewSelectionControl setSelectedSegment:targetIndex];

    // remove current view.
    [self.currentViewController.view removeFromSuperview];

    // set up new view controller.
    self.currentViewController = controller;
    [[self.window contentView] addSubview:controller.view];

    // adjust for window margin.
    NSWindow* window = self.window;
    CGFloat padding = [window contentBorderThicknessForEdge:NSMinYEdge];
    NSRect frame    = [window.contentView frame];
    frame.size.height -= padding;
    frame.origin.y += padding;
    controller.view.frame = frame;
```

```
}

- (NSViewController*) viewControllerForName: (NSString*)name {

    // see if this view already exists.
    NSMutableDictionary* allControllers = self.viewControllers;
    NSViewController* controller = [allControllers objectForKey:name];
    if ( controller ) return controller;

    // create a new instance of the view.
    Class controllerClass = NSClassFromString( name );
    controller = [[controllerClass alloc] initWithNibName:name bundle:nil];
    [allControllers setObject:controller forKey:name];

    // use key-value coding to avoid compiler warnings.
    [controller setValue:self forKey:@"mainWindowController"];
    return [controller autorelease];
}

- (void) dealloc {

    self.viewSelectionControl  = nil;
    self.viewControllers       = nil;
    self.controllerNamesByIndex = nil;

    [super dealloc];
}

@end
```

Select the Resources group in the Xcode sidebar, and choose File → New File. Select the "User Interface" group from the Mac OS X section of the template selection window, then select Window XIB and click Next (as shown in Figure 9-21). Name the file *CBMainWindow.xib*.

Now update *Gallery_AppDelegate.m* to use this new window controller. Add the following implementation of the -applicationDidFinishLaunching: method:

```
- (void)applicationDidFinishLaunching:(NSNotification *)note {

    CBMainWindow* windowController;
    windowController = [[CBMainWindow alloc] initWithWindowNibName:@"CBMainWindow"];
    [windowController showWindow:nil];
    self.mainWindowController = windowController;
    [windowController release];
}
```

Create the View Controllers

You'll now create the three views that define the user interface for the application. Each one has a separate XIB file and a view controller that owns it.

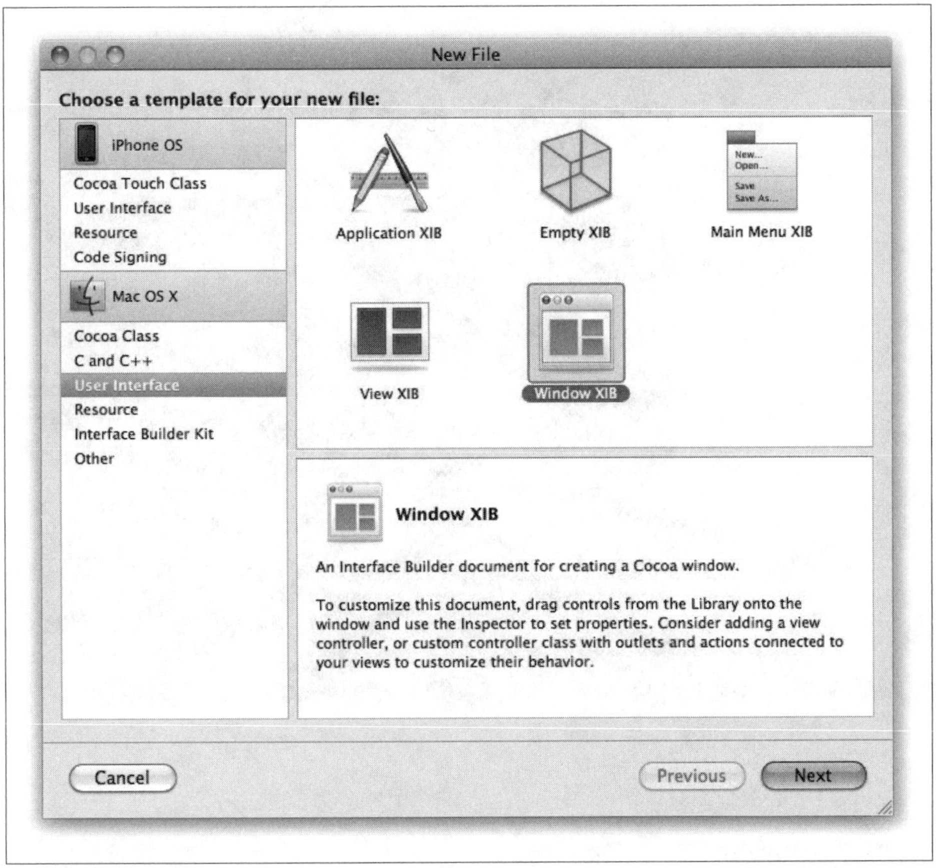

Figure 9-21. Create the CBMainWindow window XIB file

Browser view controller

The browser view is the first thing the user sees when the application launches. It shows a list of Album items on the left, and the main photo grid on the right shows all of the Photo items in the selected album (Figure 9-22). The photo grid view is an instance of `IKImageBrowserView`. You can freely drop images from the finder into the browser view and they'll be added to the Core Data store automatically.

Create a new Cocoa class with a superclass of `NSObject`. Name the class *CBBrowserView.m* (Figure 9-23). Xcode does not provide `NSViewController` as a standard superclass from the drop-down, but we can fix that with one line of code in the file itself.

Replace the contents of the *CBBrowserView.h* header file with the code from Example 9-4.

Figure 9-22. The Gallery browser view

Example 9-4. CBBrowserView.h

```
#import <Cocoa/Cocoa.h>
#import <Quartz/Quartz.h>

@class CBMainWindow;

@interface CBBrowserView : NSViewController <NSTableViewDelegate>

// parent window.
@property (assign) CBMainWindow* mainWindowController;

// xib items.
@property (retain) IBOutlet IKImageBrowserView* imageBrowser;
@property (retain) IBOutlet NSTableView*        albumsTable;
@property (retain) IBOutlet NSArrayController*  albumsArrayController;
@property (retain) IBOutlet NSArrayController*  imagesArrayController;

// additional values.
@property (retain) NSArray* imagesSortDescriptors;
@property (assign) CGFloat  thumbnailScale;

@end
```

Open the *CBBrowserView.m* implementation file and enter the code from Example 9-5.

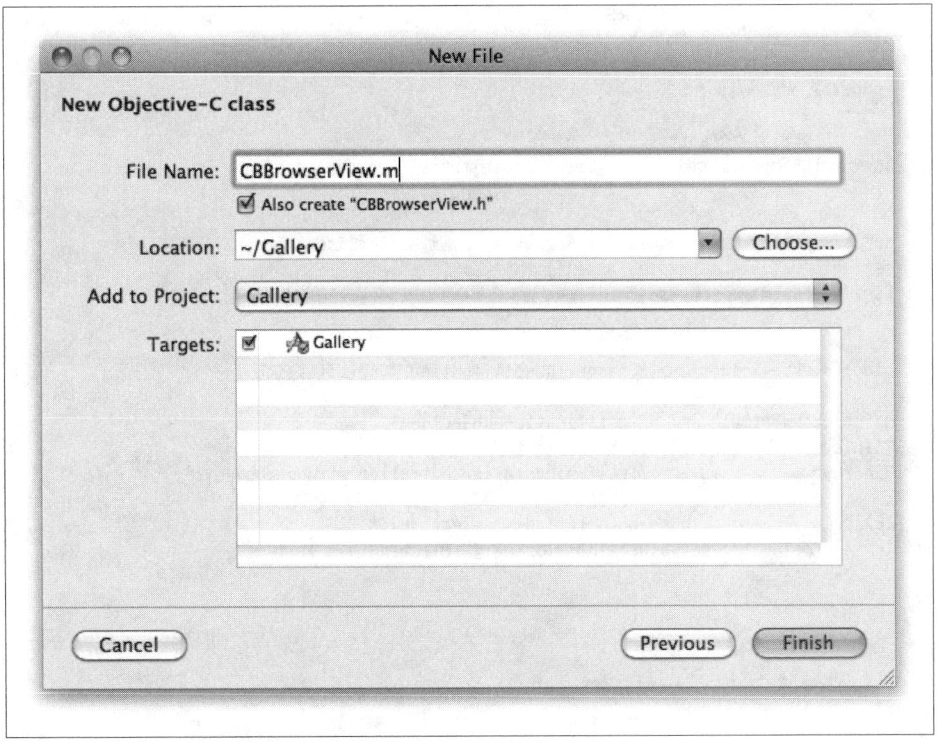

Figure 9-23. Create the CBBrowserView class

Example 9-5. CBBrowserView.m

```objc
#import "CBBrowserView.h"
#import "CBPhoto.h"
#import "CBAlbum.h"
#import "CBEditorView.h"
#import "CBMainWindow.h"


@interface CBBrowserView (Private)
- (void) setupImageBrowser;
- (void) updateSortOrderForObjects:(NSArray*)items;
@end


@implementation CBBrowserView

@synthesize mainWindowController;
@synthesize imageBrowser;
@synthesize albumsTable;
@synthesize albumsArrayController;
@synthesize imagesArrayController;
@synthesize imagesSortDescriptors;
@synthesize thumbnailScale;
```

```
- (void) loadView {

    [super loadView];

    NSSortDescriptor* sort;
    sort = [NSSortDescriptor sortDescriptorWithKey: @"orderIndex"
                                         ascending: YES];

    self.imagesSortDescriptors = [NSArray arrayWithObject:sort];
    self.albumsTable.delegate = self;
    [self setupImageBrowser];
}

- (void)tableViewSelectionDidChange:(NSNotification *)notification {

    NSTableView* table     = [notification object];
    NSInteger    selection = table.selectedRow;
    NSArray*     albums    = [self.albumsArrayController arrangedObjects];

    CBAlbum* album = [albums objectAtIndex:selection];
    [[NSApp delegate] setValue:album forKey:@"selectedAlbum"];
}



#pragma mark -
#pragma mark Image Browser

- (void) imageBrowser: (IKImageBrowserView *)browser
        cellWasDoubleClickedAtIndex: (NSUInteger)index {

    NSArray* visiblePhotos = [self.imagesArrayController arrangedObjects];
    CBPhoto* photo         = [visiblePhotos objectAtIndex:index];

    CBMainWindow* window = self.mainWindowController;
    id editor = [window viewControllerForName:@"CBEditorView"];

    if ( [editor isKindOfClass:[CBEditorView class]] )
        [(CBEditorView*)editor editPhoto:photo];
}

- (BOOL)performDragOperation:(id <NSDraggingInfo>)sender {

    IKImageBrowserView* browser = self.imageBrowser;

    NSPasteboard* pboard    = [sender draggingPasteboard];
    NSUInteger    dropIndex = [browser indexAtLocationOfDroppedItem];
    NSArray*      photos    = self.imagesArrayController.arrangedObjects;

    // indexes to place photos.
    NSMutableIndexSet* indexSet = [NSMutableIndexSet indexSet];
    [indexSet addIndex:dropIndex];
```

```
// the move might be within the view.
if ( [sender draggingSource] == browser ) {

    NSIndexSet*      selected      = browser.selectionIndexes;
    NSArray*         draggingItems = [photos objectsAtIndexes:selected];
    NSMutableArray* reorderedItems = [photos mutableCopy];

    [reorderedItems removeObjectsInArray:draggingItems];

    NSUInteger newDropIndex = dropIndex;
    NSUInteger index        = 0;
    NSUInteger firstIndex   = selected.firstIndex;

    for ( index = firstIndex; index != NSNotFound;
          index = [selected indexGreaterThanIndex:index] ) {

        if ( index < dropIndex )
            newDropIndex -= 1;
        else
            break;
    }

    NSRange     dropRange   = NSMakeRange( newDropIndex, draggingItems.count );
    NSIndexSet* dropIndexes = [NSIndexSet indexSetWithIndexesInRange:dropRange];

    [reorderedItems insertObjects:draggingItems atIndexes:dropIndexes];
    [self updateSortOrderForObjects:reorderedItems];
    [reorderedItems release];
    return YES;
}


NSMutableArray* newItems = [NSMutableArray array];
CBAlbum* album = [[NSApp delegate] valueForKey:@"selectedAlbum"];


// get list of files.
NSArray*  fileNames = [pboard propertyListForType:NSFilenamesPboardType];
NSInteger indexCount = 0;
if ( fileNames.count < 1 ) return NO;

for ( NSString* file in fileNames ) {

    CBPhoto* newItem = [CBPhoto photoInDefaultContext];
    newItem.filePath = file;
    [newItems addObject:newItem];
    [indexSet addIndex: dropIndex+indexCount];
    newItem.album = album;
    indexCount++;
}

NSMutableArray* array = [photos mutableCopy];
[array insertObjects:newItems atIndexes:indexSet];
[self updateSortOrderForObjects:array];
[array release];
```

```
    return YES;
}

- (NSDragOperation)draggingEntered:(id <NSDraggingInfo>)sender {
    return NSDragOperationCopy;
}

- (NSDragOperation)draggingUpdated:(id <NSDraggingInfo>)sender {
    return NSDragOperationCopy;
}


#pragma mark -
#pragma mark Private

- (void) setupImageBrowser {

    IKImageBrowserView* browser = self.imageBrowser;
    browser.draggingDestinationDelegate = self;
    browser.delegate        = self;
    browser.cellsStyleMask = (IKCellsStyleShadowed|IKCellsStyleTitled);
    browser.zoomValue      = 0.55;

    // base attributes.
    NSFont*  font         = [NSFont systemFontOfSize:11];
    NSColor* textColor    = [NSColor colorWithCalibratedWhite:0.8 alpha:1.0];
    NSColor* textColorAlt = [NSColor colorWithCalibratedWhite:1.0 alpha:1.0];
    NSColor* background   = [NSColor colorWithCalibratedWhite:0.2 alpha:1.0];

    // text attributes.
    NSMutableDictionary* attr;
    attr = [NSMutableDictionary dictionary];
    [attr setObject:textColor forKey:NSForegroundColorAttributeName];
    [attr setObject:font forKey:NSFontAttributeName];

    // selected text attributes.
    NSMutableDictionary* attrAlt;
    attrAlt = [NSMutableDictionary dictionary];
    [attrAlt setObject:textColorAlt forKey:NSForegroundColorAttributeName];
    [attrAlt setObject:font forKey:NSFontAttributeName];

    // set text attributes.
    [browser setValue: attr
            forKey: IKImageBrowserCellsTitleAttributesKey];
    [browser setValue: attrAlt
            forKey: IKImageBrowserCellsHighlightedTitleAttributesKey];
    [browser setValue: background
            forKey: IKImageBrowserBackgroundColorKey];
}

- (void) updateSortOrderForObjects:(NSArray*)items {

    NSMutableArray* arrangedItems = [NSMutableArray array];
    NSInteger        orderIndex    = 0;
```

```
    for ( CBPhoto* item in items ) {
        // only do each item once.
        if ( [arrangedItems containsObject:item] ) continue;
        item.orderIndex = [NSNumber numberWithInteger:orderIndex];
        [arrangedItems addObject:item];
        orderIndex++;
    }

    // reload the array controller.
    [self.imagesArrayController rearrangeObjects];
}

- (void) dealloc {

    self.imageBrowser           = nil;
    self.albumsTable            = nil;
    self.albumsArrayController  = nil;
    self.imagesArrayController  = nil;
    self.imagesSortDescriptors  = nil;

    [super dealloc];
}
@end
```

Select the Resources group in the Xcode sidebar, and choose File → New File. Select the "User Interface" group from the Mac OS X section of the template selection window, then select View XIB and click Next (Figure 9-24). Name the file *CBBrowserView.xib*.

Editor view controller

The editor view uses the `IKImageView` class, which allows you to view and edit images, as seen in Figure 9-25. If you double-click the image in the editor view, you can bring up an adjustment panel. Because this project is for demonstration purposes and I don't want it to become overwhelmingly complex, the changes in the editor view won't be saved back to the file, but you can see what it does.

Create a new Cocoa class with a superclass of `NSObject`. Name the class *CBEditorView.m*.

Replace the contents of the *CBEditorView.h* header file with the code from Example 9-6.

Example 9-6. CBEditorView.h

```
#import <Cocoa/Cocoa.h>
#import <Quartz/Quartz.h>

@class CBMainWindow;
@class CBPhoto;

@interface CBEditorView : NSViewController
```

```
@property (assign) CBMainWindow* mainWindowController;
@property (retain) IBOutlet IKImageView* imageView;

- (void) editPhoto: (CBPhoto*)photo;

@end
```

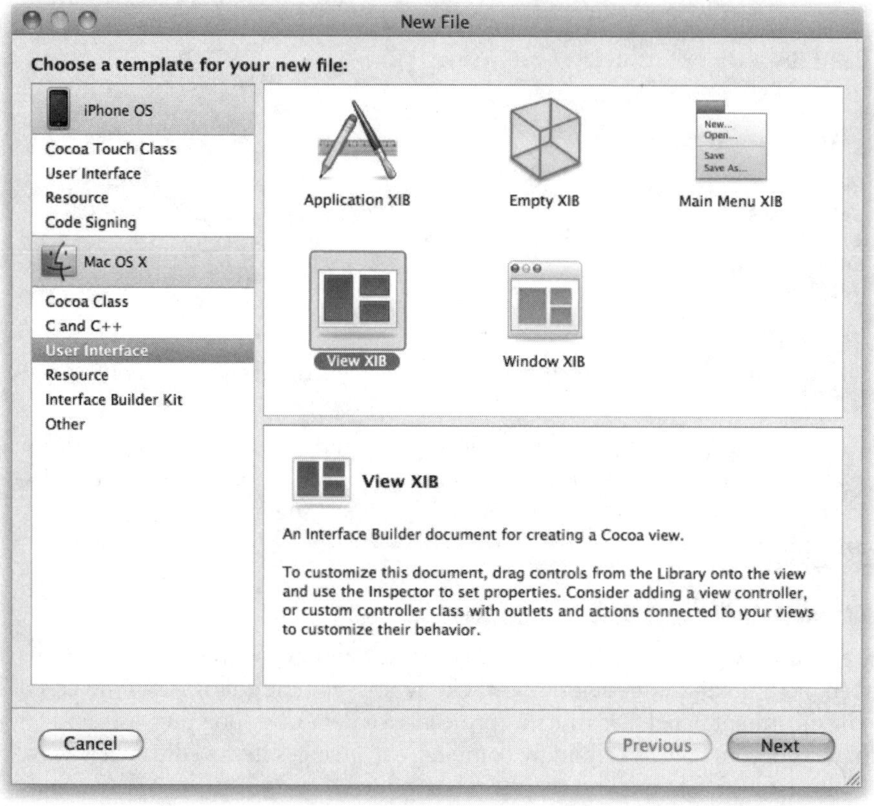

Figure 9-24. Create the CBBrowserView view XIB file

Open the *CBEditorView.m* implementation file and enter the code from Example 9-7.

Example 9-7. CBEditorView.m

```
#import "CBEditorView.h"
#import "CBPhoto.h"
#import "CBMainWindow.h"

@implementation CBEditorView

@synthesize mainWindowController;
@synthesize imageView;
```

```objc
- (void) loadView {

    [super loadView];
    [self.imageView setImageWithURL:nil];
}

- (void) editPhoto: (CBPhoto*)photo {

    if ( self.view == nil ) [self loadView];
    NSURL* url = [NSURL fileURLWithPath:photo.filePath];

    [self.imageView setImageWithURL:url];
    [self.mainWindowController activateViewController:self];
}

- (void) dealloc {

    self.imageView = nil;
    [super dealloc];
}

@end
```

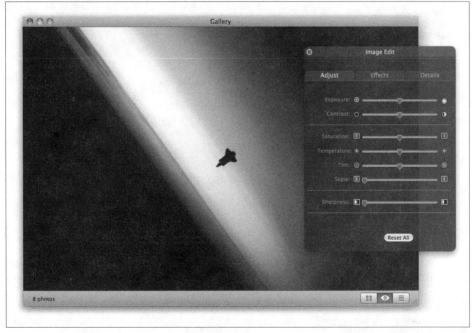

Figure 9-25. The Gallery editor view

Select the Resources group in the Xcode sidebar, and choose File → New File. Select the "User Interface" group from the Mac OS X section of the template selection window, then select View XIB and click Next. Name the file *CBEditorView.xib*.

List view controller

The third and final view is the list view. It displays a flat list of the photos across all albums in a table view (see Figure 9-26). Double-clicking a photo opens it in the editor view.

Figure 9-26. The Gallery list view

Create a new Cocoa class with a superclass of NSObject. Name the class *CBListView.m*. Replace the contents of the *CBListView.h* header file with the code from Example 9-8.

Example 9-8. CBListView.h

```
#import <Cocoa/Cocoa.h>

@class CBMainWindow;

@interface CBListView : NSViewController

@property (assign) CBMainWindow* mainWindowController;
@property (retain) IBOutlet NSTableView* imagesTable;
@property (retain) IBOutlet NSArrayController* imagesArrayController;

- (IBAction) tableViewItemDoubleClicked:(id)sender;

@end
```

Open the *CBListView.m* implementation file and enter the code from Example 9-9.

Example 9-9. CBListView.m

```
#import "CBListView.h"
#import "CBMainWindow.h"
#import "CBPhoto.h"
#import "CBEditorView.h"

@implementation CBListView

@synthesize mainWindowController;
@synthesize imagesTable;
@synthesize imagesArrayController;


- (void) loadView {

    [super loadView];

    self.imagesTable.target       = self;
    self.imagesTable.doubleAction = @selector(tableViewItemDoubleClicked:);

}


- (IBAction) tableViewItemDoubleClicked:(id)sender {

    NSInteger row          = self.imagesTable.clickedRow;
    NSArray*  visiblePhotos = [self.imagesArrayController arrangedObjects];
    CBPhoto*  photo         = [visiblePhotos objectAtIndex:row];

    CBMainWindow* window = self.mainWindowController;
    id editor = [window viewControllerForName:@"CBEditorView"];

    if ( [editor isKindOfClass:[CBEditorView class]] )
        [(CBEditorView*)editor editPhoto:photo];
}

- (void) dealloc {

    self.imagesTable           = nil;
    self.imagesArrayController = nil;
    [super dealloc];
}

@end
```

Select the Resources group in the Xcode sidebar, and choose File → New File. Select the "User Interface" group from the Mac OS X section of the template selection window, then select View XIB and click Next. Name the file *CBListView.xib*.

Create the Managed Object Classes

I mentioned before that you can use `NSManagedObject` instances as-is because the entity they're associated with has all of the information about what data can be stored. But because you're using the generic `NSManagedObject` class, you can't call getter and setter methods like `-firstName` and `-setFirstName:` to change their values. Instead, you can use generic Key-Value Coding methods:

```
NSManagedObjectContext* context = self.managedObjectContext;  ❶

NSManagedObject* photo;
photo = [NSEntityDescription insertNewObjectForEntityForName: @"Photo"  ❷
                                  inManagedObjectContext: context];

[photo setValue: @"/Library/Desktop Pictures/Nature/Earth.jpg"  ❸
        forKey: @"filePath"];

NSLog( @"photo filePath: %@", [photo valueForKey:@"filePath"] );  ❹
```

Here's the result in the console:

```
photo filePath: /Library/Desktop Pictures/Nature/Earth.jpg
```

 This code won't run correctly in the Gallery project just yet, because you're still building the application, but feel free to come back and try this example later.

Here's a quick look at what this example does:

❶ First, I get a reference to the application delegate's instance of `NSManagedObjectContext`. I need this to fetch existing managed objects, create new managed objects, or to save changes to the data.

❷ I create a new `NSManagedObject` using the entity named Photo. That is, even though I'm using the generic `NSManagedObject` class, the data it can store is defined by the entity.

❸ To set a value on a managed object, I use the Key-Value Coding `-setValue:forKey:` method, with the attribute name `filePath` as the key. I defined this attribute in the graphical model editor.

❹ To retrieve the value, I use the Key-Value Coding `-valueForKey:` method, again using the `filePath` attribute name.

This works fine, but it's somewhat limiting because you can use only the `-setValue:forKey:` and `-valueForKey:` methods. It would be better if you could declare properties, call methods directly, and add methods to the class to support features specific to each time. This also has the significant advantage of allowing the compiler to do type checking to make sure you're not trying to pass an NSNumber to a property that is defined as a string.

You can do all of this by creating a custom subclass of NSManagedObject for each entity type. You already added the custom class names in the model editor, so now you'll create the actual class files. Add two new Objective-C classes that are subclasses of NSObject. Name them CBPhoto and CBAlbum.

Implement the photo class

Replace the contents of the *CBPhoto.h* header file with the code from Example 9-10.

Example 9-10. CBPhoto.h

```objc
#import <Cocoa/Cocoa.h>

@class CBAlbum;

@interface CBPhoto : NSManagedObject

// attributes.
@property (retain) NSString* filePath;
@property (retain) NSString* uniqueID;
@property (retain) NSNumber* orderIndex;

// relationships.
@property (retain) CBAlbum*  album;

// non-modeled properties.
@property (readonly) NSImage* largeThumbnail;

// methods.
+ (id) photoInDefaultContext;

@end
```

Replace the contents of the *CBPhoto.m* implementation file with the code from Example 9-11.

Example 9-11. CBPhoto.m

```objc
#import "CBPhoto.h"
#import <Quartz/Quartz.h>

@interface CBPhoto ()
@property (retain) NSImage* thumbnail;
- (void) generateUniqueID;
@end


@implementation CBPhoto

// use 'dynamic' for Core Data properties.
@dynamic filePath;
```

```
@dynamic uniqueID;
@dynamic orderIndex;
@dynamic album;

// use 'synthesize' for normal properties.
@synthesize thumbnail;


+ (id) photoInDefaultContext {

    NSManagedObjectContext* context = [[NSApp delegate] managedObjectContext];

    CBPhoto* newItem;
    newItem = [NSEntityDescription insertNewObjectForEntityForName:@"Photo"
                                            inManagedObjectContext:context];

    newItem.filePath = nil;

    return newItem;
}

- (NSImage*) largeThumbnail {

    // 'largeThumbnail' is used by the list view.

    if ( self.thumbnail ) return self.thumbnail;

    NSSize      size = NSMakeSize( 250, 250 );
    CFStringRef path = (CFStringRef) self.filePath;
    CFURLRef    url  =
      CFURLCreateWithFileSystemPath( NULL, path, kCFURLPOSIXPathStyle, NO);

    // use QuickLook to generate a thumbnail of the image.
    CGImageRef  thumb = QLThumbnailImageCreate( NULL, url, size, nil );
    NSImage*    image = [[NSImage alloc] initWithCGImage:thumb size:size];
    self.thumbnail = image;

    CFRelease( url );
    CFRelease( thumb );
    [image release];

    return image;
}

#pragma mark -
#pragma mark Core Data Methods

- (void) awakeFromInsert {

    // called when the object is first created.
    [self generateUniqueID];
}

#pragma mark -
#pragma mark 'IKImageBrowserItem' Protocol Methods
```

```objc
-(NSString *) imageTitle {

    NSString* fullFileName = self.filePath.lastPathComponent;
    return [fullFileName stringByDeletingPathExtension];
}

- (NSString*) imageUID {

    // return uniqueID if it exists.
    NSString* uniqueID = self.uniqueID;
    if ( uniqueID ) return uniqueID;
    [self generateUniqueID];
    return self.uniqueID;
}

- (NSString *) imageRepresentationType {
    return IKImageBrowserPathRepresentationType;
}

- (id) imageRepresentation {
    return self.filePath;
}

#pragma mark -
#pragma mark Private

- (void) generateUniqueID {

    NSString* uniqueID = self.uniqueID;
    if ( uniqueID != nil ) return;
    self.uniqueID = [[NSProcessInfo processInfo] globallyUniqueString];
}

- (void) dealloc {

    // Core Data properties automatically managed.
    // Only release sythesized properties.
    self.thumbnail = nil;
    [super dealloc];
}

@end
```

CBPhoto implements the IKImageBrowserItem protocol from IKImageBrowserView, which uses protocols to support the display of items instead of providing specific classes you need to implement. The reason for this is that you may want *any* object to be an item in the browser view, and not necessarily just images. For example, you could display sound files with waveform preview icons. If the view required you to return a special "browser view item" object, you'd have to create a subclass of it just so you could add an instance variable for the sound object.

CBPhoto already has all of the necessary data needed for the image browser, but it's based on NSManagedObject, which isn't related to IKImageBrowserView at all. Because of flexible design of IKImageBrowserView, the class doesn't matter, because you just have to implement the methods that the IKImageBrowserItem protocol declares. This means you can use CBPhoto objects directly within the view.

Example 9-12 lists methods declared by the IKImageBrowserItem *protocol* (this is pulled into your project by the ImageKit framework, which is itself pulled in by the Quartz framework you added earlier).

Example 9-12. Excerpt from IKImageBrowserView.h

```
@interface NSObject (IKImageBrowserItem)

- (NSString *) imageUID;                /* required */
- (NSString *) imageRepresentationType; /* required */
- (id)         imageRepresentation;     /* required */

- (NSUInteger) imageVersion;
- (NSString *) imageTitle;
- (NSString *) imageSubtitle;
- (BOOL)       isSelectable;

@end
```

I stripped out a lot of the comments for space reasons, but go and look at them in *IKImageBrowserView.h* when you get a chance (you can search for the filename with Spotlight). This is the kind of code you should write.

In essence, this protocol is the view's way of saying, "If you give me an image, an image type, and a unique ID, I'll let you join the party." The view works exactly the same for all objects as long as it gets the data it needs, and you can add the required methods to existing classes using a category.

Implement the album class

The next step is to fill in the header and implementation for CBAlbum. Replace the contents of the *CBAlbum.h* header file with the code from Example 9-13.

Example 9-13. CBAlbum.h

```
#import <Cocoa/Cocoa.h>

@interface CBAlbum : NSManagedObject

@property (retain) NSString* title;
@property (retain) NSSet*    photos;

+ (id) defaultAlbum;
+ (id) albumInDefaultContext;

@end
```

Replace the contents of the *CBAlbum.m* implementation file with the code from Example 9-14.

Example 9-14. CBAlbum.m

```objc
#import "CBAlbum.h"

@implementation CBAlbum

// use 'dynamic' for Core Data properties.
@dynamic title;
@dynamic photos;

+ (id) albumInDefaultContext {

    NSManagedObjectContext* context =
      [[NSApp delegate] managedObjectContext];

    CBAlbum* newItem;
    newItem = [NSEntityDescription insertNewObjectForEntityForName:@"Album"
                                         inManagedObjectContext:context];

    return newItem;
}

+ (id) defaultAlbum {

    NSManagedObjectContext* context =
      [[NSApp delegate] managedObjectContext];

    NSEntityDescription* entity
        = [NSEntityDescription entityForName: @"Album"
                      inManagedObjectContext: context];

    // create a fetch request to find 'Default' album.
    NSFetchRequest* fetch   = [[NSFetchRequest alloc] init];
    fetch.entity            = entity;
    fetch.predicate
      = [NSPredicate predicateWithFormat:@"title == 'Default'"];

    // run fetch and make sure it succeeded.
    NSError* error = nil;
    NSArray* results = [context executeFetchRequest:fetch error:&error];
    [fetch release];
    if ( error ) {
        NSLog( @"error: %@", error );
        return nil;
    }

    // create the album if it doesn't exist.
    CBAlbum* album = nil;
    if ( results.count > 0 ) {
        album = [results objectAtIndex:0];
    } else {
        album = [self albumInDefaultContext];
```

```
        album.title = @"Default";
    }

    return album;
}

// used by the list view.
- (NSImage*) image {
    return [NSImage imageNamed:NSImageNameFolder];
}

@end
```

Now that the custom classes have been created and associated with their entities in the model, you can use their properties and methods directly:

```
NSManagedObjectContext* context = self.managedObjectContext;

CBPhoto* photo;
photo = [NSEntityDescription insertNewObjectForEntityForName: @"Photo"
                                     inManagedObjectContext: context];

photo.filePath = @"/Library/Desktop Pictures/Nature/Earth.jpg";

CBAlbum* album;
album = [NSEntityDescription insertNewObjectForEntityForName: @"Album"
                                     inManagedObjectContext: context];

album.title = @"Photos of Earth";
photo.album = album;

NSLog( @"photo title: %@", photo.filePath );
NSLog( @"album title: %@", album.title );
NSLog( @"Photos in '%@': %lu", album.title, album.photos.count );
```

Here's the result in the console:

```
photo title: /Library/Desktop Pictures/Nature/Earth.jpg
album title: Photos of Earth
Photos in 'Photos of Earth': 1
```

Create the User Interface

Now that you've created all of the classes, it's time to set up the interface. There are three main steps to this:

1. Remove the default window provided by the Xcode template. Because you added your own window XIB and window controller, you don't need the default one.

2. Set up the UI of the main window. The window will host each of the custom views stored in the view XIBs, but the window itself has some controls.

3. Set up the UI of each of the view XIBs. Right now, each of the views are empty. You need to add some controls to them before they're useful. You'll also bind the views to an `NSManagedObjectContext` to load data from the persistent store.

Remove the Default Window

This part is easy. Double-click *MainMenu.xib* in the Xcode sidebar to open it in Interface Builder. Select the Window icon (Figure 9-27) and press Delete to remove it. That's it. It should now look like Figure 9-28.

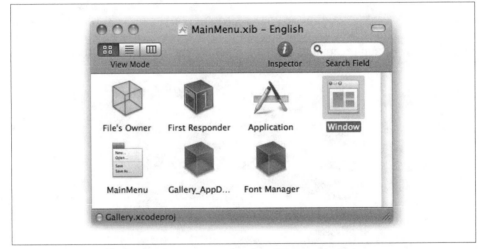

Figure 9-27. The MainMenu.xib file with the default window icon

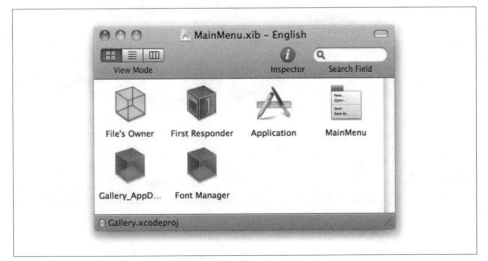

Figure 9-28. The MainMenu.xib file once the default window icon is removed

Add the album menu

There's one more thing to do in this file. Double-click the Main Menu icon to open it. Search for "submenu" in the Library and drag an NSMenuItem to the menu. Place it after the View menu and before the Window menu. Double-click the menu and rename it to Album.

Single-click the Album menu to display the menu item inside. Double-click the menu item and rename it to New Album. Select the menu item and open the Attributes Inspector by pressing Command-1. Click in the Key Equivalent box and type Command-N to bind the menu command to that key shortcut.

Click on First Responder and bring up the Attributes Inspector. Click the plus button to add a new action, and type newAlbum: for the name (see Figure 9-29). Control-drag from the New Album menu item to First Responder and select the newAlbum: action.

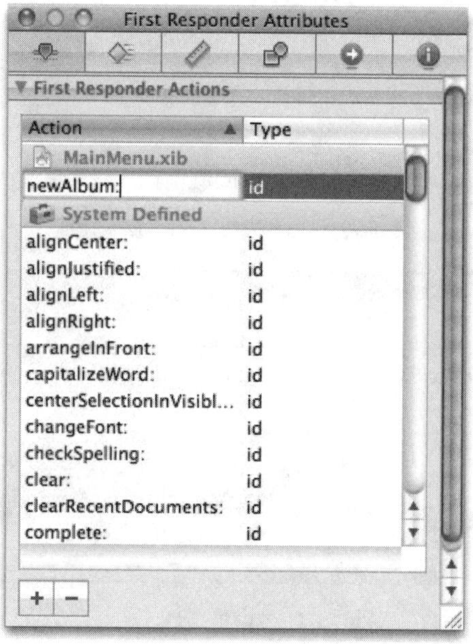

Figure 9-29. Click the plus button to add a new First Responder action, and type newAlbum: for the name

Save the file, close it (because you won't want to make any more changes to it right now), then switch back to Xcode. It's important to close documents in Interface Builder when you're no longer using them to avoid changing the wrong file.

Create the Main Window Interface

Double-click on *CBMainWindow.xib* in the Xcode sidebar to open it in Interface Builder. First and most importantly, select the File's Owner icon in the document window and press Command-6 to bring up the Identity Inspector. Type `CBMainWindow` in the Class field (Figure 9-30). This enables the window controller to manage this XIB.

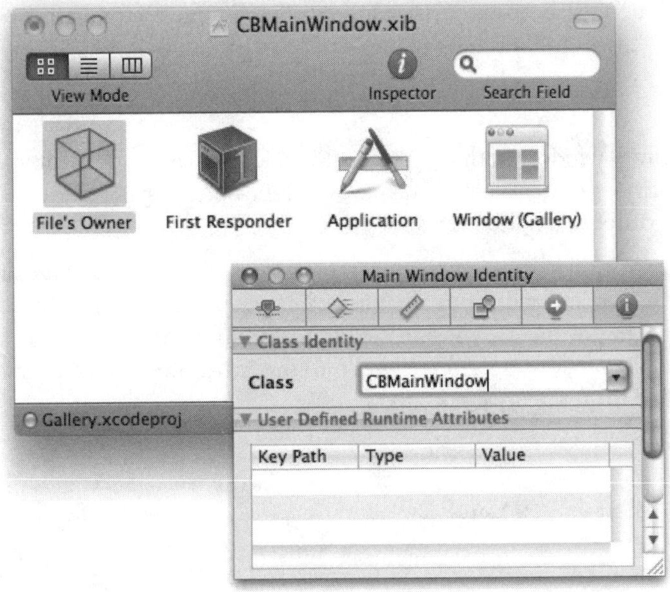

Figure 9-30. Select File's Owner and set the class to CBMainWindow using the Identity Inspector (press Command-6)

Next, Control-drag a connection from File's Owner to the Window icon and choose the `window` outlet. Then Control-drag a connection from the Window icon over to File's Owner and select the `delegate` outlet.

Set window sizing

Click the Window icon in the document window and bring up the Size Inspector (Command-3). In the Minimum Size section of the Inspector, click Use Current. This will use the window's current size as the minimum. You should always set a minimum size on windows to prevent your controls from being rendered at unusual sizes.

If you want to set the initial size and location of a window (which is always a good idea), place the prototype window wherever you like, resize it to whatever dimensions you prefer, then click Use Current in the Content Frame section of the Inspector. Save the file to apply the changes.

Select Large Bottom Border from the Content Border pop up. This will add a dragable control surface to the bottom of the window. Finally, press Command-1 to switch to the Attributes Inspector and rename the window to Gallery.

Add controls

Open the Library window with Command-Shift-L and search for "segment". Drag out an instance of `NSSegmentedControl` and place it at the bottom-right of the window, inside the content border you added earlier.

With the control still selected, bring up the Size Inspector. In the Autosizing section, disable the top and left struts, but enable the bottom and right ones so that the control stays anchored in the lower-right portion of the window. You can use the preview view in the Autosizing section as a guide. Switch to the Attributes Inspector and select Textured Rounded from the Style pop up.

Make sure to drag out `NSSegmentedControl` from the Library, not `NSSegmentedControlCell`. You can't place the cell directly on the window.

While still in the Attributes Inspector, select Segment 0 from the segment pop up. This allows you to edit settings for the first segment of the control. Type (or select) `NSIconViewTemplate` in the Image combo box. Select Segment 1 and type `NSQuickLookTemplate` for the Image name. Switch to Segment 2 and type `NSListView Template` in the Image field (see Figure 9-31).

Finally, bring the Library window back to the front and search for "label". Drag out the instance of `NSTextField` that has the name Label. Place it at the bottom-left part of the window. In the Size Inspector, choose Small from the Size pop up. In the Autosizing section, disable the top strut and enable the bottom one so it stays anchored to the bottom-left portion of the window. When you're done, the window should look like Figure 9-32.

Set up bindings

Search for "array controller" in the Library and drag an instance of `NSArrayControl ler` to the XIB document window. Select the array controller, then single-click its name and change it to Photos. Switch to the Attributes Inspector by pressing Command-1.

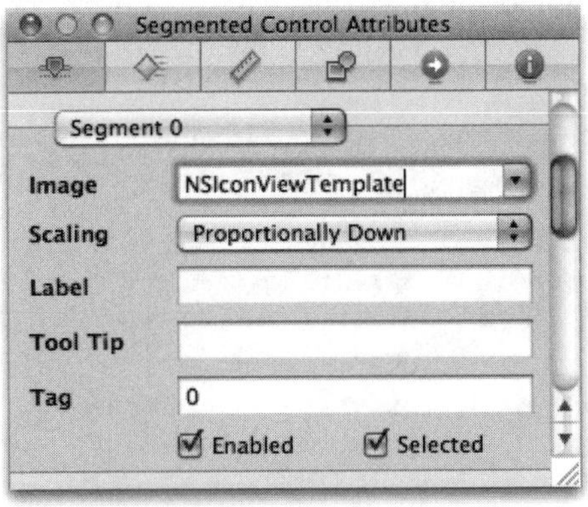

Figure 9-31. Set the image for Segment 0 to NSIconViewTemplate

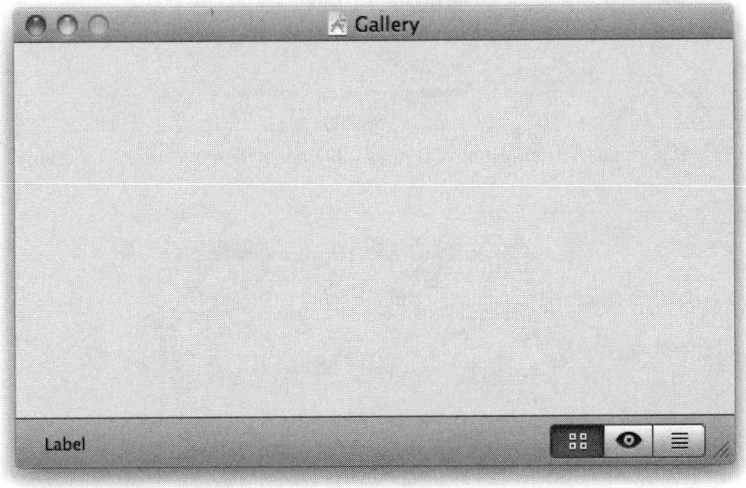

Figure 9-32. The CBMainMenu.xib window with controls added

Select Entity from the Mode pop up, and type `Photo` in the Entity Name field. Enable the Prepares Content checkbox. When you're done, it should look like Figure 9-33.

Open the Bindings Inspector with Command-4. Under the Parameters section, bind Managed Object Context to Application with a Model Key Path of `dele gate.managedObjectContext`.

Select the text field label at the bottom-left corner of the window and bring up the Bindings Inspector. Under the Value With Pattern section, open Display Pattern Value1. Bind to Photos with a Controller Key of `arrangedObjects` and a Model Key Path of `@count`. Finally, type `%{value1}@ photos` in the Display Pattern field. This will take the total count of photos and add the string "photos" on the end. It's similar to the way NSLog() formats strings. Figure 9-34 shows how the bindings should look.

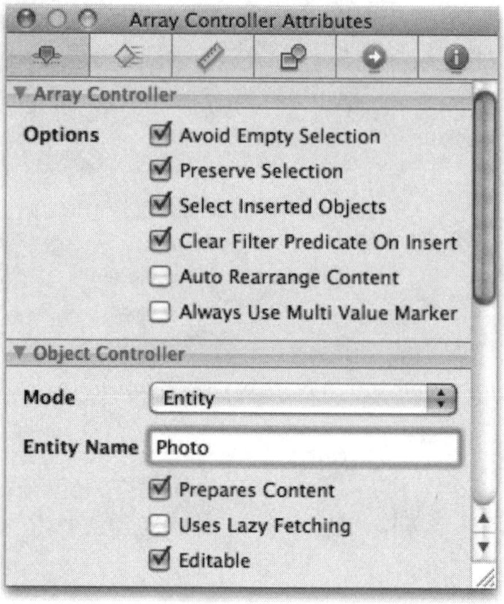

Figure 9-33. Configure the Attributes settings for the Photos array controller as shown

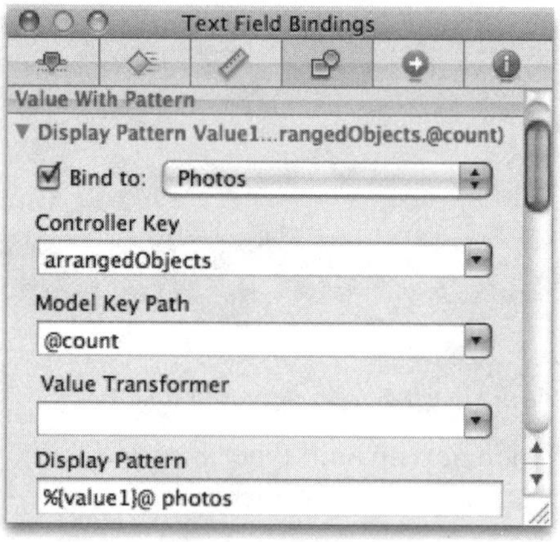

Figure 9-34. Configure the text field bindings as shown

Connect outlets and actions

Right-click File's Owner to bring up its HUD window. Connect the `viewSelec`
`tionControl` outlet to the segmented control at the bottom-right of the window. Now
control-drag from the segmented control to File's Owner, and select the `-viewSelec`
`tionDidChange:` action.

Save and close the XIB file, and switch back to Xcode.

Create the Browser Interface

Double-click *CBBrowserView.xib* to open it in Interface Builder. Select the File's Owner
icon in the document window and press Command-6 to bring up the Identity Inspector.
Type `CBBrowserView` in the Class field. This enables the view controller to manage this
XIB. Next, Control-drag a connection from File's Owner to the Custom View icon and
choose the `view` outlet.

The interface is made up of two main parts: the table view on the left side of the image
and the browser view on the right. Double-click on the Custom View icon in the document window to display the view.

Set up the album table

Drag out an `NSTableView` from the Library and place it onto the view. Resize it so it fills
the entire height of the window and roughly one-third of the width (the exact size is
not important in this case).

Make sure that the table's enclosing scroll view is selected by confirming that the Attributes Inspector's title is "Scroll View Attributes." If it isn't, Control-Command-Shift-
click on the table and select Bordered Scroll View.

Remember this technique to select a specific part of a view hierarchy,
because you'll need to use it throughout the rest of the chapter. For
example, if I say "select the table view," you must make sure that the
table itself is selected, not one of the columns or the scroll view. This is
critical when creating XIB files.

With the scroll view selected, switch to the Size Inspector. Enable the top, left, and
bottom struts, and enable the vertical springs. The idea is that the view should resize
its height to match the window, but keep a constant width and stay anchored to the
left side of the window. Next, select the table view inside of the scroll view and bring
up the Attributes Inspector.

Again, make sure the Inspector title says "Table View Attributes." If it says "Scroll View Attributes," Control-Command-Shift-click on the view and select the table view.

With the table selected and the Attributes Inspector open, choose Source List from the Highlight pop up. Make sure that the table has two columns using the Columns stepper control. Now select the table *header* view (across the top of the table), and drag the column divider to resize the left column so it's just wide enough to hold a fairly small icon, as shown in Figure 9-35.

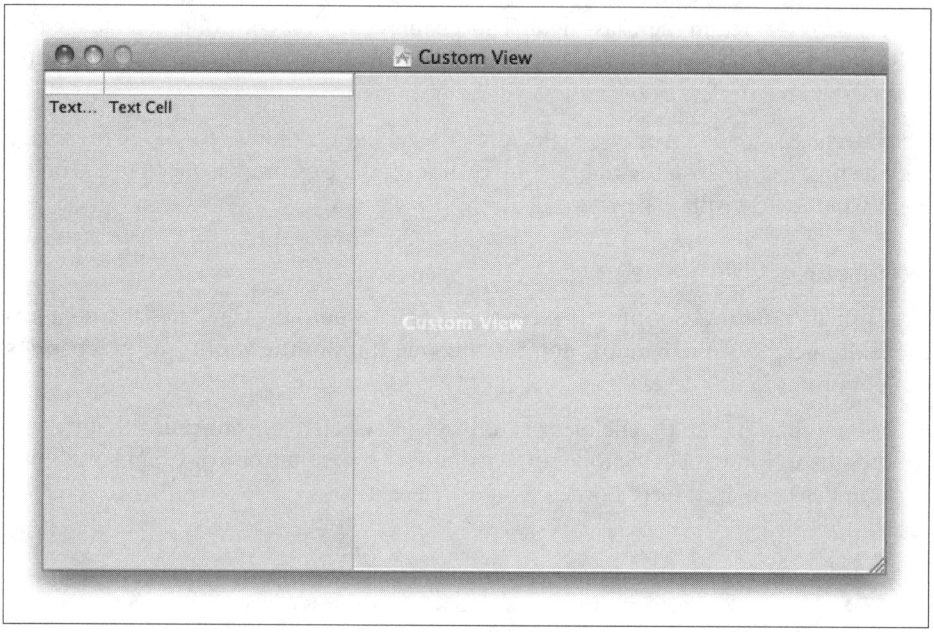

Figure 9-35. Resize the left table column so it's just wide enough for a small icon

In the Library window, search for "image cell" and drag an `NSImageCell` instance to the first column of the table. Finally, reselect the table itself and switch to the Attributes Inspector. Uncheck the Headers checkbox to hide the table columns. Select the text field cell inside of the right column, open the Size Inspector, and choose Small from the Size pop up.

This style of table is called a "source list" in Mac application design.

Set up the image browser

Search for "image browser" in the Library window, and drag an instance of IKImageBrowserView onto the custom view. Select Layout → Embed Objects In → Scroll View. Open the Attributes Inspector and enable the Automatically Hide Scrollers checkbox. Switch to the Size Inspector and enable all of the sprints and struts so the image browser resizes in both dimensions with the window. Position the browser view against the right edge of the table view, and resize it to fill the remaining space of the custom view. It should look like Figure 9-36 when you're done.

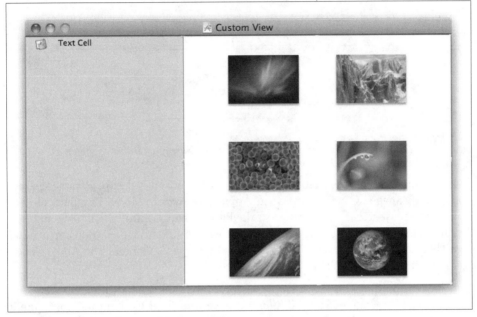

Figure 9-36. The basic layout of the browser view

Set up bindings

Add two NSArrayController objects to the XIB document window. Select one and then single-click its title to edit it. Name it Albums, and use the same technique to rename the other array controller to Photos. Select the Albums array controller and open the Attributes Inspector.

Select Entity from the Mode pop up, and type Album in the Entity Name field. Enable the Prepares Content checkbox. When you're done, it should look like Figure 9-37.

Figure 9-37. Configure the Attributes settings for the Albums array controller as shown

Switch to the Bindings Inspector by pressing Command-4. Under the Parameters section, bind Managed Object Context to Application with a Model Key Path of `dele` `gate.managedObjectContext`. Now select the Photos array controller and switch to the Attributes Inspector by pressing Command-1. Select Entity from the Mode pop up, and type `Photo` in the Entity Name field. Enable the Prepares Content checkbox. When you're done, it should look like Figure 9-38.

Switch to the Bindings Inspector by pressing Command-4. Under the Controller Content section, bind Content Set to Albums (make sure you bind Content *Set*, not Content or Content Array) with a Controller Key of `selection` and Model Key Path of `photos` (see Figure 9-39). This ensures that the browser view will display only photos that belong to the currently selected album.

> You generally use the Content Set binding when binding to Core Data collections, because to-many relationships are represented as instances of `NSMutableSet`, not `NSMutableArray`. One key point here is that all of the items in a set are unique. Even though sets don't have any inherent order, you can introduce your own ordering scheme with sort descriptors, which Gallery does with `CBPhoto` objects using the `orderIndex` property.

Under the Controller Content Parameters section, bind Sort Descriptors to File's Owner with a Model Key Path of `imagesSortDescriptors`. This will use the `imagesSort` `Descriptors` property in the `CBBrowserView` class. Then, under the Parameters section,

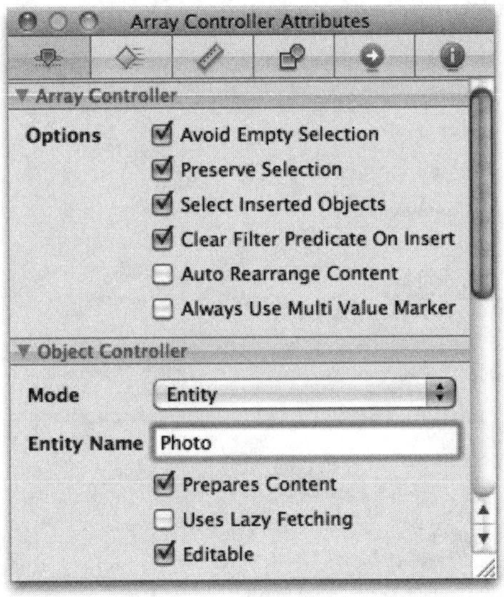

Figure 9-38. Configure the Attributes settings for the Photos array controller as shown

bind Managed Object Context to Application with a Model Key Path of dele gate.managedObjectContext.

Back, in the custom view, select the left-side image table column and open the Bindings Inspector. Bind Value to Albums, with a Controller Key of arrangedObjects and a Model Key Path of image. Select the right-side text table column. Bind Value to Albums, with a Controller Key of arrangedObjects and a Model Key Path of title.

Select the image browser view and open the Bindings Inspector. Bind Content to Photos with a Controller Key of arrangedObjects.

Connect outlets

Right-click the File's Owner icon and connect the albumsArrayController and imagesArrayController outlets to the Albums and Photos array controllers, respectively. Connect the albumsTable outlet to the table view, and the imageBrowser outlet to the image browser view. Save and close the XIB file and switch back to Xcode.

Create the Editor View Interface

The editor view interface is much simpler, because all of the hard work is done by ImageKit. Double-click *CBEditorView.xib* to open it in Interface Builder. Select the File's Owner icon in the document window and press Command-6 to bring up the Identity Inspector. Type CBEditorView in the Class field. Right-click the File's Owner icon to bring up its HUD window, and drag a connection from the view outlet to the Custom View icon, as shown in Figure 9-40.

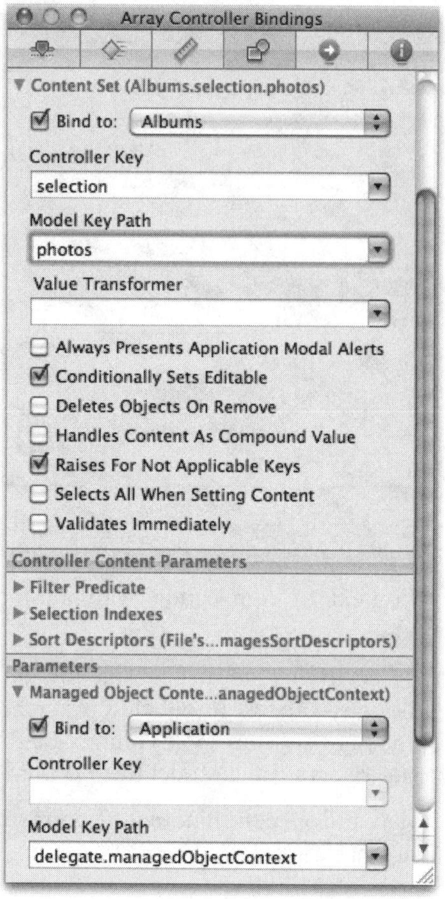

Figure 9-39. Bindings for the Photos array controller (Sort Descriptors binding not shown)

Search for "image view" in the Library and drag an instance of `IKImageView` to the custom view. Resize it to fill the entire view. With the image view still selected, bring up the Size Inspector and activate all of the springs and struts so that the view resizes with the window.

Finally, right-click on File's Owner and connect the `imageView` outlet to the image view you added. Save and close the XIB file and switch back to Xcode.

Create the List View Interface

Double-click *CBListView.xib* to open it in Interface Builder. Select the File's Owner icon in the document window and press Command-6 to bring up the Identity Inspector.

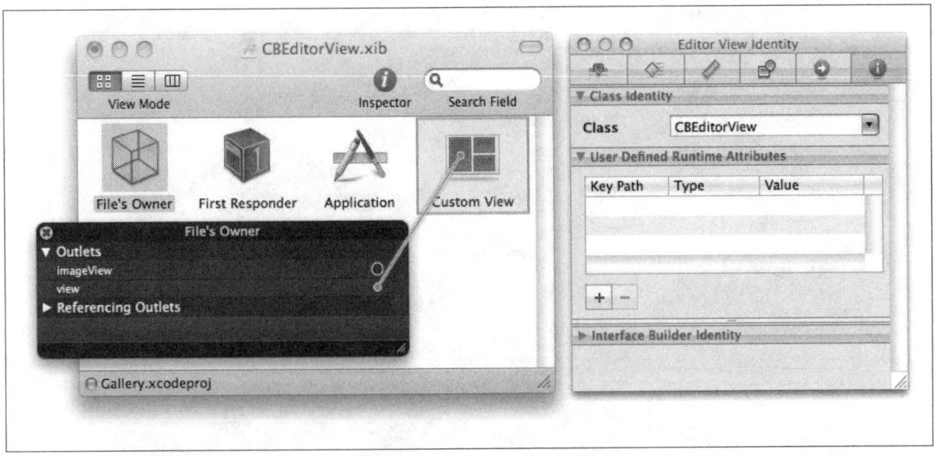

Figure 9-40. Connect the File's Owner view outlet to the Custom View icon

Type `CBListView` in the Class field. Next, Control-drag a connection from File's Owner to the Custom View icon and choose the `view` outlet.

Search for "table view" in the Library and drag an `NSTableView` to the custom view, but don't resize it yet. Select the table view (inside the scroll view) and open the Attributes Inspector. Increase the column count to 3. Reposition and resize the table view so it fills the entire custom view.

Select the Scroll View icon and open the Size Inspector. Activate all of the springs and struts so that the view resizes with the window. Rename the table columns by double-clicking them. From the left, name them Image, Album, and File Path. Search for "image cell" in the Library and drag an `NSImageCell` object onto the first column (Figure 9-41).

Set up bindings

Drag an `NSArrayController` out from the Library and drop it onto the XIB document window. Rename it to Photos. Select the array controller and open the Attributes Inspector. Choose Entity from the Mode pop up, and type `Photo` in the Entity Name field. Enable the Prepares Content checkbox.

Open the Bindings Inspector with Command-4. Under the Parameters section, bind Managed Object Context to Application with a Model Key Path of `dele gate.managedObjectContext`.

Back in the table, select the image column at the far left. Open the Bindings Inspector and bind the column's Value to Photos with a Controller Key of `arrangedObjects` and a Model Key Path of `largeThumbnail` (see Figure 9-42).

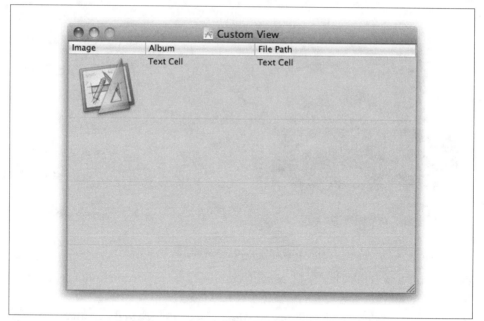

Figure 9-41. Drag an NSImageCell onto the first table column

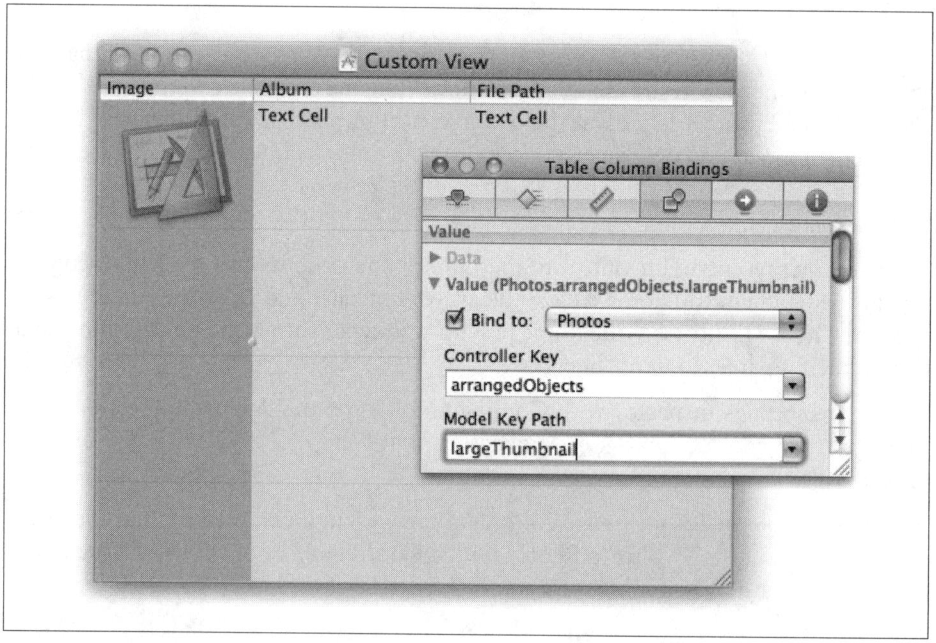

Figure 9-42. Bind the image column to Photos with a Controller Key of arrangedObjects and largeThumbnail for the Model Key Path

Select the Album table column and open the Bindings Inspector. Bind Value to Photos with a Controller Key of `arrangedObjects` and a Model Key Path of `album.title`. Finally, select the File Path table column. In the Bindings Inspector, bind Value to Photos with a Controller Key of `arrangedObjects` and a Model Key Path of `filePath`.

Connect outlets

Right-click the File's Owner icon and connect the `imagesArrayController` outlet to the Photos array controller. Connect the `imagesTable` outlet to the table view. Save and close the XIB file and switch back to Xcode.

Run the Application

At long last, you're done. Save all open files in Xcode or Interface Builder, and press Command-R to build and run the project. Once the application is running, find some photos on your Mac and drag them into the browser view (Figure 9-43). Try rearranging the photos.

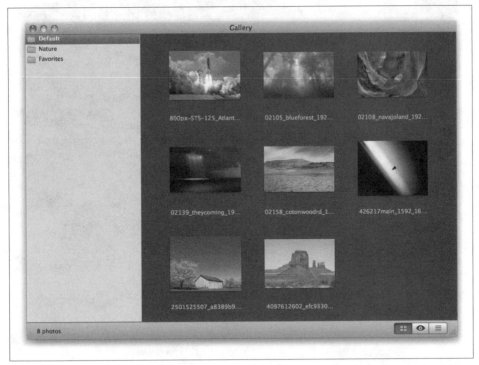

Figure 9-43. The finished Gallery application; double-click an image in the browser or list view to open it in the editor view

You can also make a new album from the Album menu, and drag different photos in. Double-click an image in the browser or list view to open it in the editor view. Double-click the image while in the editor view to bring up the image adjustment panel (Figure 9-44). Click the browser or list item in the segmented controls to switch back.

Your data is automatically saved by Core Data when you quit the application. Add some photos and albums, then press Command-Q to quit. Relaunch the application and all of your data will be back. If you want to permanently remove the saved data, delete the *CocoaBookGallery* folder in */Users/<yourusername>/Library/Application Support*.

 Your data will not be saved if you click the Tasks stop icon in the Xcode toolbar. This directly ends the program without going through the normal channels; it's equivalent to a Force Quit.

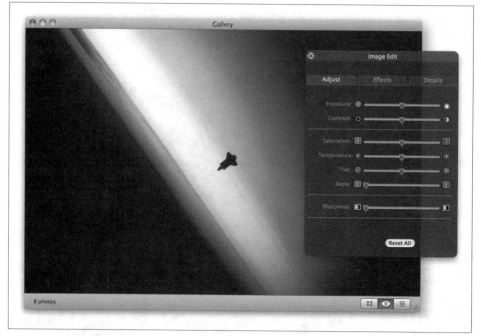

Figure 9-44. Double-click an image in the editor view to bring up the image adjustment panel

Preparing for Release

If you want to run this application outside of Xcode or on another Mac, you need to build with the Release Configuration. Select Release as the Active Configuration from the Xcode Toolbar as shown in Figure 9-45.

Figure 9-45. Select Release as the Active Configuration from the Xcode toolbar

In the same toolbar, verify that Active Architecture is x86_64. Next, double-click the Gallery project icon at the top of the Xcode sidebar to open the Project Inspector. Make sure the Architectures field is *only* 64-bit Intel (see Figure 9-46). If it contains other items, the project will not build, because Gallery uses 64-bit Objective-C features.

Press Command-R to build and run and make sure everything works. This build will probably take a bit longer than the Debug build, which is why you don't generally build as Release while you're working on the project. Finally, open the Products group near the bottom of the Xcode sidebar. Right-click on Gallery.app and choose Reveal in Finder (Figure 9-47).

This will actually take you to the finished Gallery application in the Finder, as shown in Figure 9-48 (you don't need to copy the file labeled *Gallery.app.dSYM*). You can copy this file to any other 64-bit Mac running Snow Leopard.

Now you just need to hire an icon artist.

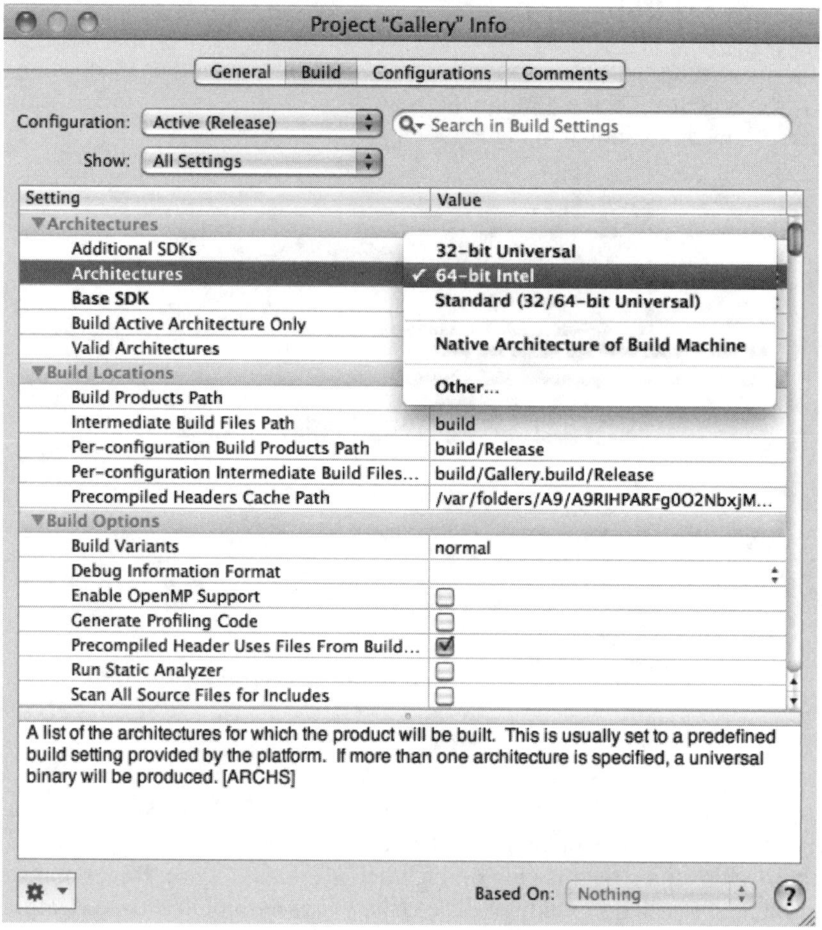

Figure 9-46. Gallery uses 64-bit Objective-C features, so make sure you're only building for 64-bit Intel

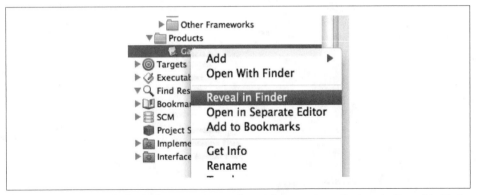

Figure 9-47. Right-click the Gallery.app item in the Products group and select the Reveal in Finder item to display it in the Finder

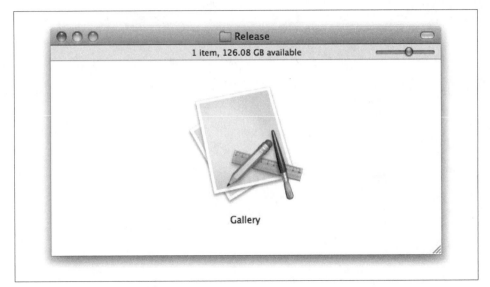

Figure 9-48. The Gallery application in the Finder

CHAPTER 10

Custom Views and Drawing

If you're looking to get started with graphics programming, you've come to the right place. Mac OS X has a lot of graphics frameworks to choose from, and each one specializes in something different. Here's a quick rundown of the main players:

AppKit
> The UI part of Cocoa has classes and methods for dealing with colors, geometry, styled text, bitmap images, and complex paths. This is the first place you should start when writing custom drawing code for the Mac UI.

Core Graphics
> This is the lower-level, C-based framework for 2D drawing in Mac OS X. Core Graphics is also part of the iPhone SDK, so you can share code easily. The drawback is that the C functions and memory management are not as convenient or as flexible as the Objective-C AppKit drawing classes.

Core Animation
> This is a relatively new framework that's part of both Mac OS X and the iPhone OS. It's based on OpenGL and allows you to use a lot of impressive 3D and transition effects, but it has an easy-to-use Objective-C interface. Because it uses the GPU, it's incredibly fast. You can also combine Core Animation with AppKit in certain cases.

Core Image
> This framework allows you to apply special effects to your images and views, such as Gaussian Blur, bloom, color adjustments, and even transitions like page curls and dissolves. This isn't an API that's useful for general drawing. Instead, you usually combine it with another framework. Core Image is currently not available in the iPhone SDK.

It's probably tempting to go straight to Core Graphics because it's available on both Mac and iPhone, and plain C functions are slightly faster. However, I think programmers who go this route are giving up a lot of features that make it fun and easy to write Cocoa code.

The Core Graphics structs and functions are easier to use than most C libraries, but they're not nearly as convenient or fault tolerant as Objective-C classes. Using AppKit means that you can use autorelease, add categories, and easily store objects in collections. You also end up writing far less code, because objects can usually keep track of their own state easily. And the amount of view drawing code you'll be able to share between Mac and iPhone is fairly low anyway, because the UIs are usually very different.

For these reasons—and others we'll eventually get to—this chapter is all about making custom views with the AppKit classes. But the concepts and even names are very similar to those in Core Graphics, so you're basically learning both at the same time.

Basic Geometry

All drawing in AppKit starts with a point—an x and y coordinate in the view. Views use the NSPoint struct to describe these points. Many of the AppKit geometry types, though, are actually aliases to the Core Graphics geometry types. So an NSPoint is actually another name for a CGPoint. There is no performance penalty for this, because they are just linked by a typedef statement.

 The bridging of the AppKit and Core Graphics geometry types is only automatic for 64-bit applications. If you're writing 32-bit Mac applications, you have to convert these types manually.

Here's the definition for the NSPoint struct and its counterpart, CGPoint:

```
typedef CGPoint NSPoint;

struct CGPoint {
  CGFloat x;
  CGFloat y;
};
typedef struct CGPoint CGPoint;
```

Looking past the slightly odd C syntax, you can see that an NSPoint is just a CGPoint, which has two fields: x and y. Both fields hold floating-point values, so you can create a point with an x value of 1.5, and a y value of 1.0. This might be surprising, because you *technically* can't have "half a pixel" on a monitor, but there's a reason for this.

Cocoa uses a scalable graphics systems, which means that it's designed to work well at different resolutions. Using floating-point values makes this arrangement work better, as a high-resolution display might have 1.5 times more pixels per inch than another monitor. The main way this affects you is that you may need to round coordinate values to whole numbers to get pixel-exact drawing.

That said, this chapter is about drawing UI elements on Mac OS X. To avoid awkward language, I'll use the term "pixels" to describe coordinates, but remember that Cocoa technically considers them *units*.

You can either create an NSPoint directly or use the NSMakePoint() function. This is an *inline* function, which means the code is effectively copied directly into the place where it's called. In other words, you don't incur the overhead you normally would when calling a function. Here are some examples of creating NSPoint structs:

```
NSPoint point1;
point1.x = 4;
point1.y = 11;

NSPoint point2;
point2.x = 12;
point2.y = 21;

NSPoint point3 = NSMakePoint ( 19, 8 );
NSPoint point4 = NSMakePoint ( 24, 18 );
```

The NSSize type has two floating-point values: width and height. It's interchangeable with the CGSize type:

```
typedef CGSize NSSize;

struct CGSize {
  CGFloat width;
  CGFloat height;
};
typedef struct CGSize CGSize;
```

You can either create NSSize structs directly or use the NSMakeSize() function. Here are some examples:

```
NSSize size1;
size1.width  = 1920;
size1.height = 1200;

NSSize size2;
size2.width  = 16;
size2.height = 16;

NSSize size3 = NSMakeSize ( 1024, 768 );
NSSize size4 = NSMakeSize ( 640, 480 );
```

An NSRect is simply a combination of an NSPoint field called origin, and an NSSize field called size. As with the other types, it's based on its CGRect counterpart:

```
typedef CGRect NSRect;

struct CGRect {
  CGPoint origin;
  CGSize size;
};
typedef struct CGRect CGRect;
```

You'll see NSRect used everywhere in Cocoa view and image classes. Like the other geometry types, you can create an NSRect manually or use the NSMakeRect() function:

```
// create a rect from separate point and size variables.
NSPoint origin1 = NSMakePoint (  0,  0 );
NSSize  size1   = NSMakeSize ( 40, 40 );

NSRect rect1;
rect1.origin = origin1;
rect1.size   = size1;

// create a rect one field at a time.
NSRect rect2;
rect2.origin.x   = 4;
rect2.origin.y   = 4;
rect2.size.width = 32;
rect2.size.height = 32;

// create the whole rect in a single line.
rect3 = NSMakeRect ( 20, 80, 200, 200 );
```

Geometry Structs As Strings

Once you've created a rect, size, or point, you may want to convert it into a string to display in the console, and there are built-in functions to do that: NSStringFrom Rect(), NSStringFromSize(), and NSStringFromPoint(). All take one of the geometry types as input and return a descriptive string:

```
NSRect    rect1       = NSMakeRect ( 0, 0 , 200, 400 );
NSString* rectString1 = NSStringFromRect ( rect1 );
NSLog ( @"rect1: %@", rectString1 );

NSSize    size1       = NSMakeSize ( 256, 256 );
NSString* sizeString1 = NSStringFromSize ( size1 );
NSLog ( @"size1: %@", sizeString1 );

NSPoint   point1      = NSMakePoint ( 100, 100 );
NSString* pointString1 = NSStringFromPoint ( point1 );
NSLog ( @"point1: %@", pointString1 );
```

The result:

```
rect1: {{0, 0}, {200, 400}}
size1: {256, 256}
point1: {100, 100}
```

It also works the other way. Once you have one of these nicely formatted strings, you can use them to create actual structs using NSRectFromString(), NSSizeFromString(), and NSPointFromString():

```
NSString* rectPlist  = @"{{0, 0}, {200, 400}}";
NSString* sizePlist  = @"{256, 256}";
NSString* pointPlist = @"{100, 100}";

NSRect rect1 = NSRectFromString ( rectPlist );
```

```
NSSize    size1  = NSSizeFromString  ( sizePlist );
NSPoint   point1 = NSPointFromString ( pointPlist );
```

It probably seems strange to convert a rect to a string and then back to a rect again, but this is useful for quickly saving geometry data using the NSString methods for reading and writing files, or if you're copying data between applications.

Geometry Structs As NSValues

Geometry structs are not objects, so you can't store them in collections; you need to convert them. You can use NSValue to wrap the struct, and then store the NSValue object in the collection. For example, to create an NSValue that wraps an NSRect, you use the +valueWithRect: method. As a bonus, NSValue is actually smart enough to do the conversion of the struct for you when you display the value object in the console:

```
NSRect    newRect      = NSMakeRect ( 10, 10, 100, 100 );
NSSize    newSize      = NSMakeSize ( 40, 40 );
NSPoint   newPoint     = NSMakePoint ( 4, 4 );

NSValue* rectObject    = [NSValue valueWithRect:newRect];
NSValue* sizeObject    = [NSValue valueWithSize:newSize];
NSValue* pointObject   = [NSValue valueWithPoint:newPoint];

NSMutableArray* array = [NSMutableArray array];
[array addObject:rectObject];
[array addObject:sizeObject];
[array addObject:pointObject];

NSLog ( @"NSValue 0: %@", [array objectAtIndex:0] );
NSLog ( @"NSValue 1: %@", [array objectAtIndex:1] );
NSLog ( @"NSValue 2: %@", [array objectAtIndex:2] );
```

The result in the console:

```
NSValue 0: NSRect:  {{10, 10}, {100, 100}}
NSValue 1: NSSize:  {40, 40}
NSValue 2: NSPoint: {4, 4}
```

When you need to get the actual geometry struct back out, you just call either -rectValue, -sizeValue, or -pointValue on the value object:

```
NSRect    newRect      = NSMakeRect ( 0, 0, 80, 180 );
NSSize    newSize      = NSMakeSize ( 16, 16 );
NSPoint   newPoint     = NSMakePoint ( 0, 0 );

NSValue* rectObject    = [NSValue valueWithRect:newRect];
NSValue* sizeObject    = [NSValue valueWithSize:newSize];
NSValue* pointObject   = [NSValue valueWithPoint:newPoint];

// convert the contents of the NSValue object back
// into a geometry struct.

NSRect    storedRect  = rectObject.rectValue;
```

```
NSSize  storedSize  = sizeObject.sizeValue;
NSPoint storedPoint = pointObject.pointValue;
```

Cocoa View Coordinates

Most onscreen controls in Cocoa apps are subclasses of NSView. The view system gives you a canvas on which to draw images for the user to see, as well as gets input from the keyboard, mouse, and even touch events on newer hardware. But let's start with drawing.

First, it's important to understand that views don't live out on their own. They're a part of a *view hierarchy*. The window has a *content view*, which is the root view for that window. The content view has any number of *subviews*, and each of *those* can have its own subviews. So each window essentially has a view "tree" that starts with the content view.

A view has two NSRect properties that describe its size and location: *bounds* and *frame*. The bounds is the view's internal coordinate system, and the frame is the view's coordinates *inside its parent*. If you want to move a view around inside the window, you have to change its frame.

Because it's based on the PDF drawing model, Cocoa uses the *Cartesian coordinate system* by default, which means the origin is in the bottom left, and higher values go up and to the right (see Figure 10-1). This is different than iPhone and HTML/CSS coordinates, where the origin is in the upper left.

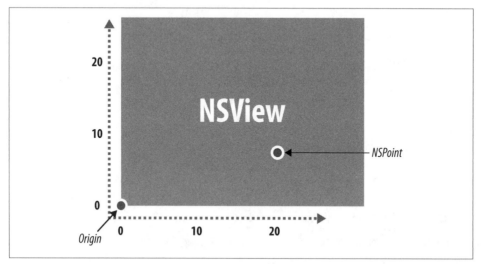

Figure 10-1. The default Cartesian coordinate system in NSView, with the origin in the bottom left

You can change this behavior by implementing -isFlipped in your NSView subclass and returning YES. Once you do this, the view's origin will be in the upper left:

```
- (BOOL) isFlipped {
    return YES;
}
```

However, I don't strongly recommend this. I *do* think it's more natural to describe coordinates starting in the upper left, but most of Cocoa uses the Cartesian system, so you can end up swimming upstream a lot. You can use a flipped coordinate system in your view, but my recommendation is to use the standard system, especially if you're using Core Animation.

Derived Rects

Cocoa provides functions that take an existing NSRect, make a copy, and alter it in some way before returning it. For example, NSOffsetRect() takes a rect and returns a copy that's shifted by some amount. This is useful if you want to create a photo mosaic with several images side by side. Remember, in the default Cartesian system, positive values given to NSOffsetRect() move the rect up and to the right, and negative values move the rect down and to the left:

```
NSRect rect1;
rect1.origin.x    = 100;
rect1.origin.y    = 100;
rect1.size.width  = 30;
rect1.size.height = 25;

// In the NSView Cartesian system, rect2 will be
// 10 units to the right of and 5 units above rect1.
NSRect rect2 = NSOffsetRect ( rect1, 5, 10 );

// In the NSView Cartesian system, rect2 will be
// 40 units to the left of and 60 units below rect1.
NSRect rect3 = NSOffsetRect ( rect1, -40, -60 );
```

The NSIntersectionRect() function takes two rects and returns a *new* rect covering only the overlapping area between the two:

```
// get the common area between two rects.

NSRect rect1 = NSMakeRect ( 0, 0, 30, 25 );
NSRect rect2 = NSMakeRect ( 5, 5, 30, 25 );

NSRect rect3 = NSIntersectionRect ( rect1, rect2 );
```

You can use the NSUnionRect() function to get a rect that completely surrounds both of the smaller input rects:

```
// get a combination of two rects.
NSRect rect1;
rect1.origin.x    = 0;
rect1.origin.y    = 0;
rect1.size.width  = 30;
rect1.size.height = 25;
```

```
// you can use standard C operators to adjust rects.
NSRect rect2 = rect1;
rect2.origin.x += 5;
rect2.origin.y += 10;

NSRect rect3 = NSUnionRect ( rect1, rect2 );
```

The NSInsetRect() function is useful when creating one rectangle embedded in another, such as drawing a frame and then an image inside:

```
NSRect rect1;
rect1.origin.x    = 0;
rect1.origin.y    = 0;
rect1.size.width  = 30;
rect1.size.height = 25;

// get the "inset" version of a rect.
NSRect rect2 = NSInsetRect ( rect1, 2, 2 );

// you can use negative values to create an "outset" rect.
NSRect rect3 = NSInsetRect ( rect1, -10, -20 );
```

Comparison Functions

Because the geometry structs aren't objects, you can't use -isEqual: to compare them. Instead, you use a few comparison functions made specifically for this purpose: NSEqualPoints(), NSEqualRects(), and NSEqualSizes():

```
NSRect  rect1  = NSMakeRect ( 0, 0, 280, 101);
NSRect  rect2;
rect2.origin.x    = 0;
rect2.origin.y    = 0;
rect2.size.width  = 280;
rect2.size.height = 101;

if ( NSEqualRects ( rect1, rect2 ) )
    NSLog (@"rect1 and rect2 are equal");

NSSize size1 = NSMakeSize ( 42, 42 );
NSSize size2 = NSMakeSize ( 24, 24 );

if ( NSEqualSizes ( size1, size2) )
    NSLog (@"size1 and size2 are equal");

// comparison functions are useful when testing
// for the 'zero' constants like NSZeroPoint.

NSPoint point1 = NSMakePoint ( 0, 0 );

if ( NSEqualPoints ( point1, NSZeroPoint ) )
    NSLog (@"point1 and NSZeroPoint are equal");
```

The result in the console:

```
rect1 and rect2 are equal
point1 and NSZeroPoint are equal
```

There are also a few functions to do spatial comparisons (Table 10-1). These are useful for user interactions like drag-and-drop.

Table 10-1. Spatial comparison functions

Method	Description
NSIntersectsRect()	Returns YES if the rects at least partially overlap
NSContainsRect()	Returns YES if the first rect completely contains the second
NSPointInRect()	Returns YES if the point is inside the rect

Here are some examples, including one practical case where you want to see if a point is inside the frame of a view:

```
NSRect rect1  = NSMakeRect ( 10, 10,  40,  40 );
NSRect rect2  = NSMakeRect ( 10, 10, 500, 500 );

if ( NSIntersectsRect ( rect1, rect2 ))
    NSLog (@"rect1 intersects rect2");

if ( NSContainsRect ( rect1, rect2 ))
    NSLog (@"rect1 contains rect2");

// check to see if a point is inside the view.

NSPoint point1 = NSMakePoint ( 10, 10 );
NSRect  rect3  = NSMakeRect  ( 0, 0, 200, 200 );
NSView* view   = [[NSView alloc] initWithFrame:rect3];

if ( NSPointInRect ( point1, view.frame ))
    NSLog (@"point1 is inside the view");

[view release];
```

Here's the result in the console:

```
rect1 intersects rect2
point1 is inside the view
```

Basic Drawing

There are two absolute essentials if you want to do any drawing: a color and something to draw. You use the NSColor class to create colors, and the "something" can be a simple rectangle to start. Well, actually, there's a third thing: you need somewhere to draw. In this case, the "somewhere" will be a view.

NSColor

The NSColor class can do some fairly impressive tricks, but I just want to introduce you to the basics. Here's a simple set of examples that demonstrates almost everything you'll need on a day-to-day basis:

```
// basic color constants.
NSColor* color1 = [NSColor redColor];
NSColor* color2 = [NSColor greenColor];
NSColor* color3 = [NSColor blueColor];
NSColor* color4 = [NSColor purpleColor];
NSColor* color5 = [NSColor yellowColor];
NSColor* color6 = [NSColor orangeColor];

// completely transparent.
NSColor* color7 = [NSColor clearColor];

// color by channel, including alpha.
NSColor* color8 = [NSColor colorWithCalibratedRed: 0.25
                                            green: 0.30
                                             blue: 0.45
                                            alpha: 1.0];

// white value with alpha.
NSColor* color9 = [NSColor colorWithCalibratedWhite: 0.45
                                              alpha: 0.8];
```

Each of the color channels is a value between 0.0 and 1.0. If your reference colors are RGBA values between 0 and 255, you can do some quick math to get a floating-point value:

```
// divide by 255 to get floating-point value between 0.0 and 1.0.
NSColor* color = [NSColor colorWithCalibratedRed: (122.0/255.0)
                                           green: (224.0/255.0)
                                            blue: (185.0/255.0)
                                           alpha: (128.0/255.0) ];
```

Once you have a color, you usually set it with the -[NSColor set] method and then draw a shape or text. You can also set the stroke and fill colors separately:

```
NSColor* color1 = [NSColor redColor];
[color1 set];

NSColor* color2 = [NSColor greenColor];
[color2 setStroke];

NSColor* color3 = [NSColor blueColor];
[color3 setFill];
```

Subclassing NSView

Create a new Cocoa project called "BasicCocoaDrawing" and place it in ~/*CocoaBook/ ch10/*. Add to the project an Objective-C class that is a subclass of NSView, as shown in Figure 10-2.

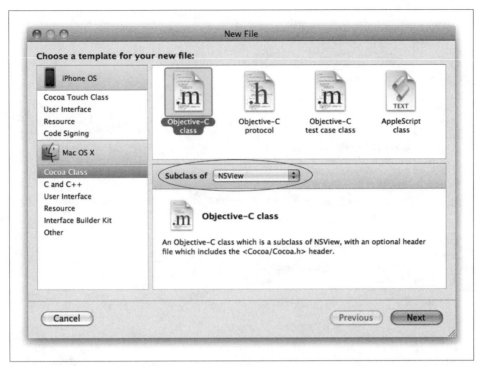

Figure 10-2. Creating a new NSView subclass in Xcode

On the second screen, name the file *ShapesAndColorsView.m*, and make sure the checkboxes for "Also create ShapesAndColorsView.h" and the BasicCocoaDrawing item in the Targets section are both checked, as shown in Figure 10-3.

Be sure to select NSView from the "Subclass of" drop-down or the view will not work.

Xcode will create a basic version of the class implementation that looks something like this:

```
#import "ShapesAndColorsView.h"

@implementation ShapesAndColorsView

- (id)initWithFrame:(NSRect)frame {
    self = [super initWithFrame:frame];
    if (self) {
        // Initialization code here.
    }
    return self;
}
```

```
- (void)drawRect:(NSRect)dirtyRect {
    // Drawing code here.
}

@end
```

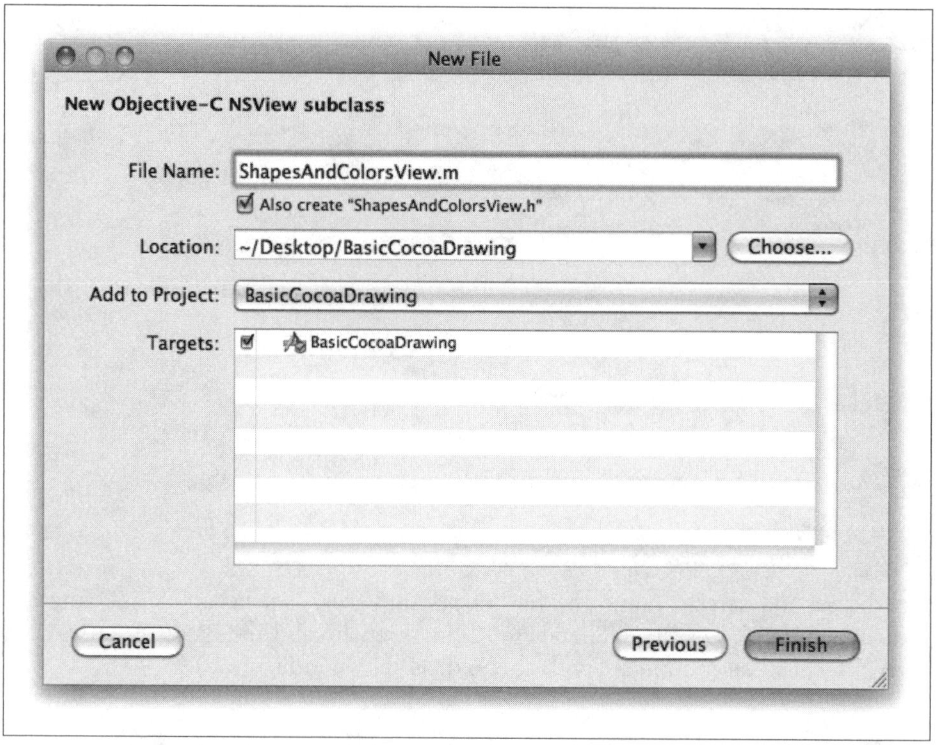

Figure 10-3. Name the file ShapesAndColorsView.m and add it to the BasicCocoaDrawing target

The -initWithFrame: method is like the -init method in most classes, but it takes a frame as an initial location and size for the view. You don't need to set up any default values yet, but let's change the formatting so it's more familiar (see Example 10-1).

Example 10-1. ShapesAndColorsView.m -initWithFrame:

```
- (id)initWithFrame:(NSRect)frame {

    if ( self = [super initWithFrame:frame] ) {

    }
    return self;
}
```

Functionally, this is exactly the same as the stock version. I just want you to understand there's nothing strange going on in this method. The -drawRect: method is brand new, though. This is where you get your hands dirty with pixels. You're going to use the NSRectFill() function to draw, and it takes a single rect as input. Rewrite the -drawRect: method so it looks like this:

```
- (void)drawRect:(NSRect)dirtyRect {

    NSColor* backgroundColor = [NSColor orangeColor];
    NSColor* foregroundColor = [NSColor yellowColor];

    // get the view geometry and fill the background.

    NSRect bounds = self.bounds;
    [backgroundColor set];
    NSRectFill ( bounds );

    // inset each side by 25%. when added together, this
    // means the shape will be half the width and height
    // of the view.

    CGFloat insetX  = ( NSWidth  (bounds) * 0.25 );
    CGFloat insetY  = ( NSHeight (bounds) * 0.25 );
    NSRect  shape   = NSInsetRect ( bounds, insetX, insetY );

    [foregroundColor set];
    NSRectFill ( shape );
}
```

If you're not a geometry expert, don't worry: this is simple math. I want the shape to be exactly half the size of the view. The NSWidth() and NSHeight() functions return the width and height of the bounds rect. I multiply both by 0.25 to get 25% of each value, and pass the rect and the inset amounts into NSInsetRect() to get a shape in the middle of the view.

But if I want to make a shape with *half* the width and height, why am I using 0.25? The NSInsetRect() function applies the inset amount to *each side*. If I ask for a 50% inset for the height, I'll end up with 50% off the top and 50% off the bottom, for a total of 100%. The shape would end up with a height of 0, and I'd never see it onscreen.

When to draw

As an application developer, you don't directly tell your views to draw—Cocoa handles that. You just need to wait for the -drawRect: method to be called. This method may be called *many times per second*, so make sure it's efficient. For example, if you have code that figures out where objects should appear, you should calculate that once and save the result as an instance variable so that it's cached.

If any data that affects the view changes—such as the location of an object—update your caches, then call [myView setNeedsDisplay:YES] to tell Cocoa that you need an update. The view system collects all of those requests and combines them into a single call to -drawRect: when it's time to draw.

If you're trying to call -drawRect: directly, you may want to rethink how your classes are set up. The drawing system is designed to make things easier for you, and trying to work outside of it will usually make the view draw incorrectly or just cause the app to crash.

Instantiate the View

There are two ways to add a view to a window, and it's important to know about both. First, let's do it in code. Change *BasicCocoaDrawingAppDelegate.m* to look like the following:

```
#import "BasicCocoaDrawingAppDelegate.h"
#import "ShapesAndColorsView.h"

@implementation BasicCocoaDrawingAppDelegate

@synthesize window;

- (void)applicationDidFinishLaunching:(NSNotification *)aNotification {

    NSRect viewFrame = [self.window.contentView bounds];

    ShapesAndColorsView* shapeView;
    shapeView = [[ShapesAndColorsView alloc] initWithFrame:viewFrame];
    [self.window.contentView addSubview:shapeView];
    [shapeView release];
}

@end
```

 Make sure to add the #import "ShapesAndColorsView.h" statement at the top of the file to avoid build errors.

Bounds and Frames

I used the *bounds* of the window's content view (the root view) as the frame for the ShapesAndColorsView. This is an easy way to get a rect that fills the whole window, but you don't have to do it this way. In fact, I could also use the content view's *frame*, but that won't always do what you expect in other cases. Here's why.

You might think giving the parent and child the same frame would make them equal, but a view's frame is *relative to its parent*, so an origin of 10,10 isn't a location in the window; it's a location in the parent view. Using the parent's bounds for this often works out better because the origin is usually 0,0:

```
NSRect frame = NSMakeRect ( 10, 10, 100, 100 );
NSView* parentView = [[NSView alloc] initWithFrame:frame];

// this will completely fill the parent view because the origin is 0,0.
NSView* childView = [[NSView alloc] initWithFrame:parentView.bounds];
[parentView addSubview:childView];
```

In the next listing, giving the parent and the child the same frame places the child at 10,10 in the parent, so there will be empty space at the bottom-left corner of the view:

```
NSRect frame = NSMakeRect ( 10, 10, 100, 100 );
NSView* parentView = [[NSView alloc] initWithFrame:frame];

// this will leave ten pixels empty at the left and the bottom.
NSView* childView = [[NSView alloc] initWithFrame:parentView.frame];
[parentView addSubview:childView];
```

That said, the origin of bounds is *not always* 0,0, but this is the most common behavior in simple cases.

Save the file and run the project. You should see a big square in the middle of the window (Figure 10-4).

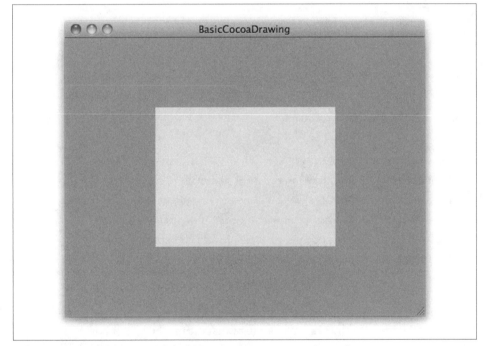

Figure 10-4. The first run of BasicCocoaDrawing

Remember, you haven't edited the XIB file yet—this is all in code. If you resize the window, though, you'll see the view isn't resizing with it. In Interface Builder, you could fix this with the Size Inspector, but you can also do it in code using the NSView autoresizingMask property.

Setting resizing values in code

The `autoresizingMask` property uses a bitmask value, which we haven't talked about much yet. It's a lower-level C technique for combining multiple "flags" into a single value. Sometimes you need only one value, but if there are more, you combine them using the pipe symbol, which is formally called the *bitwise OR* operator:

```
NSInteger bitmask = ( FirstValue | SecondValue | ThirdValue );
```

The possible values for the `autoresizingMask` property are listed at the top of *NSView.h* (Example 10-2).

Example 10-2. Excerpt of NSView.h; possible values for the autoresizingMask property

```
enum {
    NSViewNotSizable      = 0,
    NSViewMinXMargin      = 1,
    NSViewWidthSizable    = 2,
    NSViewMaxXMargin      = 4,
    NSViewMinYMargin      = 8,
    NSViewHeightSizable   = 16,
    NSViewMaxYMargin      = 32
};
```

Each of these describe a different resizing switch that you can "turn on" for the view (see Table 10-2).

Table 10-2. NSView resizing mask values

Value	Description
NSViewNotSizable	No resizing at all
NSViewMinXMargin	The left margin resizes, anchoring the view to the right
NSViewMaxXMargin	The right margin resizes, anchoring the view to the left
NSViewMinYMargin	The bottom margin resizes, anchoring the view to the top
NSViewMaxYMargin	The top margin resizes, anchoring the view to the bottom
NSViewWidthSizable	The view's width changes with its parent
NSViewHeightSizable	The view's height changes with its parent

To put this in context, using the `NSViewMinYMargin` means the "minimum *y* margin" will be allowed to resize. In the Cartesian system, that means the bottom of the view. So if you apply `NSViewMinYMargin` to a view's resizing mask, you are saying that the empty space on the *bottom* should flexible, effectively "anchoring" the view to the *top* of its parent.

In this example, the view completely fills the window, so all you need to do is tell the view to resize its width and height with its parent. Here is the method with the autoresizing mask applied:

```
- (void)applicationDidFinishLaunching:(NSNotification *)aNotification {

    NSRect viewFrame = [self.window.contentView bounds];

    ShapesAndColorsView* shapeView;
    shapeView = [[ShapesAndColorsView alloc] initWithFrame:viewFrame];
    [self.window.contentView addSubview:shapeView];

    // resize with the window.
    NSInteger resizingMask = ( NSViewWidthSizable | NSViewHeightSizable );
    [shapeView setAutoresizingMask:resizingMask];

    [shapeView release];
}
```

Save the file and rerun the project; you should see that the view now resizes with the window. As a bonus, you now understand what the Size Inspector is doing behind the scenes when you click on the resize arrows.

The Graphics Context

The thing I found most confusing when I was first learning drawing in Cocoa was the -[NSColor set] method. Usually you set *something* on an object—using some value as input. I couldn't figure out what "set" meant if I wasn't providing a value. What's actually happening here is that there is an invisible force in the background called the *graphics context*, which is an instance of NSGraphicsContext (see Table 10-3).

Table 10-3. Common methods for NSGraphicsContext

Name	Description
+currentContext	Returns the "current" context
+saveGraphicsState:	Creates and activates a new working copy of the context
+restoreGraphicsState	Restores the previously saved context
-isDrawingToScreen	Returns NO if not drawing to the screen, such as for printing
-setShouldAntialias:	Defines if lines and text should be antialiased (YES by default)
-setCompositingOperation:	Sets compositing style, such as NSCompositeSourceOver

The graphics context keeps track of settings that affect drawing, including the current color. Calling the -set method on an NSColor assigns it to the graphics context. When NSRectFill() function is called, it uses that color for drawing. Graphic contexts are stacked, which means you can create a copy of the current context using +saveGraphicsState, make some changes, draw something, then restore the original context with +restoreGraphicsState, as shown here:

```
// make the current color 'blue'.
[[NSColor blueColor] set];
NSRectFill ( outerRectangle );
```

```
[NSGraphicsContext saveGraphicsState];

    // make the current color 'white'.
    [[NSColor whiteColor] set];
    NSRectFill ( innerRectangle );

[NSGraphicsContext restoreGraphicsState];

// after restoring, the current color is blue again.
NSRectFill ( innerRectangle );
```

 Just like with retain and release, you have to balance each
+saveGraphicsState with exactly one +restoreGraphicsState. If you restore too many times, you'll see errors in the console and your view will
likely draw indirectly.

When the -drawRect: method is called on a view class, Cocoa automatically sets up a
graphics context for you. This means that you don't have to worry about where to draw
on the screen. One important note about this, though, is that the method actually passes
in a rect:

```
- (void)drawRect:(NSRect)rect;
```

This rect is the *invalidated region* in your view, meaning that anything inside of it needs
to be redrawn. You *can* redraw the entire view, but drawing just the invalidated area
may be much more efficient. The catch is that figuring out how to redraw just this
section can be difficult. In some cases, running the calculations could actually take
longer than just redrawing the entire view. So the rect is more a guideline about where
to draw than a rule.

Bezier Paths

Only very simple shapes can be described as rectangles, but you can use NSBezier
Path to create any kind of 2D shape you can imagine.

Bezier paths are the heart of Cocoa's vector drawing system; they allow you to draw
without being tied to a specific resolution. This makes it possible, for example, to
implement a zooming feature in a drawing program. Unlike NSRect structs,
NSBezierPath instances are full objects that can draw themselves into a view.

Drawing Polygons

An instance of NSBezierPath isn't necessarily curved; you can use paths to create multi-
sided polygons one point at a time. Create a project as shown in "Subclassing
NSView" on page 316, but use the following -drawRect: method instead:

```
- (void)drawRect:(NSRect)dirtyRect {
```

```
    [[NSColor blueColor] set];
    NSRectFill (self.bounds);

    NSRect  bounds = self.bounds;
    CGFloat width  = bounds.size.width;
    CGFloat height = bounds.size.height;

    NSBezierPath* path = [NSBezierPath bezierPath];

    // use -moveToPoint to go to the starting point.
    [path moveToPoint: NSMakePoint(width*0.35, height*0.1)];

    // use -lineToPoint for all lines.
    [path lineToPoint: NSMakePoint(width*0.65, height*0.1)];
    [path lineToPoint: NSMakePoint(width*0.65, height*0.6)];
    [path lineToPoint: NSMakePoint(width*0.9,  height*0.6)];
    [path lineToPoint: NSMakePoint(width*0.5,  height*0.9)];
    [path lineToPoint: NSMakePoint(width*0.1,  height*0.6)];
    [path lineToPoint: NSMakePoint(width*0.35, height*0.6)];

    // close the path at the end.
    [path closePath];

    [[NSColor whiteColor] set];
    [path fill];
}
```

Calling the -fill method on a path will draw the contents in the current graphics context. Figure 10-5 shows the result when drawn into a view.

Drawing Curved Paths

The NSBezierPath class has quite a few methods for adding curves to a shape. In the previous example, you added straight lines to a path using -lineToPoint. This is the curved version:

```
- (void)curveToPoint: (NSPoint)endPoint
      controlPoint1: (NSPoint)controlPoint1
      controlPoint2: (NSPoint)controlPoint2;
```

The control points literally control the curve, acting like a form of gravity. In the following example, the start and end points of the path are at the bottom-left and top-right corners of the view. The control points are at the bottom-right and top-left corners:

```
- (void)drawRect:(NSRect)dirtyRect {

    [[NSColor colorWithDeviceRed:0.2 green:0.6 blue:0.1 alpha:1.0] set];
    NSRectFill(self.bounds);

    NSBezierPath * path = [NSBezierPath bezierPath];
    path.lineWidth = 6.0;

    NSRect  bounds = self.bounds;
    CGFloat width  = NSWidth ( bounds );
```

```
    CGFloat height = NSHeight ( bounds );

    NSPoint startPoint = NSMakePoint ( width * 0.1, height * 0.1 );
    NSPoint endPoint   = NSMakePoint ( width * 0.9, height * 0.9 );

    [path moveToPoint: startPoint];

    [path curveToPoint: endPoint
        controlPoint1: NSMakePoint ( width * 0.9, height * 0.1 )
        controlPoint2: NSMakePoint ( width * 0.1, height * 0.9 )];

    [[NSColor colorWithDeviceRed:0.2 green:0.8 blue:0.3 alpha:0.9] set];
    [path fill];

    [[NSColor colorWithDeviceWhite:1.0 alpha:1.0] set];
    [path stroke];
}
```

Figure 10-5. An arrow created with NSBezierPath

Figure 10-6 shows the result when drawn into a view.

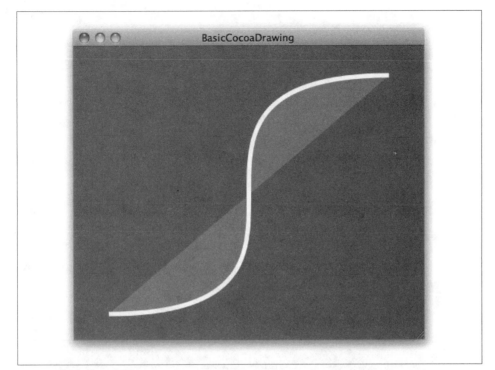

Figure 10-6. A curved shape created with NSBezierPath

You can also add arcs to a path using one of the following methods:

```
- (void)appendBezierPathWithArcWithCenter: (NSPoint)center
                                   radius: (CGFloat)radius
                               startAngle: (CGFloat)startAngle
                                 endAngle: (CGFloat)endAngle
                                clockwise: (BOOL)clockwise;

- (void)appendBezierPathWithArcFromPoint: (NSPoint)point1
                                 toPoint: (NSPoint)point2
                                  radius: (CGFloat)radius;
```

The "from point" method is similar to the other methods you've used; it draws an arc from one point to another. The "with center" method starts at **center** and draws a circle with the radius you supply. You can draw portions of a circle if you want to create shapes in the style of pie charts. Here's an example of drawing an arc from the center:

```
- (void)drawRect:(NSRect)dirtyRect {

    [[NSColor purpleColor] set];
    NSRectFill(self.bounds);

    NSBezierPath * path = [NSBezierPath bezierPath];
    path.lineWidth = 6;
```

```
NSPoint origin;
origin.x = NSWidth(self.bounds) * 0.5;
origin.y = NSHeight(self.bounds) * 0.5;

CGFloat radius = NSWidth(self.bounds) *0.25;

[path moveToPoint: origin];
[path appendBezierPathWithArcWithCenter: origin
                                 radius: radius
                             startAngle: 0
                               endAngle: 321
                              clockwise: NO];

[[NSColor magentaColor] set];
[path fill];

[[NSColor whiteColor] set];
[path stroke];
}
```

Figure 10-7 shows the result when drawn into a view.

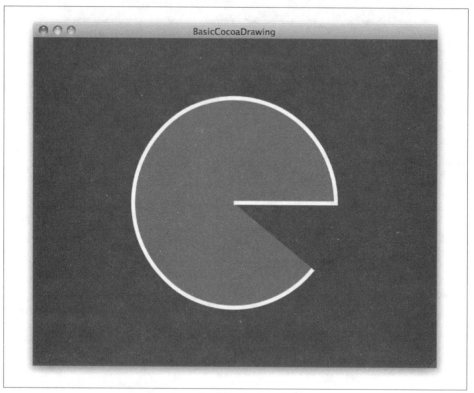

Figure 10-7. An arc created with NSBezierPath

Images

There are many different image types available to you as a Mac programmer, but the two most common are `NSImage` and `CGImage` (formally called `CGImageRef`). These used to be very different and not easily interchangeable, but that changed in Snow Leopard. The guts of `NSImage` are now backed by `CGImage`, so it's much easier to switch between them. You can't cast them directly, but you can use these two `NSImage` methods:

```
- (id)initWithCGImage: (CGImageRef)cgImage
               size: (NSSize)size;

- (CGImageRef)CGImageForProposedRect: (NSRect *)rect
                             context: (NSGraphicsContext *)context
                               hints: (NSDictionary *)hints;
```

Your first instinct when reading this might be to think, "OK, `CGImage` is the main type, so I'll just use that." The major drawback, though, is that `CGImage` is not actually an Objective-C class. Like Core Foundation's `CFStringRef` type, `CGImageRef` is an opaque struct type. That means you can't add categories to it, or use any of the generic programming techniques that Cocoa is known for. Instead, you have to use it as a data container, and pass it around to various C functions like `CGContextDrawImage()`.

Instead, I suggest using the more flexible `NSImage` class, which has all of the Objective-C goodness built right in. The other major advantage is that several of the standard Cocoa view classes already know how to display an `NSImage` without any conversion. And if you decide you want to use garbage collection, it will just work out of the box. The only downside is that `NSImage` does not exist on the iPhone, but there *is* a class that's roughly equivalent called `UIImage`.

Loading Image Data

The two main ways to load existing image data are to read in the contents of an existing image file, or to request standard artwork from Cocoa. Using standard artwork is helpful if you want to use the same icons Mac OS X itself uses for things like the color picker or the computer itself. If you're loading a custom image from a file, though, you usually want to copy it into your project because there's no way to guarantee which files will be on your user's machine.

Loading an image from your project

First, track down an image that you want to use. Almost any image will work, such as a PNG or JPEG file. You can download it from a website or just use something from your photo library. You probably want to use something that isn't too big—around 1,000 × 1,000 pixels is good. Drag the file from the Finder to your *Resources* folder in your project, and when Xcode asks, confirm that you want to *copy* the file and add it to the target, as shown in Figure 10-8. (You can use the project shown in "Subclassing NSView" on page 316 as a starting point for this.)

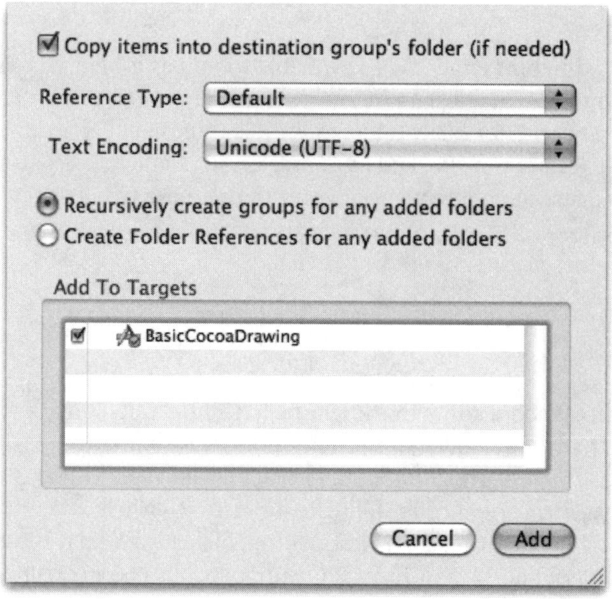

Figure 10-8. Confirm that you want the file copied into the project and added to the target

Once the image is in the project, you can use the NSImage class method +imageNamed: to automatically load it (*let's hear it for object-oriented design*). My file is called *SpaceShuttle.jpg*,* so here's the code I would use to load it as an NSImage object:

```
NSImage* mainImage = [NSImage imageNamed:@"SpaceShuttle"];
```

Even though it would be really easy to add this to the -drawRect: method, I don't want to do that, because it means the image would be re-created every single time, which could be really slow. So instead, I'm only going to load it *once*, when the application starts up.

Loading standard Cocoa artwork

You use the same +imageNamed: method to load standard artwork, but instead of providing a filename, you use one of the constants declared in AppKit's *NSImage.h* header file. Example 10-3 lists a few of the more interesting ones.

Example 10-3. Excerpts from NSImage.h—standard artwork constants

```
NSString *const NSImageNameComputer;
NSString *const NSImageNameColorPanel;
NSString *const NSImageNameUser;
NSString *const NSImageNameNetwork;
```

---

* Public domain image from NASA: *http://commons.wikimedia.org/wiki/File:STS-125_Atlantis_Liftoff_02.jpg*.

For example, here's how I can create an image that represents the computer:

```
NSImage* computerImage = [NSImage imageNamed:NSImageNameComputer];
```

The great thing about this is that the image itself will change depending on the computer that is actually being used. So this same line of code will return a laptop icon if the user has a portable Mac, but it will return a different icon if the app is running on a desktop machine.

One important note here is that the actual artwork for an image name is not guaranteed to be the same for each release of Mac OS X, but the *intent* of the image is. In other words, use the `NSImageNameColorPanel` only if you really want to indicate a color panel. Using it to represent something else that roughly fits the icon's appearance may cause confusion for the user if the artwork suddenly changes.

 Cocoa's standard artwork image names are global variables, so don't add quotes around them. Even if the variable name and the string contents of that variable *happen* to be the same (for example: `NSString* NSImageNameComputer = @"NSImageNameComputer"`), it's better to let the compiler make sure the constant you asked for actually exists.

The complete list of standard artwork names is located at the bottom of *NSImage.h*, but you can also see some of the names in Interface Builder by opening the Library panel and clicking on the Media tab (see Figure 10-9). This won't necessarily show you the *complete* list, but it's an easy way to get a quick glance at some of the most common items. Even better, this tab will also show you all of the images that you've added to the project.

Drawing Images in a View

`NSImage` is a fairly complex class, but basic drawing is easy. These are the two most common methods for drawing:

```
- (void)drawAtPoint: (NSPoint)point
           fromRect: (NSRect)fromRect
          operation: (NSCompositingOperation)op
           fraction: (CGFloat)delta;

- (void)drawInRect: (NSRect)rect
          fromRect: (NSRect)fromRect
         operation: (NSCompositingOperation)op
          fraction: (CGFloat)delta;
```

One takes an `NSPoint` as the first input item, and the other takes an `NSRect`. All of the other input items are the same. The main difference between the two is if you specify a rect, the image you draw will be scaled to fill the entire area of the rectangle. If you specify a point, the natural image size will be used (but no larger than the size of `fromRect`).

Figure 10-9. The Media tab in Interface Builder's Library panel shows some of Cocoa's standard artwork

You can use `fromRect` if you want to draw only a portion of the source image in a view. For example, if the source image is 1,000 × 1,000, but the view you're drawing into is only 200 × 200, you can specify a `fromRect` that is 200 × 200. This is useful for panning around inside large images, for example. You can also pass in `NSZeroRect` here to just draw the whole thing.

The *operation* value is a bit harder to explain. Some image editing programs have a concept called *blend mode*, which is basically the same thing as a compositing operation in Cocoa. This is an advanced topic that I won't cover in detail here. Instead, I'll just use `NSCompositeSourceOver`.

The last input item is a floating-point value called `fraction`. You use this to draw images with different levels of transparency. For example, to draw an image at 50% opacity, you would use a `fraction` value of `0.5`.

In Xcode, add a new `NSView` class to the BasicCocoaDrawing project. Name the class *StyledImageView.m*, and make sure the checkboxes for "Also create StyledImage-View.h" and the BasicCocoaDrawing item in the Targets section are both checked.

Add the properties from Example 10-4 to *StyledImageView.h*.

Example 10-4. StyledImageView.h

```
#import <Cocoa/Cocoa.h>


@interface StyledImageView : NSView

@property (retain) NSImage* mainImage;
@property (retain) NSColor* backgroundColor;
@property (retain) NSColor* borderColor;

@end
```

In *StyledImageView.m*, change the implementation of the view to that in Example 10-5.

Example 10-5. StyledImageView.m

```
#import "StyledImageView.h"


@implementation StyledImageView

    @synthesize mainImage;
    @synthesize backgroundColor;
    @synthesize borderColor;

- (id)initWithFrame:(NSRect)frame {

    if ( self = [super initWithFrame:frame] ) {

    }
    return self;
}

- (void)drawRect:(NSRect)rect {

    NSRect bounds = self.bounds;

    // draw a background color.
    [self.backgroundColor set];
    NSRectFill ( bounds );

    CGFloat insetX      = NSWidth     ( bounds ) * 0.10;
    CGFloat insetY      = NSHeight    ( bounds ) * 0.10;
    NSRect  imageRect   = NSInsetRect ( bounds, insetX, insetY );

    // draw the image.
    NSImage* image = self.mainImage;

    [image drawInRect: imageRect
            fromRect: NSZeroRect
           operation: NSCompositeSourceOver
            fraction: 1.0];

    // draw a border around the image.
    [self.borderColor set];
```

```
    NSBezierPath* imageFrame = [NSBezierPath bezierPathWithRect:imageRect];
    imageFrame.lineWidth = 4;
    [imageFrame stroke];
}

- (void) dealloc {

    self.mainImage       = nil;
    self.backgroundColor = nil;
    self.borderColor     = nil;

    [super dealloc];
}

@end
```

Now in *BasicCocoaDrawingAppDelegate.m*, change the implementation of
-applicationDidFinishLaunching: so that it uses StyledImageView instead of the shape
view you used before. Be sure to replace @"SpaceShuttle" with the name of the image
you added to the project earlier:

```
#import "BasicCocoaDrawingAppDelegate.h"
#import "StyledImageView.h"

@implementation BasicCocoaDrawingAppDelegate

@synthesize window;

- (void)applicationDidFinishLaunching:(NSNotification *)aNotification {

    NSRect viewFrame = [self.window.contentView bounds];

    StyledImageView* imageView;
    imageView = [[StyledImageView alloc] initWithFrame:viewFrame];

    // set properties for this instance of the view.
    imageView.mainImage       = [NSImage imageNamed:@"SpaceShuttle"];
    imageView.backgroundColor = [NSColor darkGrayColor];
    imageView.borderColor     = [NSColor whiteColor];

    // resize with the window.
    NSInteger resizingMask = ( NSViewWidthSizable | NSViewHeightSizable );
    [imageView setAutoresizingMask:resizingMask];

    // add to content view and release.
    [self.window.contentView addSubview:imageView];
    [imageView release];
}

@end
```

Now save all of the files and rerun the application. You should see your image drawn
in the center of the view with a border around the outside, like in Figure 10-10.

Figure 10-10. StyledImageView drawing an image

Preserving aspect ratio

The one thing you might notice while resizing the window is that the view doesn't keep the image proportional, so you can end up with a really skinny or flat image. That's usually not what the user would want to see, so let's fix it with a category on NSImage.

In Xcode, create a new Objective-C class file called *NSImage-Utilities.m* (with the header file), and make sure it's added to the target. You don't actually want a class in this case, so change *NSImage-Utilities.h* to look like this:

```
#import <Cocoa/Cocoa.h>

@interface NSImage (Utilities)

@end
```

Now add the declaration to *NSImage-Utilities.h* for the method that will figure out the correct *proportional* rect to draw into:

```
#import <Cocoa/Cocoa.h>

@interface NSImage (Utilities)
- (NSRect) proportionalRectForTargetRect:(NSRect)targetRect;
@end
```

The implementation of this method is pretty easy if you understand the theory behind it; figure out if the width or height will require a larger amount of adjustment, and apply that adjustment equally to both sides. So if the width is 50% less and the height is 25% less, reduce *both sides* by 50% to keep the image proportions. Got it? Good. See Example 10-6 for the code for *NSImage-Utilities.m*.

Example 10-6. NSImage-Utilities.m

```
#import "NSImage-Utilities.h"


@implementation NSImage (Utilities)

- (NSRect) proportionalRectForTargetRect:(NSRect)targetRect {

    // if the sizes are the same, we're already done.
    if ( NSEqualSizes(self.size, targetRect.size) ) return targetRect;

    NSSize  imageSize    = self.size;
    CGFloat soureWidth   = imageSize.width;
    CGFloat sourceHeight = imageSize.height;

    // figure out the difference in size for each side, and use
    // the larger adjustment for both edges (maintains aspect ratio).
    CGFloat widthAdjust  = targetRect.size.width  / soureWidth;
    CGFloat heightAdjust = targetRect.size.height / sourceHeight;
    CGFloat scaleFactor  = 1.0;

    if ( widthAdjust < heightAdjust )
        scaleFactor = widthAdjust;
    else
        scaleFactor = heightAdjust;

    // resize both edges by the same amount.
    CGFloat finalWidth  = soureWidth   * scaleFactor;
    CGFloat finalHeight = sourceHeight * scaleFactor;
    NSSize  finalSize   = NSMakeSize ( finalWidth, finalHeight );

    // actual rect we'll use for the image.
    NSRect finalRect;
    finalRect.size = finalSize;

    // use the same base origin as the target rect, but adjust
    // for the resized image.
    finalRect.origin    = targetRect.origin;
    finalRect.origin.x += (targetRect.size.width  - finalWidth)  * 0.5;
    finalRect.origin.y += (targetRect.size.height - finalHeight) * 0.5;

    // return exact coordinates for a sharp image.
    return NSIntegralRect ( finalRect );
}

@end
```

The last step is to use this category in the view. Add the code for the category at the top of *StyledImageView.m*:

```
#import "StyledImageView.h"
#import "NSImage-Utilities.h"
```

Then, add a line to call the category method to get a proportional rect for the image, right below where the image is fetched from the property:

```
NSImage* image = self.mainImage;
imageRect = [image proportionalRectForTargetRect:imageRect];
```

Now rerun the app; you should see that the aspect ratio is maintained for any window size as shown in Figures 10-11 and 10-12.

Figure 10-11. The "stretched" image before the fix

Figure 10-12. The proportionately sized image after the fix

Shadows

The `NSShadow` class adds shadows to shapes or text. Using a shadow is very similar to using a color—you create one and call `-set` to apply it to the current graphics context. The shadow will be applied to all drawing after that point. Here's a simple example:

```
NSShadow* dropShadow = [[NSShadow alloc] init];

dropShadow.shadowBlurRadius  = 8.0;
dropShadow.shadowOffset      = NSMakeSize(0,-6);
dropShadow.shadowColor       = [NSColor blackColor];
[dropShadow set];

NSRect fillRect = NSMakeRect ( 20, 20, 100, 100 );
[[NSColor whiteColor] set];
[NSBezierPath fillRect:fillRect];

[dropShadow release];
```

 You can set the `shadowColor` property to `+[NSColor whiteColor]` to create a glow effect around an object.

The one important detail is that there's no way to *unset* a shadow. You can try to set the blur radius to zero or the color to `+[NSColor clearColor]`, but I think it's usually better to save the graphic context right before you set the shadow, then restore the previous context (which doesn't have the shadow) when you're done. There is a cost to save and restore the context, but to me, it makes more sense to remove the shadow from the equation when you're done using it instead of trying to make it invisible.

Add a Shadow to StyledImageView

To see how all of this works, let's add a shadow to the image in `StyledImageView`. First, add a new property to the class to control whether the shadow should be used. It's usually a good idea to add these sorts of settings to increase reusability of the class. Add the line shown in bold to *StyledImageView.h*:

```
#import <Cocoa/Cocoa.h>

@interface StyledImageView : NSView

@property (retain) NSImage* mainImage;
@property (retain) NSColor* backgroundColor;
@property (retain) NSColor* borderColor;
@property (assign) BOOL     shouldAddShadow;

@end
```

Now, in *StyledImageView.m*, add a category interface with an empty name and declare the private `imageShadow` property and the private `+defaultImageShadow` class method (see Example 10-7). You can declare private properties only in *class continuations* (categories without names), not named categories.

Example 10-7. Excerpt of StyledImageView.m

```
#import "StyledImageView.h"
#import "NSImage-Utilities.h"

@interface StyledImageView ()
// private properties.
@property (retain) NSShadow* imageShadow;
// private methods.
+ (NSShadow*) defaultImageShadow;
@end
```

Then, not far below that, add `synthesize` statements for the new properties:

```
@implementation StyledImageView

@synthesize mainImage;
@synthesize backgroundColor;
@synthesize borderColor;
@synthesize shouldAddShadow;
@synthesize imageShadow;
```

In this case, I want you to actually override the setter for `shouldAddShadow` only. If the input value is `YES`, you'll create the shadow and save it as an instance variable. If it's `NO`, you'll set the instance variable to `nil`. We don't need to do anything special for the getter, so you'll just keep the default implementation.

I'm also going to have you implement the `+defaultImageShadow` class method to return a preconfigured shadow object, so that we don't have to stuff all of that code in the setter method. Add these methods to the bottom of the class (but obviously before the `@end`):

```
- (void) setShouldAddShadow:(BOOL)shouldAdd {

    // if the new value is the same, just return.
    if ( shouldAddShadow == shouldAdd ) return;

    // set the new value.
    shouldAddShadow = shouldAdd;

    if ( shouldAddShadow )
        self.imageShadow = [[self class] defaultImageShadow];
    else
        self.imageShadow = nil;

    // redraw.
    [self setNeedsDisplay:YES];
}
```

```
#pragma mark Private

+ (NSShadow*) defaultImageShadow {

    NSShadow* newShadow        = [[NSShadow alloc] init];
    newShadow.shadowBlurRadius = 8.0;
    newShadow.shadowOffset     = NSMakeSize(0,-6);
    newShadow.shadowColor      = [NSColor blackColor];

    return [newShadow autorelease];
}
```

Because NSShadow is an object, you need to release it in -dealloc, so add the line shown in bold to that method:

```
- (void) dealloc {

    self.mainImage       = nil;
    self.backgroundColor = nil;
    self.borderColor     = nil;
    self.imageShadow     = nil;

    [super dealloc];
}
```

Now, add code to the -drawRect: method to apply the shadow:

```
// save the graphics context, apply the shadow, and draw the image.
[NSGraphicsContext saveGraphicsState];

    [self.imageShadow set];

[image drawInRect: imageRect
         fromRect: NSZeroRect
        operation: NSCompositeSourceOver
         fraction: 1.0];

// restore the context so the frame doesn't get a shadow.
[NSGraphicsContext restoreGraphicsState];
```

There's a subtle point here. If the shouldAddShadow property is set to NO, the imageShadow object will be nil. But because you can freely send messages to nil, it's absolutely fine to call [self.imageShadow set] every time through. The only downside is that the graphics context is saved and restored each time, regardless of whether the shadow is there. I left it in for this example to make the code more clear, but you can choose whichever approach works best for you. Just keep in mind that you may never see any practical difference in speed, and simpler code is easier to improve and debug.

The last step is to go back to *BasicCocoaDrawingAppDelegate.m*, and specify that you want the shadow added:

```
// set properties for this instance of the view.
imageView.mainImage       = [NSImage imageNamed:@"SpaceShuttle"];
imageView.backgroundColor = [NSColor darkGrayColor];
```

```
imageView.borderColor     = [NSColor whiteColor];
imageView.shouldAddShadow = YES;
```

Now save all of the edited files and rerun the application. As shown in Figure 10-13, you should see that the image now has a drop shadow behind it. The effect is subtle, but that's intentional. The ideal case is that the user isn't consciously aware of the drop shadow, but the image presentation simply seems more elegant. You don't want to hit the user over the head with a "Hey, look at this shadow here."

Figure 10-13. The image drawn with a drop shadow applied; it's subtle, but effective

Gradients

In the world of Cocoa graphics programming, gradients are a master's tool. If used properly, they can help you hit the UI presentation out of the park. But used carelessly, they can bring down the entire experience. Just like shadows, the key is to use gradients to *accent* the user interface, not overwhelm it.

You use the NSGradient class to create gradients in Cocoa, but they work differently from colors or shadows. You don't set a gradient on the graphics context. Instead, you draw it directly into a rect or a bezier path. NSGradient supports multiple-segment gradients (formally called *multistop gradients*), and you can draw them either linearly or radially.

The most common use for gradients in Mac and iPhone apps is to simulate a light source. So if you start with a light color at the top of the screen, and transition to a darker color, you're creating the illusion of light shining down from the top of the window. In this case, I want you to draw a gradient on the view's canvas, behind the main image.

Drawing a Gradient Background

Open *StyledImageView.h* and add a new property for the gradient:

```
@interface StyledImageView : NSView

@property (retain) NSImage* mainImage;
@property (retain) NSColor* backgroundColor;
@property (retain) NSColor* borderColor;
@property (assign) BOOL shouldAddShadow;
@property (retain) NSGradient* backgroundGradient;

@end
```

In *StyledImageView.m*, add a synthesize statement for the property:

```
@implementation StyledImageView

@synthesize mainImage;
@synthesize backgroundColor;
@synthesize borderColor;
@synthesize shouldAddShadow;
@synthesize imageShadow;
@synthesize backgroundGradient;
```

Because gradients are objects, you also need to remove the reference in the dealloc method:

```
- (void) dealloc {

    self.mainImage          = nil;
    self.backgroundColor    = nil;
    self.borderColor        = nil;
    self.imageShadow        = nil;
    self.backgroundGradient = nil;

    [super dealloc];
}
```

Right now, the -drawRect: method has all of the drawing code inline. But now that drawing the background will include two separate steps, it makes sense to break it off into a separate method. Add this private method declaration to the class continuation in *StyledImageView.m*:

```
@interface StyledImageView ()
// private properties.
@property (retain) NSShadow* imageShadow;
// private methods.
```

```
+ (NSShadow*) defaultImageShadow;
- (void) drawBackgroundInRect:(NSRect)rect;
@end
```

Grouping drawing code into several methods doesn't just make the code easier to read—it also makes it easier to create subclasses later. For example, if I wanted to make a subclass of this view with a different background, I can override only -drawBackgroundInRect: instead of having to reimplement the entire -drawRect: method.

Now, add the method itself to the class:

```
- (void) drawBackgroundInRect:(NSRect)rect {

    // draw a background color.
    [self.backgroundColor set];
    NSRectFill ( rect );

    // draw background gradient.
    [self.backgroundGradient drawInRect:rect angle:90.0];
}
```

Change -drawRect: to call this new method:

```
- (void)drawRect:(NSRect)rect {

NSRect bounds = self.bounds;
[self drawBackgroundInRect:bounds];

CGFloat insetX     = NSWidth    ( bounds ) * 0.10;
CGFloat insetY     = NSHeight   ( bounds ) * 0.10;
```

Some new Mac programmers are surprised you can call draw outside of -drawRect: method. The key is that you can draw from methods that -drawRect: calls directly. But you don't want to draw any other time, because the graphics context won't be set up correctly.

Now you just need to create a gradient and set it on the view. Here's how to do that in *BasicCocoaDrawingAppDelegate.m*:

```
StyledImageView* imageView;
imageView = [[StyledImageView alloc] initWithFrame:viewFrame];

// create background gradient.
NSColor* gradientBottom = [NSColor colorWithCalibratedWhite:0.18 alpha:1.0];
NSColor* gradientTop    = [NSColor colorWithCalibratedWhite:0.35 alpha:1.0];

NSGradient* gradient = [[NSGradient alloc] initWithStartingColor:gradientBottom
                                                      endingColor:gradientTop];

// set properties for this instance of the view.
```

```
imageView.mainImage          = [NSImage imageNamed:@"SpaceShuttle"];
imageView.backgroundColor    = [NSColor darkGrayColor];
imageView.borderColor        = [NSColor whiteColor];
imageView.shouldAddShadow     = YES;
imageView.backgroundGradient = gradient;

[gradient release];

// resize with the window.
NSInteger resizingMask = ( NSViewWidthSizable | NSViewHeightSizable );
```

Save all the files and rerun the project. You will now see a background gradient behind the main image, as shown in Figure 10-14.

Figure 10-14. The StyledImageView with a background gradient

The gradient is subtle, but that's intentional. You don't want to hit the user over the head with a gradient—you just want to make the lighting more convincing.

Drawing an Image Sheen

Drawing a sheen over an image simulates a glass surface material. Just like with shadows and gradients, the key is to use the sheen effect sparingly. In this case, you're going to draw a sheen over the main image in StyledImageView. The secret behind this effect is to use a gradient that fades from a white color with an alpha value of around 0.8 to a white color with an alpha of 0.0. You'll also use a multistop gradient to refine the look.

Calculate the sheen path

Create a new Objective-C category in the project, and name it *NSBezierPath-Utilities.m*. Change *NSBezierPath-Utilities.h* (the header file) to look like Example 10-8.

Example 10-8. NSBezierPath-Utilities.h

```
#import <Cocoa/Cocoa.h>

@interface NSBezierPath (Utilities)
+ (NSBezierPath*) sheenPathForRect:(NSRect)myRect;
@end
```

Change the implementation to look like Example 10-9.

Example 10-9. NSBezierPath-Utilities.m

```
#import "NSBezierPath-Utilities.h"

@implementation NSBezierPath (Utilities)

+ (NSBezierPath*) sheenPathForRect:(NSRect)myRect {

    CGFloat minX = NSMinX(myRect);
    CGFloat maxX = NSMaxX(myRect);
    CGFloat maxY = NSMaxY(myRect);

    // scale the base of the sheen with the image.
    CGFloat bottomLeftY  = myRect.origin.y + (myRect.size.height * 0.25);
    CGFloat bottomRightY = myRect.origin.y + (myRect.size.height * 0.9);

    NSPoint point1  = NSMakePoint ( minX, bottomLeftY );
    NSPoint point2  = NSMakePoint ( maxX, bottomRightY );
    NSPoint point3  = NSMakePoint ( maxX, maxY );
    NSPoint point4  = NSMakePoint ( minX, maxY );

    // for the arc that crosses the image.
    NSPoint control1 = NSMakePoint ( minX * 0.9, maxY * 0.9 );
    NSPoint control2 = NSMakePoint ( maxX * 0.9, maxY * 0.9 );

    // create the path.
    NSBezierPath* sheenPath = [NSBezierPath bezierPath];

    // starting point.
    [sheenPath moveToPoint: point1];

    // arc to the other side.
    [sheenPath curveToPoint: point2
            controlPoint1: control1
            controlPoint2: control2];

    [sheenPath lineToPoint:point3];
    [sheenPath lineToPoint:point4];
    [sheenPath closePath];
```

```
    return sheenPath;
}

@end
```

Unlike the other category, this is a class method that creates a new instance of `NSBezierPath`, which can be used for a sheen. Another approach is to add a category instance method on `NSImage` that returns a copy with a sheen drawn on top, but this approach is a bit more flexible, and increases the chances I can use this in another application later.

 Category class methods *technically* don't have to be attached to the type of thing you're creating. I *could* add this method to `NSImage`, or even `NSNumber`, but that's really bad style. It will also cause confusion for anyone who looks at my code later. Whenever possible, add the method to the class of the thing you're creating.

Add the `import` statement at the top of *StyledImageView.m*:

```
#import "StyledImageView.h"
#import "NSImage-Utilities.h"
#import "NSBezierPath-Utilities.h"
```

Add sheen properties and methods

Like with the image shadow, you don't want the view to re-create the sheen each time `-drawRect:` is called. It's much more efficient to create it *once* and save it as a private property. You'll also add a *public* property to turn the sheen on or off. First, add the public property to enable the sheen to *StyledImageView.h*:

```
@interface StyledImageView : NSView

@property (retain) NSImage* mainImage;
@property (retain) NSColor* backgroundColor;
@property (retain) NSColor* borderColor;
@property (assign) BOOL shouldAddShadow;
@property (retain) NSGradient* backgroundGradient;
@property (assign) BOOL shouldAddSheen;

@end
```

Now add the private sheen property and methods to *StyledImageView.m*:

```
@interface StyledImageView ()
// private properties.
@property (retain) NSShadow* imageShadow;
@property (retain) NSGradient* imageSheen;
// private methods.
+ (NSShadow*) defaultImageShadow;
+ (NSGradient*) defaultImageSheen;
- (void) drawBackgroundInRect:(NSRect)rect;
```

```
- (void) drawImageSheenInRect:(NSRect)rect;
@end
```

Add synthesize statements for the two new properties:

```
@implementation StyledImageView

@synthesize mainImage;
@synthesize backgroundColor;
@synthesize borderColor;
@synthesize shouldAddShadow;
@synthesize imageShadow;
@synthesize backgroundGradient;
@synthesize shouldAddSheen;
@synthesize imageSheen;
```

Be sure to release the sheen gradient in dealloc:

```
- (void) dealloc {

    self.mainImage         = nil;
    self.backgroundColor   = nil;
    self.borderColor       = nil;
    self.imageShadow       = nil;
    self.backgroundGradient = nil;
    self.imageSheen        = nil;

    [super dealloc];
}
```

Now, override the setter for shouldAddSheen so that the view will regenerate the gradient when it's turned on:

```
- (void) setShouldAddSheen:(BOOL)shouldAdd {

    // if the new value is the same, just return.
    if ( shouldAddSheen == shouldAdd ) return;

    // set the new value.
    shouldAddSheen = shouldAdd;

    if ( shouldAddSheen )
        self.imageSheen = [[self class] defaultImageSheen];
    else
        self.imageSheen = nil;

    // redraw.
    [self setNeedsDisplay:YES];
}
```

One optimization you could do here is to keep the gradient around even after it's "turned off" so that you don't have to re-create it if it's turned back on later. I'd call this *obsessive optimization*. It takes more code, and the gain is so small that the user will never see a difference. *And* the gradient still takes up memory in the meantime. If your optimization won't actually result in anything tangible, you're better off spending the same time on something else.

Add the private class method to generate the sheen gradient:

```
+ (NSGradient*) defaultImageSheen {

    NSColor* color1 = [NSColor colorWithDeviceWhite:1.0 alpha:0.80];
    NSColor* color2 = [NSColor colorWithDeviceWhite:1.0 alpha:0.10];
    NSColor* color3 = [NSColor colorWithDeviceWhite:1.0 alpha:0.0];

    // a location of 0.0 is the 'start' of the gradient; 1.0 is the 'end'.
    NSGradient* sheen = [[NSGradient alloc] initWithColorsAndLocations:
                    color1, 0.0, color2, 0.4, color3, 0.8, nil];

    return [sheen autorelease];
}
```

Now implement the method that draws the sheen:

```
- (void) drawImageSheenInRect:(NSRect)rect {

    NSBezierPath* sheenPath = [NSBezierPath sheenPathForRect:rect];

    // draw at 280.0 degees to simulate a light source from the upper-left.
    [self.imageSheen drawInBezierPath:sheenPath angle:280.0];
}
```

And add a line to call this method in `-drawRect:` after the image has been drawn:

```
// restore the context so the frame doesn't get a shadow.
[NSGraphicsContext restoreGraphicsState];

// draw the sheen.
[self drawImageSheenInRect:imageRect];

// draw a border around the image.
[self.borderColor set];
NSBezierPath* imageFrame = [NSBezierPath bezierPathWithRect:imageRect];
imageFrame.lineWidth = 4;
[imageFrame stroke];
```

Finally, add a line to activate the sheen in *BasicCocoaDrawingAppDelegate.m*:

```
imageView.shouldAddShadow      = YES;
imageView.backgroundGradient   = gradient;
imageView.shouldAddSheen       = YES;
```

Save all of the files and rerun the project. You should now see a sheen applied to the image, as shown in Figure 10-15.

Figure 10-15. The StyledImageView with a sheen gradient added to the image

Refactoring View Code

You've added a lot of new code to this view while working through the chapter, and now it's a bit harder to follow. When you hit this point, you basically have three options.

Allow the code to be messy
> This is the path of least resistance. You wrote the code once and don't see any reason to write it again. A rookie move. You get no points.

Rewrite the code
> You've painted yourself into a corner and want to rewrite everything from scratch. Your heart is in the right place, but rewriting is tricky. Rewriting the big parts is obvious; it's all of the subtle issues you fixed along the way that will be hard to reimplement. That said, sometimes there's no other option and rewriting is the only clear course (maybe about 15 percent of the time), but usually it's overkill.

Refactor the code
> *Refactoring* is a middle ground. You take what already works and rearrange it in a way that makes more sense. One version of refactoring is where you just rename variables and methods; another is where you change how the methods are

connected. You still risk breaking something that works, but not nearly as much as with rewriting. And this is much better than allowing the code to be a mess.

Why You Should Refactor

If your code is messy, you'll have a harder time debugging it and other people will have an even harder time understanding what it does. You might think, "Well, no one is ever going to see this code other than me," but there's a good chance the universe will prove you wrong. Code has a way of finding a path out into the world through the smallest cracks. You may hand the project over to someone else, or you may show the code to someone who is considering hiring you. The *last thing* you want to preface an email with is, "Sorry, this code is sort of a mess."

But even if you don't believe *that*, there's another reason. Messy code slows progress— it's like trying to run a race in the snow. Yes, you can technically move forward, but not nearly as fast as you'd like. Clean code is easy to improve. If you layer new features on top of messy code, it's probably going to fall over and take you down with it. And if the existing code is disorganized, any new code you add will probably end up the same. It's easier to throw dirty clothes on the floor of an already messy room.

Most importantly, though, you may forget how your code works. This often happens to developers who come back to a project after working on something else for a while. Always consider "future you" when you think about how well-written your code is.

Some programmers don't see any of this as a problem. They think that it's good enough if the code compiles and runs. But you don't want to be just *some programmer*, do you? Since we're in the process of making you a *superstar engineer*, you need to fix this. So let's keep the core of the view intact, but move some parts around so it makes more sense. Then you'll be ready to add new functionality.

The other major benefit that refactoring has over rewriting is that you can do it in chunks, which means the app continues to work in the meantime. You should always have a version of the app running, even if it's missing some features.

Goals for Refactoring

There are a few goals I have in mind for refactoring the `StyledImageView` class:

- Make the code easier to read.
- Make the view easier to customize.
- Make the methods more symmetrical.

"Easier to read" is somewhat subjective. Coding styles are like fingerprints. Everyone's brain works a bit differently and each person has different opinions about what good code looks like, so two versions of the same class never turn out exactly the same. But just because it's subjective doesn't mean it's irrelevant, so let's come up with the best version of the class we can.

"Easier to customize" is a bit different. You can make life easier on yourself and other people you work with by making it easy to change how a class works. A key difference between a *good programmer* and a *great engineer* is the ability to design a class that is both easy to use as-is and friendly to customization.

 It *is* possible to have too many customization options. If you have to wade through dozens of properties just to do something basic, the class is probably too complex. An expert engineer knows where the sweet spot is between simplicity and flexibility, but this mostly comes with experience.

The "symmetrical" part is a bit more objective (so to speak). Let me explain what symmetry means in this context. If you have two methods that do similar things, they should have similar names. This is *asymmetrical* code (something you can improve):

```
- (NSArray*)itemsSortedByName;
- (NSArray*)dateSortedItems;
```

This is the symmetrical version:

```
- (NSArray*)itemsSortedByName;
- (NSArray*)itemsSortedByDate;
```

The advantage of this is clear. You don't have to mentally deconstruct the design and think, "Ah, these do the same thing; they just use a different sort value." If your class, method, and variable names are symmetrical, the similarities will be obvious. The more symmetrical the methods are, the easier the view is to use and customize.

Symmetry in practice

This symmetry thing is really important—it's another one of those "good programmer" versus "great engineer" things—but a lot of new Mac programmers don't get enough guidance about it early on, so I want to give you one more example. This isn't just about naming things consistently, but about using similar input and output types as well. Here's an example of some code that needs fixing:

```
NSRect textBounds = [self textBounds];
NSRect bounds     = self.boundsOfContainer;
NSSize size       = [self sizeOfShape];
```

The local variable names are inconsistent—*bounds of what?*—and there's a mix of dot syntax and standard messaging syntax. But the bigger problem is the methods themselves. For this example, let's assume the implementations look like this:

```
- (NSRect) textBounds {
    return text.bounds;
}
```

```
- (NSRect) boundsOfContainer {
    return container.bounds;
}

- (NSSize) sizeOfShape {
    return shape.bounds.size;
}
```

The methods should have the same naming pattern and return types, if possible. Keep the big picture of your code in mind. Even if there's one of line of code *somewhere* in the app that wants an NSSize value, it's better for this method to be consistent with the others and return an NSRect. The other code calling this method can get the size value out of it later. Here are the updated versions of the methods:

```
- (NSRect) textBounds {
    return text.bounds;
}

- (NSRect) containerBounds {
    return container.bounds;
}

- (NSRect) shapeBounds {
    return shape.bounds;
}
```

Now, let's fix the calling code:

```
NSRect textBounds       = self.textBounds;
NSRect containerBounds  = self.containerBounds;
NSSize shapeSize        = self.shapeBounds.size;
```

If you prefer using the standard messaging syntax with square brackets for properties, you can also do this:

```
NSRect textBounds       = [self textBounds];
NSRect containerBounds  = [self containerBounds];
NSSize shapeSize        = [[self shapeBounds] size];
```

Changing the method and variables took very little effort, but the code is far more symmetrical. It's much easier to see the meaning at a glance. The one note here is that I kept shapeSize as an NSSize because I presumably still need to use that value somewhere else, but I do the conversion on the *caller* side, so that all of the accessor methods are consistent.

Refactored Header

Replace the current contents of the *StyledImageView.h* header file with the following refactored version. I split the file up into three main sections: the delegate protocol, public properties for the view, and methods that view subclasses can override. I marked them with the #pragma mark statements so that they're divided up in Xcode's method drop-down list:

```
#import <Cocoa/Cocoa.h>

#pragma mark -
#pragma mark Delegate Protocols

❶ // allows another class to calculate the geometry.
@protocol StyleImageViewGeometryDelegate <NSObject>
- (NSRect)imageRectForContentRect:(NSRect)contentRect;
@end


#pragma mark -
#pragma mark Class Definiton

@interface StyledImageView : NSView

#pragma mark -
#pragma mark Main Properties

❷ // content.
@property (copy) NSImage* mainImage;

❸ // colors and gradients.
@property (retain) NSGradient* backgroundGradient;
@property (retain) NSColor*     backgroundColor;
@property (retain) NSColor*     borderColor;

❹ // display options.
@property (assign) BOOL shouldAddShadow;
@property (assign) BOOL shouldAddSheen;

❺ // delegate.
@property (assign) id<StyleImageViewGeometryDelegate> delegate;


#pragma mark -
#pragma mark Drawing Methods

❻ // drawing methods for subclasses to override.
- (void) drawBackground;
- (void) drawImage;
- (void) drawImageBorder;
- (void) drawImageSheen;

@end
```

The two main sections are split up into six subsections:

❶ A protocol that lists methods for the delegate to respond to. The protocol inherits from the NSObject protocol, so that I can call -respondsToSelector: without getting warnings.

❷ The content section lists properties that store the actual data being displayed. For now, it's just the mainImage property, but I can add other content here later.

❸ The colors and gradients section lists individual drawing attributes that the owner of this view can set.

❹ The display options section has properties that turn special features on or off. These are different from the colors and gradients, because the caller only has to specify that the attributes should be used. The details are worked out by the view automatically.

❺ The delegate responds to the geometry protocol messages.

❻ The drawing methods actually draw the view in separate steps. These could be overridden by subclasses to customize the drawing. There's no reasonable way to make these properties.

There isn't an "official" layout for Cocoa classes; this is just one example. The goal is to group things that are related to each other, and make it as clear as possible what the most important properties and methods are. In this header, I put `mainImage` and the color-related properties near the top, because they'll be used for every instance of this view. The other methods that can be overridden by subclasses are farther down because they're not quite as critical.

Refactored Implementation

I've also reorganized *StyledImageView.m* a bit, partially to bring it in line with the header. Ideally, you always want your properties to appear in the same order. So since I list `mainImage` as the first property in the header, I put the `@synthesize` statement for `mainImage` first, and release it first in `-dealloc`. The more you can stay consistent like this, the less likely it is that you'll forget a property.

I've broken the implementation up into a few separate parts. Delete the contents of *StyledImageView.m*, then type each part into Xcode as you go so that you can try the new version when you're done. Here's the top of *StyledImageView.m*:

```
#import "StyledImageView.h"
#import "NSImage-Utilities.h"
#import "NSBezierPath-Utilities.h"


@interface StyledImageView ()
// private properties.
@property (assign)   NSRect        contentRect;
@property (readonly) NSRect        imageRect;
@property (retain)   NSShadow*     imageShadow;
@property (retain)   NSGradient*   imageSheen;

// private methods.
+ (NSShadow*)   defaultImageShadow;
+ (NSGradient*) defaultImageSheen;
@end


@implementation StyledImageView
```

```objc
// content.
@synthesize mainImage;
@synthesize contentRect;

// colors and gradients.
@synthesize backgroundGradient;
@synthesize backgroundColor;
@synthesize borderColor;

// display options.
@synthesize shouldAddShadow;
@synthesize shouldAddSheen;
@synthesize imageShadow;
@synthesize imageSheen;

// delegate.
@synthesize delegate;


- (id)initWithFrame:(NSRect)frame {

    if ( self = [super initWithFrame:frame] ) {

    }
    return self;
}

- (void) dealloc {

    self.mainImage          = nil;
    self.backgroundGradient = nil;
    self.backgroundColor    = nil;
    self.borderColor        = nil;
    self.imageShadow        = nil;
    self.imageSheen         = nil;
    self.delegate           = nil;

    [super dealloc];
}
```

This is mostly the same as before, except the methods are reorganized a bit. All of the drawing methods have been moved out into the public header file, but the class methods that return the default shadow and image sheen are still in place. There are two new private properties: contentRect and imageRect. The content rect contains all drawing, and the image rect is the where the actual image is drawn. I made the imageRect property readonly because there's no instance variable—it's calculated each time -drawRect: is called by calling -imageRect.

In my experience, not many developers use the **readonly** keyword for private properties. The more common way to do this is to define an -imageRect method. Personally, I like using properties not just to synthesize instance variables and accessors, but to describe *any* property-like values.

Here are the accessor method implementations for *StyledImageView.m*:

```
#pragma mark -
#pragma mark Property Accessors

- (void) setShouldAddShadow:(BOOL)shouldAdd {

    if ( shouldAddShadow == shouldAdd ) return;
    shouldAddShadow = shouldAdd;

    if ( shouldAddShadow )
        self.imageShadow = [[self class] defaultImageShadow];
    else
        self.imageShadow = nil;

    [self setNeedsDisplay:YES];
}

- (void) setShouldAddSheen:(BOOL)shouldAdd {

    if ( shouldAddSheen == shouldAdd ) return;
    shouldAddSheen = shouldAdd;

    if ( shouldAddSheen )
        self.imageSheen = [[self class] defaultImageSheen];
    else
        self.imageSheen = nil;

    [self setNeedsDisplay:YES];
}


#pragma mark -
#pragma mark Geometry

- (NSRect) imageRect {

    // first, check with the delegate.
    if ( [self.delegate respondsToSelector:@selector(imageRectForContentRect:)] )
        return [self.delegate imageRectForContentRect:self.contentRect];

    // if delegate didn't return a value, calculate it.
    NSImage* image = self.mainImage;
    return [image proportionalRectForTargetRect:self.contentRect];
}
```

The shadow and sheen methods are basically the same, other than the fact that I removed the comments. The -imageRect method is the implementation for the imageRect property definition. I start by asking the delegate if it responds to -imageRectForContentRect:. If it does, I just use the value it returns. Otherwise, I will pass the contentRect value into the -[NSImage proportionalRectForTargetRect:] category method I added before to get an imageRect value. Previously, I was just using the view bounds property directly, but adding an intermediate content rect is a bit more flexible without adding much complexity.

 I don't need to check for a valid delegate first, because the delegate instance variable defaults to nil, which will always respond NO for methods that return BOOL values. When I call -respondsToSelector: on a nil delegate, it will be the same as if an actual object didn't respond to the method.

Now let's add the drawing methods that do the bulk of the work:

```
#pragma mark -
#pragma mark Drawing

- (void)drawRect:(NSRect)rect {

    // set up the content rect that will be used by the other
    // drawing methods.
    NSRect  bounds    = self.bounds;
    CGFloat insetX    = NSWidth ( bounds ) * 0.10;
    CGFloat insetY    = NSHeight ( bounds ) * 0.10;
    self.contentRect  = NSInsetRect ( bounds, insetX, insetY );

    // call each drawing method separately.
    [self drawBackground];
    [self drawImage];
    [self drawImageBorder];
    [self drawImageSheen];
}

- (void) drawBackground {

    [self.backgroundColor set];
    NSRectFill ( self.bounds );

    [self.backgroundGradient drawInRect:self.bounds angle:90.0];
}

- (void) drawImage {

    NSImage* image = self.mainImage;
    [NSGraphicsContext saveGraphicsState];

        [self.imageShadow set];
```

```
        [image drawInRect: self.imageRect
                  fromRect: NSZeroRect
                 operation: NSCompositeSourceOver
                  fraction: 1.0];

    [NSGraphicsContext restoreGraphicsState];
}

- (void) drawImageBorder {

    [self.borderColor set];
    NSBezierPath* imageFrame = [NSBezierPath bezierPathWithRect:self.imageRect];
    imageFrame.lineWidth = 4;
    [imageFrame stroke];
}

- (void) drawImageSheen {

    NSRect rect = self.imageRect;
    NSBezierPath* sheenPath = [NSBezierPath sheenPathForRect:rect];

    // draw at 280.0 degrees to simulate a light source from the upper-left.
    [self.imageSheen drawInBezierPath:sheenPath angle:280.0];
}
```

Again, because I'm *refactoring* instead of rewriting, most of the code is the same. The main difference is that -drawRect: sets the contentRect property first, then calls the other drawing methods that use that contentRect value to figure out where to draw. Another (slightly faster) way to do this is to pass the contentRect into each method, but that makes the code harder to change later. If I decided I wanted to pass in an NSSize instead, I'd have to change all of the methods. In this case, I've decided that the flexibility is worth the tiny performance hit of saving the rect as a property each time.

 It's always important to think about how to make your code flexible, but it's even more important when you make a class that others can reuse and customize. If you change the core methods of the class, other developers will have to go back and rewrite their code. They may never get around to that, so you'll be stuck supporting an older version.

Finally, there are two methods that provide default values for drawing properties. These were private methods before, but they're now listed in the public class header. They're unchanged from the previous version, but I'm including them for completeness:

```
#pragma mark -
#pragma mark Default Values

+ (NSShadow*) defaultImageShadow {

    NSShadow* newShadow          = [[NSShadow alloc] init];
    newShadow.shadowBlurRadius   = 8.0;
    newShadow.shadowOffset       = NSMakeSize(0,-6);
```

```
    newShadow.shadowColor      = [NSColor blackColor];

    return [newShadow autorelease];
}

+ (NSGradient*) defaultImageSheen {

    NSColor* color1 = [NSColor colorWithDeviceWhite:1.0 alpha:0.80];
    NSColor* color2 = [NSColor colorWithDeviceWhite:1.0 alpha:0.10];
    NSColor* color3 = [NSColor colorWithDeviceWhite:1.0 alpha:0.0];

    NSGradient* sheen = [[NSGradient alloc] initWithColorsAndLocations:
                         color1, 0.0, color2, 0.4, color3, 0.8, nil];

    return [sheen autorelease];
}

@end
```

Test the Refactored Version

Of course, refactoring is only useful if the app still builds and runs. So save all of the files, and then build and rerun the application. Everything should look the same as before. Now we can start adding new features.

Text

The built-in `NSTextField` and `NSTextView` classes are extremely versatile, and they should work for many common cases. But you still may want to draw text in a custom way, or maybe you want to draw a lot of text without the overhead of many `NSTextView` instances, or maybe you just need to draw text directly on top of a button. For all of these reasons and more, it helps to know something about text.

Keep in mind that the text system is one of the most complex parts of Cocoa. The idea of text *seems* simple until you factor in things like Unicode, writing direction, kerning, completions, and so on. AppKit handles all of these things, so the code has to exist to deal with them. As a result, there may be times when you have to look through a lot of methods to find what you need. But eventually, you may need those *exact methods* that you skipped over before.

Fonts

The `NSFont` class allows you to select fonts at different sizes and styles. Once you have a font object, you can apply it to an attributed string. Like the rest of the Cocoa text system, fonts have a lot of knobs and dials, but you can get some basic things done very easily. To create a font object with 18-pt. Helvetica, for example, all I need to do is this:

```
NSFont* myFont = [NSFont fontWithName:@"Helvetica" size:18.0];
```

There's another class you should know about here that will make your life much easier. It's called NSFontManager. This class does the grunt work for the font panel that pops up in most Mac apps. In addition to its main function, though, it's a great way to apply font attributes in just a few lines of code. Here's how you can create 18-pt. Helvetica Bold:

```
NSFont* myFont = [NSFont fontWithName:@"Helvetica" size:18.0];
NSFontManager* fontManager = [NSFontManager sharedFontManager];
myFont = [fontManager convertFont:myFont toHaveTrait:NSBoldFontMask];
```

It's just as easy to create 18-pt. Helvetica Oblique (also known as Helvetica Italic):

```
NSFont* myFont = [NSFont fontWithName:@"Helvetica" size:18.0];
NSFontManager* fontManager = [NSFontManager sharedFontManager];
myFont = [fontManager convertFont:myFont toHaveTrait:NSItalicFontMask];
```

The other class that does all this is NSFontDescriptor. It's a far more comprehensive take on fonts, with a much finer-grained level of control for things that typography experts need to do their jobs. But it's arguably overkill if you just want a bold or italic font. So for this chapter, we can just use NSFontManager and let it work out the details for us. (*Hooray for encapsulation!*)

Attributed Strings

In most cases, use NSAttributedString to draw text in AppKit. This class is actually not a direct subclass of NSString. Instead, it implements -initWithString: and -string to convert between the two types. The *attributed* part of the name means that the text has style attributes like font and color.

You customize the appearance of text by creating dictionaries of attributes. Although the core NSAttributedString is part of Foundation, many of the important parts— including the actual attribute keys—are added by AppKit. Example 10-10 shows some of the most commonly used keys.

Example 10-10. Excerpt of AppKit.framework/Headers/NSAttributedString.h

```
NSString *NSFontAttributeName;
NSString *NSParagraphStyleAttributeName;
NSString *NSForegroundColorAttributeName;
NSString *NSUnderlineStyleAttributeName;
NSString *NSSuperscriptAttributeName;
NSString *NSBackgroundColorAttributeName;
NSString *NSUnderlineColorAttributeName;
NSString *NSStrikethroughStyleAttributeName;
NSString *NSStrikethroughColorAttributeName;
NSString *NSShadowAttributeName;
NSString *NSObliquenessAttributeName;
```

Here's how to set a text color and font and draw the result in a view. Create a project as shown in "Subclassing NSView" on page 316, but use the following -drawRect: method instead (Figure 10-16 shows the results):

```
- (void)drawRect:(NSRect)rect {

    [[NSColor darkGrayColor] set];
    NSRectFill ( self.bounds );

    NSString* text = @"All of this text is Times white.";
    NSMutableDictionary* attributes = [NSMutableDictionary dictionary];

    // use white text.
    [attributes setObject: [NSColor whiteColor]
                forKey: NSForegroundColorAttributeName];

    // use 72pt Times.
    [attributes setObject: [NSFont fontWithName: @"Times" size: 72.0]
                forKey: NSFontAttributeName];

    NSAttributedString* styledText = nil;
    styledText = [[NSAttributedString alloc] initWithString: text
                                            attributes: attributes];
    [styledText drawInRect:self.bounds];
    [styledText release];

}
```

Figure 10-16. Drawing an NSAttributedString in a view

You can also skip the intermediate step of creating an NSAttributedString object, and just draw a regular NSString with a dictionary of attributes:

```
[[NSColor darkGrayColor] set];
NSRectFill ( self.bounds );

NSString* text = @"All of this text is Times white.";
NSMutableDictionary* attributes = [NSMutableDictionary dictionary];

[attributes setObject: [NSColor whiteColor]
```

```
                forKey: NSForegroundColorAttributeName];

    [attributes setObject: [NSFont fontWithName: @"Times" size: 72.0]
                forKey: NSFontAttributeName];

    [text drawInRect:self.bounds withAttributes:attributes];
```

The interesting thing about this is that **NSString** is a Foundation class, so it doesn't have any built-in support for drawing. Instead, AppKit includes a file called *NSStringDrawing.h*,[†] which adds category methods to **NSString** for drawing.

The **NSAttributedString** class has a major limitation, though. All of the text has the same set of attributes. The more flexible *NSMutableAttributedString* class allows you to add, remove, or change attributes in individual parts of the string using **NSRange** values to identify specific blocks of text. Here's an example of applying one attribute to the whole string, and another attribute to only part of the string:

```
    [[NSColor whiteColor] set];
    NSRectFill ( self.bounds );

    NSString* text = @"Regular Text. Bold Text.";

    NSMutableAttributedString* styledText;
    styledText = [[NSMutableAttributedString alloc] initWithString:text];

    // create a 48pt Helvetica font.
    NSFont* font = [NSFont fontWithName: @"Helvetica" size: 48.0];

    // add font attribute to all text using the entire range.
    [styledText addAttribute: NSFontAttributeName
                        value: font
                        range: [text rangeOfString:text]]; // not a typo!

    // create a bold font.
    NSFontManager* fontManager = [NSFontManager sharedFontManager];
    NSFont* boldFont = [fontManager convertFont:font toHaveTrait:NSBoldFontMask];

    // add bold font to part of the string.
    [styledText addAttribute: NSFontAttributeName
                        value: boldFont
                        range: [text rangeOfString:@"Bold Text."]];

    [styledText drawInRect: self.bounds];
    [styledText release];
```

Figure 10-17 shows what it looks like when rendered in a view.

Paragraph styles

Most of the base text attributes like fonts and colors apply to groups of characters. **NSParagraphStyle** and **NSMutableParagraphStyle** give you control over the bigger picture

---

† */System/Library/Frameworks/AppKit.framework/Headers/NSStringDrawing.h.*

Figure 10-17. A string with multiple attributes

of how entire blocks of text are arranged in the view, using properties like alignment, line spacing, and indentation. Here's how to center text in an attributed string:

```
[[NSColor colorWithDeviceRed: 168.0 / 255.0
                       green: 128.0 / 255.0
                        blue:   0.0 / 255.0
                       alpha: 255.0 / 255.0] set];

NSRectFill ( self.bounds );

NSString* text = @"Centered Text.";
NSMutableDictionary* attributes = [NSMutableDictionary dictionary];

[attributes setObject: [NSFont fontWithName:@"Helvetica" size:85.0]
              forKey: NSFontAttributeName];

[attributes setObject: [NSColor yellowColor]
              forKey: NSForegroundColorAttributeName];


// center text with paragraph style.
NSMutableParagraphStyle* centerStyle = [[NSMutableParagraphStyle alloc] init];
[centerStyle setAlignment:NSCenterTextAlignment];

[attributes setObject: centerStyle
              forKey: NSParagraphStyleAttributeName];


NSRect textRect = NSInsetRect ( self.bounds, 30, 30 );
[text drawInRect: textRect withAttributes: attributes];

[centerStyle release];
```

Figure 10-18 shows the result in the view.

Text sizes and vertical alignment

NSAttributedString has a method called -size that calculates the size of the string—with all of the attributes factored in—before it's actually drawn. This helps you

Figure 10-18. Drawing centered text using NSParagraphStyle

rearrange your view before drawing to accommodate text. In this example, I use the height of the string to vertically center the text rect in the view:

```
[[NSColor blackColor] set];
NSRect viewBounds = self.bounds;
NSRectFill ( viewBounds );

NSString* text = @"Red Orange Yellow";

NSMutableAttributedString* styledText = nil;
styledText = [[NSMutableAttributedString alloc] initWithString:text];

NSString* colorKey = NSForegroundColorAttributeName;

// apply color to each word.
[styledText addAttribute: colorKey
                    value: [NSColor redColor]
                    range: [text rangeOfString:@"Red"]];

[styledText addAttribute: colorKey
                    value: [NSColor orangeColor]
                    range: [text rangeOfString:@"Orange"]];

[styledText addAttribute: colorKey
                    value: [NSColor yellowColor]
                    range: [text rangeOfString:@"Yellow"]];

// apply a 32pt Helvetica font to all of the text.
[styledText addAttribute: NSFontAttributeName
```

```
                    value: [NSFont fontWithName: @"Helvetica" size: 32.0]
                    range: [text rangeOfString:text]];

// center the text horizontally and truncate any text that doesn't fit.
NSMutableParagraphStyle* pStyle = [[NSMutableParagraphStyle alloc] init];
pStyle.alignment      = NSCenterTextAlignment;
pStyle.lineBreakMode = NSLineBreakByTruncatingTail;

[styledText addAttribute: NSParagraphStyleAttributeName
                   value: pStyle
                   range: [text rangeOfString:text]];

[pStyle release];


CGFloat viewWidth  = viewBounds.size.width;
CGFloat viewHeight = viewBounds.size.height;
CGFloat textHeight = styledText.size.height;

// make the rect the entire width of the view, but only as
// high as the text itself. center it vertically.

NSRect textRect;
textRect.size    = NSMakeSize ( viewWidth, textHeight );
textRect.origin = NSMakePoint ( 0, (viewHeight - textHeight) * 0.5 );

// add some padding around the edges.
textRect = NSInsetRect ( textRect, 30, 0 );
[styledText drawInRect: textRect];

[styledText release];
```

Figure 10-19 shows the final result.

> If this seems too complex, remember that these classes aren't only for
> drawing small bits of text in views. The Cocoa text system is also used
> as the basis for full-fledged word-processing applications. That said, you
> can often let the built-in classes like NSTextField, NSTextView, and
> NSFontManger do the hard work for you.

Add a Title to StyledImageView

Using your new knowledge of attributed strings, you're going to add an image title to
StyledImageView, so open the BasicCocoaDrawing project. First, add a title property
to *StyledImageView.h*:

```
@interface StyledImageView : NSView

#pragma mark -
#pragma mark Main Properties

// content.
```

```
@property (copy) NSImage* mainImage;
@property (copy) NSString* title;
```

In the same file, declare a method that draws the title in the view:

```
#pragma mark -
#pragma mark Drawing Methods

// drawing methods for subclasses to override.
- (void) drawBackground;
- (void) drawImage;
- (void) drawImageBorder;
- (void) drawImageSheen;
- (void) drawTitle;
```

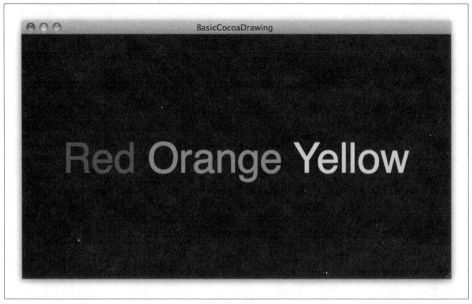

Figure 10-19. Centering text vertically by calculating the height before drawing

While you're here, go to the top of the file and add another method to the geometry protocol so the delegate can return a custom rect for the title if it wants to:

```
#pragma mark -
#pragma mark Delegate Protocols

// allows another class to calculate the geometry.
@protocol StyleImageViewGeometryDelegate <NSObject>
- (NSRect)imageRectForContentRect:(NSRect)contentRect;
- (NSRect)titleRectForContentRect:(NSRect)contentRect;
@end
```

Save the file and switch over to *StyledImageView.m* to update the implementation. First add new private properties for `titleRect` and `textAttributes`, and a private method for configuring the text attributes:

```
@interface StyledImageView ()
// private properties.
@property (assign)   NSRect        contentRect;
@property (readonly) NSRect        imageRect;
@property (readonly) NSRect        titleRect;
@property (copy)     NSDictionary* textAttributes;
@property (retain)   NSShadow*     imageShadow;
@property (retain)   NSGradient*   imageSheen;

// private methods.
+ (NSShadow*)   defaultImageShadow;
+ (NSGradient*) defaultImageSheen;
- (void)        setupTextAttributes;
@end
```

The -setupTextAttributes method will create a dictionary with the text styles, then assign it to the textAttributes property. Add synthesize statements for the new properties and release them in -dealloc:

```
@implementation StyledImageView

// content.
@synthesize mainImage;
@synthesize title;
@synthesize contentRect;
@synthesize textAttributes;

// colors and gradients.
@synthesize backgroundGradient;
@synthesize backgroundColor;
@synthesize borderColor;

// display options.
@synthesize shouldAddShadow;
@synthesize shouldAddSheen;
@synthesize imageShadow;
@synthesize imageSheen;

// delegate.
@synthesize delegate;


- (id)initWithFrame:(NSRect)frame {

    if ( self = [super initWithFrame:frame] ) {

    }
    return self;
}

- (void) dealloc {

    self.mainImage      = nil;
    self.title          = nil;
    self.textAttributes = nil;
```

```
self.backgroundGradient = nil;
self.backgroundColor    = nil;
self.borderColor        = nil;
self.imageShadow        = nil;
self.imageSheen         = nil;
self.delegate           = nil;

[super dealloc];
}
```

 The imageRect and titleRect properties are **readonly**, so I don't need to @synthesize the accessors or manage the memory. I *only* implement a single method for each, which returns the value.

Now I need to rework the geometry methods a bit, because there are now two things in the view: the image and the title. Both of these need a separate rect to draw into, though both will be inside of the overall **contentRect** property. I'm going to add the -titleRect method, but I'm also going to change -imageRect to take the title into account. Use these method implementations in your copy of the project:

```
#pragma mark -
#pragma mark Geometry

- (NSRect) imageRect {

    // first, check with the delegate.
    if ( [self.delegate respondsToSelector:@selector(imageRectForContentRect:)] )
        return [self.delegate imageRectForContentRect:self.contentRect];

    NSRect imageRect = self.contentRect;

    // if there's a title, make room for it in the view.
    if ( self.title ) {
        imageRect.size.height -= 34;
        imageRect.origin.y    += 34;
    }

    // if delegate didn't retun a value, calculate it.
    NSImage* image = self.mainImage;
    return [image proportionalRectForTargetRect:imageRect];
}

- (NSRect) titleRect {

    // first, check with the delegate.
    if ( [self.delegate respondsToSelector:@selector(titleRectForContentRect:)] )
        return [self.delegate titleRectForContentRect:self.contentRect];

    // use the imageRect as a base value, but resize and reposition
    // so that it doesn't overlap the image.
    NSRect titleRect       = self.imageRect;
    titleRect.size.height  = 24;
```

```
        titleRect.origin.y    -= 40;
        return titleRect;
}
```

Next, I need an implementation for the -drawTitle method. Instead of just drawing the text, though, I want to place it in a container (or make it "anchored" as they say in the design biz). To make it look a bit nicer, I'm going to create a round rect using the NSBezierPath method designed for this. And as one extra feature, I want to display the size that the image is currently rendered at—such as 256 × 256—after the title itself. Add this code right below the -drawImageSheen method in *StyledImageView.m*:

```
- (void) drawTitle {

    if ( self.title == nil) return;

    NSRect titleRect = self.titleRect;

    NSBezierPath* titleContainer;
    titleContainer = [NSBezierPath bezierPathWithRoundedRect: titleRect
                                                    xRadius: 8.0
                                                    yRadius: 8.0];

    [[NSColor colorWithDeviceWhite:0.18 alpha:1.0] set];
    [titleContainer fill];


    CGFloat    imageWidth    = self.imageRect.size.width;
    CGFloat    imageHeight   = self.imageRect.size.height;
    NSString* formatString = @"%@ - %1.0f x %1.0f";
    NSString* titleString  = [NSString stringWithFormat: formatString,
                                                         self.title,
                                                         imageWidth,
                                                         imageHeight];

    if ( self.textAttributes == nil )
        [self setupTextAttributes];

    NSAttributedString* drawingString;
    drawingString = [[NSAttributedString alloc] initWithString: titleString
                                                   attributes: self.textAttributes];

    [drawingString drawInRect: NSInsetRect(titleRect, 10, 2)];
    [drawingString release];
}
```

Now, add the implementation for the private -setupTextAttributes method that was declared at the top of the file:

```
- (void) setupTextAttributes {

    NSMutableParagraphStyle * pStyle = [[NSMutableParagraphStyle alloc] init];
    [pStyle setAlignment: NSCenterTextAlignment];

    // create the font and color.
    NSColor* color = [NSColor whiteColor];
```

```
NSFont*  font  = [NSFont boldSystemFontOfSize:[NSFont systemFontSize]];

// combine into an attributes dictionary for an attributed string.
NSMutableDictionary * attrs = [NSMutableDictionary dictionaryWithObjectsAndKeys:
                                font,   NSFontAttributeName,
                                color,  NSForegroundColorAttributeName,
                                pStyle, NSParagraphStyleAttributeName,
                                nil];
[pStyle release];

self.textAttributes = attrs;
}
```

Add a line in -drawRect: to call the -drawTitle method:

```
[self drawBackground];
[self drawImage];
[self drawImageBorder];
[self drawImageSheen];
[self drawTitle];
```

Finally, in *BasicCocoaDrawingAppDelegate.m*, add a line to -applicationDidFinish
Launching: to set the title for the image:

```
imageView.mainImage        = [NSImage imageNamed:@"SpaceShuttle"];
imageView.title            = @"SpaceShuttle";
imageView.backgroundColor  = [NSColor darkGrayColor];
imageView.borderColor      = [NSColor whiteColor];
```

> You have to set the title manually on the view, because an NSImage object
> isn't directly associated with a file. You *can* set the name of an image
> object using image.name = @"My Title", but that's no easier than setting
> the title on the view itself.

Save all of the files and rebuild the app. You should see the title and the size below the
image, like Figure 10-20.

Handling Mouse and Keyboard Events

The one missing piece to all of this is how to handle user interaction in a custom view.
The event system in Cocoa is very sophisticated and has a lot of options, but just to get
you started, I'm going to show you how to handle a mouse click-and-drag event and a
single key press. When this example is complete, you will be able to drag the image
around the view, and press the "r" key to reset its location.

The main player in all of this is NSEvent. NSResponder declares a number of built-in
methods related to user input, most of which take an NSEvent object as input. Here are
the most common ones to implement in a view:

```
- (void) mouseDown:    (NSEvent *)event;
- (void) mouseDragged: (NSEvent *)event;
```

```
- (void) mouseUp:        (NSEvent *)event;
- (void) keyDown:        (NSEvent *)event;

- (BOOL) acceptsFirstResponder;
- (BOOL) becomeFirstResponder;
```

I first introduced you to the first responder methods in Chapter 8. In this case, you'll return YES from both -acceptsFirstResponder and -becomeFirstResponder to indicate that you'd like your view to receive user keyboard events.

Figure 10-20. The image title and size rendered in the view

Keyboard Events

The most common way to start accepting keyboard events is to implement the method -[NSResponder keyDown:] in your view. There are two main approaches to take in your implementation. You can manually check the characters in the event object by calling the -characters: or -charactersIgnoringModifiers: methods:

```
- (void) keyDown:(NSEvent *)event {

    NSString* characters = [event charactersIgnoringModifiers];

    // use 'v' key to go full screen.
    if ( [characters isEqualToString:@"v"] ) {
        [self enableFullScreenView];
```

```
        }
    }
```

Another approach is to hand off processing to the `-interpretKeyEvents:` method. The advantage to this is that it allows `NSResponder` to convert common key shortcuts into calls to methods on your view. For example, the Command-Right Arrow key sequence is converted into a call to the `-moveToEndOfLine:` method on your view. In general, it's better to use this approach when you can, because Cocoa will do more work for you.

Mouse Events

A normal mouse click is handled by implementing the `-[NSResponder mouseDown:]` method. You can get the number of clicks for the event with `-clickCount`, and the location of the mouse during the click with `-locationInWindow`. In many cases, though, you want the location of the mouse *in your view*, which you can get by using the `-[NSView convertPointFromBase]` method:

```
- (void) mouseDown:(NSEvent *)event {

    NSPoint pointInWindow = event.locationInWindow;
    NSPoint pointInView   = [self convertPointFromBase:pointInWindow];

    if ( event.clickCount > 1 ) {
        NSLog(@"double click at: %@", pointInView);
    } else {
        NSLog(@"single click at: %@", pointInView);
    }
}
```

You can use all of the same techniques within the `-mouseDragged:` and `-mouseUp:` methods in your view.

Add Event Support to StyledImageView

The implementation of this feature is actually quite simple. Open *StyledImageView.m* and add the two new private properties shown in bold:

```
@property (retain)  NSShadow*    imageShadow;
@property (retain)  NSGradient*  imageSheen;
@property (assign)  NSRect       customImageRect;
@property (assign)  NSPoint      mouseDownPointInImage;
```

And add `synthesize` statements for them as well, as shown in bold here:

```
// delegate.
@synthesize delegate;

// events.
@synthesize customImageRect;
@synthesize mouseDownPointInImage;
```

Add default values for them to `-initWithFrame:`, as shown here:

```
- (id)initWithFrame:(NSRect)frame {

    if ( self = [super initWithFrame:frame] ) {
        self.customImageRect      = NSZeroRect;
        self.mouseDownPointInImage = NSZeroPoint;
    }
    return self;
}
```

Add two lines to the top of the -imageRect implementation to check for a custom image rect value:

```
- (NSRect) imageRect {

    if ( NSEqualRects(self.customImageRect, NSZeroRect) == NO )
        return self.customImageRect;

    // first, check with the delegate.
    if ( [self.delegate respondsToSelector:@selector(imageRectForContentRect:)] )
        return [self.delegate imageRectForContentRect:self.contentRect];
```

And finally, add the method implementations themselves to the bottom of the class:

```
#pragma mark -
#pragma mark Events

- (void) mouseDown:(NSEvent *)event {

    NSPoint pointInWindow = event.locationInWindow;
    NSPoint pointInView   = [self convertPointFromBase:pointInWindow];
    NSRect  newRect       = self.customImageRect;

    // if the user rect is empty, use the default image rect.
    if ( NSEqualRects(newRect, NSZeroRect) )
        newRect = self.imageRect;

    // make sure.
    if ( NSPointInRect(pointInView, newRect) ) {

        NSPoint pointInImage = pointInView;
        pointInImage.x -= newRect.origin.x;
        pointInImage.y -= newRect.origin.y;

        self.mouseDownPointInImage = pointInImage;
        self.customImageRect       = newRect;
    }
}

- (void) mouseDragged:(NSEvent *)event {

    // don't do anything if mouse is outside of image.
    if ( NSEqualPoints(self.mouseDownPointInImage, NSZeroPoint) ) return;

    NSPoint pointInWindow = event.locationInWindow;
    NSPoint pointInView   = [self convertPointFromBase:pointInWindow];
```

```
    // start with current customImageRect.
    NSRect newRect = self.customImageRect;
    newRect.origin.x = pointInView.x;
    newRect.origin.y = pointInView.y;
    newRect.origin.x -= self.mouseDownPointInImage.x;
    newRect.origin.y -= self.mouseDownPointInImage.y;

    self.customImageRect = newRect;
    [self setNeedsDisplay:YES];
}

- (void) mouseUp:(NSEvent *)event {

    self.mouseDownPointInImage = NSZeroPoint;
}

- (void)keyDown:(NSEvent *)event {

    [self interpretKeyEvents:[NSArray arrayWithObject:event]];
}

- (void)insertText:(id)string {

    // reset if the key pressed was 'r'.
    NSString* resetKey = @"r";
    if ( [string isEqual:resetKey] ) {
        self.customImageRect = NSZeroRect;
        [self setNeedsDisplay:YES];
    }
}

- (BOOL) acceptsFirstResponder {
    return YES;
}

- (BOOL) becomeFirstResponder {
    return YES;
}
```

Save the file. Rebuild and rerun the project with Command-R. You can now drag the image around inside the view, and press the "r" key to reset its size and location to the default value for the current size of the window (see Figure 10-21).

Figure 10-21. You can set a custom image location by dragging it around the view, and hit the "r" key to reset the size and location

CHAPTER 11

The Final Word

You've made it to the end of the book. I'm thrilled, amazed, and impressed. Although I hope this is different from any programming book you've ever read, it's still a lot of reading. So now that you're here, what's next? Hopefully, you're going to go write some apps. To help you with that, I want to give you a few last pointers.

But first, a few essentials. The home base for this book is at *http://cocoabook.com*, and the official O'Reilly catalog page can be found at *http://www.oreilly.com/catalog/9780596804794/*. My personal site is *http://theocacao.com*, and I'm *@scottstevenson* on Twitter. You can email me at *cocoahelp@me.com*.

The List

Being a Cocoa developer is about more than just writing a lot of code. There are a few key things you must know to make world-class apps for Mac, iPhone, iPad, and iPod touch:

Presentation matters
> Many developers come to Mac or iPhone from other platforms and miss this. I cannot possibly overstate how critical it is to have a well-designed user interface, application icon, and website. These things tell your users that you care about your software. Your audience appreciates quality user experiences by definition—that's why they bought a Mac in the first place. If two apps occupy the same space with roughly the same features, the one with the better UI usually wins. Invest in the user experience.

Trust the frameworks
> Another thing I see come up with some new Cocoa programmers is an inexplicable resistance to using the built-in frameworks. The reasoning is usually either that they're not sure if the built-in frameworks are good, or they want to have complete control. The frameworks built into Mac OS X *are* good, and get better with each release; you want to get on that train so that you get new features in the future. It's almost always in your best interest to bend the frameworks to your will instead of

trying to write something from scratch. Trust the frameworks, and don't worry about not having enough code to write; there's plenty of interesting work to do.

Use Interface Builder

Along the same lines as frameworks, some new Cocoa developers want to figure out how to write apps without using XIB files. Don't waste time trying to do this. Interface Builder is there to help you do your job. It's been around for a long time, and the concept is battle-tested. The best Cocoa programmers in the world use Interface Builder every day.

Write code

This sure seems obvious, doesn't it? The best way to become a better Cocoa programmer is to do more of it. Don't worry about doing it right the first time. I wrote some absolutely horrible code when I first started, because I simply didn't know what I was doing. But I did it more and more, and got better each time I made something. Spend five hours working on some Cocoa project—any project—every single week.

Simplify

When in doubt, simplify. If you don't know where to start with your app or don't know how to design your user interface, start with the simplest thing that will work and build on it. This approach will never steer you wrong, because you won't build anything you don't need. All great apps are built on a few great ideas. Don't waste time thinking up more complexity for your app. Simplify.

The user is in control

If you only take one thing away from the list, make it this. The user is always in control. Never do things behind his back, even with good intentions. Never change the user's data, rearrange preferences, or autoupdate anything without asking. This was once phrased to me as something along the lines of, "If you place a book on a table, you expect it to still be there the next time you come into the room." Ask before changing anything.

Have fun!

Writing software is very demanding. You can produce world-class apps only if you enjoy doing it. The best engineers I've ever worked with are not driven by a need to work hard, but a deep desire to make the best thing they possibly can, and they stay at it long after everyone else would have given up. They do it because they love making great things. If you're not having fun writing software, why are you doing it?

Websites

There are some websites out there that can help you learn more about Cocoa. I'm involved with some of them, but others are simply things that I've found to be incredibly useful:

CocoaBook.com

The home base for this book is *http://cocoabook.com*. This is where you can find examples from the book and any news that I think is relevant to you as a reader. You may also be able to find some expanded versions of projects from the book here.

O'Reilly catalog page

The O'Reilly page for this book is *http://www.oreilly.com/catalog/ 9780596804794/*. This is another way to get information on the book, including corrections and other extra information you might find helpful.

Theocacao

My personal site is at *http://theocacao.com*. I usually write about Cocoa, general programming, or user interface design. There are years of articles in the archives, and you'll probably find at least some of it useful. I also sometimes announce upcoming events in the San Francisco Bay Area for Cocoa programmers.

Cocoa Dev Central

The long-running Cocoa tutorial site at *http://cocoadevcentral.com* contains many articles that I've written over the years. Although I'm not the original founder, I've been running it since 2004. The tutorials I've written since were the inspiration for this book.

CocoaHeads

An international user group for Mac, iPhone, iPad, and iPod touch programmers is at *http://cocoaheads.org*. Chances are pretty good that there's a chapter near you. If there isn't, consider starting one. Meeting with other Cocoa programmers in person is one of the best ways to get better at what you do.

NSCoder Night

NSCoder Night events at *http://nscodernight.com* are weekly "hands-on" meetings where Cocoa programmers get together to write and collaborate on code. There are many locations listed on the site, and this may be one of your best tools for getting help on a weekly basis. If you don't see a chapter, consider starting one.

Daring Fireball

John Gruber has one of the most well-written and useful sites devoted to goings-on in the world of Mac, iPhone, iPad, and iPod touch. If you want to keep pace with the overall ecosystem that you're writing software for, bookmark *http://dar ingfireball.net*. I read this site every day.

Well-Placed Pixels

http://wellplacedpixels.com has an ever-growing collection of exceptional Mac and iPhone apps. Browsing through the gallery gives you a feel for what the best apps on the platform look like and how they work. These should be your model.

Last Thought

I have one last thing I'd like to leave you with: the quote that sits at the top of my personal site. It's a lyric by Peter Gabriel that I think perfectly sums up how to think about your potential in this line of work:

"All of the buildings, all of those cars were once just a dream in somebody's head."

Any piece of software—or, for that matter, any *thing*—you've seen and admired was dreamed up by someone who then decided to make it real. If you have some version of that in your head today, stop reading this and get back to Xcode right now. Don't wait until tomorrow or next week. Go write it *now*.

Index

We'd like to hear your suggestions for improving our indexes. Send email to *index@oreilly.com*.

W

X